Motion Picture Market Place

Motion Picture Market Place 1976-1977

Tom Costner
Editor

Little, Brown and Company
Boston – Toronto

FIRST EDITION

T04/76

While every effort has been made to assure the accuracy and completeness of all directory listings, neither the publisher nor the editor assumes legal responsibility for errors or omissions.

Please notify the editor promptly of changes of address or telephone at the address given below so that your file can be updated. If you have not been listed and should be, request a questionnaire from the editor.

TOM COSTNER, EDITOR
435 HUDSON STREET
NEW YORK, NEW YORK 10014

Library of Congress Cataloging in Publication Data

Costner, Tom, 1933–
    Motion picture market place, 1976–1977.

    1. Moving-picture industry — United States — Directories. I. Title.
PN1998.A1C6   338.4'7'7914302573   76–104
ISBN 0-316-15770-8

*Published simultaneously in Canada
by Little, Brown & Company (Canada) Limited*

PRINTED IN THE UNITED STATES OF AMERICA

Preface

Motion Picture Market Place — 1976 – 1977 surveys in directory format all aspects of doing business in the theatrical and television film community in the United States. This business directory, the first in a series to be published at least annually, supplies the current "who, what, and where" information necessary for individuals and organizations interested in and involved with the American film industry. *Motion Picture Market Place — 1976 – 1977* has been arranged and edited to provide easy access to the people and companies involved in all phases of theatrical and television film production, distribution, and exhibition, as well as suppliers to the motion picture industry throughout the United States.

The *Motion Picture Market Place* series has been specifically designed to promote and encourage film production in the United States by serving as the complete professional talent, production, services, and equipment directory for the industry on a nationwide basis. The annual concentrates its coverage on films produced for theatrical and television exhibition. The industrial film and educational audio-visual markets are covered only incidentally. The directory has been compiled with the needs of student users, as well as industry professionals, in mind. According to statistics released by the American Film Institute, approximately 35,000 students are currently enrolled in 6,000 courses dealing with film and television production. For the film student, *Motion Picture Market Place* can serve as an introduction to the business of film.

Access to entries contained in *Motion Picture Market Place — 1976 – 1977* has been arranged by subject classification. If the reader wishes to locate, for example, an underwater photographer in Hawaii, he should first determine the correct subject heading from the table of contents, in this case "Underwater Photography & Equipment." He should then locate and note the listings for Hawaii under "Underwater Photography & Equipment" in the directory.

A unique feature of this directory is the listing of the film production assistance staff and facilities available in all fifty states, plus Puerto Rico and the U.S. Virgin Islands. Of the fifty states, seventeen now have film commissions or maintain formal production assistance programs, in addition to the programs initiated by the city governments in New York and San Francisco. Other states are able to offer visiting filmmakers considerable assistance on an informal basis.

Another feature not found elsewhere is the inclusion of a list of distributors of X-rated films. This list has been prepared principally as an aid to young or neophyte filmmakers who are often obliged, because of the realities of the marketplace, to break into feature production via the X-rated film route. Francis Ford Coppola, recently described as "the single most powerful creative artist in film," got his start after UCLA in nudie flicks like *Peeper*. The X rating of the Motion Picture Association of America is not, of course, given only for on-screen sexual athletics. Objectionable language and on-screen violence are also the basis for an MPAA X rating.

No listing of film directors is included in this edition for two reasons: space limitations preclude listing all 5,000-odd members of the Directors Guild of America, and the Guild has for some nine years published its own membership directory. The Guild directory is available from the Directors Guild of America, Inc., 7950 Sunset Boulevard, Los Angeles, California 90046. Telephone: 213-656-1220.

Individual members of motion picture crafts' and performers' organizations and guilds can be located through their respective guild offices. These organizations are included in this directory under "Associations & Organizations" and "Guilds & Unions." It is the policy of many such organizations not to give out the address or telephone number of guild members, but the office will generally forward the information to the member or have the member telephone back. It should be noted that the guilds or unions listed will not undertake to forward or process bulk mailings addressed to their membership in care of the organization's office.

Movie people are creatures of the telephone; written communication is generally reserved for occasions such as executing contracts or signing one's name in cement. This holds true even with the word-oriented "ad-pub" (advertising-publicity) people, the industry's communicators. If a rapid reply is important, it is advisable to telephone rather than chance getting a written response.

The film industry is one characterized by high flux and mobility of industry professionals. Individuals and organizations are requested to notify the editor promptly of address and telephone changes so that the directory can be kept accurate and current. Requests for new or additional listings should likewise be addressed to the editor at 435 Hudson Street, New York, New York 10014.

                                    — Tom Costner
                                    New York, New York
                                    June 30, 1975

Contents

Motion Picture Market Place

Advertising Agencies

Included here are the principal advertising agencies servicing the motion picture industry, and that segment of the television industry which is involved with the television exhibition of theatrical films and made-for-television movies. The listed agencies are concentrated, predictably, in Los Angeles and New York.

California:

Allen, Dorsey & Hatfield
3727 West Sixth Street
Los Angeles, California 90020
Tel: 213-383-3147

Anderson-McConnell-Oakner, Inc.
7050 Hollywood Boulevard
Los Angeles, California 90028
Tel: 213-463-4154

Averill Advertising, Inc.
6269 Selma Avenue
Los Angeles, California 90026
Tel: 213-464-7341

Ayer/Jorgensen/MacDonald
5900 Wilshire Boulevard
Los Angeles, California 90036
Tel: 213-937-6211

David D. Bates Advertising
1777 North Vine Street
Los Angeles, California 90028
Tel: 213-464-2161

Batten, Barton, Durstine &
   Osborn, Inc.
5670 Wilshire Boulevard
Los Angeles, California 90036
Tel: 213-938-3188

M. J. Beckman & Associates
6464 Sunset Boulevard
Los Angeles, California 90028
Tel: 213-469-3101

Walter F. Bennett & Company
1717 North Highland Avenue
Los Angeles, California 90028
Tel: 213-464-8291

Benton & Bowles, Inc.
1800 North Highland Avenue
Los Angeles, California 90028
Tel: 213-464-9151

Braverman-Mirisch, Inc.
9255 Sunset Boulevard
Los Angeles, California 90069
Tel: 213-274-5204

Leo Burnett Company, Inc.
1777 North Vine Street
Los Angeles, California 90028
Tel: 213-464-7373

Campbell-Ewald Company
1717 North Highland Avenue
Los Angeles, California 90028
Tel: 213-461-3211

The Carlin Company
1801 Century Park East
Los Angeles, California 90067
Tel: 213-553-2404

Compton Advertising, Inc.
5670 Wilshire Boulevard
Los Angeles, California 90036
Tel: 213-937-3610

Cunningham & Walsh
1888 Century Park East
Los Angeles, California 90067
Tel: 213-556-1600

Dailey & Associates
3807 Wilshire Boulevard
Los Angeles, California 90010
Tel: 213-386-7823

Dancer-Fitzgerald-Sample
5670 Wilshire Boulevard
Los Angeles, California 90036
Tel: 213-937-2710

Dolan/Hammond/Hess
6300 Wilshire Boulevard
Los Angeles, California 90048
Tel: 213-655-6040

Doyle Dane Bernbach, Inc.
5900 Wilshire Boulevard
Los Angeles, California 90036
Tel: 213-937-5100

The Dreyfus Agency
1880 Century Park East
Los Angeles, California 90067
Tel: 213-879-2114

Eisaman, Johns & Laws
6290 Sunset Boulevard
Los Angeles, California 90028
Tel: 213-466-8101

Erwin Wasey, Inc.
5455 Wilshire Boulevard
Los Angeles, California 90036
Tel: 213-931-1211

Foote, Cone & Belding
2727 West Sixth Street
Los Angeles, California 90057
Tel: 213-381-6966

Grey Advertising, Inc.
3435 Wilshire Boulevard
Los Angeles, California 90010
Tel: 213-380-0530

Honig-Cooper & Harrington
3600 Wilshire Boulevard
Los Angeles, California 90010
Tel: 213-388-3301

Hunter-Willhite Advertising
721 North La Brea Avenue
Los Angeles, California 90038
Tel: 213-933-7353

Kenyon & Eckhardt Advertising,
    Inc.
120 El Camino Drive
Beverly Hills, California 90212
Tel: 213-274-7611

Jay M. Kholos Advertising
16055 Ventura Boulevard
Encino, California 91316
Tel: 213-981-3951

McCann-Erickson, Inc.
3325 Wilshire Boulevard
Los Angeles, California 90010
Tel: 213-385-3301

Ogilvy & Mather, Inc.
5900 Wilshire Boulevard
Los Angeles, California 90036
Tel: 213-937-7900

Sullivan, Stauffer, Colwell &
  Bayles, Inc.
1800 North Highland Avenue
Los Angeles, California 90028
Tel: 213-464-2119

J. Walter Thompson Company
6505 Wilshire Boulevard
Los Angeles, California 90048
Tel: 213-653-0300

The Tullis Company, Inc.
8730 Sunset Boulevard
Los Angeles, California 90069
Tel: 213-657-7333

Weinberg Advertising Company
6523 Wilshire Boulevard
Los Angeles, California 90048
Tel: 213-653-2300

Young & Rubicam, Inc.
3435 Wilshire Boulevard
Los Angeles, California 90010
Tel: 213-380-6400

Colorado:

Broyles, Allebaugh & Davis, Inc.
No. 2 Executive Park
Englewood, Colorado 80110
Tel: 303-771-5230

Crested Butte
1812 Market Street
Denver, Colorado 80202
Tel: 303-534-8459

Florida:

Carson Chern Communications
4845 N.W. Seventh Street
Miami, Florida 33105
Tel: 306-443-4168

Cine Unlimited, Inc.
801 N.W. 111th Street
Miami, Florida 33101
Tel: 305-754-4141

Coronado Studios
260 N.E. 70th Street
Miami, Florida 33104
Tel: 305-751-1853

Image Devices, Inc.
811 N.W. 111th Street
Miami, Florida 33101
Tel: 305-751-1818

M. J. Productions
4555 Ponce De Leon Boulevard
Coral Gables, Florida 33134
Tel: 305-666-8055

H. W. Pettingill & Associates
350 Sevilla Avenue
Coral Gables, Florida 33134
Tel: 305-553-9032

Woroner Films, Inc.
1995 N.E. 150th Street
North Miami, Florida 33161
Tel: 305-945-5465

Illinois:

Albert Frank Guenther Law, Inc.
1 North La Salle Street
Chicago, Illinois 60601
Tel: 312-332-6424

N. W. Ayer & Son
111 East Wacker Drive
Chicago, Illinois 60601
Tel: 312-645-8800

Leo Burnett Co. USA
Prudential Plaza
Chicago, Illinois 60601
Tel: 312-236-5959

D'Arcy, MacManus & Masius
Prudential Plaza
Chicago, Illinois 60601
Tel: 312-329-5000

Doremus & Company
208 South La Salle Street
Chicago, Illinois 60604
Tel: 312-236-9132

Foote, Cone & Belding, Inc.
401 North Michigan Avenue
Chicago, Illinois 60611
Tel: 312-467-9200

Clinton E. Frank, Inc.
120 South Riverside Plaza
Chicago, Illinois 60606
Tel: 312-451-5500

Fuller & Smith & Ross, Inc.
410 North Michigan Avenue
Chicago, Illinois 60611
Tel: 312-467-6800

Kenyon & Eckhardt, Inc.
10 South Riverside Plaza
Chicago, Illinois 60606
Tel: 312-356-4020

McCann-Erickson, Inc.
10 South Riverside Plaza
Chicago, Illinois 60606
Tel: 312-454-7700

Needham, Harper, Steers
   Advertising, Inc.
401 North Michigan Avenue
Chicago, Illinois 60611
Tel: 312-527-3400

Post-Keyes-Gardner, Inc.
875 North Michigan Avenue
Chicago, Illinois 60611
Tel: 312-943-9400

J. Walter Thompson Company
875 North Michigan Avenue
Chicago, Illinois 60611
Tel: 312-664-6700

Young & Rubicam International,
   Inc.
1 East Wacker Drive
Chicago, Illinois 60601
Tel: 312-329-0750

New York:

Albert Frank Guenther Law, Inc.
61 Broadway
New York, New York 10006
Tel: 212-248-5200

Carl Alley
437 Madison Avenue
New York, New York 10022
Tel: 212-688-5300

N. W. Ayer & Son, Inc.
1345 Avenue of the Americas
New York, New York 10019
Tel: 212-974-7400

Ted Bates & Company
1515 Broadway
New York, New York 10036
Tel: 212-869-3131

Batten, Barton, Durstine &
   Osborn, Inc.
383 Madison Ave.
New York, New York 10017
Tel: 212-355-5800

Benton & Bowles, Inc.
909 Third Avenue
New York, New York 10022
Tel: 212-758-6200

Blaine Thompson Company, Inc.
234 West 44th Street
New York, New York 10036
Tel: 212-564-0800

Bozell & Jacobs
505 Park Avenue
New York, New York 10022
Tel: 212-751-1400

Leo Burnett Company, Inc.
767 Fifth Avenue
New York, New York 10022
Tel: 212-759-5959

Campbell-Ewald Company
620 Fifth Avenue
New York, New York 10020
Tel: 212-489-6200

Compton Advertising, Inc.
625 Madison Avenue
New York, New York 10022
Tel: 212-754-1100

Cunningham & Walsh, Inc.
260 Madison Avenue
New York, New York 10016
Tel: 212-683-4900

Dancer-Fitzgerald-Sample, Inc.
347 Madison Avenue
New York, New York 10017
Tel: 212-679-0600

Daniel & Charles, Inc.
261 Madison Avenue
New York, New York 10016
Tel: 212-661-0200

D'Arcy, MacManus & Masius,
  Inc.
437 Madison Avenue
New York, New York 10022
Tel: 212-754-2300

Della Femina, Travisano &
  Partners
625 Madison Avenue
New York, New York 10022
Tel: 212-421-7180

Diener-Hauser-Greenthal Company,
  Inc.
25 West 43rd Street
New York, New York 10036
Tel: 212-564-2100

Doremus & Company
120 Broadway
New York, New York 10005
Tel: 212-964-0700

Dreher Advertising, Inc.
45 Rockefeller Plaza
New York, New York 10020
Tel: 212-581-9300

William Estey Co., Inc.
100 East 42nd Street
New York, New York 10017
Tel: 212-697-1600

Fairfax, Inc.
270 Madison Avenue
New York, New York 10016
Tel: 212-684-4484

Foote, Cone & Belding, Inc.
200 Park Avenue
New York, New York 10017
Tel: 212-937-7000

Clinton E. Frank, Inc.
866 Third Avenue
New York, New York 10022
Tel: 212-832-6060

Fuller & Smith & Ross, Inc.
666 Fifth Avenue
New York, New York 10019
Tel: 212-582-9000

Gardner Advertising Company
767 Fifth Avenue
New York, New York 10022
Tel: 212-759-8940

Grant Advertising, Inc.
90 Park Avenue
New York, New York 10016
Tel: 212-661-6930

Grey Advertising, Inc.
777 Third Avenue
New York, New York 10017
Tel: 212-751-3500

Hicks & Greist
850 Third Avenue
New York, New York 10022
Tel: 212-421-4200

Interpublic Group of Companies
1271 Avenue of the Americas
New York, New York 10019
Tel: 212-867-1122

Kenyon & Eckhardt, Inc.
200 Park Avenue
New York, New York 10017
Tel: 212-973-2000

Ketchum, MacLeod & Grove,
  Inc.
90 Park Avenue
New York, New York 10019
Tel: 212-983-8000

Krone-Olim Advertising, Inc.
1540 Broadway
New York, New York 10019
Tel: 212-869-8090

Al Paul Lefton Co., Inc.
71 Vanderbilt Avenue
New York, New York 10017
Tel: 212-689-7470

Lieberman-Harrison, Inc.
880 Third Avenue
New York, New York 10022
Tel: 212-751-2820

Lois Holland Calloway, Inc.
745 Fifth Avenue
New York, New York 10022
Tel: 212-688-1525

Lord, Geller, Federico, Peterson,
  Inc.
1414 Avenue of the Americas
New York, New York 10019
Tel: 212-421-6050

The Marschalk Company
1345 Avenue of the Americas
New York, New York 10019
Tel: 212-974-7700

McCaffrey & McCall, Inc.
575 Lexington Avenue
New York, New York 10022
Tel: 212-421-7500

McCann-Erickson, Inc.
485 Lexington Avenue
New York, New York 10017
Tel: 212-697-6000

The Media Stock Exchange
477 Madison Avenue
New York, New York 10022
Tel: 212-935-9810

Needham & Grohmann, Inc.
30 Rockefeller Plaza
New York, New York 10020
Tel: 212-245-6200

Needham, Harper & Steers, Inc.
909 Third Avenue
New York, New York 10022
Tel: 212-758-7600

Norman Craig & Kummel, Inc.
919 Third Avenue
New York, New York 10022
Tel: 212-751-0900

Ogilvy & Mather, Inc.
2 East 48th St.
New York, New York 10017
Tel: 212-688-6100

Shaller-Rubin Co., Inc.
909 Third Avenue
New York, New York 10022
Tel: 212-758-3600

Shorlane-Benet Company, Inc.
229 West 42nd Street
New York, New York 10036
Tel: 212-563-1643

Smith-Greenland Company
1414 Avenue of the Americas
New York, New York 10019
Tel: 212-752-5500

Sullivan, Stauffer, Colwell &
    Bayles
575 Lexington Avenue
New York, New York 10022
Tel: 212-688-1600

Tatham-Laird & Kudner, Inc.
605 Third Avenue
New York, New York 10016
Tel: 212-972-9000

Tinker, Dodge & Delano, Inc.
1345 Avenue of the Americas
New York, New York 10019
Tel: 212-245-1030

Trahey Advertising, Inc.
919 Third Avenue
New York, New York 10022
Tel: 212-759-9200

Warwick, Welsh & Miller
375 Park Avenue
New York, New York 10022
Tel: 212-751-4700

Lawrence Weiner & Associates,
    Inc.
230 West 41st Street
New York, New York 10036
Tel: 212-736-8270

Weiss & Geller, Inc.
880 Third Avenue
New York, New York 10022
Tel: 212-421-0600

Young & Rubicam, Inc.
285 Madison Avenue
New York, New York 10017
Tel: 212-576-1212

Aerial Services & Aircraft

Fixed-wing aircraft as well as helicopters are included in this category. Mo suppliers have the necessary camera mounts, and some operators can furnis SAG-accredited story pilots as well as camera ship and crew.

EQUIPMENT & PHOTOGRAPHY

Arizona:

Arizona Helicopters, Inc.
Scottsdale Municipal Airport
7600 East Butheris Drive
Scottsdale, Arizona 85260
Tel: 602-948-2150

Madison Aviation, Inc.
2301 North Greenfield Road
Mesa, Arizona 85205
Tel: 602-832-1420

California:
Los Angeles area:

Aerial Sign Towing and
  Skywriting
1112 Via Mirabel
Palos Verdes Estates, California
  90274
Tel: 213-326-6353

Art Scholl Aviation
4130 Mennes
Riverside, California 92509
Tel: 714-686-0510

R. B. Chenoweth Films
1860 East North Hills Drive
La Habre, California 90631
Tel: 213-691-1652

Continental Camera Systems
Van Nuys Airport
Van Nuys, California 91406
Tel: 213-989-5222

Free Fall Films
14940 Martha Street
Van Nuys, California 91401
Tel: 213-994-1368

Freestyle Sales Company, Inc.
5124 Sunset Boulevard
Los Angeles, California 90027
Tel: 213-660-3460

Alan Gordon Enterprises, Inc.
1430 North Cahuenga Boulevarc
Los Angeles, California 90028
Tel: 213-466-3561

Alan Gordon Enterprises, Inc.
5362 North Cahuenga Boulevard
North Hollywood, California
  91601
Tel: 213-985-5500

Hardwick Aircraft Company
1612 Chico
South El Monte, California 91733
Tel: 213-444-9922

Image Films, Inc.
8563 Beverly Boulevard
Los Angeles, California 90048
Tel: 213-657-5141

Los Angeles International Airport
  Photography
801 World Way
Los Angeles, California 90045
Tel: 213-646-3950

Matrix Image
6622 Variel Avenue
Canoga Park, California 91303
Tel: 213-883-6622

Movie Tech
6518 Santa Monica Boulevard
Hollywood, California 90038
Tel: 213-467-8491

National Helicopter Service
16800 Roscoe Boulevard
Van Nuys, California 91406
Tel: 213-345-5222

David Sutton
11502 Dona Teresa Drive
Studio City, California 91604
Tel: 213-654-7979

Tallmantz Aviation, Inc.
Orange County Airport
19051 Airport Way South
Santa Ana, California 92707
Tel: 213-629-2770

Tyler Camera Systems
6335 Homewood Avenue
Los Angeles, California 90028
Tel: 213-875-7469

Tyler Camera Systems
14218 Aetna Street
Van Nuys, California 91401
Tel: 213-873-7469

San Francisco area:

Astrocopters Limited
Oakland International Airport
P.O. Box 2563
Oakland, California 94614
Tel: 415-635-6880

Holger Kreuzhage Photography
231 Sixth Street
San Francisco, California 94103

Sequoia Helicopters
2500 Cunningham Avenue
San Jose, California 95122
Tel: 408-926-3060

Colorado:

Cinema Services
Box 398
Eldorado Springs, Colorado
  80025
Tel: 303-443-4913
Tel: 303-499-9430

Dillion Aerial Photography
450 Lincoln Street
Denver, Colorado 80203
Tel: 303-778-7758

Sky Choppers, Inc.
Aspen, Colorado 81611
Tel: 303-925-1550

Sky Choppers, Inc.
Denver, Colorado 80202
Tel: 303-469-3972

Sky Choppers, Inc.
Durango, Colorado 81301
Tel: 303-247-0861

Sky Choppers, Inc.
Grand Junction, Colorado 81501
Tel: 303-243-9313

Hawaii:

David Cornwell Productions, Inc.
1358 Kapiolani Boulevard
Honolulu, Hawaii 96814
Tel: 808-949-7000

Hawaii Helicopters International
P.O. Box 1401
Lihue, Hawaii 96766
Tel: 808-245-2131

Hawaii Production Center
1534 Kapiolani Boulevard
Honolulu, Hawaii 96814
Tel: 808-941-3011

House of Photography
1943 North King
Honolulu, Hawaii 96819
Tel: 808-845-2872

The Nelson Photo Company
863 Halekauwila Street
Honolulu, Hawaii 96814
Tel: 808-521-6136

Pacific Instrumentation
5388 Papai Street
Honolulu, Hawaii 96821
Tel: 808-373-1287
Tel: 808-373-9398

Photographics Hawaii, Inc.
905-C Keaumoku
Honolulu, Hawaii 96814
Tel: 808-949-0846
Tel: 808-955-1058

Idaho:

Sky Choppers, Inc.
Boise, Idaho 83707
Tel: 208-344-6589

Montana:

Butte Aero
Airport
Butte, Montana 59701
Tel: 406-494-2455

Combe Airways, Inc.
Logan Field
Billings, Montana 59101
Tel: 406-245-6407

Lynch Flying Service
Logan Field
Billings, Montana 59101
Tel: 406-252-0508

Nebraska:

Chapman/Spittler, Inc.
1908 California Street
Omaha, Nebraska 68102
Tel: 402-348-1600

New Mexico:

Sky Choppers, Inc.
Albuquerque, New Mexico 87101
Tel: 505-898-7160

Utah:

Sky Choppers, Inc.
Provo, Utah 84601
Tel: 801-373-1508

Sky Choppers, Inc.
Salt Lake City, Utah 84101
Tel: 801-359-2085

Washington:

Gardner/Marlow/Maes Corporation
Seattle Towers, Penthouse
Seattle, Washington 98101
Tel: 206-624-9090

HELICOPTERS

California:
Los Angeles area:

Art Scholl Aviation
4130 Mennes
Riverside, California 92509
Tel: 714-686-0510

Briles Wing and Helicopter
3011 Airport Avenue
Santa Monica, California 90405
Tel: 213-390-3554

Continental Camera Systems
16800 Roscoe Boulevard
Van Nuys, California 91406
Tel: 213-989-5222

Dean Engelhardt
404 North Danehearst
Covina, California 91724
Tel: 213-339-7183

Hardwick Aircraft Company
1612 Chico
South El Monte, California 91733
Tel: 213-283-6236

National Helicopter Service
16800 Roscoe Boulevard
Van Nuys, California 91406
Tel: 213-345-5222

Tallmantz Aviation, Inc.
Orange County Airport
Orange, California 92668
Tel: 213-629-2770

San Francisco area:

Astrocopters Limited
Oakland International Airport
P.O. Box 2563
Oakland, California 94614
Tel: 415-635-6880

Golden Gate Helicopters, Inc.
San Francisco International
  Airport
San Francisco, California 94128
Tel: 415-873-3971

Sequoia Helicopters
2500 Cunningham Avenue
San Jose, California 95122
Tel: 408-926-3060

Colorado:

Helicopters Unlimited, Inc.
8895 Montview Boulevard
Denver, Colorado 80220
Tel: 303-321-3344

12

Motion Picture Market Place

Sky Choppers, Inc.
Aspen, Colorado 81611
Tel: 303-925-1550

Sky Choppers, Inc.
Durango, Colorado 81301
Tel: 303-247-0861

Sky Choppers, Inc.
Grand Junction, Colorado 81501
Tel: 303-243-9313

Florida:

Miami Helicopter Service
Opa Locka Airport
Opa Locka, Florida 33054
Tel: 305-688-6778

Sunline Helicopters
1050 McArthur Bay
Miami, Florida 33101
Tel: 305-377-0934

Georgia:

Executive Hele-Opters
DeKalb Peachtree Airport
Atlanta, Georgia 30305
Tel: 404-458-6082

Mobley's Aviation
3999 Gordon Road, S.W.
Atlanta, Georgia 30336
Tel: 404-691-2786

Hawaii:

Hawaii Helicopters International
P.O. Box 1401
Lihue, Hawaii 96766
Tel: 808-245-2131

Idaho:

Skychoppers, Inc.
Boise, Idaho 83707
Tel: 208-344-6589

Illinois:
Aviation Service Division

Shirley Hamilton, Inc.
360 North Michigan Avenue
Chicago, Illinois 60611
Tel: 312-332-1803

Chicago Helicopter
5240 West 63rd Street
Chicago, Illinois 60638
Tel: 312-735-0200

Montana:

Central Air Service
Lewistown Airport
Lewistown, Montana 59457
Tel: 406-538-3767

Central Helicopter, Inc.
Gallatin Field
Bozeman, Montana 59715
Tel: 406-586-9185

Commercial Helicopter, Inc.
1616 Patricia Lane
Billings, Montana 59101
Tel: 406-656-5020

Helicopter Associates, Inc.
2442 Grand Avenue
Billings, Montana 59101
Tel: 406-656-1313

Johnson Flying Service
Johnson-Bell Field
Missoula, Montana 59801
Tel: 406-549-4158

Kruger Flying Service
211 Third Avenue S.E.
Cut Bank, Montana 59427
Tel: 406-938-2147

Minutemen Aviation
Conrad, Montana 59425
Kenneth G. Mamuzich
Tel: 406-278-3730

Montana Helicopters
Ulm, Montana 59485
Tel: 406-866-3341

Strand Aviation
Highway 93
City Field
Kalispell, Montana 59901
Tel: 406-756-7678

New Jersey:

Metropolitan Helicopter
  Corporation
7700 River Road
North Bergen, New Jersey 07047
Tel: 201-868-1200

Ronson Helicopters, Inc.
Mercer County Airport
Trenton, New Jersey
Tel: 212-431-3930

New York:

Butler Aviation
La Guardia Airport
Flushing, New York 11371
Tel: 212-478-1000

Utah:
Sky Choppers, Inc.
Provo, Utah 84601
Tel: 801-373-1508

Sky Choppers, Inc.
Salt Lake City, Utah 84101
Tel: 801-359-2085

Virgin Islands:

Caribbean Air Service
P.O. Box 1149
Christiansted, St. Croix, Virgin
  Islands 00820
John Jackson
Tel: 809-773-0082

PARACHUTING

California:

Art Scholl Aviation
4130 Mennes
Riverside, California 92509
Tel: 714-686-0510

Hardwick Aircraft Company
1612 Chico Street
South El Monte, California 91733
Tel: 213-444-9922

Parachuting Associates
Los Angeles, California 90052
Tel: 213-464-7124

Pro Chuting Enterprises
12619 South Manor Drive
Hawthorne, California 90250
Tel: 213-678-0163

STUNT FLYING

California:
Los Angeles area:

Aerial Sign Towing and
  Skywriting
1112 Via Mirabel
Palos Verdes Estates, California
  90274
Tel: 213-326-6353

Continental Camera Systems
16800 Roscoe Boulevard
Van Nuys, California 91406
Tel: 213-989-5222

Hardwick Aircraft Company
1612 Chico Street
South El Monte, California 91733
Tel: 213-444-9922

Rockwell International
Bob Hoover
1700 East Imperial Highway
El Segundo, California 90245
Tel: 213-647-5283

OBS Airshows Inc.
P.O. Box 1253
Santa Ana, California 92701
Tel: 714-547-2888

Tallmantz Aviation, Inc.
Orange County Airport
19051 Airport Way South
Santa Ana, California 92701
Tel: 213-629-2770

San Francisco area:

Golden Gate Helicopters, Inc.
San Francisco International
  Airport
San Francisco, California 94128
Tel: 415-873-3971

Hawaii:

Pacific Instrumentation
5388 Papai Street
Honolulu, Hawaii 96821
Tel: 808-373-1287

Agents (Literary)

Many literary agents will not undertake to read or return unsolicited manuscripts and screenplays. Writers are cautioned not to make a submission without first determining a particular agent's policies.

California:

Los Angeles area:

Ackerman Sci-Fi Agency
2495 Glendower Avenue
Los Angeles, California 90027
Tel: 213-666-6326

Adams, Ray & Rosenberg
9220 Sunset Boulevard, Suite 210
Los Angeles, California 90069
Tel: 213-278-3000

Associated Booking Corporation
9477 Brighton Way
Beverly Hills, California 90210
Tel: 213-273-5600

The Barksin Agency
8721 Sunset Boulevard, Room 205
Los Angeles, California 90069
Tel: 213-657-5740

Belcourt Artists Corporation
222 North Canon Drive
Beverly Hills, California 90210
Tel: 213-276-6205

Mel Bloom & Associates
328 South Beverly Drive
Beverly Hills, California 90212
Tel: 213-553-0820

The Brand Agency
8721 Sunset Boulevard
Los Angeles, California 90069
Tel: 213-657-2870

Alex Brewis Agency
9145 Sunset Boulevard
Los Angeles, California 90069
Tel: 213-274-9874

Ned Brown Associates
407 North Maple Drive
Beverly Hills, California 90210
Tel: 213-276-1131

The Calder Agency
8749 Sunset Boulevard
Los Angeles, California 90069
Tel: 213-652-3380

The Cambridge Company
9000 Sunset Boulevard
Los Angeles, California 90069
Tel: 213-657-2125

Chartwell Artists, Ltd.
9720 Wilshire Boulevard
Beverly Hills, California 90212
Tel: 213-273-6700

Chasin-Park-Citron Agency
10889 Wilshire Boulevard
Los Angeles, California 90024
Tel: 213-879-0450

Shirley Collier Agency
1127 Stradella Road
Los Angeles, California 90024
Tel: 213-270-3500

Kingsley Colton & Associates, Inc.
321 South Beverly Drive
Beverly Hills, California 90212
Tel: 213-277-5491

Contemporary/Korman Artists
Ltd.
132 South Lasky Drive
Beverly Hills, California 90212
Tel: 213-278-8250

Ben F. Conway & Associates
999 North Doheny Drive, Suite
403
Los Angeles, California 90069
Tel: 213-271-8133

John F. Dugan Enterprises
9229 Sunset Boulevard
Los Angeles, California 90069
Tel: 213-271-7231

Eisenbach-Greene, Inc.
760 North La Cienega Boulevard
Los Angeles, California 90069
Tel: 213-659-3420

FCA Agency, Inc.
9000 Sunset Boulevard
Los Angeles, California 90069
Tel: 213-278-1460

Peter Fleming Agency
9046 Sunset Boulevard
Los Angeles, California 90069
Tel: 213-271-5693

J. Carter Gibson Agency
9000 Sunset Boulevard
Los Angeles, California 90069
Tel: 213-274-8813

The Ivan Green Agency
1900 Avenue of the Stars, Suite
840
Los Angeles, California 90067
Tel: 213-277-1541

Reece Halsey Agency
8733 Sunset Boulevard
Los Angeles, California 90069
Tel: 213-652-2409

Mitchell J. Hamilburg Agency
292 La Cienega Boulevard, Suite
212
Los Angeles, California 90011
Tel: 213-478-0896

International Creative
Management
9255 West Sunset Boulevard
Los Angeles, California 90069
Tel: 213-273-8811

Kahn/Penney Agency
7466 Beverly Boulevard
Los Angeles, California 90036
Tel: 213-938-4114

Irving Paul Lazar Agency
211 South Beverly Drive, Suite
100
Beverly Hills, California 90212
Tel: 213-275-6153

William Morris Agency, Inc.
151 El Camino Drive
Beverly Hills, California 90212
Tel: 213-274-7451

Mildred O. Portnoy Agency
13111 Ventura Boulevard
Studio City, California 91604
Tel: 213-783-5886

Glenn Shaw Agency
8440 Sunset Boulevard
Los Angeles, California 90069
Tel: 213-654-6110

Don Shepherd Agency
1680 Vine Street
Los Angeles, California 90028
Tel: 213-467-3535

H. N. Swanson, Inc.
8523 Sunset Boulevard
Los Angeles, California 90069
Tel: 213-652-5385

Tobinson-Weintraub Associates,
Inc.
8438 Melrose Place
Los Angeles, California 90069
Tel: 213-653-5802

James Warren Associates
5647 Lemona Avenue
Van Nuys, California 91401
Tel: 213-780-7921

Lew Weitzman & Associates
9171 Wilshire Boulevard
Beverly Hills, California 90212
Tel: 213-278-5562

Ziegler-Ross, Inc.
9255 West Sunset Boulevard
Los Angeles, California 90069
Tel: 213-278-0070

San Francisco area:

Informagency West
570 Sutter Street
San Francisco, California 94102
Tel: 415-986-0212

Elizabeth Pomada/Michael
Larsen
1350 Pine Street
San Francisco, California 94109
Tel: 415-673-0939

Illinois:

Marjorie Peters & Pierre Long
5744 South Harper Avenue
Chicago, Illinois 60637
Tel: 312-752-8377

Porter, Gould & Dierks
1236 Sherman Avenue
Evanston, Illinois 60201
Tel: 312-944-3243

Austin Wahl Agency, Inc.
21 East Van Buren Street
Chicago, Illinois 60605
Tel: 312-922-3329

New York:

Maxwell Aley Associates
145 East 35th Street
New York, New York 10016
Tel: 212-679-5377

Alice Bach
222 East 75th Street
New York, New York 10021
Tel: 212-988-2643

Julian Bach Literary Agency
3 East 48th Street
New York, New York 10017
Tel: 212-753-2605

Barber & Merrill
333 West 22nd Street
New York, New York 10011
Tel: 212-924-1439

Scott Bartlett Associates
3 East 65th Street
New York, New York 10021
Tel: 212-628-4654

Maximilian Becker
115 East 82nd Street
New York, New York 10028
Tel: 212-988-3887

Bill Berger Associates
535 East 72nd Street
New York, New York 10021
Tel: 212-249-2771

Lois Berman
530 East 72nd Street
New York, New York 10021
Tel: 212-288-1424

Bethel Agency
125 West 79th Street
New York, New York 10024
Tel: 212-724-3840

Lurton Blassingame
60 East 42nd Street
New York, New York 10017
Tel: 212-687-7491

Georges Borchardt
145 East 52nd Street
New York, New York 10022
Tel: 212-753-5785

Brandt & Brandt
101 Park Avenue
New York, New York 10017
Tel: 212-683-5890

Helen Brann Literary Agency
14 Sutton Place South
New York, New York 10022
Tel: 212-751-0137

Anita Helen Brooks
155 East 55th Street
New York, New York 10022
Tel: 212-755-4498

Curtis Brown, Ltd.
60 East 56th Street
New York, New York 10022
Tel: 212-755-4200

James Brown Associates
22 East 60th Street
New York, New York 10022
Tel: 212-355-4182

Knox Burger Associates
39 1/2 Washington Square South
New York, New York 10012
Tel: 212-533-2360

Shirley Burke
370 East 76th Street
New York, New York 10021
Tel: 212-861-2309

Ruth Cantor
156 Fifth Avenue
New York, New York 10010
Tel: 212-243-3246

Bertha Case
42 West 53rd Street
New York, New York 10019
Tel: 212-581-6280

Jacques Chambrun
745 Fifth Avenue
New York, New York 10022
Tel: 212-755-9464

The Collins Agency
225 East 57th Street
New York, New York 10022
Tel: 212-688-7296

Collins-Knowlton-Wing, Inc.
60 East 56th Street
New York, New York 10022
Tel: 212-755-4200

John Cushman Associates
25 West 43rd Street
New York, New York 10036
Tel: 212-685-2052

Joan Daves
515 Madison Avenue
New York, New York 10022
Tel: 212-759-6250

Anita Diamant
51 East 42nd Street
New York, New York 10017
Tel: 212-687-1122

Sarah B. Dona
20 West 72nd Street
New York, New York 10023
Tel: 212-787-0845

Candida Donadio & Associates
111 West 57th Street
New York, New York 10019
Tel: 212-757-5076

Ann Elmo Agency
52 Vanderbilt Avenue
New York, New York 10017
Tel: 212-686-9282

Frieda Fishbein
353 West 57th Street
New York, New York 10019
Tel: 212-247-4398

Barthold Fles
507 Fifth Avenue
New York, New York 10017
Tel: 212-687-7248

The Foley Agency
34 East 38th Street
New York, New York 10016
Tel: 212-686-6930

The Fox Chase Agency
60 East 42nd Street
New York, New York 10017
Tel: 212-682-6910

Blanche Gaines
350 West 57th Street
New York, New York 10019
Tel: 212-757-0537

Jay Garon-Brooke Associates
415 Central Park West
New York, New York 10025
Tel: 212-866-3654

Max Gartenberg
331 Madison Avenue
New York, New York 10017
Tel: 212-661-5270

Larney Goodkind
30 East 60th Street
New York, New York 10022
Tel: 212-355-6560

The Graham Agency
317 West 45th Street
New York, New York 10036
Tel: 212-489-8288

Sanford J. Greenburger
757 Third Avenue
New York, New York 10017
Tel: 212-753-8581

Blanche Gregory, Inc.
2 Tudor City Place
New York, New York 10017
Tel: 212-697-0828

Helen Harvey Associates
1697 Broadway
New York, New York 10019
Tel: 212-581-5610

Shirley Hector Agency
29 West 46th Street
New York, New York 10036
Tel: 212-246-4314

Kurt Hellmer
52 Vanderbilt Avenue
New York, New York 10017
Tel: 212-686-2222

Ronald Hobbs Literary Agency
211 East 43rd Street
New York, New York 10017
Tel: 212-687-1417

Holub & Associates
432 Park Avenue South
New York, New York 10016
Tel: 212-889-6626

International Creative
  Management
40 West 57th Street
New York, New York 10019
Tel: 212-586-0440

Alex Jackinson
55 West 42nd Street
New York, New York 10036
Tel: 212-563-0156

Margot Johnson Agency
405 East 54th Street
New York, New York 10022
Tel: 212-688-7638

Marvin Josephson Associates, Inc.
1301 Avenue of the Americas
New York, New York 10019
Tel: 212-556-5618

Bertha Klausner
71 Park Avenue
New York, New York 10016
Tel: 212-685-2642

Otto R. Kozak
1089 West Park Street
Long Beach, New York 11561
Tel: 516-889-4370

Lucy Kroll Agency
390 West End Avenue
New York, New York 10024
Tel: 212-877-0627

The Lantz Office, Inc.
114 East 55th Street
New York, New York 10022
Tel: 212-751-2107

Phoebe Larmore
5 Milligan Place
New York, New York 10011
Tel: 212-255-1329

Irving Paul Lazar Agency
680 Madison Avenue
New York, New York 10021
Tel: 212-355-1177

Lenniger Literary Agency
437 Fifth Avenue
New York, New York 10016
Tel: 212-532-9278

Robert Lescher
155 East 71st Street
New York, New York 10021
Tel: 212-249-7600

Lester Lewis Associates
Carolyn Willyoung Stagg
156 East 52nd Street
New York, New York 10022
Tel: 212-753-5082

Patricia Lewis/Ingrid Hallen
450 Seventh Avenue
New York, New York 10001
Tel: 212-947-6902

Sterling Lord Agency
660 Madison Avenue
New York, New York 10021
Tel: 212-751-2533

Donald MacCampbell
12 East 41st Street
New York, New York 10017
Tel: 212-683-5580

Betty Marks
51 East 42nd Street
New York, New York 10017
Tel: 212-687-1122

Elisabeth Marton
96 Fifth Avenue
New York, New York 10011
Tel: 212-255-1908

Harold Matson Co., Inc.
22 East 40th Street
New York, New York 10016
Tel: 212-679-4490

McIntosh & Otis, Inc.
475 Fifth Avenue
New York, New York 10017
Tel: 212-689-1050

McIntosh, McKee & Dodds
22 East 40th Street
New York, New York 10016
Tel: 212-679-4490

Toni Mendez
140 East 56th Street
New York, New York 10022
Tel: 212-838-6740

Scott Meredith, Inc.
845 Third Avenue
New York, New York 10022
Tel: 212-245-5500

Toni Milford
50 East 86th Street
New York, New York 10028
Tel: 212-288-7371

Robert P. Mills, Ltd.
156 East 52nd Street
New York, New York 10022
Tel: 212-752-6132

Howard Moorepark
444 East 82nd Street
New York, New York 10028
Tel: 212-737-3961

William Morris Agency, Inc.
1350 Avenue of the Americas
New York, New York 10019
Tel: 212-586-5100

Henry Morrison, Inc.
311 1/2 West 20th Street
New York, New York 10011
Tel: 212-691-1440

Charles Neighbors
240 Waverly Place
New York, New York 10014
Tel: 212-924-8296

Bonita K. Nelson
210 East 47th Street
New York, New York 10017
Tel: 212-755-9111

Ellen Neuwald, Inc.
905 West End Avenue
New York, New York 10025
Tel: 212-663-1586

Harold Ober Associates
40 East 49th Street
New York, New York 10017
Tel: 212-759-8600

David Obst
34 Perry Street
New York, New York 10014
Tel: 212-929-0964

Dorothea Oppenheimer
866 United Nations Plaza
New York, New York 10017
Tel: 212-421-3789

Park Avenue Literary Agency
230 Park Avenue
New York, New York 10017
Tel: 212-684-3640

Phoenix Literary Agency
225 East 49th Street
New York, New York 10017
Tel: 212-838-4060

Arthur Pine Associates
1780 Broadway
New York, New York 10019
Tel: 212-265-7330

Susan Ann Protter
18 West 55th Street
New York, New York 10019
Tel: 212-541-4972

Theron Raines Agency
244 Madison Avenue
New York, New York 10016
Tel: 212-683-7012

Paul R. Reynolds
599 Fifth Avenue
New York, New York 10017
Tel: 212-688-4767

Flora Roberts, Inc.
116 East 59th Street
New York, New York 10022
Tel: 212-355-4165

Jane Rotrosen
212 East 48th Street
New York, New York 10017
Tel: 212-752-1038

Russell & Volkening
551 Fifth Avenue
New York, New York 10017
Tel: 212-682-5340

Gloria Safier–Bob Barry, Inc.
667 Madison Avenue
New York, New York 10021
Tel: 212-838-4868

Leah Salisbury
790 Madison Avenue
New York, New York 10021
Tel: 212-628-4404

John Schaffner
425 East 51st Street
New York, New York 10022
Tel: 212-688-4763

David H. Scott
225 East 57th Street
New York, New York 10022
Tel: 212-688-5892

Seligmann & Collier
280 Madison Avenue
New York, New York 10016
Tel: 212-679-3383

Southgate Literary Agency
41 Fifth Avenue
New York, New York 10003
Tel: 212-473-1308

Renee Spodheim
698 West End Avenue
New York, New York 10025
Tel: 212-222-4083

Toni Strassman
130 East 18th Street
New York, New York 10003
Tel: 212-473-5030

Gunther Stuhlmann
65 Irving Place
New York, New York 10003
Tel: 212-677-2580

Roslyn Targ Literary Agency
250 West 57th Street, Suite 1932
New York, New York 10019
Tel: 212-582-7847

J. H. VanDaele
225 East 57th Street
New York, New York 10022
Tel: 212-758-7643

WB Agency, Inc.
156 East 52nd Street
New York, New York 10022
Tel: 212-751-8330

Wallace, Aitken & Sheil, Inc.
118 East 61st Street
New York, New York 10021
Tel: 212-751-1944

A. Watkins, Inc.
77 Park Avenue
New York, New York 10016
Tel: 212-532-0080

Wender & Associates
30 East 60th Street
New York, New York 10022
Tel: 212-832-8330

Mary Yost
141 East 55th Street
New York, New York 10022
Tel: 212-755-4682

Agents (Talent)

Presented here is a listing of talent agents active in the motion picture and television movie areas. Under the bylaws of the Screen Actors Guild, SAG members are prohibited from accepting employment from any agent or agency that is not SAG-franchised. For this reason the most recent listing of SAG-franchised agencies is appended.

Arizona:

Arizona Talent Service
627 East Indian School Road
Phoenix, Arizona 85012
Tel: 602-277-8683

Bobby Ball Talent Agency
3443 North Central Avenue
Phoenix, Arizona 85012
Tel: 602-264-5007

Fosis Modeling & Talent Agency
2777 North Campbell Avenue
Tucson, Arizona 85719
Tel: 602-795-3534

Plaza Three Talent Agency
4343 North Sixteenth Street
Phoenix, Arizona 85016
Tel: 602-279-4179

Southern Arizona Casting
  Company
2777 North Campbell Avenue
Tucson, Arizona 85719
Tel: 602-327-7341

Studio East
6317 East 22nd Street
Tucson, Arizona 85710
Tel: 602-296-1711

Tor-Ann Talent Agency
32825 North Scottsdale Road
Cave Creek, Arizona 85331
Tel: 602-488-9660

Tor-Ann Talent Agency
3000 East Thomas Road
Phoenix, Arizona 85016
Tel: 602-263-8708

California:
Los Angeles area:

Aberle & Associates
9100 Sunset Boulevard
Los Angeles, California 90069
Tel: 213-274-9801

Abrams-Rubaloff & Associates,
  Inc.
9012 Beverly Boulevard
Los Angeles, California 90048
Tel: 213-273-5711

Adams, Ray & Rosenberg
9220 Sunset Boulevard
Los Angeles, California 90069
Tel: 213-278-3000

Agency for the Performing Arts
9000 Sunset Boulevard
Los Angeles, California 90069
Tel: 213-273-0744

Aimee Entertainment Association
8383 Wilshire Boulevard
Beverly Hills, California 90212
Tel: 213-655-0701

Carlos Alvarado Agency
8820 Sunset Boulevard
Los Angeles, California 90069
Tel: 213-652-0272

Amaral Agency
9172 Sunset Boulevard
Los Angeles, California 90069
Tel: 213-271-8161

Armstrong-Deuser Agency
449 South Beverly Drive
Beverly Hills, California 90212
Tel: 213-553-8611

Artists' Career Management
10929 Weyburn Avenue
Los Angeles, California 90024
Tel: 213-270-4902

Associated Booking Corporation
9477 Brighton Way
Beverly Hills, California 90210
Tel: 213-273-5600

William Barnes Agency
8721 Sunset Boulevard
Los Angeles, California 90069
Tel: 213-659-2773

Rick Barr/Georgia Gilly
8721 Sunset Boulevard
Los Angeles, California 90069
Tel: 213-659-0141

The Barskin Agency
8721 Sunset Boulevard
Los Angeles, California 90069
Tel: 213-657-5740

Bart/Levy Associates Inc.
8601 Wilshire Boulevard
Beverly Hills, California 90211
Tel: 213-659-5570

The Blake Agency, Ltd.
409 North Camden Drive
Beverly Hills, California 90210
Tel: 213-278-6885

Nina Blanchard Agency
1717 North Highland Avenue
Los Angeles, California 90028
Tel: 213-462-7274

Mel Bloom & Associates
328 South Beverly Drive
Beverly Hills, California 90212
Tel: 213-553-0820

Blumenthal Artists Agency
435 South La Cienega Boulevard
Los Angeles, California 90048
Tel: 213-656-1451

Bresler, Wolff, Cota & Livingston
190 North Canon Drive
Beverly Hills, California 90210
Tel: 213-278-3200

Alex Brewis Agency
9145 Sunset Boulevard
Los Angeles, California 90069
Tel: 213-274-9874

The Calder Agency
8749 Sunset Boulevard
Los Angeles, California 90069
Tel: 213-652-3380

Carey-Phelps-Colvin Agency
7813 Sunset Boulevard
Los Angeles, California 90046
Tel: 213-874-7780

Century Artists, Ltd.
9470 Santa Monica Boulevard
Beverly Hills, California 90210
Tel: 213-273-4366

Charter Management
9000 Sunset Boulevard
Los Angeles, California 90069
Tel: 213-278-1690

Chartwell Artists, Ltd.
9720 Wilshire Boulevard
Beverly Hills, California 90212
Tel: 213-273-6700

Chasin-Park-Citron Agency
10889 Wilshire Boulevard
Los Angeles, California 90024
Tel: 213-879-0450

Kingsley Colton & Associates, Inc.
321 South Beverly Drive
Beverly Hills, California 90212
Tel: 213-277-5491

Allen Connor–Alexis Corfino
 Theatrical Agency
14241 Ventura Boulevard
Sherman Oaks, California 91403
Tel: 213-981-1133

Contemporary-Korman Artists,
 Ltd.
132 North Lasky Drive
Beverly Hills, California 90212
Tel: 213-278-8250

Conway and Rumar Associates
999 North Doheny Drive
Los Angeles, California 90069
Tel: 213-271-8133

Doug Cooper Agency
10850 Riverside Drive
North Hollywood, California
 91602
Tel: 213-980-6100

Coralie Jr. Agency
5107 Hollywood Boulevard
Los Angeles, California 90027
Tel: 213-663-1268

Genevieve Cordier Agency
9426 Santa Monica Boulevard
Beverly Hills, California 90210
Tel: 213-273-8501

Kerwin Coughlin Agency
10850 Riverside Drive
North Hollywood, California
 91602
Tel: 213-980-7200

Creative Artists Agency, Inc.
9300 Wilshire Boulevard
Beverly Hills, California 90212
Tel: 213-550-1020

Lil Cumber Attractions Agency
6515 Sunset Boulevard
Los Angeles, California 90028
Tel: 213-469-1919

William D. Cunningham &
Associates
5900 Wilshire Boulevard
Los Angeles, California 90036
Tel: 213-937-8500

Dade/Rosen Associates
999 North Doheny Drive
Los Angeles, California 90069
Tel: 213-278-7077

Kenneth Daniels Agency
7188 Sunset Boulevard
Los Angeles, California 90046
Tel: 213-874-6560

Diamond Artists, Ltd.
8400 Sunset Boulevard
Los Angeles, California 90069
Tel: 213-654-5960

The Dietrich Agency
10701 Riverside Drive
North Hollywood, California
  91602
Tel: 213-985-4824

Eisenbach-Greene, Inc.
760 North La Cienega Boulevard
Los Angeles, California 90069
Tel: 213-659-3420

FCA Agency, Inc.
9000 Sunset Boulevard
Los Angeles, California 90069
Tel: 213-278-1460

William Felber Agency
6636 Hollywood Boulevard
Los Angeles, California 90028
Tel: 213-466-7629

Jack Fields & Associates
9255 Sunset Boulevard
Los Angeles, California 90069
Tel: 213-278-1333

The Flaire Agency
473 South Robertson Boulevard
Beverly Hills, California 90211
Tel: 213-278-2292

Peter Fleming Agency
9046 Sunset Boulevard
Los Angeles, California 90069
Tel: 213-271-5693

Kurt Frings Agency, Inc.
9025 Wilshire Boulevard
Beverly Hills, California 90211
Tel: 213-274-8881

Marion Garner Agency
800 North El Centro
Los Angeles, California 90038
Tel: 213-661-2035

Dale Garrick International
8831 Sunset Boulevard
Los Angeles, California 90069
Tel: 213-657-2661

Phil Gersh Agency, Inc.
222 North Canon Drive
Beverly Hills, California 90210
Tel: 213-274-6611

Carter J. Gibson Agency
9000 Sunset Boulevard
Los Angeles, California 90069
Tel: 213-274-8813

Herman Gold Agency, Inc.
9034 Sunset Boulevard
Los Angeles, California 90069
Tel: 213-274-1621

Stanley R. Goldberg & Associates
999 North Doheny Drive
Los Angeles, California 90069
Tel: 213-274-8545

Goldin, Dennis & Masser
470 South San Vicente Boulevard
Los Angeles, California 90048
Tel: 213-651-1700

Allen Goldstein & Associates, Ltd.
9171 Wilshire Boulevard
Beverly Hills, California 90210
Tel: 213-278-2742

Gordean–Friedman Agency, Inc.
9229 Sunset Boulevard
Los Angeles, California 90069
Tel: 213-273-4195

Della Gower Artists' Agency
1680 Vine Street
Los Angeles, California 90028
Tel: 213-464-2117

The Granite Agency
1920 South La Cienega Boulevard
Los Angeles, California 90034
Tel: 213-934-8383

Mauri Grashin Agency
8730 Sunset Boulevard
Los Angeles, California 90069
Tel: 213-652-5168

Ivan Green Agency
1900 Avenue of the Stars
Los Angeles, California 90067
Tel: 213-277-1541

The Greenevine Agency
9021 Melrose Avenue
Los Angeles, California 90069
Tel: 213-278-5800

Grossman-Raison Agency, Inc.
8730 Sunset Boulevard
Los Angeles, California 90069
Tel: 213-657-3040

Jeanne Halliburton Agency
5205 Hollywood Boulevard
Los Angeles, California 90027
Tel: 213-466-6138

Reece Halsey Agency
8733 Sunset Boulevard
Los Angeles, California 90069
Tel: 213-652-2409

Mitchell J. Hamilburg Agency
1105 Glendon Avenue
Los Angeles, California 90024
Tel: 213-478-0896

Beverly Hecht Agency
8949 Sunset Boulevard
Los Angeles, California 90069
Tel: 213-278-3544

The Hiller Agency
9220 Sunset Boulevard
Los Angeles, California 90069
Tel: 213-271-5601

George B. Hunt & Associates
8350 Santa Monica Boulevard
Los Angeles, California 90069
Tel: 213-654-6600

Robert G. Hussong Agency
9000 Sunset Boulevard
Los Angeles, California 90069
Tel: 213-274-7652

Hyland-Chandler Agency
9100 Sunset Boulevard
Los Angeles, California 90069
Tel: 213-271-8188

Miles Ingalls Agency
205 South Beverly Drive
Beverly Hills, California 90212
Tel: 213-276-7017

George Ingersoll Agency
716 1/2 Sunset Boulevard
Los Angeles, California 90069
Tel: 213-874-6434

Lou Irwin Agency, Inc.
9901 Durant Drive
Beverly Hills, California 90212
Tel: 213-553-4775

J. M. Associates
8400 Sunset Boulevard
Los Angeles, California 90069
Tel: 213-656-2607

Jones/Hunter & Associates
7033 Sunset Boulevard
Los Angeles, California 90028
Tel: 213-461-3793

Junior Artists Unlimited
4914 Lankershim Boulevard
North Hollywood, California
91601
Tel: 213-763-9000

Kahn-Penny Agency
7466 Beverly Boulevard
Los Angeles, California 90036
Tel: 213-938-4114

Toni Kelman Agency
8537 3/8 Sunset Boulevard
Los Angeles, California 90069
Tel: 213-657-3670

Paul Kohner, Inc.
9169 Sunset Boulevard
Los Angeles, California 90069
Tel: 213-271-5165

Kumin-Olenick Agency
400 South Beverly Drive, Room
216
Beverly Hills, California 90212
Tel: 213-553-8561

Irving Paul Lazar Agency
211 South Beverly Drive
Beverly Hills, California 90212
Tel: 213-275-6153

Caroline Leonetti Agency
6526 Sunset Boulevard
Los Angeles, California 90028
Tel: 213-462-2345

Sidney M. Levee Agency
8721 Sunset Boulevard
Los Angeles, California 90069
Tel: 213-652-0012

Levin-Karg Agency
328 South Beverly Drive
Beverly Hills, California 90212
Tel: 213-277-8881

Henry Lewis Agency
9172 Sunset Boulevard
Los Angeles, California 90069
Tel: 213-275-5129

George Litto Agency, Inc.
9000 Sunset Boulevard
Los Angeles, California 90069
Tel: 213-278-0017

Robert Longnecker Agency
8438 Melrose Place
Los Angeles, California 90069
Tel: 213-653-3770

Grace Lyons Agency
8730 Sunset Boulevard
Los Angeles, California 90069
Tel: 213-652-5290

M.E.W. Company
151 North San Vicente Boulevard
Beverly Hills, California 90211
Tel: 213-653-4731

MGA Mary Grady Agency
10850 Riverside Drive
North Hollywood, California
91602
Tel: 213-985-9800

M-M-C Agency
5400 Hollywood Boulevard
Los Angeles, California 90028
Tel: 213-467-7278

M.T.A. Artists Manager
4615 Melrose Avenue
Los Angeles, California 90029
Tel: 213-661-9888

Mitzi MacGregor Agency
13455 Ventura Boulevard
Sherman Oaks, California 94403
Tel: 213-872-1146

Major Media Management
3330 Barham Boulevard
Los Angeles, California 90068
Tel: 213-876-3110

Major Talent Agency, Inc.
113 North San Vicente Boulevard
Beverly Hills, California 90211
Tel: 213-655-4870

Alvin G. Manuel Agency
1649 Selby Avenue
Los Angeles, California 90024
Tel: 213-474-6842

Paul Marion Agency
9110 Sunset Boulevard
Los Angeles, California 90069
Tel: 213-274-8285

Ernestine McClendon
Enterprises, Inc.
8440 Sunset Boulevard
Los Angeles, California 90069
Tel: 213-654-4425

James McHugh Agency
8150 Beverly Boulevard
Los Angeles, California 90048
Tel: 213-651-2770

Hazel McMillan & Associates
Agency
9426 Santa Monica Boulevard
Beverly Hills, California 90210
Tel: 213-276-9823

Ben Medford Agency
9000 Sunset Boulevard
Los Angeles, California 90069
Tel: 213-271-7021

William Meiklejohn Associates
9250 Wilshire Boulevard
Beverly Hills, California 90212
Tel: 213-273-2566

Fred Messenger Agency
8265 Sunset Boulevard
Los Angeles, California 90046
Tel: 213-654-3800

The Mishkin Agency, Inc.
9255 Sunset Boulevard
Los Angeles, California 90069
Tel: 213-274-5261

Molson-Stanton Associates
Agency, Inc.
10889 Wilshire Boulevard
Los Angeles, California 90024
Tel: 213-477-1262

Eve Montaigne Agency
7906 Santa Monica Boulevard
Los Angeles, California 90046
Tel: 213-654-3083

William Morris Agency, Inc.
151 El Camino Drive
Beverly Hills, California 90212
Tel: 213-274-7451

Burton Moss Agency
118 South Beverly Drive, Suite
217
Beverly Hills, California 90212
Tel: 213-275-6195

H. David Moss & Associates
409 North Camden Drive
Beverly Hills, California 90212
Tel: 213-273-4530

Marvin Moss Agency
9229 Sunset Boulevard
Los Angeles, California 90069
Tel: 213-274-8483

Mary Murphy Agency
9172 Sunset Boulevard
Los Angeles, California 90069
Tel: 213-273-5836

Fran O'Bryan Agency
1648 Wilshire Boulevard
Los Angeles, California 90017
Tel: 213-483-7452

O'Bryan's Talent West, Inc.
1648 Wilshire Boulevard
Los Angeles, California 90017
Tel: 213-483-7452

Maurine Oliver & Associates
8746 Sunset Boulevard
Los Angeles, California 90069
Tel: 213-657-1250

Dorothy Day Otis Agency
6430 Sunset Boulevard
Los Angeles, California 90028
Tel: 213-461-4911

Pacific Artists Ltd.
515 North La Cienega Boulevard
Los Angeles, California 90048
Tel: 213-657-5990

Ben Pearson Agency
6399 Wilshire Boulevard
Los Angeles, California 90048
Tel: 213-651-3381

The Pickman Company, Inc.
148 South Beverly Boulevard
Beverly Hills, California 90212
Tel: 213-273-8273

Mildred O. Portnoy Agency
13111 Ventura Boulevard
Studio City, California 91604
Tel: 213-783-5886

Premiere Artists & Productions
Agency
6399 Wilshire Boulevard
Los Angeles, California 90048
Tel: 213-651-3381

Guy Prescott Agency
8920 Wonderland Avenue
Los Angeles, California 90046
Tel: 213-656-1963

R & I Enterprises
12429 Ventura Court
Studio City, California 91604
Tel: 213-762-4478

Raison-Grossman Agency
8730 Sunset Boulevard
Los Angeles, California 90069
Tel: 213-657-3040

Victor Ray
6331 Hollywood Boulevard
Los Angeles, California 90028
Tel: 213-469-3509

Bill Robards Agency
4421 Riverside Drive
Burbank, California 91505
Tel: 213-845-8547

Robinson & Associates, Inc.
132 South Rodeo Drive
Beverly Hills, California 90212
Tel: 213-275-6114

Robinson-Weintraub &
Associates, Inc.
8438 Melrose Place
Los Angeles, California 90069
Tel: 213-653-5802

Harold Rose Artists, Ltd.
8530 Wilshire Boulevard
Beverly Hills, California 90211
Tel: 213-652-3961

Howard Rose
9720 Wilshire Boulevard
Beverly Hills, California 90212
Tel: 213-273-6700

Sam Rubins Agency
9033 Wilshire Boulevard
Beverly Hills, California 90211
Tel: 213-556-2247

Betty Ruby Talent Agency
1741 North Ivar Street, Suite 119
Los Angeles, California 90028
Tel: 213-466-6652

Art Rush, Inc.
10221 Riverside Drive
North Hollywood, California
  91602
Tel: 213-985-3033

The Sackheim Agency
222 North Canon Drive
Beverly Hills, California 90210
Tel: 213-276-3151

Irving Salkow Agency
450 North Roxbury Drive
Beverly Hills, California 90210
Tel: 213-276-3141

Norah Sanders Agency
9301 Wilshire Boulevard
Beverly Hills, California 90210
Tel: 213-278-8080

James L. Saphier Agency, Inc.
9229 Sunset Boulevard, Suite 408
Los Angeles, California 90069
Tel: 213-271-7231

William Schuller Agency
9110 Sunset Boulevard
Los Angeles, California 90069
Tel: 213-273-4000

Don Schwartz & Associates
8721 Sunset Boulevard
Los Angeles, California 90069
Tel: 213-657-8910

Scott & Smith Associates
280 South Beverly Drive
Beverly Hills, California 90212
Tel: 213-273-3773

Hal Shafer Agency
4421 Riverside Drive
Burbank, California 91505
Tel: 213-980-6333

Shapiro-Lichtman, Inc.
116 North Robertson Boulevard
Los Angeles, California 90048
Tel: 213-652-9893

Glenn Shaw Agency
8440 Sunset Boulevard
Los Angeles, California 90069
Tel: 213-654-6110

Lew Sherrell Agency, Ltd.
7060 Hollywood Boulevard
Los Angeles, California 90028
Tel: 213-461-9955

The Shiffrin Agency
941 North La Cienega Boulevard
Los Angeles, California 90069
Tel: 213-659-3550

Shipley-Ishimoto Agency
9163 Sunset Boulevard
Los Angeles, California 90069
Tel: 213-276-6251

A. Frederick Shorr, Inc.
1717 North Highland Avenue
Los Angeles, California 90028
Tel: 213-461-9344

Dorothy Shreve Agency
13444 Ventura Boulevard
Sherman Oaks, California 91403
Tel: 213-872-2603

Jerome Siegel Associates
8733 Sunset Boulevard
Los Angeles, California 90069
Tel: 213-652-6033

The Sindell Agency
257 Tavistock Avenue
Los Angeles, California 90049
Tel: 213-472-5714

George Soares Associates
12735 Ventura Boulevard
Studio City, California 91604
Tel: 213-980-0400

Charles H. Stern Agency, Inc.
9220 Sunset Boulevard
Los Angeles, California 90069
Tel: 213-273-6890

Norman Stevens Agency
10929 Weyburn Avenue
Los Angeles, California 90024
Tel: 213-270-4902

Larry Sugho Agency
1017 North La Cienega
Boulevard
Los Angeles, California 90069
Tel: 213-657-1450

H. N. Swanson Agency, Inc.
8523 Sunset Boulevard
Los Angeles, California 90069
Tel: 213-652-5385

Talent, Inc.
1421 North McCadden Place
Los Angeles, California 90028
Tel: 213-462-0913

Herb Tannen & Associates
6640 Sunset Boulevard
Los Angeles, California 90028
Tel: 213-461-3055

Taylor-Kubik, Ltd.
8235 Santa Monica Boulevard
Los Angeles, California 90046
Tel: 213-656-7590

Herb Tobias & Associates, Inc.
1901 Avenue of the Stars
Los Angeles, California 90067
Tel: 213-277-6211

Twentieth Century Artists
4749 Vineland Avenue
North Hollywood, California
91602
Tel: 213-980-5552

George Ullman Agency
8983 Sunset Boulevard
Los Angeles, California 90069
Tel: 213-980-8552

Angela Vitt Agency
9172 Sunset Boulevard
Los Angeles, California 90069
Tel: 213-276-1646

Ruth Webb Ltd.
9229 Sunset Boulevard
Los Angeles, California 90069
Tel: 213-274-4311

Jack Weiner Agency
8721 Sunset Boulevard
Los Angeles, California 90069
Tel: 213-652-1140

✓Murray Weintraub Agency
1017 North La Cienega
Boulevard
Los Angeles, California 90069
Tel: 213-652-3892

✓ Lew Weitzman & Associates
9171 Wilshire Boulevard
Beverly Hills, California 90210
Tel: 213-278-5562

Jerry B. Wheeler Artists'
Management
8721 Sunset Boulevard
Los Angeles, California 90069
Tel: 213-656-0032

Ted Wilk Agency
9172 Sunset Boulevard
Los Angeles, California 90069
Tel: 213-273-0801

Peter Witt Associates, Inc.
321 South Beverly Drive
Beverly Hills, California 90212
Tel: 213-277-8711

✓ Witzer & Small Agency
9441 Wilshire Boulevard
Beverly Hills, California 90212
Tel: 213-278-1926

Jack Wormser Agency, Inc.
1717 North Highland Avenue
Los Angeles, California 90028
Tel: 213-466-9111

Sylvia Wosk Agency
439 South La Cienega Boulevard
Los Angeles, California 90048
Tel: 213-274-8063

Ann Wright Associates, Ltd.
8422 Melrose Place
Los Angeles, California 90069
Tel: 213-655-5040

Ziegler-Ross, Inc.
9255 Sunset Boulevard
Los Angeles, California 90069
Tel: 213-278-0070

Herman Zimmerman Agency
12077 Ventura Place
Studio City, California 91604
Tel: 213-766-8119

San Francisco area:

Brebner Agency
1615 Polk Street
San Francisco, California 94109
Tel: 415-771-3488

Demeter Agency
2087 Union Street
San Francisco, California 94123
Tel: 415-567-5226

San Francisco Casting
1615 Polk Street
San Francisco, California 94104
Tel: 415-771-3492

Colorado:

Athena Enterprises, Inc.
1515 Monroe Street
Denver, Colorado 80206
Tel: 303-399-8681

Illinois Talent
2664 South Krameria Street
Denver, Colorado 80222
Tel: 303-757-8675

Image Developers
1422 North Hancock
Colorado Springs, Colorado
80901
Tel: 303-471-1266

J. F. Images, Inc.
1776 South Jackson Street, Suite
702
Denver, Colorado 80210
Tel: 303-758-7777

Joe McKenna Productions
470 South Colorado Boulevard
Denver, Colorado 80222
Tel: 303-322-0106

John Robert Powers Agency
1550 Court Place
Denver, Colorado 80202
Tel: 303-222-7991

Georgia:

Atlanta Models & Talent
2581 Piedmont Road, N.E.
Atlanta, Georgia 30324
Tel: 404-261-9627

Ray Belue & Associates
100 Colony Square
Atlanta, Georgia 30361
Tel: 404-892-0660

House of Talent of Cain
996 Lindridge
Atlanta, Georgia 30324
Tel: 404-261-5543

The Peachtrees
15 Baltimore Place, N.W.
Atlanta, Georgia 30308
Tel: 404-881-8118

Hawaii:

B & B Talent Agency
657 Kapiolani, Suite 13
Honolulu, Hawaii 96813
Tel: 808-533-3583

Illinois:

A-Plus, Inc.
615 North Wabash Avenue
Chicago, Illinois 60611
Tel: 312-642-8151

Agency for the Performing Arts,
Inc.
203 North Wabash Avenue
Chicago, Illinois 60611
Tel: 312-664-7703

Willard Alexander, Inc.
333 North Michigan Avenue
Chicago, Illinois 60611
Tel: 312-236-2460

Associated Booking Corporation
919 North Michigan Avenue
Chicago, Illinois 60611
Tel: 312-751-2000

Burns Sports Celebrity Service,
Inc.
One IBM Plaza
Chicago, Illinois 60611
Tel: 312-321-1650

Exclusively Yours, Inc.
535 North Michigan Avenue
Chicago, Illinois 60611
Tel: 312-329-9051

Geddes Agency
3148 Hancock Center
Chicago, Illinois 60611
Tel: 312-664-9890

Guys & Dolls
333 East Ontario Street
Chicago, Illinois 60611
Tel: 312-337-0276

Shirley Hamilton, Inc.
500 North Michigan Avenue, 7th
Floor
Chicago, Illinois 60611
Tel: 312-644-0300

Helpmate, Inc.
8 South Michigan Avenue
Chicago, Illinois 60603
Tel: 312-372-6875

Frank J. Hogan, Inc.
307 North Michigan Avenue
Chicago, Illinois 60601
Tel: 312-263-6910

Emilia Lorence, Ltd.
619 North Wabash Avenue
Chicago, Illinois 60611
Tel: 312-943-4558

William Morris Agency, Inc.
435 North Michigan Avenue
Chicago, Illinois 60611
Tel: 312-467-1744

Playboy Models, Inc.
Playboy Building
919 North Michigan Avenue
Chicago, Illinois 60611
Tel: 312-664-9024

Jimmy Richards Productions
919 North Michigan Avenue
Chicago, Illinois 60611
Tel: 312-664-1552

Jack Russell & Associates
1010 Dixie Highway
Chicago Heights, Illinois 60411
Tel: 312-765-7060

Norman Schucart Enterprises
1417 Green Bay Road
Highland Park, Illinois 60201
Tel: 312-433-1113

Howard W. Schultz
2525 West Peterson
Chicago, Illinois 60659
Tel: 312-769-2244

Seymour Shapiro
166 East Superior Street
Chicago, Illinois 60611
Tel: 312-266-7620

Eileen Slater Associates
5445 North Sheridan Road
Chicago, Illinois 60640
Tel: 312-275-9565

The Talent Registry
400 North Michigan Avenue,
   Room 2002
Chicago, Illinois 60611
Tel: 312-828-0166

New Mexico:

Chaparral Casting & Services,
   Inc.
928 Avenida Manana, N.E.
Albuquerque, New Mexico 87110
Tel: 505-266-0460
Carmen Martines, President

Cinema Services of New Mexico
712 Sundown Place, S.E.
Albuquerque, New Mexico 87108
Tel: 505-255-7003
Jeanne Swain, President

Professional Personnel, Inc.
2521 San Pedro Drive, N.E.
Albuquerque, New Mexico 87110
Tel: 505-256-9866
Harold Mohart, President

New York:

ATI
888 Seventh Avenue
New York, New York 10019
Tel: 212-977-2300

Abrams-Rubaloff & Associates
10 East 53rd Street
New York, New York 10022
Tel: 212-758-3636

Rose Adair
250 West 57th Street
New York, New York 10019
Tel: 212-582-1957

Bret Adams, Ltd.
36 East 61st Street
New York, New York 10021
Tel: 212-752-7864

Ceil Adler Agency, Inc.
67 West 55th Street
New York, New York 10019
Tel: 212-757-2535

Agency for Performing Arts
120 West 57th Street
New York, New York 10019
Tel: 212-581-8860

Willard Alexander, Inc.
660 Madison Avenue
New York, New York 10021
Tel: 212-751-7070

Maria Almonte
160 West 46th Street
New York, New York 10036
Tel: 212-246-7481

American Artists Management
303 West 42nd Street
New York, New York 10036
Tel: 212-265-0430

American International Talent
   Agency
166 West 125th Street
New York, New York 10027
Tel: 212-663-4626

Beverly Anderson Agency
1472 Broadway, Suite 806
New York, New York 10036
Tel: 212-279-5553

Artists Management Associates
200 West 57th Street
New York, New York 10019
Tel: 212-757-2157

Associated Booking Corporation
445 Park Avenue
New York, New York 10022
Tel: 212-421-5200

Richard Astor Agency
119 West 57th Street
New York, New York 10019
Tel: 212-581-1970

Richard Bauman Agency
1650 Broadway
New York, New York 10019
Tel: 212-757-0098

Lola M. Bishop
853 Seventh Avenue
New York, New York 10019
Tel: 212-245-4775

J. Michael Bloom, Ltd.
400 Madison Avenue, Suite 1009
New York, New York 10017
Tel: 212-838-0982

Jane Broder
35 Park Avenue
New York, New York 10016
Tel: 212-685-6729

Bernard Burke–Max Roth
48 West 48th Street
New York, New York 10036
Tel: 212-757-4540

Bertha Case
42 West 53rd Street
New York, New York 10019
Tel: 212-581-6280

Central Casting Corporation
200 West 54th Street
New York, New York 10019
Tel: 212-582-4933

The Cereghetti Agency
1564 Broadway
New York, New York 10036
Tel: 212-765-5260

Chartwell Agency
1345 Avenue of the Americas
New York, New York 10019
Tel: 212-765-6900

Circle Artists
200 West 57th Street
New York, New York 10019
Tel: 212-757-4668

Toby Cole Actors Agency
234 West 44th Street
New York, New York 10036
Tel: 212-279-7770

Coleman-Rosenberg Agency
667 Madison Avenue
New York, New York 10021
Tel: 212-838-0734

Charles W. Conaway
345 East 56th Street
New York, New York 10022
Tel: 212-759-8479

Bill Cooper Associates
16 East 52nd Street
New York, New York 10022
Tel: 212-758-6491

Frank Cooper Associates
16 East 52nd Street
New York, New York 10022
Tel: 212-758-6491

Jane Deacy Agency
119 East 54th Street
New York, New York 10022
Tel: 212-752-4865

Diamond Artists
119 West 57th Street
New York, New York 10019
Tel: 212-247-3025

Stephen Draper Agency
37 West 57th Street
New York, New York 10019
Tel: 212-421-5780

Ford Men
344 East 59th Street
New York, New York 10022
Tel: 212-753-6500

Ford Model Agency
344 East 59th Street
New York, New York 10022
Tel: 212-688-8538

Foster-Fell Agency, Inc.
515 Madison Avenue
New York, New York 10022
Tel: 212-355-7227

The Gage Group, Inc.
1650 Broadway
New York, New York 10019
Tel: 212-541-5250

Robert W. Gewald
2 West 59th Street
New York, New York 10019
Tel: 212-753-0450

George Goldsmith
360 West 22nd Street
New York, New York 10011
Tel: 212-242-7060

Martin Goodman
654 Madison Avenue
New York, New York 10021
Tel: 212-751-3555

Janet Hall Artists Bureau
200 West 58th Street
New York, New York 10019
Tel: 212-265-1673

Michael Hartig Agency
850 Seventh Avenue
New York, New York 10019
Tel: 212-489-8484

Helen Harvey Associates
1697 Broadway
New York, New York 10019
Tel: 212-581-5610

Henderson/Hogan Agency, Inc.
200 West 57th Street
New York, New York 10019
Tel: 212-765-5190

Hesseltine-Baker Associates, Ltd.
119 West 57th Street
New York, New York 10019
Tel: 212-489-0966

Hans J. Hofmann
200 West 58th Street
New York, New York 10019
Tel: 212-246-1557

Diana Hunt
246 West 44th Street
New York, New York 10036
Tel: 212-279-0009

Jeff Hunter
119 West 57th Street
New York, New York 10019
Tel: 212-757-4995

International Attractions
342 Madison Avenue
New York, New York 10017
Tel: 212-867-3887

International Creative
   Management
40 West 57th Street
New York, New York 10019
Tel: 212-586-0440

International Management, Inc.
767 Third Avenue
New York, New York 10022
Tel: 212-832-4973

Leonard Jacobson
1650 Broadway
New York, New York 10019
Tel: 212-757-3920

Joe Jordan Talent Agency
400 Madison Avenue
New York, New York 10017
Tel: 212-755-2198

Kahn, Lifflander & Rhodes, Inc.
853 Seventh Avenue
New York, New York 10019
Tel: 212-582-1280

Kaplan-Veidt Ltd.
667 Madison Avenue
New York, New York 10021
Tel: 212-421-7370

Kennedy Artists Representatives
881 Seventh Avenue
New York, New York 10019
Tel: 212-675-3944

Archer King, Ltd.
1271 Avenue of the Americas
New York, New York 10020
Tel: 212-581-8513

Kolmar-Luth Entertainment, Inc.
1776 Broadway
New York, New York 10019
Tel: 212-581-5833

Lloyd Kolmer Enterprises
62 East 55th Street
New York, New York 10022
Tel: 212-582-4735

L.B.H. Associates
1775 Broadway
New York, New York 10019
Tel: 212-582-4940

Lionel Larner, Ltd.
850 Seventh Avenue
New York, New York 10019
Tel: 212-246-3105

Irving Paul Lazar
465 Park Avenue
New York, New York 10022
Tel: 212-355-1177

Gary Leaverton, Inc.
1650 Broadway
New York, New York 10019
Tel: 212-541-9640

Sanford Leigh
527 Madison Avenue
New York, New York 10022
Tel: 212-752-4450

Lenny-Debin, Inc.
140 West 58th Street
New York, New York 10019
Tel: 212-582-0270

Julie Leonard
245 West 104th Street
New York, New York 10025
Tel: 212-663-6911

Lester Lewis Associates, Inc.
156 East 52nd Street
New York, New York 10022
Tel: 212-753-5082

M.E.W. Company
Mary Ellen White
370 Lexington Avenue
New York, New York 10017
Tel: 212-889-7272

Magna Artists
1370 Avenue of the Americas
New York, New York 10019
Tel: 212-489-8027

Marje/Fields
250 West 57th Street
New York, New York 10019
Tel: 212-581-7240

Marge McDermott Enterprises
215 East 37th Street
New York, New York 10016
Tel: 212-687-4363

Josh Meyer Agency
527 Madison Avenue
New York, New York 10022
Tel: 212-752-0505

William Morris Agency, Inc.
1350 Avenue of the Americas
New York, New York 10019
Tel: 212-586-5100

Ellen Neuwald, Inc.
905 West End Avenue
New York, New York 10025
Tel: 212-663-1586

Newborn Associates
Plaza Hotel
New York, New York 10019
Tel: 212-688-6818

Fifi Oscard Agency, Ltd.
19 West 44th Street
New York, New York 10036
Tel: 212-764-1100

Barna Ostertag
501 Fifth Avenue
New York, New York 10017
Tel: 212-697-6339

Paramuse Artists Associates
745 Fifth Avenue
New York, New York 10022
Tel: 212-758-5055

Cye Perkins Agency
139 East 52nd Street
New York, New York 10022
Tel: 212-752-4488

Barron Polan, Ltd.
250 East 49th Street
New York, New York 10017
Tel: 212-759-4727

Premier Talent Associates, Inc.
888 Seventh Avenue
New York, New York 10019
Tel: 212-757-4300

Queen Booking Corporation
1650 Broadway
New York, New York 10019
Tel: 212-489-1400

Rapp Enterprises
1650 Broadway
New York, New York 10019
Tel: 212-247-6646

Rice-McHugh Agency, Inc.
136 East 57th Street
New York, New York 10022
Tel: 212-752-0222

Tony Rivers
154 West 54th Street
New York, New York 10019
Tel: 212-581-1466

Paul Rosen
39 West 55th Street
New York, New York 10019
Tel: 212-541-8641

Eddie Ross
1564 Broadway
New York, New York 10036
Tel: 212-757-8170

Lynn Rosselli Agency
1650 Broadway
New York, New York 10019
Tel: 212-489-7227

Bernard Rubenstein
342 Madison Avenue
New York, New York 10017
Tel: 212-986-1317

Dick Rubin, Ltd.
501 Madison Avenue
New York, New York 10022
Tel: 212-751-0445

Charles Vernon Ryan
35 West 53rd Street
New York, New York 10019
Tel: 212-245-2225

Gus Schirmer, Jr.
667 Madison Avenue
New York, New York 10021
Tel: 212-838-3413

William Schuller Agency, Inc.
667 Madison Avenue
New York, New York 10021
Tel: 212-758-1919

Mort Schwartz Agency
156 East 52nd Street
New York, New York 10022
Tel: 212-753-1529

Joan Scott, Inc.
162 West 56th Street
New York, New York 10019
Tel: 212-246-9029

Monty Silver
850 Seventh Avenue
New York, New York 10019
Tel: 212-765-4040

Smith-Stevens, Inc.
1650 Broadway
New York, New York 10019
Tel: 212-582-8040

Anthony Soglio
423 Madison Avenue
New York, New York 10017
Tel: 212-751-1850

Stewart Artists Corporation
405 Park Avenue
New York, New York 10022
Tel: 212-752-0944

Stroud Management
18 East 48th Street
New York, New York 10016
Tel: 212-688-0226

Talent Representatives, Inc.
20 East 53rd Street
New York, New York 10022
Tel: 212-752-1835

Jean Thomas Agency, Inc.
850 Seventh Avenue
New York, New York 10019
Tel: 212-586-4616

Michael Thomas Agency, Inc.
22 East 60th Street
New York, New York 10022
Tel: 212-755-2616

Tranum, Robertson & Hughes,
Inc.
2 Dag Hammarskjold Plaza
New York, New York 10017
Tel: 212-371-7500

Gloria Troy Talent Agency
1790 Broadway
New York, New York 10019
Tel: 212-582-0260

Universal Attractions, Inc.
888 Seventh Avenue
New York, New York 10019
Tel: 212-582-7575

Paul Vance
150 West 55th Street
New York, New York 10019
Tel: 212-581-0030

Ruth Webb, Ltd.
200 West 57th Street
New York, New York 10019
Tel: 212-265-4311

Wender & Associates
30 East 60th Street
New York, New York 10022
Tel: 212-832-8330

Henry William Wiese
350 West 55th Street
New York, New York 10019
Tel: 212-265-1930

Wilhelmina Men
9 East 37th Street
New York, New York 10016
Tel: 212-532-7715

Wilhelmina Model Agency
9 East 37th Street
New York, New York 10016
Tel: 212-532-7141

Joe Williams
1650 Broadway
New York, New York 10019
Tel: 212-245-9310

Peter Witt Associates, Inc.
37 West 57th Street
New York, New York 10019
Tel: 212-759-7966

Hanns Wolters Agency
342 Madison Avenue
New York, New York 10017
Tel: 212-867-9177

Ann Wright Representatives
137 East 57th Street
New York, New York 10022
Tel: 212-832-0110

Babs Zimmerman Productions
1414 Avenue of the Americas
New York, New York 10019
Tel: 212-421-9555

SAG-FRANCHISED TALENT AGENTS

Arizona:

Bobby Ball Agency
4831 Eleventh Street
Phoenix, Arizona 85014

Dar Lu Modeling and Talent
Agency
2302 East Speedway
Tucson, Arizona 85719

Fosi's Talent Agency
2777 North Campbell Avenue
Tucson, Arizona 85719

Plaza Three
4343 North Sixteenth Street
Phoenix, Arizona 85016

Red Wing American Indian
Talent Agency
711 East Palo Verde
Phoenix, Arizona 85014

Tor/Ann Talent And Booking
3000 East Thomas Road
Phoenix, Arizona 85016

California:
  Los Angeles area:

Aberle & Associates
9100 Sunset Boulevard
Los Angeles, California 90069
Tel: 213-274-9801

Abrams-Rubaloff & Associates,
  Inc.
9012 Beverly Boulevard
Los Angeles, California 90048
Tel: 213-273-5711

Bret Adams
8440 Sunset Boulevard
Los Angeles, California 90069
Tel: 213-656-6420

Agency for the Performing Arts
9000 Sunset Boulevard
Los Angeles, California 90069
Tel: 213-273-0744

Aimee Entertainment
8383 Wilshire Boulevard
Beverly Hills, California 90213
Tel: 213-655-0701

Carlos Alvarado Agency
8820 Sunset Boulevard
Los Angeles, California 90069
Tel: 213-652-0272

Amaral Agency
10000 Riverside Drive
Toluca Lake, California 90612
Tel: 213-980-1013

Velvet Amber Agency
6515 Sunset Boulevard
Los Angeles, California 90028
Tel: 213-464-8184

Armstrong-Deuser
449 South Beverly Drive
Beverly Hills, California 90213
Tel: 213-553-8611

Artists' Career Management
10929 Weyburn
Los Angeles, California 90024
Tel: 213-270-4902

Associated Booking Corporation
9595 Wilshire Boulevard
Beverly Hills, California 90213
Tel: 213-273-5600

Miles Bohm Auer
8344 Melrose Avenue, Suite 29
Los Angeles, California 90069
Tel: 213-462-6416

Barr/Gilly Agency
8721 Sunset Boulevard
Los Angeles, California 90069
Tel: 213-659-0141

The Barskin Agency
8721 Sunset Boulevard
Los Angeles, California 90069
Tel: 213-657-5740

Richard Bauman Associates
409 North Camden
Beverly Hills, California 90213
Tel: 213-274-6385

Belcourt Artists
222 North Canon Drive
Beverly Hills, California 90213
Tel: 213-276-6205

Belson Agency
211 South Beverly Drive
Beverly Hills, California 90213
Tel: 213-274-9169

The Blake Agency, Ltd.
409 North Camden Drive
Beverly Hills, California 90210
Tel: 213-278-6885

William Blake Agency
9012 West Olympic
Beverly Hills, California 90213
Tel: 213-274-0321

Nina Blanchard Agency
1717 North Highland Avenue
Los Angeles, California 90028
Tel: 213-462-7274

Blumenthal Artists Agency
435 South La Cienega Boulevard
Los Angeles, California 90048
Tel: 213-656-1451

Paul Brandon
9046 Sunset Boulevard
Los Angeles, California 90069
Tel: 213-273-6173

Bresler, Wolff, Cota & Livingston
190 North Canon Drive
Beverly Hills, California 90210
Tel: 213-278-3200

Alex Brewis Agency
9145 Sunset Boulevard
Los Angeles, California 90069
Tel: 213-274-9874

Iris Burton
1450 Belfast
Los Angeles, California 90069
Tel: 213-652-0954

The Calder Agency
8749 Sunset Boulevard
Los Angeles, California 90069
Tel: 213-652-3380

Carey-Phelps-Colvin Agency
7813 Sunset Boulevard
Los Angeles, California 90046
Tel: 213-874-7780

Casselman Agency
141 1/2 North Beverly Glen
Los Angeles, California 90024
Tel: 213-279-1537

Century Artists, Ltd.
9470 Santa Monica Boulevard
Beverly Hills, California 90210
Tel: 213-273-4366

Charter Management
9000 Sunset Boulevard
Los Angeles, California 90069
Tel: 213-278-1690

Chasin-Park-Citron Agency
9255 Sunset Boulevard
Los Angeles, California 90069
Tel: 213-273-7190

Chutuk & Associates
9905 Santa Monica Boulevard
Beverly Hills, California 90213
Tel: 213-552-1773

Kingsley Colton & Associates, Inc.
321 South Beverly Drive
Beverly Hills, California 90212
Tel: 213-277-5491

Commercial Talent Agency
6922 Hollywood Boulevard
Los Angeles, California 90028
Tel: 213-466-6433

Commercials Unlimited
7461 Beverly Boulevard
Los Angeles, California 90036
Tel: 213-937-2220

Connor-Corfino Associates, Inc.
14241 Ventura Boulevard
Sherman Oaks, California 91403
Tel: 213-981-1133

Contemporary-Korman Artists,
Ltd.
132 North Lasky Drive
Beverly Hills, California 90212
Tel: 213-278-8250

Doug Cooper Agency
10850 Riverside Drive
North Hollywood, California
91603
Tel: 213-980-6100

Coralie Jr. Agency
5107 Hollywood Boulevard
Los Angeles, California 90027
Tel: 213-663-1268

Robert Cosden
15233 Ventura
Sherman Oaks, California 91403
Tel: 213-788-1881

Kerwin Coughlin Agency
10850 Riverside Drive
North Hollywood, California
91603
Tel: 213-980-7200

Bernyce Cronin Agency
439 South La Cienega Boulevard
Los Angeles, California 90048
Tel: 213-273-8144

Lil Cumber Attractions Agency
6515 Sunset Boulevard
Los Angeles, California 90028
Tel: 213-469-1919

William D. Cunningham &
Associates
5900 Wilshire Boulevard
Los Angeles, California 90036
Tel: 213-937-8500

Dade/Rosen Associates
999 North Doheny Drive
Los Angeles, California 90069
Tel: 213-278-7077

Diamond Artists, Ltd.
8400 Sunset Boulevard
Los Angeles, California 90069
Tel: 213-654-5960

The Dietrich Agency
10701 Riverside Drive
North Hollywood, California
91603
Tel: 213-985-4824

John Dugan Entertainment
9229 Sunset Boulevard
Los Angeles, California 90069
Tel: 213-278-5616

Entertainment Enterprises
1680 Vine Street
Los Angeles, California 90028
Tel: 213-462-6001

FCA Agency, Inc.
9000 Sunset Boulevard
Los Angeles, California 90069
Tel: 213-278-1460

William Felber Agency
6636 Hollywood Boulevard
Los Angeles, California 90028
Tel: 213-466-7629

Carol Ferrell
6331 Hollywood Boulevard
Los Angeles, California 90028
Tel: 213-466-8311

Jack Fields & Associates
9255 Sunset Boulevard
Los Angeles, California 90069
Tel: 213-278-1333

Film Artists Management
   Enterprises
8278 Sunset Boulevard
Los Angeles, California 90046
Tel: 213-656-7590

The Flaire Agency
155 South Robertson Boulevard
Beverly Hills, California 90213
Tel: 213-659-6721

Paul D. Flowers
5427 Sepulveda Boulevard
Culver City, California 90230
Tel: 213-839-1812

Kurt Frings Agency, Inc.
9025 Wilshire Boulevard
Beverly Hills, California 90213
Tel: 213-274-8881

Dale Garrick International
8831 Sunset Boulevard
Los Angeles, California 90069
Tel: 213-657-2661

Phil Gersh Agency, Inc.
222 North Canon Drive
Beverly Hills, California 90210
Tel: 213-274-6611

Carter J. Gibson
9000 Sunset Boulevard
Los Angeles, California 90069
Tel: 213-274-8813

Herman Gold Agency, Inc.
9034 Sunset Boulevard
Los Angeles, California 90069
Tel: 213-274-1621

Goldin, Dennis & Masser
470 South San Vicente Boulevard
Los Angeles, California 90048
Tel: 213-651-1700

Goldstein-Shapira
9171 Wilshire Boulevard
Beverly Hills, California 90213
Tel: 213-278-2742

Gordean-Friedman Agency, Inc.
9229 Sunset Boulevard
Los Angeles, California 90069
Tel: 213-273-4195

Della Gower Artists' Agency
1680 Vine Street
Los Angeles, California 90028
Tel: 213-464-2117

The Granite Agency
1920 South La Cienega Boulevard
Los Angeles, California 90034
Tel: 213-934-8383

Ivan Green Agency
1900 Avenue of the Stars
Los Angeles, California 90067
Tel: 213-277-1541

The Greenvine Agency
9021 Melrose Avenue
Los Angeles, California 90069
Tel: 213-278-5800

Milton Grossman
8730 Sunset Boulevard
Los Angeles, California 90069
Tel: 213-657-3040

Jeanne Halliburton Agency
5205 Hollywood Boulevard
Los Angeles, California 90027
Tel: 213-466-6138

Mitchell Hamilburg
292 South La Cienega Boulevard
Beverly Hills, California 90213
Tel: 213-657-1501

Beverly Hecht Agency
8949 Sunset Boulevard
Los Angeles, California 90069
Tel: 213-278-3544

Henderson-Wardlow-Hogan
247 South Beverly Drive
Beverly Hills, California 90213
Tel: 213-274-7815

The Hiller Agency
9220 Sunset Boulevard
Los Angeles, California 90069
Tel: 213-271-5601

Mark Hudson Agency
10960 Ventura Boulevard
North Hollywood, California
    91603
Tel: 213-766-8116

George B. Hunt & Associates
8350 Santa Monica Boulevard
Los Angeles, California 90069
Tel: 213-654-6600

Robert G. Hussong Agency
9000 Sunset Boulevard
Los Angeles, California 90069
Tel: 213-274-7652

Hyland-Chandler Agency
9100 Sunset Boulevard
Los Angeles, California 90069
Tel: 213-271-8188

George Ingersoll Agency
7167 1/2 Sunset Boulevard
Los Angeles, California 90069
Tel: 213-874-6434

Lou Irwin Agency, Inc.
9901 Durant Drive
Beverly Hills, California 90212
Tel: 213-553-4775

J. M. Associates
8400 Sunset Boulevard
Los Angeles, California 90069
Tel: 213-656-2086

Jones/Hunter & Associates
7033 Sunset Boulevard
Los Angeles, California 90028
Tel: 213-461-3793

Junior Artists Unlimited
4914 Lankershim Boulevard
North Hollywood, California
   91603
Tel: 213-763-9000

Kahn-Penny Agency
7466 Beverly Boulevard
Los Angeles, California 90036
Tel: 213-938-4114

Michael Karg Agency
328 South Beverly Drive
Beverly Hills, California 90213
Tel: 213-277-8881

Toni Kelman Agency
8537 3/8 Sunset Boulevard
Los Angeles, California 90069
Tel: 213-657-3670

Paul Kohner, Inc.
9169 Sunset Boulevard
Los Angeles, California 90069
Tel: 213-271-5165

Kumin-Olenick
400 South Beverly Drive, Room
   216
Beverly Hills, California 90213
Tel: 213-553-8561

Irving Paul Lazar Agency
211 South Beverly Drive
Beverly Hills, California 90212
Tel: 213-275-6153

Leaverton-Fields, Ltd.
434 North Rodeo Drive
Beverly Hills, California 90213
Tel: 213-273-7570

Caroline Leonetti Agency
6526 Sunset Boulevard
Los Angeles, California 90028
Tel: 213-462-2345

Sidney M. Levee Agency
8721 Sunset Boulevard
Los Angeles, California 90069
Tel: 213-652-0012

Mark Levin Associates
328 South Beverly Drive
Beverly Hills, California 90212
Tel: 213-277-8881

Robert Longenecker Agency
8438 Melrose Place
Los Angeles, California 90069
Tel: 213-653-3770

Bessie Loo
8746 Sunset Boulevard
Los Angeles, California 90069
Tel: 213-657-5888

Grace Lyons Agency
8730 Sunset Boulevard
Los Angeles, California 90069
Tel: 213-652-5290

M.E.W. Company
151 North San Vicente Boulevard
Beverly Hills, California 90211
Tel: 213-653-4731

MGA Mary Grady Agency
10850 Riverside Drive
North Hollywood, California
 91603
Tel: 213-985-9800

M-M-C Agency
5400 Hollywood Boulevard
Los Angeles, California 90028
Tel: 213-467-7278

M.T.A. Artists' Manager
4615 Melrose Avenue
Los Angeles, California 90029
Tel: 213-661-9888

Ernestine McClendon
 Enterprises, Inc.
8440 Sunset Boulevard
Los Angeles, California 90069
Tel: 213-654-4425

Mitzi McGregor
13455 Ventura Boulevard
Sherman Oaks, California 91403
Tel: 213-872-1146

James McHugh Agency
8150 Beverly Boulevard
Los Angeles, California 90048
Tel: 213-651-2770

Hazel McMillan & Associates
 Agency
9426 Santa Monica Boulevard
Beverly Hills, California 90210
Tel: 213-276-9823

William Meiklejohn Associates
9250 Wilshire Boulevard, Suite
 412
Beverly Hills, California 90213
Tel: 213-273-2566

Fred Messenger Agency
8265 Sunset Boulevard
Los Angeles, California 90046
Tel: 213-654-3800

The Mishkin Agency, Inc.
9255 Sunset Boulevard
Hollywood, California 90069
Tel: 213-274-5261

Eve Montaigne Agency
7906 Santa Monica Boulevard
Los Angeles, California 90046
Tel: 213-654-3083

Lola D. Moore
9172 Sunset Boulevard
Los Angeles, California 90069
Tel: 213-276-6097

William Morris Agency, Inc.
151 El Camino Drive
Beverly Hills, California 90213
Tel: 213-274-7451

Burton Moss Agency
118 South Beverly Drive, Suite
 217
Beverly Hills, California 90213
Tel: 213-275-6195

H. David Moss & Associates
409 North Camden Drive
Beverly Hills, California 90212
Tel: 213-273-4530

Marvin Moss Agency
9200 Sunset Boulevard
Los Angeles, California 90069
Tel: 213-274-8483

Mary Murphy Agency
10701 Riverside Drive
North Hollywood, California
91603
Tel: 213-985-4241

Marc Newman Agency
8530 Wilshire Boulevard
Beverly Hills, California 90213
Tel: 213-652-3419

Fran O'Bryan Agency
600 South San Vicente Boulevard
Los Angeles, California 90048
Tel: 213-653-0450

Maurine Oliver & Associates
8746 Sunset Boulevard
Los Angeles, California 90069
Tel: 213-657-1250

Dorothy Day Otis Agency
6430 Sunset Boulevard
Los Angeles, California 90028
Tel: 213-461-4911

Pacific Artists Ltd.
515 North La Cienega Boulevard
Los Angeles, California 90048
Tel: 213-657-5990

Pathway Artists' Management
1777 North Vine Street
Los Angeles, California 90028
Tel: 213-466-8156

Ben Pearson Agency
6399 Wilshire Boulevard
Los Angeles, California 90048
Tel: 213-651-3381

Pinnacle Artists Agency
211 South Beverly Drive
Beverly Hills, California 90213
Tel: 213-278-4822

Premiere Artists & Productions
    Agency
6399 Wilshire Boulevard
Los Angeles, California 90048
Tel: 213-651-3381

Guy Prescott Agency
8920 Wonderland Avenue
Los Angeles, California 90046
Tel: 213-656-1963

RPM Limited
400 South Beverly Drive
Beverly Hills, California 90213
Tel: 213-277-6730

Robert Raison
9575 Lime Orchard Road
Beverly Hills, California 90213
Tel: 213-274-7217

Edward Rakestraw Agency
7805 Sunset Boulevard
Los Angeles, California 90046
Tel: 213-876-1622

Regency Artists, Ltd.
9200 Sunset Boulevard
Los Angeles, California 90069
Tel: 213-273-7103

Rifkin-David
9615 Brighton Way
Beverly Hills, California 90213
Tel: 213-276-7598

Bill Robards Agency
4421 Riverside Drive
Burbank, California 91505
Tel: 213-845-8547

Robinson & Associates, Inc.
132 South Rodeo Drive
Beverly Hills, California 90212
Tel: 213-275-6114

Harold Rose Artists, Ltd.
8530 Wilshire Boulevard
Beverly Hills, California 90211
Tel: 213-652-3961

Betty Ruby Talent Agency
1741 North Ivar Street, Suite 119
Los Angeles, California 90028
Tel: 213-466-6652

Art Rush, Inc.
10221 Riverside Drive
North Hollywood, California
  91603
Tel: 213-985-3033

The Sackheim Agency
222 North Canon Drive
Beverly Hills, California 90210
Tel: 213-276-3151

Norah Sanders Agency
12198 1/2 Ventura Boulevard
Studio City, California 91614
Tel: 213-769-2162

James L. Saphier Agency, Inc.
9229 Sunset Boulevard, Suite 408
Los Angeles, California 90069
Tel: 213-271-7231

William Schuller Agency
9110 Sunset Boulevard
Los Angeles, California 90069
Tel: 213-273-4000

Don Schwartz & Associates
8721 Sunset Boulevard
Los Angeles, California 90069
Tel: 213-657-8910

Scott & Smith Associates
9720 Wilshire Boulevard
Beverly Hills, California 90212
Tel: 213-273-3773

Hal Shafer Agency
4421 Riverside Drive
Burbank, California 90505
Tel: 213-980-6333

Glenn Shaw Agency
8440 Sunset Boulevard
Los Angeles, California 90069
Tel: 213-654-6110

Lew Sherrell Agency, Ltd.
7060 Hollywood Boulevard
Los Angeles, California 90028
Tel: 213-461-9955

The Shiffrin Agency
941 North La Cienega Boulevard
Los Angeles, California 90069
Tel: 213-659-3550

Shipley-Ishimoto Agency
9163 Sunset Boulevard
Los Angeles, California 90069
Tel: 213-276-6251

A. Frederick Shorr, Inc.
1717 North Highland
Los Angeles, California 90028
Tel: 213-461-9344

Harvey Shotz
666 North Robertson Boulevard
Los Angeles, California 90069
Tel: 213-659-4030

Dorothy Shreve Agency
13444 Ventura Boulevard
Sherman Oaks, California 91403
Tel: 213-872-2603

Smith-Stevens Representation
434 North Rodeo Drive
Beverly Hills, California 90213
Tel: 213-278-1236

Phillomena Smyth
8005 Santa Monica Boulevard
Los Angeles, California 90046
Tel: 213-650-0376

George Soares Associates
12735 Ventura Boulevard
Studio City, California 91614
Tel: 213-980-0400

Charles H. Stern Agency, Inc.
9220 Sunset Boulevard
Los Angeles, California 90069
Tel: 213-273-6890

Larry Sugho's Agency
1017 North La Cienega
  Boulevard
Los Angeles, California 90069
Tel: 213-657-1450

Talent, Inc.
1421 North McCadden Place
Los Angeles, California 90028
Tel: 213-462-0913

Herb Tannen & Associates
6640 Sunset Boulevard
Los Angeles, California 90028
Tel: 213-461-3055

Herb Tobias & Associates, Ltd.
1901 Avenue of the Stars
Los Angeles, California 90067
Tel: 213-277-6211

Twentieth Century Artists
4749 Vineland
North Hollywood, California
  91602
Tel: 213-980-5552

Angela Vitt Agency
9172 Sunset Boulevard
Los Angeles, California 90069
Tel: 213-276-1646

Ruth Webb Ltd.
9229 Sunset Boulevard
Los Angeles, California 90069
Tel: 213-274-4311

Jack Weiner Agency
8721 Sunset Boulevard
Los Angeles, California 90069
Tel: 213-652-1140

Murry Weintraub Agency
1017 North La Cienega
Boulevard
Los Angeles, California 90069
Tel: 213-652-3892

Warren Wever
1104 South Robertson Boulevard
Los Angeles, California 90035
Tel: 213-276-7065

Jerry B. Wheeler Artists'
Management
8721 Sunset Boulevard
Los Angeles, California 90069
Tel: 213-656-0032

Ted Wilk Agency
9172 Sunset Boulevard
Los Angeles, California 90069
Tel: 213-273-0801

Peter Witt Associates, Inc.
321 South Beverly Drive
Beverly Hills, California 90212
Tel: 213-277-8711

Witzer & Small Agency
9441 Wilshire Boulevard
Beverly Hills, California 90212
Tel: 213-278-1926

Jack Wormser Agency, Inc.
1717 North Highland Avenue
Los Angeles, California 90028
Tel: 213-466-9111

Sylvia Wosk Agency
439 South La Cienega Boulevard
Los Angeles, California 90048
Tel: 213-274-8063

Ann Wright Associates, Ltd.
8422 Melrose Place
Los Angeles, California 90069
Tel: 213-655-5040

Ziegler*Ross, Inc.
9255 Sunset Boulevard
Los Angeles, California 90069
Tel: 213-278-0070

Herman Zimmerman Agency
12077 Ventura Place
Studio City, California 91604
Tel: 213-766-8119

San Diego area:

Commercial Artists Management
Agency
2232 Fifth Avenue
San Diego, California 92101

Crosby Talent Agency
3611 Fifth Avenue
San Diego, California 92103

Tina Real
3108 Fifth Avenue
San Diego, California 92103

San Francisco area:

Brebner Agency
1615 Polk Street
San Francisco, California 94109
Tel: 415-771-3488

Ann Demeter Agency
2087 Union Street
San Francisco, California 94123
Tel: 415-567-5226

Grimme Agency
41 Grant Avenue
San Francisco, California 94108

House of Charm
157 Maiden Lane
San Francisco, California 94108

Irma Kay and Associates
24 Mount View
Fairfax, California 94930

Ranmarc Agency
681 Market Street
San Francisco, California 94104

Colorado:

Illinois Talent
2664 South Krameria Street
Denver, Colorado 80222
Tel: 303-757-8675

J. F. Images, Inc.
1776 South Jackson Street, Suite
   702
Denver, Colorado 80210
Tel: 303-758-7777

John Robert Powers Agency
1550 Court Place
Denver, Colorado 80202

Connecticut:

Connecticut Modeling Agency
1326 Shippan
Stamford, Connecticut 06904
Tel: 203-325-0576

Ridgefield Model Agency
54 Main Street
Ridgefield, Connecticut 06877
Tel: 203-438-7711

Florida:

Act 1 Casting
3361 S.W. Third Avenue
Miami, Florida 33312

Agency for the Performing Arts
7630 Biscayne Boulevard
Miami, Florida 33138

Camelot Talent Agency
2233 Lee Road
Winter Park, Florida 32789

Creative Management Associates
7630 Biscayne Boulevard
Miami, Florida 33168

Florida Talent Agency
2631 East Oakland Park
   Boulevard
Fort Lauderdale, Florida 33310

Jerry Grant Agency, Inc.
220 71st Street
Miami, Florida 33126

Jean Henderson
709 South Federal Highway
Pompano Beach, Florida 33060

MarBea Agency
104 Crandon Boulevard
Key Biscayne, Florida 32656

Marks Talent Agency
600 Lincoln Road
Miami Beach, Florida 33139

Beverly McDermott Talent
  Agency
923 North Golf Drive
Hollywood, Florida 33022

Marian Polan Talent
111 S.E. Seventh Street
Miami, Florida 33136

Talent Enterprises
1603 N.E. 123rd Street
North Miami, Florida 33161

Wright-Florida Casting Talent
333 Alcazar Avenue
Coral Gables, Florida 33134

Illinois:

A-Plus Talent Agency
615 North Wabash Avenue
Chicago, Illinois 60611
Tel: 312-642-8151

Agency for the Performing Arts,
  Inc.
203 North Wabash Avenue
Chicago, Illinois 60601
Tel: 312-664-7703

Associated Booking Corporation
919 North Michigan Avenue
Chicago, Illinois 60611
Tel: 312-751-2000

Creative Management Associates
600 North McClurg Court
Chicago, Illinois 60611

Exclusively Yours
535 North Michigan Avenue
Chicago, Illinois 60611
Tel: 312-329-9051

Ann Geddes Inc.
875 North Michigan Avenue
Chicago, Illinois 60611

Guys & Dolls
333 East Ontario Street
Chicago, Illinois 60611
Tel: 312-337-0276

Shirley Hamilton, Inc.
500 North Michigan Avenue, 7th
  floor
Chicago, Illinois 60611

Emilia Lorence, Ltd.
619 North Wabash Avenue
Chicago, Illinois 60611

William Morris Agency, Inc.
435 North Michigan Avenue
Chicago, Illinois 60611
Tel: 312-467-1744

Jimmy Richards Productions
919 North Michigan Avenue
Chicago, Illinois 60611
Tel: 312-664-1552

Jack Russell
333 North Michigan Avenue
Chicago, Illinois 60601

Norman Schucart Enterprises
1417 Green Bay Road
Highland Park, Illinois 60035
Tel: 312-433-1113

Eileen Slater Associates
5445 Sheridan Road
Chicago, Illinois 60640
Tel: 312-275-9565

The Talent Registry
400 North Michigan Avenue,
Room 2002
Chicago, Illinois 60611
Tel: 312-828-0166

Indiana:

Wilhelmina Klinger
Box 36
Buck Creek, Indiana 47924

Michigan:

Advertisers Casting Service
15324 East Jefferson
Grosse Point Park, Michigan
48230

Leslie Fargo Agency
811 Fisher Building
Detroit, Michigan 48226

Gail and Rice Talent
24453 Grand River
Detroit, Michigan 48219

Martin-Rosenberg
28021 Southfield Road
Lathrup Village, Michigan 48235

New Jersey:

Jo Anderson Models
400 Route 38
Maple Shade, New Jersey 08052
Tel: 212-779-2447

Entertainment Associates
6027 Prodigy Building, Route 130
Pennsauken, New Jersey 08110
Tel: 609-662-3444

New York:

Abrams-Rubaloff & Associates
10 East 53rd Street
New York, New York 10022
Tel: 212-758-3636

Bret Adams, Ltd.
36 East 61st Street
New York, New York 10021
Tel: 212-752-7864

Agency for the Performing Arts
120 West 57th Street
New York, New York 10019
Tel: 212-581-8860

Willard Alexander, Inc.
660 Madison Avenue
New York, New York 10021
Tel: 212-751-7070

American International Talent
  Agency
166 West 125th Street
New York, New York 10027
Tel: 212-663-4626

American Talent, Inc.
888 Seventh Avenue
New York, New York 10026
Tel: 212-765-1896

Beverly Anderson Agency
1472 Broadway, Suite 806
New York, New York 10036
Tel: 212-279-5553

Associated Booking Corporation
445 Park Avenue
New York, New York 10022
Tel: 212-421-5200

Associated Talent Agency
56 West 45th Street
New York, New York 10036
Tel: 212-867-2287

Richard Astor Agency
119 West 57th Street
New York, New York 10019
Tel: 212-581-1970

Richard Bauman Agency
1650 Broadway
New York, New York 10019
Tel: 212-757-0098

Lola M. Bishop
853 Seventh Avenue
New York, New York 10019
Tel: 212-245-4775

Black Beauty, Inc.
145 East 52nd Street
New York, New York 10022
Tel: 212-935-9360

J. Michael Bloom, Ltd.
400 Madison Avenue, Suite 1009
New York, New York 10017
Tel: 213-838-0982

Jane Broder
35 Park Avenue
New York, New York 10016
Tel: 212-685-6729

Molly Bryant Agency
667 Madison Avenue
New York, New York 10021
Tel: 212-371-7010

Carnegie Talent Agency
300 Northern Boulevard
Great Neck, New York 11022
Tel: 212-487-2260

Bertha Case
42 West 53rd Street
New York, New York 10019
Tel: 212-581-6280

Cataldi Agency
250 West 57th Street
New York, New York 10019
Tel: 212-582-1960

The Cereghetti Agency
1564 Broadway
New York, New York 10036
Tel: 212-765-5260

Toby Cole (The Actors Agency)
234 West 44th Street
New York, New York 10036
Tel: 212-279-7770

Coleman-Rosenberg Agency
667 Madison Avenue
New York, New York 10021
Tel: 212-838-0734

Bill Cooper Association
16 East 52nd Street
New York, New York 10019
Tel: 212-758-6491

Cunningham & Associates
919 Third Avenue
New York, New York 10022
Tel: 212-832-2700

D.M.I. Talent Association
250 West 57th Street
New York, New York 10019
Tel: 212-246-4650

Jane Deacy Agency
119 East 54th Street
New York, New York 10022
Tel: 212-752-4865

Del Marco, Inc.
55 West 42nd Street
New York, New York 10036
Tel: 212-695-3820

Diamond Artists, Ltd.
119 West 57th Street
New York, New York 10019
Tel: 212-247-3025

Frances Dilworth
19 West 44th Street
New York, New York 10017
Tel: 212-661-0070

Stephen Draper Agency
37 West 57th Street
New York, New York 10019
Tel: 212-421-5780

Dee Edwards Models
145 East 49th Street
New York, New York 10017
Tel: 212-755-1393

Entertainment Agency
1564 Broadway
New York, New York 10036
Tel: 212-246-7175

Marje Fields
250 West 57th Street
New York, New York 10019
Tel: 212-581-7240

Filor Talent Agency
110 East 55th Street
New York, New York 10019
Tel: 212-832-1636

Ford Model Agency
344 East 59th Street
New York, New York 10022
Tel: 212-688-8538

Foster-Fell Agency, Inc.
515 Madison Avenue
New York, New York 10022
Tel: 212-355-7227

The Gage Group, Inc.
1650 Broadway
New York, New York 10019
Tel: 212-541-5250

George Goldsmith
360 West 22nd Street
New York, New York 10011
Tel: 212-242-7060

Bonny Golub Agency
850 Seventh Avenue
New York, New York 10019
Tel: 212-757-5021

Ellen Harth
515 Madison Avenue
New York, New York 10022
Tel: 212-593-2332

Michael Hartig Agency
850 Seventh Avenue
New York, New York 10019
Tel: 212-489-8484

Helen Harvey Associates
110 West 57th Street
New York, New York 10019
Tel: 212-581-5610

Sallee Held
5 East 57th Street
New York, New York 10022
Tel: 212-371-9754

Henderson/Hogan Agency, Inc.
200 West 57th Street
New York, New York 10019
Tel: 212-765-5190

Hesseltine-Baker Associates, Ltd.
119 West 57th Street
New York, New York 10019
Tel: 212-489-0966

Diana Hunt
246 West 44th Street
New York, New York 10036
Tel: 212-279-0009

Jeff Hunter
119 West 57th Street
New York, New York 10019
Tel: 212-757-4995

Jacobson Enterprises
1650 Broadway
New York, New York 10019
Tel: 212-757-3920

Jacobson/Wilder, Inc.
400 Madison Avenue
New York, New York 10017
Tel: 212-759-0860

Jan J. Agency
224 East 46th Street
New York, New York 10017
Tel: 212-490-1875

Merrill Jonas
119 West 57th Street
New York, New York 10019
Tel: 212-581-6005

Joe Jordan Talent Agency
400 Madison Avenue
New York, New York 10017
Tel: 212-755-2198

Kahn, Lifflander & Rhodes, Inc.
853 Seventh Avenue
New York, New York 10019
Tel: 212-582-1280

Kaplan-Veidt Ltd.
667 Madison Avenue
New York, New York 10021
Tel: 212-421-7370

Kennedy Artists Representatives
881 Seventh Avenue
New York, New York 10019
Tel: 212-675-3944

Bonnie Kid
250 West 57th Street
New York, New York 10019
Tel: 212-246-0223

Archer King
Time & Life Building
New York, New York 10020
Tel: 212-581-8513

Lucy Kroll
390 West End Avenue
New York, New York 10024
Tel: 212-877-0556

Robert Lantz, Ltd.
111 West 57th Street
New York, New York 10019
Tel: 212-757-5076

Lantz Office, Inc.
114 East 55th Street
New York, New York 10019
Tel: 212-751-2107

Lionel Larner, Ltd.
850 Seventh Avenue
New York, New York 10019
Tel: 212-246-3105

Gary Leaverton, Inc.
1650 Broadway
New York, New York 10019
Tel: 212-541-9640

Sanford Leigh
527 Madison Avenue
New York, New York 10022
Tel: 212-752-4450

Lester Lewis Associates, Inc.
156 East 52nd Street
New York, New York 10022
Tel: 212-753-5082

M.E.W. Company
370 Lexington Avenue
New York, New York 10017
Tel: 212-889-7272

Martinelli Attractions
888 Eighth Avenue
New York, New York 10019
Tel: 212-586-0963

Marge McDermott Enterprises
215 East 37th Street
New York, New York 10016
Tel: 212-687-4363

Meade Talent
119 West 57th Street
New York, New York 10019
Tel: 212-582-5760

William Morris Agency, Inc.
1350 Avenue of the Americas
New York, New York 10019
Tel: 212-586-5100

Neuwirth and Palmer
250 West 57th Street
New York, New York 10019
Tel: 212-765-4280

Oppenheim-Christie Associates
565 Fifth Avenue
New York, New York 10017
Tel: 212-661-4330

Fifi Oscard Agency, Ltd.
19 West 44th Street
New York, New York 10036
Tel: 212-764-1100

Barna Ostertag
501 Fifth Avenue
New York, New York 10017
Tel: 212-697-6339

Cye Perkins Agency
139 East 52nd Street
New York, New York 10022
Tel: 212-752-4488

Richard Pitman Agency
229 West 42nd Street
New York, New York 10036
Tel: 212-947-5555

Joel Pitt Agency
250 West 57th Street
New York, New York 10019
Tel: 212-765-6373

Premier Talent Associates
888 Seventh Avenue
New York, New York 10019
Tel: 212-757-4300

Professional Artists
667 Madison Avenue
New York, New York 10021
Tel: 212-838-3413

Rice-McHugh Agency Inc.
136 East 57th Street
New York, New York 10022
Tel: 212-752-0222

Tony Rivers
154 West 54th Street
New York, New York 10019
Tel: 212-581-1466

Mike Roscoe
119 West 57th Street
New York, New York 10019
Tel: 212-541-5400

Lynn Rosselli Agency
1650 Broadway
New York, New York 10019
Tel: 212-489-7227

Royal Model and Talent
185 Madison Avenue
New York, New York 10021
Tel: 212-889-9111

Bernard Rubenstein
342 Madison Avenue
New York, New York 10017
Tel: 212-986-1317

Charles Vernon Ryan
35 West 53rd Street
New York, New York 10019
Tel: 212-245-2225

Gloria Safier–Bob Barry
667 Madison Avenue
New York, New York 10021
Tel: 212-838-4868

William Schuller Agency, Inc.
667 Madison Avenue
New York, New York 10021
Tel: 212-758-1919

Mort Schwartz Agency
156 East 52nd Street
New York, New York 10022
Tel: 212-753-1529

Joan Scott, Inc.
162 West 56th Street
New York, New York 10019
Tel: 212-246-9029

Jack Segal
850 Seventh Avenue
New York, New York 10019
Tel: 212-265-7489

Monty Silver
850 Seventh Avenue
New York, New York 10019
Tel: 212-765-4040

Smith-Stevens, Inc.
1650 Broadway
New York, New York 10019
Tel: 212-582-8040

Stewart Artists Corporation
405 Park Avenue
New York, New York 10022
Tel: 212-752-0944

Stewart Personal Management
405 Park Avenue
New York, New York 10022
Tel: 212-753-4610

Stroud Management
18 East 48th Street
New York, New York 10017
Tel: 212-688-0226

Talent Group, Inc.
527 Madison Avenue
New York, New York 10022
Tel: 212-371-8600

Talent Representatives, Inc.
20 East 53rd Street
New York, New York 10022
Tel: 212-752-1835

Jean Thomas Agency, Inc.
850 Seventh Avenue
New York, New York 10019
Tel: 212-586-4616

Michael Thomas Agency, Inc.
22 East 60th Street
New York, New York 10022
Tel: 212-755-2616

Tranum, Robertson & Hughes,
    Inc.
2 Dag Hammarskjold Place
New York, New York 10017
Tel: 212-371-7500

Gloria Troy Talent Agency
1790 Broadway
New York, New York 10019
Tel: 212-582-0260

Bob Waters Agency
510 Madison Avenue
New York, New York 10022
Tel: 212-593-0543

Wender & Associates
30 East 60th Street
New York, New York 10022
Tel: 212-832-8330

Henry William Wiese
350 West 55th Street
New York, New York 10019
Tel: 212-265-1930

Wilhelmina Model Agency
9 East 37th Street
New York, New York 10016
Tel: 212-532-7141

Peter Witt Associates, Inc.
37 West 57th Street
New York, New York 10019
Tel: 212-759-7966

Hanns Wolters Agency
342 Madison Avenue
New York, New York 10017
Tel: 212-867-9177

Ann Wright Representatives
137 East 57th Street
New York, New York 10022
Tel: 212-832-0110

Young Talent Agency
322 East 39th Street
New York, New York 10016
Tel: 212-686-5000

Babs Zimmerman Productions
1414 Avenue of the Americas
New York, New York 10022
Tel: 212-421-9555

Zoli Management, Inc.
121 East 62nd Street
New York, New York 10021
Tel: 212-758-5959

Pennsylvania:

Jolly Joyce
2028 Chestnut Street
Philadelphia, Pennsylvania 19103
Tel: 215-564-0982

Midiri Models
1902 Chestnut Street
Philadelphia, Pennsylvania 19103
Tel: 215-561-5028

Models' Guild Philadelphia
1512 Spruce Street
Philadelphia, Pennsylvania 19102
Tel: 215-735-4067

Joseph Rocco
21 South Fifth Street
Philadelphia, Pennsylvania 19106
Tel: 215-462-2603
Tel: 215-582-8040

Texas:

Kim Dawson Agency
1143 Apparel Mart
2300 Stemmons Freeway
Dallas, Texas 75207

Professional Talent Agency
6318 Gaston Avenue
Dallas, Texas 75214

Peggy Taylor Agency
4228 North Central Expressway
Dallas, Texas 75206

Animals (Trained)

The American Humane Society is watchdog for animal actors. Local office of the society should be contacted for guidance when any on-screen action could be potentially hazardous to an animal. The listing below of sources of movie-trained animals includes reptiles, marine animals, and birds. Livestock suppliers are grouped in a special category.

California:

Los Angeles area:

Accurate Animal Action
P.O. Box 824
Arleta, California 91331
Tel: 213-767-4519

Africa USA
Ralph Helfer
2930 E. Guiberson Road
Fillmore, California 93015
Tel: 805-521-1785

Allied Movie Dogs
16555 Lassen Street
Sepulveda, California 91343
Tel: 213-893-1441

American Wild Life
13618 Van Nuys Boulevard
Pacoima, California 91331
Tel: 213-899-4905

Animal Actors of Hollywood
1285 1/2 Thousand Oaks
    Boulevard
Thousand Oaks, California 91360
Tel: 213-889-3340

Animal Actors of Wild Country
6800 Soledad Canyon Road
Acton, California 93510
Tel: 805-947-4039

C A T Creative Animal
    Techniques
Division of Marriott Corporation
15840 Cedarfort Drive
Saugus, California 91351
Tel: 805-252-7188

Lionel Comport
12265 Branford Avenue
Sun Valley, California 91352
Tel: 213-899-4101

Ted Derby's Animal Kingdom,
    Inc.
286 East Highway 246
Buellton, California 93427
Tel: 805-688-3634

Moe Di Sesso's Trained Wildlife
13618 Van Nuys Boulevard
Pacoima, California 91331
Tel: 213-899-4905

Entertainment Enterprises
1680 Vine Street, Suite 519
Los Angeles, California 90028
Tel: 213-462-6001

Four C's Kennels
421 North Moss Street
Burbank, California 91502
Tel: 213-849-5029

Frank Inn, Inc.
12265 Branford Street
Sun Valley, California 91352
Tel: 213-899-1534

Hermosa Reptile and Wild
Animal Farm
219 Pacific Coast Highway
Hermosa Beach, California 90254
Tel: 213-376-5017

Hollywood Dog Training School
10805 Vanowen Street
North Hollywood, California
91605
Tel: 213-762-1262

Gene Holter's Movieland
Animals, Inc.
Bloomington, California 92316
Tel: 714-877-2827

Fat Jones Stables
1800 Devonshire
Northridge, California 91324
Tel: 213-885-0771

Jungle Land
Thousand Oaks, California 91360
Tel: 805-495-2122

Pat La Coss
6905 Tujunga Avenue
North Hollywood, California
91603
Tel: 213-705-7909

The Lion Wild Animal Rentals
P.O. Box 259
Ventura, California 93001
Tel: 805-648-6550

Marineland of Pacific
Los Angeles, California 90052
Tel: 213-772-2661

Miller Karl Lewis
9125 Crawford, Box 824
Arleta, California 91331
Tel: 213-767-4519

Myers & Wills Stables
11035 Osborne Street Lakeview
Terrace
San Fernando, California 91342
Tel: 213-896-1333

Randall Ranch
23870 Pine Street
Newhall, California 91321
Tel: 213-365-2119

Lou Schumacher
14453 Cavette Place
Baldwin Park, California 91706
Tel: 213-338-4614

Studio Dog Training School
25078 Sea Vista Drive
Malibu, California 90265
Tel: 213-457-7528

Dick Webb Stables
23868 Pine Street
Newhall, California 91321
Tel: 213-365-2921

San Diego area:

Sea World of San Diego
1720 South Shores Road
San Diego, California 92109
Tel: 714-222-6363

San Francisco area:

Brebner Agency
1615 Polk Street
San Francisco, California 94109
Tel: 415-775-1802

Grimme Agency
41 Grant Avenue
San Francisco, California 94108
Tel: 415-392-9175

Marine World
Marine World Parkway
Redwood City, California 94065
Tel: 415-591-7676

Colorado:

Wide Acres Ranch
1205 Hawthorne Road
Golden, Colorado 80401
Tel: 303-237-9787

Ernest Wilkinson
Monte Vista, Colorado 81144
Tel: 303-852-3277

Georgia:

Arden Farms
Crabapple Road
Alpharetta, Georgia 30201
Tel: 404-475-4034

Jim Dodd
3906 Land O'Lakes Drive
Buford, Georgia 30518
Tel: 404-526-6001

Kennesaw Kennels
Route 2
Marietta, Georgia 30060
Tel: 404-971-3226

Illinois:

Animal Kingdom, Inc.
2980 North Milwaukee
Chicago, Illinois 60611
Tel: 312-227-4444

Stuart Kennels
599 East Rosevelt Road
Lombard, Illinois 61614
Tel: 312-627-4029

New York:

A-OK Corral, Inc.
24 Spook Rock Road
Suffern, New York 10901
Tel: 212-832-0822

All-Tame Animals, Inc.
37 West 57th Street
New York, New York 10019
Tel: 212-752-5885

Animal Talent Scouts, Inc.
331 West 18th Street
New York, New York 10011
Tel: 212-243-2700

Chateau Theatrical Animals
608 West 48th Street
New York, New York 10036
Tel: 212-246-0520

Dawn Animal Agency
1545 Broadway
New York, New York 10019
Tel: 212-582-5729

Captain Haggerty's Theatrical
  Dogs
16 East Tremont
Bronx, New York 10453
Tel: 212-299-8600

Hollywood Dogs
600 Grand Concourse
Bronx, New York 10451
Tel: 212-665-6700

Pennsylvania:

Animal Kingdom Talent Service
Mitchell Creek
Tioga, Pennsylvania 16946
Tel: 717-835-5470

LIVESTOCK

California:

Fat Jones Livestock and
  Horse-Drawn Vehicles
1800 Devonshire
Northridge, California 91324
Tel: 213-885-0771

H. H. Magee (HAP) Ranches
1025 Lagonda Way
Danville, California 94526
Tel: 415-837-7228

Myers & Wills Stables
11035 Osborne Street Lakeview
  Terrace
San Fernando, California 91342
Tel: 213-899-8633

Ralph McCutcheon's Motion
  Picture Livestock
1742 Riverside Drive
Glendale, California 91201
Tel: 213-240-4066

Randall Ranch
23870 Pine Street
Newhall, California 91321
Tel: 213-365-2119

Sawyer Rental and Sales
6820 Santa Monica Boulevard
Los Angeles, California 90038
Tel: 213-466-6114

Topanga Stables
121 Old Topanga, Box 147
Topanga, California 90290
Tel: 213-455-2244

Dick Webb Motion Picture
  Livestock and Equipment
23868 Pine Street
Newhall, California 91321
Tel: 213-365-3921

Colorado:

Ernest Wilkinson
Monte Vista, Colorado 81144
Tel: 303-852-3277

Montana: **Nevada:**

William Brogan   Bonnie Springs Old Nevada
Corwin Springs, Montana 59021   830 East Sahara Avenue, Suite
                                          One
James Burnett   Las Vegas, Nevada 89105
Luther, Montana 59051   Tel: 702-732-2115
                                      Tel: 702-875-9103
Jack Gehring
Helena, Montana 59601   H. H. Magee (HAP) Ranches
                                      Carson City, Nevada 89701
Bob Shall   Tel: 702-882-8176
Arlee, Montana 59821
                                      Nevada Motion Pictures Service
                                      2025 Paradise Road
                                      Las Vegas, Nevada 89105
                                      Tel: 702-734-0975

Animation

Animation designers, photographers, and equipment suppliers are included here by location. Computer animation systems, operators, and suppliers are listed as well.

Arizona:

Don Douglass Creative Design
4449 North 12th Street
Phoenix, Arizona 85014
Tel: 602-248-8089

Don Heraldson Animated Films,
Inc.
8213 East Fairmont Avenue
Scottsdale, Arizona 85251
Tel: 602-947-0696

California:

ABC Films, Inc.
1313 North Vine Street
Los Angeles, California 90028
Tel: 213-663-3311
Ext: 1515

Ablidon Enterprises, Inc.
13063 Ventura Boulevard
Studio City, California 91604
Tel: 213-981-7575

Acme Camera Corporation
820 South Mariposa Street
Burbank, California 91506
Tel: 213-849-6251

Acre Enterprises, Inc.
1041 North Formosa Avenue
Los Angeles, California 90046
Tel: 213-851-1234

Action Animation, Inc.
4270 Artesia
Fullerton, California 92631
Tel: 714-523-4800

Anicam
6331 Homewood
Los Angeles, California 90028
Tel: 213-465-4114

Animation Camera Service
4368-A Tujunga Avenue
North Hollywood, California
91604
Tel: 213-980-1178

Animedia
13107 Ventura Boulevard
Studio City, California 91604
Tel: 213-981-6540

Bakshi-Krantz Animation, Inc.
6725 Sunset Boulevard
Los Angeles, California 90028
Tel: 213-461-4242

Saul Bass & Associates
7039 Sunset Boulevard
Los Angeles, California 90046
Tel: 213-466-9701

Bemiller Productions
2350 Hyperion Avenue
Los Angeles, California 90027
Tel: 213-665-5137

Tony Benedict Productions
13701 Riverside Drive
Sherman Oaks, California 91403
Tel: 213-981-5577

Stephen Bosustow Productions
1649 Eleventh Street
Santa Monica, California 90404
Tel: 213-394-0218

Braverman Productions
8961 Sunset Boulevard
Los Angeles, California 90069
Tel: 213-278-5444

Wally Bulloch Animation
  Camera Service, Inc.
1113 North Formosa
Los Angeles, California 90046
Tel: 213-851-0400

Fred Calvert Productions
5352 Laurel Canyon Boulevard
North Hollywood, California
  91607
Tel: 213-985-1414

Bob Clampett Productions
729 Seward Street
Los Angeles, California 90038
Tel: 213-466-0264

Consolidated Film Industries
959 Seward Street
Los Angeles, California 90038
Tel: 213-462-3161

Cornerstone Productions
6087 Sunset Boulevard
Los Angeles, California 90028
Tel: 213-462-0071

Dawn Studio
6725 Sunset Boulevard, Suite 215
Los Angeles, California 90028
Tel: 213-466-0338

DePatie-Freleng Enterprises, Inc.
6859 Havenhurst
Van Nuys, California 91406
Tel: 213-988-3890

Dickson-Vasu, Inc.
633 North La Brea Avenue
Los Angeles, California 90036
Tel: 213-936-5184

Leo Diner Films, Inc.
332-350 Golden Gate Avenue
San Francisco, California 94102
Tel: 415-775-3664

Walt Disney Productions
500 South Buena Vista Street
Burbank, California 91503
Tel: 213-845-3141

Richard Einfeld, Inc.
1512 North Las Palmas Avenue
Los Angeles, California 90028
Tel: 213-461-3731

Angel Esparza
11729 Kling Street
North Hollywood, California
  91607
Tel: 213-763-8023

F&B/Ceco of California, Inc.
7051 Santa Monica Boulevard
Los Angeles, California 90038
Tel: 213-466-9361

Film Effects of Hollywood, Inc.
1140 North Citrus
Los Angeles, California 90038
Tel: 213-469-5808

Film Technology Company, Inc.
6900 Santa Monica Boulevard
Los Angeles, California 90038
Tel: 213-465-4908

Filmation Associates
18107 Sherman Way
Reseda, California 91335
Tel: 213-734-7414

Format Productions, Inc.
12754 Ventura Boulevard
Studio City, California 91604
Tel: 213-769-3610

Sherman Glas Productions, Inc.
7015 Sunset Boulevard
Los Angeles, California 90028
Tel: 213-462-1873

Glenar Productions
6618 Sunset Boulevard
Los Angeles, California 90028
Tel: 213-464-0406

Alan Gordon Enterprises, Inc.
1430 North Cahuenga Boulevard
Los Angeles, California 90028
Tel: 213-466-3561

Alan Gordon Enterprises, Inc.
5632 North Cahuenga Boulevard
North Hollywood, California
  91601
Tel: 213-985-5500

Grantray-Lawrence Animation,
  Inc.
1537 North La Brea Avenue
Los Angeles, California 90028
Tel: 213-469-7968

Graphic Films Corporation
3341 Cahuenga Boulevard
Los Angeles, California 90068
Tel: 213-851-4100

Bernard Gruver
429 North Larchmont Boulevard
Los Angeles, California 90004
Tel: 213-463-4101

The Haboush Company
6611 Santa Monica Boulevard
Los Angeles, California 90038
Tel: 213-466-4111

Hanna-Barbera Productions, Inc.
3400 Cahuenga Boulevard, West
Los Angeles, California 90028
Tel: 213-466-1371

Hogan-Lee Images
12849 Magnolia Avenue
North Hollywood, California
  91607
Tel: 213-980-3566

Hollywood Animators
7401 Sunset Boulevard
Los Angeles, California 90046
Tel: 213-876-1190

Bill Hurtz
6345 Ranchito Avenue
Van Nuys, California 91401
Tel: 213-785-9778

Jacques, Jean-Guy et Compagnie
633 North La Brea Avenue
Los Angeles, California 90036
Tel: 213-936-7177

Chris Jenkyns
3497 Cahuenga Boulevard
Los Angeles, California 90068
Tel: 213-851-3443

Kaleidoscope Films Ltd.
6345 Fountain Avenue
Los Angeles, California 90028
Tel: 213-465-1151

Llewellyn Keller
6824 Apperson Street
Tujunga, California 91042
Tel: 213-353-1316

Korty Films, Inc.
200 Miller Avenue
Mill Valley, California 94941
Tel: 415-383-6900

Krofft Enterprises, Inc.
11347 Vanowen
North Hollywood, California
    91603
Tel: 213-877-3361

Kurtz & Friends Films
6532 Sunset Boulevard
Los Angeles, California 90028
Tel: 213-461-8188

Walter Lantz Productions, Inc.
861 Seward Street
Los Angeles, California 90038
Tel: 213-469-2907

Levitow/Hanson Films, Inc.
861 Seward Street
Los Angeles, California 90038
Tel: 202-832-2600

Edward Levitt
439 North Larchmont Boulevard
Los Angeles, California 90004
Tel: 213-463-4101

MGM Animation
6290 Sunset Boulevard
Los Angeles, California 90028
Tel: 213-466-3393

Matrix Image
6622 Vairel Avenue
Canoga Park, California 91303
Tel: 213-883-6622

Bill Melendez Productions, Inc.
439 North Larchmont Boulevard
Los Angeles, California 90004
Tel: 213-463-4101

Ray Mercer & Company
4241 Normal Avenue
Los Angeles, California 90029
Tel: 213-663-9331

Louis Meyer Studios
6337 Santa Monica Boulevard
Los Angeles, California 90038
Tel: 213-469-8209

Murakami Wolf Films
1463 Tamarind Street
Los Angeles, California 90028
Tel: 213-462-6474

Ernie Nemeth
810 North Highland Avenue
Los Angeles, California 90038
Tel: 213-469-0158

National Screen Service
  Corporation
7026 Santa Monica Boulevard
Los Angeles, California 90038
Tel: 213-453-3136

Gerald Nevius Company
6335 Homewood Avenue
Los Angeles, California 90028
Tel: 213-465-7757

Nicholson Films, Inc.
6335 Homewood Avenue
Los Angeles, California 90028
Tel: 213-462-0878

The Odyssey Corporation
1333 Camino Del Rio South,
  Suite 316
San Diego, California 92108
Tel: 714-291-6830

Orsatti Productions
10331 Riverside Drive
North Hollywood, California
  91602
Tel: 213-980-6430

Paint Box Films
135 Lindero Avenue
Long Beach, California 90803
Tel: 213-438-5412

Pantomime Pictures, Inc.
12144 Riverside Drive
North Hollywood, California
  91607
Tel: 213-980-5555

Ray Patin Productions
6650 Sunset Boulevard
Los Angeles, California 90028
Tel: 213-462-1147

Pearson Photographics
10530 Burbank Boulevard
North Hollywood, California
  91601
Tel: 213-769-7929

Photo-Sonics, Inc.
820 South Mariposa Street
Burbank, California 91506
Tel: 213-849-6251

Jack Pill & Associates
6370 Santa Monica Boulevard
Los Angeles, California 90038
Tel: 213-466-5391

Progress Industries
8766 Amigo
Norwood, California 91340
Tel: 213-349-5399

Quartet Films, Inc.
5631 Hollywood Boulevard
Los Angeles, California 90046
Tel: 213-464-9225

SOS/Photo-Cine-Optics, Inc.
7051 Santa Monica Boulevard
Los Angeles, California 90038
Tel: 213-466-9361

The Schmeltzer Organization
P.O. Box 1036
Alameda, California 94501
Tel: 415-775-2634

Fletcher Smith Studios, Inc.
177 South Beverly Drive
Beverly Hills, California 90213
Tel: 213-275-4451

Solis-Navarro
1051 Santa Cruz Avenue
Menlo Park, California 94025
Tel: 415-322-6937

Storyboard Studio
341 1/2 South Western Avenue
Los Angeles, California 90020
Tel: 213-382-8503

Temple-Toons Productions, Inc.
9363 Wilshire Boulevard
Beverly Hills, California 90213
Tel: 213-276-8423
TV and Industrial Films Division

Twentieth Century–Fox Pictures
    Corporation
P.O. Box 900
Beverly Hills, California 90213
Tel: 213-277-2211

U.P.A. Pictures, Inc.
4440 Lakeside Drive
Burbank, California 91505
Tel: 213-849-6666

United Producers
8310 Beverly Boulevard
Los Angeles, California 90048
Tel: 213-653-2430

Warner Brothers Cartoons
461 South California Street
Burbank, California 91503
Tel: 213-469-1251

Norman Wright Productions, Inc.
27963 Cabot Road
South Laguna, California 92677
Tel: 714-831-1480

Felix Zelenka
818 North La Brea Avenue
Los Angeles, California 90038
Tel: 213-466-3263

Colorado:

Computer Animation
1405 Race Street, No. 404
Denver, Colorado 80218
Tel: 303-388-5171

Computer Image Corporation
2475 West Second Avenue
Denver, Colorado 80223
Tel: 303-934-5801

Spencer Nelson
1420 Larimer Square, c/o JPI
Denver, Colorado 80202
Tel: 303-623-0167

District of Columbia:

Creative Arts
2323 Fourth Street, N.E.
Washington, D.C. 20002
Tel: 202-832-2600

Florida:

International Animated Cartoons
14875 N.E. Twentieth Avenue
North Miami, Florida 33161
Tel: 305-947-2983

Nationwide Pictures
69 Merrick Way
Coral Gables, Florida 33134
Tel: 305-443-3395

Reela Films, Inc.
17 N.W. Third Street
Miami, Florida 33128

Soundac Productions, Inc.
2133 N.W. Eleventh Avenue
Miami, Florida 33127
Tel: 305-374-2655

Georgia:

AND, Inc.
1428-B Mason Street, N.E.
Atlanta, Georgia 30324
Tel: 404-876-1033

Cinetron Computer Systems, Inc.
6700 I-85 N.E. Access Road
Norcross, Georgia 30071
Tel: 404-448-9463

Thumbprint, Inc.
6700 I-85 North
Norcross, Georgia 30071
Tel: 404-449-0166

Hawaii:

Cine-Pic Hawaii
1847 Pacific Heights Road
Honolulu, Hawaii 96813
Tel: 808-533-2677

Pacific Instrumentation
5388 Papai Street
Honolulu, Hawaii 96821
Tel: 808-373-1287

Illinois:

AGS & R Studios
425 North Michigan Avenue
Chicago, Illinois 60611
Tel: 312-527-4070

Animated Film Producers of
   America
159 East Chicago Avenue
Chicago, Illinois 60611
Tel: 312-943-2424

Atlas Film Corporation
1111 South Boulevard
Oak Park, Illinois 60301
Tel: 312-287-8620

Computer Animation
400 North Michigan Avenue
Chicago, Illinois 60611
Tel: 312-467-0787

Computer Image Corporation
1920 North Lincoln Avenue
Chicago, Illinois 60614
Tel: 312-787-7230

Consolidated Film Industries
333 North Michigan Avenue
Chicago, Illinois 60601
Tel: 312-641-0028

Crocus Productions
926 Chicago
Evanston, Illinois 60602
Tel: 312-481-0200

Goldsholl Associates, Inc.
420 Frontage Road
Northfield, Illinois 60628
Tel: 312-446-8300

Insight, Inc.
100 East Ohio Street
Chicago, Illinois 60611
Tel: 312-467-4350

Kling Film Productions
1058 West Washington Boulevard
Chicago, Illinois 60607
Tel: 312-738-4181

Producers Technical Services, Inc.
160 East Grand Avenue
Chicago, Illinois 60611
Tel: 312-644-6910

Programming Technologies, Inc.
215 West Chicago Avenue
Chicago, Illinois 60610
Tel: 312-787-2700

George M. Ricci & Associates
625 North Michigan Avenue
Chicago, Illinois 60602
Tel: 312-787-5221

Ritter-Waxberg & Associates, Inc.
600 North McClurg Street
Chicago, Illinois 60611
Tel: 312-664-3934

Scientificom
708 North Dearborn Street
Chicago, Illinois 60610
Tel: 312-787-8656

Telecine Film Studios, Inc.
100 South Northwest Highway
Park Ridge, Illinois 60068
Tel: 312-823-1418

V.I.P. Studios, Inc.
800 East Northwest Highway
Mt. Prospect, Illinois 60056
Tel: 312-394-3900

Visual Effects, Inc.
57 West Grand Avenue
Chicago, Illinois 60610
Tel: 312-642-8441

Kentucky:

Kent Lane Films, Inc.
1253 South Third Street
Louisville, Kentucky 40203
Tel: 502-636-3911

Maryland:

John H. Battison Productions
4515 Saul Road
Kensington, Maryland 20795
Tel: 202-657-9593

Friar Graphics
9232 Warren Street
Silver Springs, Maryland 20901
Tel: 301-588-5900

Pilgrim Film Service
2504 50th Avenue
Hyattsville, Maryland 20781
Tel: 301-773-7072

Massachusetts:

Sherrill F. Martin
117 Anson Road
Concord, Massachusetts 01742
Tel: 617-259-0809

Michigan:

Video Films
1004 East Jefferson Avenue
Detroit, Michigan 48207
Tel: 313-962-3440

Nebraska:

Keith Film Productions
2820 Harney Street
Omaha, Nebraska 68131
Tel: 402-523-5596

New York:

Alexsa Corporation
619 West 54th Street
New York, New York 10019
Tel: 212-246-3035

Animated Motion Picture Artists
 Co.
663 Fifth Avenue
New York, New York 10022
Tel: 212-757-6454

Animated Productions, Inc.
1600 Broadway
New York, New York 10019
Tel: 212-265-2942

Animatic Productions, Ltd.
2 West 45th Street
New York, New York 10036
Tel: 212-661-7290

Animation Services, Inc.
47 West 57th Street
New York, New York 10019
Tel: 212-688-6225

Ariel Productions, Inc.
210 Fifth Avenue
New York, New York 10010
Tel: 212-679-8554

B & B
145 East 52nd Street
New York, New York 10022
Tel: 212-752-3750

Bebell & Bebell Color
 Laboratories, Inc.
416 West 45th Street
New York, New York 10036
Tel: 212-245-8900

Howard Beckerman
24 West 45th Street
New York, New York 10036
Tel: 212-869-0595

Berkey Video Services
322 East 45th Street
New York, New York 10017
Tel: 212-889-3790

Elinor Bunin Productions, Inc.
30 East 60th Street
New York, New York 10022
Tel: 212-688-0759

Cartoon Company Films, Inc.
1154 Second Avenue
New York, New York 10021
Tel: 212-935-1440

Cel-Art Film Service, Inc.
16 West 46th Street
New York, New York 10036
Tel: 212-247-7771

Cine Image–Synthavision
9 East 37th Street
New York, New York 10016
Tel: 212-679-1101

Cineffects, Inc.
115 West 45th Street
New York, New York 10036
Tel: 212-246-0950

Cineplast, Inc.
149 Madison Ave.
New York, New York 10016
Tel: 212-684-5910

Ian Clark
229 East 96th Street
New York, New York 10025
Tel: 212-289-0998

Coastal Film Service, Inc.
45 West 45th Street
New York, New York 10036
Tel: 212-582-7780

Computer Visuals
3 Westchester Plaza
Elmsford, New York 10523
Tel: 914-592-4646

Consolidated Film Industries
15 Columbus Circle
New York, New York 10023
Tel: 212-581-1090

Creativision, Inc.
295 West Fourth Street
New York, New York 10014
Tel: 212-924-3935

Dolphin Productions
140 East 80th Street
New York, New York 10021
Tel: 212-628-5930

Film Planning Associates
305 East 46th Street
New York, New York 10017
Tel: 212-755-9170

Fordel Films, Inc.
1079 Nelson Avenue
Bronx, New York 10452
Tel: 212-992-5000

Granato Animation Photography
8 West 40th Street
New York, New York 10018
Tel: 212-244-4744

Haberstroh Special Effects
   Studios
9 West 19th Street
New York, New York 10003
Tel: 212-255-1827

Hallas & Batchelor Animation
80 East End Avenue
New York, New York 10021
Tel: 212-752-2310

Harvey Famous Cartoons
1860 Broadway
New York, New York 10023
Tel: 212-582-2244

R. P. Heath Productions, Inc.
1627 Scott Avenue
West Islip, New York 11795
Tel: 516-661-5935

Hubley Studio, Inc.
815 Park Avenue
New York, New York 10021
Tel: 212-744-8050

I. F. Studios, Inc.
328 East 44th Street
New York, New York 10017
Tel: 212-683-4747

O. A. Kaufman
866 United Nations Plaza
New York, New York 10017
Tel: 212-758-9480

Phil Kimmelman & Associates,
  Inc.
65 East 55th Street
New York, New York 10022
Tel: 212-371-1850

L & L Eastern Effects, Inc.
219 East 44th Street
New York, New York 10036
Tel: 212-889-3790

Leo Animation Camera Service
15 West 46th Street
New York, New York 10036
Tel: 212-582-2515

Lippman Film Service, Inc.
18 West 45th Street
New York, New York 10036
Tel: 212-869-0838

Looking Glass Studios
305 East 46th Street
New York, New York 10017
Tel: 212-755-1776

MPO-Peridot Animation
222 East 45th Street
New York, New York 10036
Tel: 212-867-8200

Sal Maimone, Inc.
16 West 46th Street
New York, New York 10036
Tel: 212-581-4558

John McCrory, Studios
Visual Education Center Building
Floral Park, New York 11001
Tel: 212-347-3109

National Telepix, Inc.
747 Third Avenue
New York, New York 10017
Tel: 212-759-7770

The Optical House
25 West 45th Street
New York, New York 10036
Tel: 212-757-7840

Ovation Films, Inc.
33 West 46th Street
New York, New York 10036
Tel: 212-581-4406

Albert Paganelli
21 West 46th Street
New York, New York 10036
Tel: 212-582-2899

Pelican Films, Inc.
270 Madison Avenue
New York, New York 10017
Tel: 212-679-0670

David Piel, Inc.
300 Central Park West
New York, New York 10024
Tel: 212-873-9492

Willis Pyle Productions
781 Seventh Avenue
New York, New York 10019
Tel: 212-246-9400

Rainbow Film Effects, Inc.
45 West 45th Street
New York, New York 10036
Tel: 212-247-1676

Rembrandt Films
59 East 54th Street
New York, New York 10022
Tel: 212-758-1024

Screen Gems, Inc.
711 Fifth Avenue
New York, New York 10022
Tel: 212-751-4432

Hal Seeger
45 West 45th Street
New York, New York 10036
Tel: 212-586-4311

Fletcher Smith Studios, Inc.
321 East 44th Street
New York, New York 10017
Tel: 212-685-9010

Al Stahl Productions
1600 Broadway
New York, New York 10019
Tel: 212-265-2942

Telemated Motion Pictures
8 West 40th Street
New York, New York 10018
Tel: 212-565-5341

Terrytoons
38 Centre Avenue
New Rochelle, New York 10801
Tel: 914-632-3466

Richard H. Ullman, Inc.
295 Delaware Avenue
Buffalo, New York 14202

Van Praag Productions
250 West 54th Street
New York, New York 10019
Tel: 212-245-1050

Videart, Inc.
62 West 45th Street
New York, New York 10036
Tel: 212-682-2363

Wylde Films & Associates, Inc.
352 Park Avenue South
New York, New York 10010
Tel: 212-685-1000

Zander's Animation Parlour
285 Madison Avenue
New York, New York 10017
Tel: 212-725-1331

Pennsylvania:

The Animators
247 Fort Pitt Boulevard
Pittsburgh, Pennsylvania 15222
Tel: 412-391-2550

Brian Cartoons
1729 Sansom Street
Philadelphia, Pennsylvania 19103
Tel: 215-563-3892

Warren R. Smith, Inc.
117 Fourth Avenue
Pittsburgh, Pennsylvania 15222
Tel: 412-391-4410

K & H Productions
3601 Oak Grove
Dallas, Texas 75204
Tel: 214-526-5268

Texas:

Virginia:

A-V Corporation
2518 North Boulevard
Houston, Texas 77006
Tel: 713-523-6701

Dunn Productions
205 Nineteenth Street
Virginia Beach, Virginia 23451
Tel: 804-425-9422

P. D. Closser
3875 Dunhaven Road
Dallas, Texas 75220
Tel: 214-352-2090

Washington:

Know Productions, Inc.
1003 Lenora Street
Seattle, Washington 98121
Tel: 206-682-6931

William M. Hayes Productions
303 South Alamo Street
San Antonio, Texas 78205
Tel: 512-227-4073

Associations & Organization

Professional organizations and associations related to the movie industry a cataloged here. Labor organizations, guilds, and unions are presented und the heading "Guilds & Unions." Due to an overlap in the functions a purposes of some industry groups, the "Guilds & Unions" category should consulted if the desired organization is not found here.

California:

Academy of Motion Picture Arts
  and Sciences
9038 Melrose Avenue
Los Angeles, California 90069
Tel: 213-278-8990
Walter Mirisch, President

Academy of Television Arts and
  Sciences (Hollywood Chapter)
6363 Sunset Boulevard
Los Angeles, California 90028
Tel: 213-465-1131

Academy of Television Arts and
  Sciences (National Office)
291 South La Cienega Boulevard
Beverly Hills, California 90211
Tel: 213-659-0990

Actors Agency Directory
8480 Beverly Boulevard
Los Angeles, California 90048
Tel: 213-938-2521
Dorothy Dahlgren, Executive
  Secretary

Actors Equity Association
6430 Sunset Boulevard
Los Angeles, California 90028
Tel: 213-462-2334
Edward Weston, Assistant Exec.
  Secretary

Adult Film Association of
  America
1654 Cordova Street
Los Angeles, California 90007
Tel: 213-731-7236
David F. Friedman, President

Advertising Club of Los Ange
3105 Wilshire Boulevard
Los Angeles, California 90010
Tel: 213-382-1228
Alfred B. Lee, President

Affiliated Property Craftsman
7429 Sunset Boulevard
Los Angeles, California 90046
Tel: 213-876-2320
Frank O'Connor, President

Allied Casting
3518 Cahuenga Boulevard, W
Los Angeles, California 90068
Tel: 213-851-3515
John McLaughlin, Secretary

American Association of
  Advertising Agencies
8500 Wilshire Boulevard
Beverly Hills, California 902
Tel: 213-657-3711
Robert Stephens, Vice-Preside

American Association of
  Newspaper Representatives
4311 Wilshire Boulevard
Beverly Hills, California 90010
Tel: 213-937-1930
William Black, Vice-President

American Cinema Editors, Inc.
422 South Western Avenue
Los Angeles, California 90020
Tel: 213-384-0588
Axel R. Hubert, President

American Federation of
  Television & Radio Artists
  (AFTRA)
1717 North Highland Avenue
Los Angeles, California 90028
Tel: 213-461-8111
Claude McCue, Executive
  Secretary

American Film Institute
501 Doheny Road
Beverly Hills, California 90210
Tel: 213-278-8777
George Stevens, Jr., Director

American Guild of Authors and
  Composers
6331 Hollywood Boulevard
Los Angeles, California 90028
Tel: 213-462-1108
Helen King, West Coast
  Coordinator

American Guild of Musical
  Artists
6430 Sunset Boulevard
Los Angeles, California 90028
Tel: 213-461-3714
Francis Barnes, So. Calif.
  Representative

American Guild of Variety Artists
  (AGVA)
6331 Hollywood Boulevard
Los Angeles, California 90028
Tel: 213-464-8281
Alon Cory, Field Representative

The American Humane
  Association
8480 Beverly Boulevard
Los Angeles, California 90048
Tel: 213-653-3394

American Society of
  Cinematographers
1782 North Orange Drive
Los Angeles, California 90028
Tel: 213-876-5080

American Society of Composers,
  Authors and Publishers
6450 Sunset Boulevard
Los Angeles, California 90028
Tel: 213-466-7681

American Society of Lighting
  Directors
4949 Hollywood Boulevard, Suite
  214
Los Angeles, California 90027
Tel: 213-663-1915
Bill Shaw, President

Artists Managers Guild
7046 Hollywood Boulevard
Los Angeles, California 90028
Tel: 213-465-7107
Adrian McCalman, President

Association of Motion Picture and
  Television Producers, Inc.
8480 Beverly Boulevard
Los Angeles, California 90048
Tel: 213-653-2200
Jack Valenti, President

Black Stuntmen's Association
8949 West 24th Street
Los Angeles, California 90034
Tel: 213-837-2985

Broadcast Music, Inc. (BMI)
6255 Sunset Boulevard
Los Angeles, California 90028
Tel: 213-465-2111
Richard Kirk, Vice-President

California Newspaper Publishers
  Association
9841 Airport Boulevard
Los Angeles, California 90045
Tel: 213-641-8300

Central Casting Corporation
8480 Beverly Boulevard
Los Angeles, California 90048
Tel: 213-938-2325

Chamber of Commerce
  (Hollywood)
6520 West Sunset Boulevard
Los Angeles, California 90028
Tel: 213-469-8311

Cinema Audio Society
1800 North Highland Avenue
Los Angeles, California 90028
Tel: 213-463-0903

Commercial Film Producers
  Association
15300 Ventura Boulevard
Sherman Oaks, California 91403
Tel: 213-872-0833

Composers & Lyricists Guild of
  America, Inc.
6565 Sunset Boulevard
Los Angeles, California 90028
Tel: 213-462-6068
Ted Cain, Executive Director

Conference of Personal Managers
9220 Sunset Boulevard
Los Angeles, California 90069
Tel: 213-273-3060
Bette Rosenthal, Executive
  Secretary

Directors Guild of America
7950 Sunset Boulevard
Los Angeles, California 90046
Tel: 213-656-1220
Joseph Youngerman, National
  Exec. Secretary

Film Industry Workshops, Inc.
4063 Radford Avenue
Studio City, California 91604
Tel: 213-769-4146

Greater Los Angeles Press Club
600 North Vermont Avenue
Los Angeles, California 90004
Tel: 213-665-1141
James D'Arrigo, Manager

Hollywood Foreign Press
  Association
8732 Sunset Boulevard
Los Angeles, California 90069
Tel: 213-657-1731
Judy Solomon, President

Independent Casting
1523 Cross Roads of the World
Los Angeles, California 90028
Tel: 213-465-6157
Richard Graney, Exec.
  Vice-President

Independent Producers
  Association
1578 Queens Road
Los Angeles, California 90069
Tel: 213-656-0200
Edward Finney, President

Los Angeles Chamber of
  Commerce
404 South Bixel Street
Los Angeles, California 90054
Tel: 213-482-4010
Frederick Llewellyn, President

Motion Picture and Television
  Country House and Hospital
23388 Mulholland Drive
Woodland Hills, California 91364
Tel: 213-347-1591
Jack Staggs, Executive Director

Motion Picture and Television
  Credit Association
1725 Beverly Boulevard
Los Angeles, California 90026
Tel: 213-483-4694

Motion Picture and Television
  Fund
335 North La Brea Avenue
Los Angeles, California 90036
Tel: 213-937-7250
Jack Staggs, Executive Director

Motion Picture Health and
  Welfare Fund
6850 Van Nuys Boulevard
Van Nuys, California 91409
Tel: 213-997-8511

Motion Picture Industry Pension
  Plan
7423 Beverly Boulevard
Los Angeles, California 90036
Tel: 213-938-3651

National Academy of Recording
  Arts and Sciences
6430 Sunset Boulevard
Los Angeles, California 90028
Tel: 213-466-6181

National Association of Theatre
  Owners
292 South La Cienega Boulevard,
  Suite 216
Beverly Hills, California 90211
Tel: 213-657-5790

Permanent Charities Committee
  of the Entertainment Industries
463 North La Cienega Boulevard
Los Angeles, California 90048
Tel: 213-652-4680
William Arnold, Exec.
  Vice-President

Producers Guild of America, Inc.
8201 Beverly Boulevard
Los Angeles, California 90048
Tel: 213-651-0084

Producers-Writers Guild of
  America Pension Plan
8455 Beverly Boulevard
Los Angeles, California 90048
Tel: 213-651-0931
Andrew B. MacDonald,
  Administrator

Screen Actors Guild
7750 Sunset Boulevard
Los Angeles, California 90046
Tel: 213-876-3030
Dennis Weaver, President
Chester Migden, National Exec.
  Secretary

Screen Composers Association
9250 Wilshire Boulevard
Beverly Hills, California 90210
Tel: 213-276-3123
Nathan Scott, President

Screen Extras Guild
3629 Cahuenga Boulevard, West
Los Angeles, California 90068
Tel: 213-851-4301
Norman Stevans, President

Society of Motion Picture Art
  Directors
7715 Sunset Boulevard
Los Angeles, California 90046
Tel: 213-876-4330
Gene Allen, Executive Director

Southern California Broadcasters
  Association
1800 North Highland Avenue
Los Angeles, California 90028
Tel: 213-466-4481
Robert Light, President

Stunt Women of America
202 Vanoe Street
Pacific Palisades, California
  90272
Tel: 213-454-8228
Jeannie Eppers, President

Stuntmen's Association of Motion
  Pictures, Inc.
4810 Whitsett Avenue
North Hollywood, California
  91607
Tel: 213-766-4334

Television Bureau of Advertising,
  Inc.
444 North Larchmont Boulevard
Los Angeles, California 90004
Tel: 213-469-8231
Norm Cash, President

Underwater Motion Picture
  Association
1500 South Second Street
Alhambra, California 91801
Tel: 213-282-4117

Western States Advertising
  Agencies Association
5900 Wilshire Boulevard
Los Angeles, California 90036
Tel: 213-933-7337

Women of the Motion Picture
  Industry
3430 Sepulveda Boulevard,
  Apartment 80
Los Angeles, California 90034
Tel: 213-838-7928

Writers Guild of America—West
8955 Beverly Boulevard
Los Angeles, California 90048
Tel: 213-274-8601
Michael Franklin, Executive
    Director

District of Columbia:

The American Film Institute
The John F. Kennedy Center for
    the Performing Arts
Washington, D.C. 20566
Tel: 202-833-9300
Charlton Heston, Chairman
George Stevens, Jr., Director

Motion Picture Association of
    America, Inc.
1600 Eye Street, N.W.
Washington, D.C. 20006
Tel: 202-293-1966
Jack Valenti, President

National Endowment for the Arts
One McPherson Square, N.W.
Washington, D.C. 20005
Tel: 202-382-6085
Nancy Hanks, Chairman

New York:

Actors Equity Association
165 West 46th Street
New York, New York 10036
Tel: 212-757-7660

Actors Fund of America
1619 Broadway
New York, New York 10019
Tel: 212-265-6400

American Federation of
    Musicians
641 Lexington Avenue
New York, New York 10022
Tel: 212-758-0600

American Federation of
    Television and Radio Artists
    (AFTRA)
1350 Avenue of the Americas
New York, New York 10019
Tel: 212-265-7700

American Guild of Authors &
    Composers
50 West 57th Street
New York, New York 10013
Tel: 212-757-8833

American Guild of Musical
    Artists
1841 Broadway
New York, New York 10023
Tel: 212-265-3687

American Guild of Variety Artists
1540 Broadway
New York, New York 10036
Tel: 212-765-0800

American National Theatre and
    Academy
245 West 52nd Street
New York, New York 10019
Tel: 212-757-4133

American Society of Composers,
    Authors and Publishers
1 Lincoln Plaza
New York, New York 10023
Tel: 212-595-3050

American Theatre Society, Inc.
226 West 47th Street
New York, New York 10036
Tel: 212-765-2950

American Theatre Wing
225 Park Avenue South
New York, New York 10003
Tel: 212-533-1600

Artists Representatives
 Association, Inc.
1270 Avenue of the Americas
New York, New York 10020
Tel: 212-246-1379

Associated Actors and Artists of
 America
165 West 46th Street
New York, New York 10036
Tel: 212-245-8046
Mortimer Becker, Counsel

Associated Councils of the Arts
1564 Broadway
New York, New York 10036
Tel: 212-586-3731

Association of Theatrical Press
 Agents and Managers
268 West 47th Street
New York, New York 10036
Tel: 212-582-3750

Authors Guild, Inc.
234 West 44th Street
New York, New York 10036
Tel: 212-582-3750

Authors League of America, Inc.
234 West 44th Street
New York, New York 10036
Tel: 212-736-4811

Broadcast Music, Inc. (BMI)
40 West 57th Street
New York, New York 10019
Tel: 212-586-2000

Catholic Actors Guild of America
227 West 45th Street
New York, New York 10036
Tel: 212-245-4646

Conference of Motion Picture and
 Television Unions
236 West 55th Street
New York, New York 10019
Tel: 212-245-5986

Conference of Personal Managers
850 Seventh Avenue
New York, New York 10021
Tel: 212-265-7489
Jack Segal, Secretary

Council of Motion Picture
 Organizations, Inc.
1501 Broadway
New York, New York 10036
Tel: 212-594-3325

Directors Guild of America, Inc.
110 West 58th Street
New York, New York 10019
Tel: 212-581-0370

Dramatists Guild, Inc.
234 West 44th Street
New York, New York 10036
Tel: 212-563-2233

Episcopal Actors Guild, Inc.
1 East 29th Street
New York, New York 10016
Tel: 212-685-2927

Hebrew Actors Union, Inc.
31 East Seventh Street
New York, New York 10003
Tel: 212-674-1923

The Jewish Theatrical Guild of
America, Inc.
1619 Broadway
New York, New York 10019
Tel: 212-757-5237

Motion Picture Association of
America, Inc.
522 Fifth Avenue
New York, New York 10036
Tel: 212-867-1200

Motion Picture Export
Association of America, Inc.
522 Fifth Avenue
New York, New York 10036
Tel: 212-867-1200

National Academy of Television
Arts and Sciences
1270 Avenue of the Americas
New York, New York 10020
Tel: 212-582-0190

National Association of Broadcast
Employees & Technicians
135 West 50th Street
New York, New York 10020
Tel: 212-757-3065

National Association of
Broadcasters
485 Madison Avenue
New York, New York 10022
Tel: 212-752-8050

National Association of Theatre
Owners, Inc.
1501 Broadway
New York, New York 10036
Tel: 212-594-3325

National Board of Review of
Motion Pictures
210 East 68th Street
New York, New York 10021
Tel: 212-988-4916

National Cartoonists Society
9 Ebony Court
Brooklyn, New York 11229
Tel: 212-743-6510

National Society of Film Critics
(see Critics)

Negro Actors Guild of America,
Inc.
1674 Broadway
New York, New York 10019
Tel: 212-245-4343

New York Film Critics Circle (see
Critics)

Recording Industry Association of
America, Inc.
1 East 57th Street
New York, New York 10022
Tel: 212-688-3778

Screen Actors Guild, Inc.
551 Fifth Avenue
New York, New York 10017
Tel: 212-687-4623

Screen Composers Association
c/o Zissu, Marcus & Stein
270 Madison Avenue
New York, New York 10016
Tel: 212-683-5320

Society of Authors
  Representatives
101 Park Avenue
New York, New York 10016
Tel: 212-683-5890

Society of Illustrators
128 East 63rd Street
New York, New York 10021
Tel: 212-838-2560

Society of Stage Directors and
  Choreographers, Inc.
1619 Broadway
New York, New York 10019
Tel: 212-246-5118

Television Bureau of Advertising,
  Inc.
1 Rockefeller Plaza
New York, New York 10020
Tel: 212-757-9420

Writers Guild of America—East
22 West 48th Street
New York, New York 10036
Tel: 212-575-5060

Business Managers

Having a business manager appears to be largely a Hollywood institution. New York–based celebrities and film industry professionals tend to leave the tax sheltering of investments and other business to their lawyers.

California:

Los Angeles area:

Vincent Andrews Management
Corporation
315 South Beverly Drive
Beverly Hills, California 90212
Tel: 213-553-0260

Babette Enterprises, Inc.
1560 North La Brea Avenue,
Suite M
Los Angeles, California 90028
Tel: 213-464-0411

Henry J. Bamberger
280 South Beverly Drive, Room
310
Beverly Hills, California 90212
Tel: 213-274-6315

Fred Barman & Associates
9255 Sunset Boulevard
Los Angeles, California 90069
Tel: 213-652-2222

Bash, Barkin & Gesas
9401 Wilshire Boulevard
Beverly Hills, California 90212
Tel: 213-278-7700

Samuel Berke & Company
9350 Wilshire Boulevard
Beverly Hills, California 90212
Tel: 213-272-9194

Beverly Management
Corporation
9470 Santa Monica Boulevard
Beverly Hills, California 90210
Tel: 213-271-5611

Bisgeier, Breslauer & Company
9134 Sunset Boulevard
Los Angeles, California 90069
Tel: 213-276-4174

Lurie Braverman & Company
233 South Beverly Drive
Beverly Hills, California 90212
Tel: 213-272-8456

Brent, Silverman & Berkowitz
15300 Ventura Boulevard, Suite
405
Sherman Oaks, California 91403
Tel: 213-872-1717

Annabelle Lewis Brown &
Associates
9465 Wilshire Boulevard
Beverly Hills, California 90212
Tel: 213-273-5580
Tel: 213-878-5202

Brown Kraft & Company
8530 Wilshire Boulevard, Suite
303
Beverly Hills, California 90211
Tel: 213-657-1550

Stanley Bushell
9025 Wilshire Boulevard
Beverly Hills, California 90211
Tel: 213-274-8881

Business Administration
Company
118 South Beverly Drive, Suite
222
Beverly Hills, California 90212
Tel: 213-276-7071

CMI-Howorth Wormser
1560 North La Brea Avenue,
Suite M
Los Angeles, California 90028
Tel: 213-464-0411

CPB Management
1901 Avenue of the Stars, Suite
650
Los Angeles, California 90067
Tel: 213-552-2124

Cabot Entertainment
6640 Sunset Boulevard, Suite 201
Los Angeles, California 90028
Tel: 213-466-5181

Caldin, Kalman, Hartman &
Sampson
9454 Wilshire Boulevard, Suite
209
Beverly Hills, California 90212
Tel: 213-272-9041

David Capell and Company
315 South Beverly Drive, Suite
500
Beverly Hills, California 90212
Tel: 213-553-0310

Carlin, Levy and Company
449 South Beverly Drive
Beverly Hills, California 90202
Tel: 213-277-4733

Carman Productions, Inc.
15456 Cabrito Road
Van Nuys, California 91406
Tel: 213-873-7370

Milton Cashy
8833 Sunset Boulevard
Los Angeles, California 90069
Tel: 213-652-9790

Samuel N. Chilkov
280 South Beverly Drive
Beverly Hills, California 90212
Tel: 213-273-2905

Hammer Cohen Company
8920 Wilshire Boulevard
Beverly Hills, California 90211
Tel: 213-657-3880

Coulter & Gray
430 North Rodeo Drive
Beverly Hills, California 90210
Tel: 213-276-2085

Dawson Business Management
8447 Wilshire Boulevard
Beverly Hills, California 90211
Tel: 213-651-0220

Jay J. Eller, Inc.
3700 Wilshire Boulevard
Los Angeles, California 90010
Tel: 213-381-5393

Embassy Sound Productions
847 South Grand Avenue
Los Angeles, California 90017
Tel: 213-623-3266

Myron D. Emory
10850 Wilshire Boulevard
Westwood, California 90024
Tel: 213-879-3444

Epimetheus Management
8600 Melrose Avenue
Los Angeles, California 90069
Tel: 213-659-1301

Equitable Investment
  Corporation
6253 Hollywood Boulevard
Los Angeles, California 90028
Tel: 213-469-2975

Ev-Love Management
8730 Sunset Boulevard, Penthouse
  Suite
Los Angeles, California 90069
Tel: 213-652-2532

Executive Business Management,
  Inc.
132 South Rodeo Drive
Beverly Hills, California 90212
Tel: 213-278-6700

Chauncey C. Ferris & Company
260 South Rodeo Drive
Beverly Hills, California 90212
Tel: 213-274-5469

First Kensington, Inc.
1900 Avenue of the Stars, Suite
  1725
Los Angeles, California 90067
Tel: 213-277-4922

Freedman & Freedman
1801 Avenue of the Stars
Los Angeles, California 90067
Tel: 213-277-0700

Gadbois Management, Inc.
9201 Wilshire Boulevard
Beverly Hills, California 90210
Tel: 213-271-2183

Arthur Gage
1277 Sunset Plaza Drive
Los Angeles, California 90069
Tel: 213-652-4118

General Management Associates
P.O. Box 49993
Los Angeles, California 90049
Tel: 213-476-6273

Gerwin, Jamner & Pariser
760 North La Cienega Boulevard
Los Angeles, California 90069
Tel: 213-655-4410

Gilbert & Levine
1901 Avenue of the Stars, Suite
  1531
Los Angeles, California 90067
Tel: 213-277-5911

Robert H. Ginter & Company
120 El Camino Drive
Beverly Hills, California 90212
Tel: 213-278-0733

Global Business Management,
  Inc.
9601 Wilshire Boulevard
Beverly Hills, California 90210
Tel: 213-274-6788

Glusman & Halpern
9033 Wilshire Boulevard
Beverly Hills, California 90212
Tel: 213-278-8840

Owen N. Golden
9348 Santa Monica Boulevard
Beverly Hills, California 90210
Tel: 213-275-8842

Charles Goldring
8810 Sunset Boulevard
Los Angeles, California 90069
Tel: 213-655-8122

Marcel Goodwin
280 South Beverly Drive
Beverly Hills, California 90212
Tel: 213-271-9431

Eliot H. Gordon & Company
8888 West Olympic Boulevard
Beverly Hills, California 90211
Tel: 213-271-5677

George J. Gottfried
9025 Wilshire Boulevard, Suite
305
Beverly Hills, California 90210
Tel: 213-271-5261

Joe Gottfried Management
15456 Cabritto Road
Van Nuys, California 91406
Tel: 213-873-7370

Alexander Grant & Company
8920 Wilshire Boulevard
Beverly Hills, California 90212
Tel: 213-657-3880

Grillo & Grillo, Inc.
6363 Sunset Boulevard, Suite 900
Los Angeles, California 90028
Tel: 213-466-5346

Guild Management Corporation
10203 Santa Monica Boulevard
Los Angeles, California 90067
Tel: 213-277-9711

H-T Management
270 North Canon Drive
Beverly Hills, California 90210
Tel: 213-273-4077

Bart Hackley & Company
16055 Ventura Boulevard
Encino, California 91316
Tel: 213-872-2404

Ralph Handloy & Associates
13063 Ventura Boulevard
Studio City, California 91604
Tel: 213-981-7575

James Harper & Associates
13063 Ventura Boulevard
Studio City, California 91604
Tel: 213-788-8683

J. William Hayes
132 South Rodeo Drive
Beverly Hills, California 90212
Tel: 213-278-6700

Henshey, Beeman & Weyl
6253 Hollywood Boulevard
Los Angeles, California 90028
Tel: 213-462-7439

Peter W. Hopp & Company
1263 Westwood Boulevard
West Los Angeles, California
90024
Tel: 213-478-8818

International Business
Management, Ltd.
1901 Avenue of the Stars, Suite
1132
Los Angeles, California 90067
Tel: 213-277-4455

L. H. Joseph Jr. & Associates
8344 Melrose Avenue
Los Angeles, California 90069
Tel: 213-651-2322

Malvern L. Kaplan
1900 Avenue of the Stars, Suite
2535
Los Angeles, California 90067
Tel: 213-553-1944

Kelman, Greenberg & Company
7060 Hollywood Boulevard, Suite
606
Los Angeles, California 90028
Tel: 213-469-8241

Harold B. Kern Accountancy
1901 Avenue of the Stars
Los Angeles, California 90067
Tel: 213-277-2351

Fred Landau & Company
6922 Hollywood Boulevard
Los Angeles, California 90028
Tel: 213-466-9231

Leance & Kastner
9401 Wilshire Boulevard
Beverly Hills, California 90212
Tel: 213-275-0128

Julius Lefkowitz & Company
9171 Wilshire Boulevard, Suite
420
Beverly Hills, California 90210
Tel: 213-275-0111

Eli Leslie Management
9465 Wilshire Boulevard
Beverly Hills, California 90212
Tel: 213-273-4333

Walter Lipshie & Company
3345 Wilshire Boulevard
Los Angeles, California 90010
Tel: 213-380-4382

Robert E. Major & Associates
434 North Rodeo Drive, Suite 301
Beverly Hills, California 90210
Tel: 213-271-5131

The Management Tree
8961 Sunset Boulevard, Penthouse
Los Angeles, California 90069
Tel: 213-273-7211

A. Morgan Maree, Jr., &
Associates
6363 Wilshire Boulevard, Room
600
Los Angeles, California 90048
Tel: 213-653-7330

Elva McGuire
P.O. Box 1266
Beverly Hills, California 90213
Tel: 213-273-0146

George Mercader & Company
9171 Wilshire Boulevard, Suite
404
Beverly Hills, California 90210
Tel: 213-274-9911

Forest W. Monroe & Associates
420 South Beverly Drive
Beverly Hills, California 90212
Tel: 213-552-1100

Jess S. Morgan & Company, Inc.
6300 Wilshire Boulevard
Los Angeles, California 90048
Tel: 213-651-1601

Benjamin Newman
211 South Beverly Drive
Beverly Hills, California 90212
Tel: 213-278-4927

Orland, Chase & Mucci
9200 Sunset Boulevard, Suite 905
Los Angeles, California 90069
Tel: 213-279-1301

Osborne & Ward
141 El Camino Drive
Beverly Hills, California 90212
Tel: 213-276-7105

Oxford Management Enterprises
6404 Wilshire Boulevard
Los Angeles, California 90048
Tel: 213-653-1665

PBM Associates
9000 Sunset Boulevard
Los Angeles, California 90069
Tel: 213-278-4432

George Pakkala
8530 Wilshire Boulevard
Beverly Hills, California 90211
Tel: 213-657-1550

Henry Polakow Business
Management
9110 Sunset Boulevard
Los Angeles, California 90069
Tel: 213-274-0105

Samuel Pop and Company
420 South Beverly Drive
Beverly Hills, California 90212
Tel: 213-552-1100

Walter Prince
8150 Beverly Boulevard
Los Angeles, California 90048
Tel: 213-656-1665

Professional Management
Association Ltd.
9454 Wilshire Boulevard
Beverly Hills, California 90212
Tel: 213-278-6680

Renthal, Kaufman and Bernstein,
Inc.
1900 Avenue of the Stars, Suite
2270
Los Angeles, California 90067
Tel: 213-277-1900

Rosenthal & Leon
250 North Canon Drive
Beverly Hills, California 90210
Tel: 213-276-7123

Ryder, Stilwell & Company
5900 Wilshire Boulevard
Los Angeles, California 90036
Tel: 213-937-5500

M. R. Schacker
321 South Beverly Drive
Beverly Hills, California 90212
Tel: 213-553-0133

Herbert B. Schlosberg
Certified Life Tower
14724 Ventura Boulevard
Sherman Oaks, California 91403
Tel: 213-990-5600

Lucille Siegel
9348 Santa Monica Boulevard
Beverly Hills, California 90210
Tel: 213-276-5434

A. J. Silverman
12412 Ventura Boulevard
Studio City, California 91604
Tel: 213-769-5640

Bernard Skadron
P.O. Box 1065
Studio City, California 91604
Tel: 213-762-0669

William E. Stein Accounting
   Corporation
9454 Wilshire Boulevard, Suite
   801
Beverly Hills, California 90212
Tel: 213-274-6247

Sterling, Salyers, Altman, Inc.
260 South Beverly Drive
Beverly Hills, California 90212
Tel: 213-278-4201

Stutman and Varco, Inc.
1900 Avenue of the Stars, Suite
   1475
Los Angeles, California 90067
Tel: 213-556-3226

Edward Traubner & Company,
   Inc.
1800 Century Park East
Los Angeles, California 90067
Tel: 213-277-3000

Tri-Lo, Inc.
1100 North Alta Loma Road
Los Angeles, California 90069
Tel: 213-657-4040

Alexander Tucker
9200 Sunset Boulevard
Los Angeles, California 90069
Tel: 213-274-0891

Sophia Wallenstein Business
   Management
8230 Beverly Boulevard
Los Angeles, California 90048
Tel: 213-651-5110

H. B. Walls
1600 North La Brea Avenue
Los Angeles, California 90028
Tel: 213-461-8341

Weber, Lipshie & Company
3345 Wilshire Boulevard
Los Angeles, California 90005
Tel: 213-380-4382

Westheimer, Fine, Berger &
   Company
1880 Century Park East, Suite
   600
Los Angeles, California 90067
Tel: 213-553-6370

Harold Williams
9405 Brighton Way
Beverly Hills, California 90210
Tel: 213-271-9181

Reginald K. Wilson
8330 West Third Street, Suite 206
Los Angeles, California 90048
Tel: 213-653-9750

Lee Winkler
9601 Wilshire Boulevard
Beverly Hills, California 90210
Tel: 213-274-6788

Kurt E. Wolff
5451 Laurel Canyon Boulevard
North Hollywood, California
   91607
Tel: 213-877-3043

Wood/Freeman Business
   Management
6233 Hollywood Boulevard
Los Angeles, California 90028
Tel: 213-469-5196

San Francisco area:

Stephen A. Baffrey
2774 Jackson Street
San Francisco, California 94115
Tel: 415-921-3607

Steamboat Productions
273 Page Street
San Francisco, California 94102
Tel: 415-864-5100

Hawaii:

American Pacific Entertainment
3026-A Kopaka, Box 9181
Honolulu, Hawaii 96820
Tel: 808-847-4875

Len Mednick
1777 Ala Moana Boulevard #202
Honolulu, Hawaii 96744
Tel: 808-955-4000

Camera Equipment

Included within this category are sources of camera rentals and sales, equipment repairs and modifications, and suppliers of camera cars and cranes.

CAMERA CARS & CRANES

California:
Los Angeles area:

Bragg Crane and Rigging
  Company
6242 Paramount Boulevard
Long Beach, California 90805
Tel: 213-636-2421

Gil Casper Camera Cars
10797 Galvin Street
Culver City, California 90230
Tel: 213-839-6416

Chapman Studio Equipment
12950 Raymer
North Hollywood, California
  91605
Tel: 213-877-5309

Cine Group
8560 Sunset Boulevard
Los Angeles, California 90069
Tel: 213-652-4800

Coulter Brothers, Inc.
1850 East 33rd Street
Long Beach, California 90810
Tel: 213-830-8410

George Dockstader Rentals
6700 Fair Avenue
North Hollywood, California
  91606
Tel: 213-763-7167

F&B/Ceco of California, Inc.
7051 Santa Monica Boulevard
Los Angeles, California 90038
Tel: 213-466-9361

Galloway Crane and Truck
  Company
12521 Branford
Pacoima, California 91331
Tel: 213-896-2461

Alan Gordon Enterprises, Inc.
1430 North Cahuenga Boulevard
Los Angeles, California 90028
Tel: 213-466-3561

Pat Hustis Camera Cars
9315 Burnet Avenue
Sepulveda, California 91343
Tel: 213-892-8533

Hydraulic Crane Rental
10805 South Painter
Santa Fe Springs, California
    90670
Tel: 213-723-5109

Owl Crane and Rigging Service
500 South Alameda
Compton, California 90224
Tel: 213-638-8761

Porta Crane Company, Inc.
11927 Sherman Road
North Hollywood, California
    91605
Tel: 213-765-9843

SOS/Photo-Cine-Optics, Inc.
7051 Santa Monica Boulevard
Los Angeles, California 90038
Tel: 213-466-9361

Smith Crane and Rigging
    Company
1640 Compton
Los Angeles, California 90021
Tel: 213-749-3271

Ray Tostado Camera Cars and
    Cranes
915 West Kensington Road
Los Angeles, California 90026
Tel: 213-823-1843

San Francisco area:

The Phelps and Kopp Company
991 Tennessee Street
San Francisco, California 94107
Tel: 415-285-1900

New York:

Bernard Grubman
519 West 47th Street
New York, New York 10036
Tel: 212-582-1194

Texas:

Perfection Film Equipment
    Company
5915-A Star Lane
Houston, Texas 77027
Tel: 713-781-7886
Tel: 713-781-7894

REPAIRS & MODIFICATIONS

Arizona:

Camera World
7252 First Avenue
Scottsdale, Arizona 85251
Tel: 602-945-6692

Phoenix Camera Repair Inc.
2221 North Seventh Street
Phoenix, Arizona 85012
Tel: 602-252-3157

Tucson Camera Repair
6947 East 22nd Street
Tucson, Arizona 85710
Tel: 602-296-3374

California:
Los Angeles area:

Bob Adler Camera Service
8534 Corbin Avenue
Northridge, California 91324
Tel: 213-885-1038

Akkad International Products,
Inc.
8730 Sunset Boulevard
Los Angeles, California 90069
Tel: 213-657-7670

Aremac Camera Company
5609 Sunset Boulevard
Los Angeles, California 90028
Tel: 213-469-2987

Mark Armistead, Inc.
1041 North Formosa Avenue
Los Angeles, California 90046
Tel: 213-851-2424

Bach Auricon, Inc.
6950 Romaine Street
Los Angeles, California 90038
Tel: 213-462-0931

Bell & Howell
623 Rodier Drive
Glendale, California 91209
Tel: 213-245-6631

Birns & Sawyer
1026 North Highland Avenue
Los Angeles, California 90046
Tel: 213-466-8211

Camera Repair Company of
Hollywood
1255 North La Brea Avenue
Los Angeles, California 90038
Tel: 213-851-2050

Century Precision Optics, Inc.
10661 Burbank Boulevard
North Hollywood, California
91601
Tel: 213-766-3715

Cine Group
8560 Sunset Boulevard
Los Angeles, California 90069
Tel: 213-652-4800

Cinema Arts Crafts
914 North Fairfax
Los Angeles, California 90046
Tel: 213-654-0502

Continental Camera Systems
16800 Roscoe Boulevard
Van Nuys, California 91406
Tel: 213-989-5222

Herman Galli Camera Service
6804 Melrose Avenue
Los Angeles, California 90038
Tel: 213-931-4111

Gerhard's Camera Repair
137 South Vermont
Los Angeles, California 90004
Tel: 213-388-5114

Alan Gordon Enterprises, Inc.
5362 North Cahuenga Boulevard
North Hollywood, California
91601
Tel: 213-985-5500

Hill Production Service, Inc.
3518 Cahuenga Boulevard
West Hollywood, California
90068
Tel: 213-851-4706

Hollywood Camera
1255 North La Brea Avenue
Los Angeles, California 90038
Tel: 213-783-1134

Hollywood Film Company
956 Seward Street
Los Angeles, California 90038
Tel: 213-462-3284

Kenworthy Snorkel Camera
 Systems, Inc.
P.O. Box 49851
Los Angeles, California 90049
Tel: 213-476-4100

Rudy Ling Camera Service
4355 Sepulveda Boulevard
Culver City, California 90230
Tel: 213-397-0072

Lloyd's Camera Exchange
1612 Cahuenga Boulevard North
Los Angeles, California 90028
Tel: 213-467-7956

Mitchell Camera Corporation
666 West Harvard Street
Glendale, California 91204
Tel: 213-245-1088

Mole-Richardson Company
937 North Sycamore Avenue
Los Angeles, California 90038
Tel: 213-654-3660

Mel Pierce Camera
5645 Hollywood Boulevard
Los Angeles, California 90028
Tel: 213-465-2191

Jack Pill & Associates, Inc.
6370 Santa Monica Boulevard
Los Angeles, California 90038
Tel: 213-466-5391

Research Products, Inc.
6860 Lexington Avenue
Los Angeles, California 90038
Tel: 213-461-3733

Saba Camera Service
6572 Santa Monica Boulevard
Los Angeles, California 90038
Tel: 213-469-1551

Skidmore Engineering
6531 Santa Monica Boulevard
Los Angeles, California 90038
Tel: 213-464-9346

Stylecraft Engineering Company
6572 Santa Monica Boulevard
Los Angeles, California 90038
Tel: 213-464-0828

S. Walters Camera Repair
412 West Sixth Street, Suite 901
Los Angeles, California 90014
Tel: 213-622-0744

San Francisco area:

Brooks Cameras, Inc.
45 Kearny Street
San Francisco, California 94108
Tel: 415-392-1902

Cudabac Camera Repair
184 Second Street
San Francisco, California 94105
Tel: 415-982-3213

Ferco
363 Brannan Street
San Francisco, California 94107
Tel: 415-957-1787

Adolph Gasser, Inc.
5733 Geary Boulevard
San Francisco, California 92421
Tel: 415-751-0145

Lee Engineering
431 Jones Street
San Francisco, California 94102
Tel: 415-776-8360

Skinner Studio
345 Sutter Street
San Francisco, California 94108
Tel: 415-986-5040

Colorado:

Metro Camera Service, Inc.
1973 South Federal Boulevard
Denver, Colorado 80219
Tel: 303-935-5854

Hawaii:

Pacific Instrumentation
5388 Papai Street
Honolulu, Hawaii 96821
Tel: 808-373-1287

New Jersey:

Frezzolini Electronics, Inc.
7 Valley Street
Hawthorne, New Jersey 07506
Tel: 201-427-1160

New York:
New York City:

Ace Camera Exchange
689 Lexington Avenue
New York, New York 10022
Tel: 212-759-0947

Arriflex Company of America
P.O. Box 1050
Woodside, New York 10009
Tel: 212-932-3403

Camera Mart, Inc.
465 West 55th Street
New York, New York 10019
Tel: 212-757-6977

Camera Service Center
625 West 54th Street
New York, New York 10019
Tel: 212-757-0906

Cine 60, Inc.
Film Center Building
630 Ninth Avenue
New York, New York 10036
Tel: 212-586-8782

Cinekad Engineering Company
759 Tenth Avenue
New York, New York 10019
Tel: 212-757-3511

F&B/Ceco Industries, Inc.
315 West 43rd Street
New York, New York 10036
Tel: 212-586-1420

Film Equipment Rental
  Company
419 West 54th Street
New York, New York 10019
Tel: 212-581-5474

General Camera
471 Eleventh Avenue
New York, New York 10018
Tel: 212-594-8700

General Cinema Corporation
159 West 53rd Street
New York, New York 10019
Tel: 212-489-1950

Golden Camera & Lens
  Company, Inc.
1265 Broadway
New York, New York 10001
Tel: 212-684-4280

National Cine Equipment, Inc.
4140 Austin Boulevard
Island Park, New York 11558
Tel: 212-799-4602

SOS/Photo-Cine-Optics, Inc.
315 West 43rd Street
New York, New York 10036
Tel: 212-586-1420

Wall Street Camera Exchange,
  Inc.
82 Wall Street
New York, New York 10005
Tel: 212-944-0001

Willoughby Camera Stores
110 West 32nd Street
New York, New York 10001
Tel: 212-564-1600

Texas:

Victor Duncan, Inc.
2657 Fondren Drive
Dallas, Texas 75206
Tel: 214-369-1165

SALES & RENTALS

Alaska:

Films North
203 West Fifteenth Avenue
Anchorage, Alaska 99501
Tel: 907-277-8834

Arizona:

Studio Rentals of Arizona
2321 East University Drive
Phoenix, Arizona 85034
Tel: 602-252-5848

California:
Los Angeles area:

Acme Camera Corporation
820 South Mariposa Street
Burbank, California 91506
Tel: 213-849-6251

Akkad International Production,
  Inc.
8730 Sunset Boulevard
Los Angeles, California 90069
Tel: 213-657-7670

Amerton/American Electronics
Supply, Inc.
1200 North Vine Street
Los Angeles, California 90038
Tel: 213-466-4321

Aremac Camera Company
5609 Sunset Boulevard
Los Angeles, California 90028
Tel: 213-469-2987

Mark Armistead, Inc.
1041 North Formosa Avenue
Los Angeles, California 90046
Tel: 213-851-2424

Arriflex Company of America
1011 Chestnut Street
Burbank, California 91502
Tel: 213-845-7687

Bach-Auricon, Inc.
6950 Romaine Street
Los Angeles, California 90038
Tel: 213-462-0931

Bell & Howell
623 Rodier Drive
Glendale, California 91201
Tel: 213-245-6631

Berkey Marketing
1011 Chestnut Street
Burbank, California 91502
Tel: 213-843-1883

Birns & Sawyer, Inc.
1026 North Highland Avenue
Los Angeles, California 90038
Tel: 213-466-8211

Camera Service Center
4355 Sepulveda Boulevard
Culver City, California 90230
Tel: 213-397-0072

Cine Group
8560 Sunset Boulevard
Los Angeles, California 90069
Tel: 213-652-4800

Cine Services
173 South Ardmore
Los Angeles, California 90004
Tel: 213-383-9462

Cinema Beaulieu, Inc.
14225 Ventura Boulevard
Sherman Oaks, California 91405
Tel: 213-981-2395

Cinema Products Corporation
2037 Granville Avenue
Los Angeles, California 90025
Tel: 213-478-0711

Cineomobile Systems
8600 Sunset Boulevard
Los Angeles, California 90069
Tel: 213-652-4800

Eclair Camera
7262 Melrose Avenue
Los Angeles, California 90046
Tel: 213-933-7182

Elliot Periscope Lens
932 North La Brea Avenue
Los Angeles, California 90038
Tel: 213-874-9400

F&B/Ceco of California, Inc.
7051 Santa Monica Boulevard
Los Angeles, California 90038
Tel: 213-466-9361

Freestyle Sales Company, Inc.
5124 Sunset Boulevard
Los Angeles, California 90027
Tel: 213-660-3460

Herman Galli Camera Service
6804 Melrose Avenue
Los Angeles, California 90038
Tel: 213-931-4111

Alan Gordon Enterprises, Inc.
1430 North Cahuenga Boulevard
Los Angeles, California 90028
Tel: 213-466-3561

Alan Gordon Enterprises, Inc.
5362 North Cahuenga Boulevard
North Hollywood, California
 91601
Tel: 213-985-5500

Jon Hall Enterprises
2036 Stoner Avenue
Los Angeles, California 90052
Tel: 213-478-1511

Henry's Camera Corporation
516 West Eighth Street
Los Angeles, California 90014
Tel: 213-627-5514

Hill Production Service, Inc.
835 Seward Street
Los Angeles, California 90038
Tel: 213-463-0311

Stacy Keach Productions
5216 Laurel Canyon Boulevard
North Hollywood, California
 91607
Tel: 213-877-0472

Kenworthy Snorkel Camera
 Systems, Inc.
P.O. Box 49851
Los Angeles, California 90049
Tel: 213-476-4100

Lloyd-Davies Enterprises
1021 North McCadden Place
Los Angeles, California 90038
Tel: 213-462-1206

Lloyd's Camera Exchange
1612 Cahuenga Boulevard North
Los Angeles, California 90028
Tel: 213-467-7956

Mitchell Camera Corporation
666 West Harvard Street
Glendale, California 91204
Tel: 213-245-1085

Mobile Production Systems
1225 North Vine Street
Los Angeles, California 90038
Tel: 213-465-7141

Morgan Rents
1123 North Lillian Way
Los Angeles, California 90038
Tel: 213-469-2704

Movie Tech
6518 Santa Monica Boulevard
Los Angeles, California 90038
Tel: 213-467-8491

POV Helmet Camera
3518 Cahuenga Boulevard West
Los Angeles, California 90068
Tel: 213-874-0166

Photo-Sonics, Inc.
820 South Mariposa Street
Burbank, California 91506
Tel: 213-849-6251

Mel Pierce Camera
5645 Hollywood Boulevard
Los Angeles, California 90028
Tel: 213-465-2191

Jack Pill & Associates, Inc.
6370 Santa Monica Boulevard
Los Angeles, California 90038
Tel: 213-466-3238

Research Products, Inc.
6860 Lexington Avenue
Los Angeles, California 90038
Tel: 213-461-3733

SOS/Photo-Cine-Optics, Inc.
7051 Santa Monica Boulevard
Los Angeles, California 90038
Tel: 213-466-9361

Saba Camera Service
6572 Santa Monica Boulevard
Los Angeles, California 90038
Tel: 213-469-1551

Sawyer Camera Company
6820 Santa Monica Boulevard
Los Angeles, California 90038
Tel: 213-466-6113

Sol-Lux Cinema
5632 Lexington
Los Angeles, California 90038
Tel: 213-467-4646

Stereovision International, Inc.
5700 Cahuenga Boulevard
North Hollywood, California
  91601
Tel: 213-762-7200

Tech-Camera Rentals, Inc.
6370 Santa Monica Boulevard
Los Angeles, California 90038
Tel: 213-466-5391

Todd-AO Corporation
1021 North Seward Street
Los Angeles, California 90038
Tel: 213-463-1136

UPS Studio Rentals
6561 Santa Monica Boulevard
Los Angeles, California 90038
Tel: 213-461-1442

Universal City Studios
100 Universal City Plaza
Universal City, California 91608
Tel: 213-985-4321

Visual Instrumentation
239 West Olive Avenue
Burbank, California 91502
Tel: 213-849-7333

San Francisco area:

Brooks Cameras, Inc.
45 Kearny Street
San Francisco, California 94108
Tel: 415-392-1902

Camera Center
998 Market Street
San Francisco, California 94102
Tel: 415-775-5100

Eastman Kodak Company
3250 Van Ness Avenue
San Francisco, California 94109
Tel: 415-776-6055

Essanay Motion Picture
  Production Corporation
1935 Sixteenth Avenue
San Francisco, California 94116
Tel: 415-564-2886

Ferco
363 Brannan Street
San Francisco, California 94107
Tel: 415-957-1787

Adolph Gasser, Inc.
5733 Geary Boulevard
San Francisco, California 92421
Tel: 415-751-0145

W. A. Palmer Films, Inc.
611 Howard Street
San Francisco, California 94105
Tel: 415-986-5961

The Phelps & Kopp Company
991 Tennessee Street
San Francisco, California 94107
Tel: 415-285-1900

Jack Pill's Tech-Camera, Inc.
1239 Polk Street
San Francisco, California 94109
Tel: 415-771-1100

Skinner Studio
345 Sutter Street
San Francisco, California 94108
Tel: 415-986-5040

Colorado:

E. K. Edwards and Son, Inc.
2120 Holly
Denver, Colorado 80222
Tel: 303-757-5130

Western Cine Service
312 South Pearl Street
Denver, Colorado 80209
Tel: 303-744-1017

Florida:

Camera South, Inc.
1645 S.W. 27th Avenue
Miami, Florida 33101
Tel: 305-445-9461

Cine Tech, Inc.
1330 N.E. Fourth Court
Miami, Florida 33138
Tel: 305-754-2611

TOGA Film Equipment
  Company
4325 N.E. 22nd Avenue
Fort Lauderdale, Florida 33308
Tel: 305-772-1471

Hawaii:

Central Camera, Inc.
1105 Bishop
Honolulu, Hawaii 96813
Tel: 808-536-6692

Film Services of Hawaii, Ltd.
716 Cooke Street
Honolulu, Hawaii 96813
Tel: 808-538-1928

Hawaii Camera Company
1415 Kapiolani
Honolulu, Hawaii 96814
Tel: 808-949-5321

Pacific Instrumentation
5388 Papai Street
Honolulu, Hawaii 96821
Tel: 808-373-1287

Pacific Productions
700 Richards Street
Box 2881
Honolulu, Hawaii 96813
Tel: 808-531-1560

Illinois:

Behrend's, Inc.
161 East Grand Avenue
Chicago, Illinois 60611
Tel: 312-527-3060

Victor Duncan, Inc.
676 North St. Clair Street
Chicago, Illinois 60611
Tel: 312-321-9406

Helix, Ltd.
679 North Orleans Street
Chicago, Illinois 60610
Tel: 312-944-4400

Rent Com, Inc.
4734 North Austin
Chicago, Illinois 60630
Tel: 312-736-1225

Standard Photo Supply Company
43 East Chicago Avenue
Chicago, Illinois 60611
Tel: 312-787-3124

Massachusetts:

Film Associates
421 Broadway
Cambridge, Massachusetts 02138
Tel: 617-492-1062

Michigan:

Victor Duncan, Inc.
11043 Gratiot
Detroit, Michigan 48213
Tel: 313-371-4920

Missouri:

Calvin Cinequip, Inc.
215 West Pershing Road
Kansas City, Missouri 64108
Tel: 816-471-7800

Nevada:

K-B Cine Supply
P.O. Box 12611
Las Vegas, Nevada 89112
Tel: 702-451-5290

Rugar Electronics Company
4515 Industrial Road
Las Vegas, Nevada 89103
Tel: 702-736-4331

Video Sound Engineering
2130 South Highland Avenue
Las Vegas, Nevada 89102
Tel: 702-385-4691

New Jersey:

Comquip, Inc.
366 South Maple Avenue
Glen Rock, New Jersey 07452
Tel: 201-444-3800

Frezzolini Electronics, Inc.
7 Valley Street
Hawthorne, New Jersey 07506
Tel: 201-427-1160

Paillard
1900 Lower Road
Linden, New Jersey 07036
Tel: 201-381-5600

New York:

Audio Services Company
565 Fifth Avenue
New York, New York 10019
Tel: 212-972-0825

Camera Mart, Inc.
456 West 55th Street
New York, New York 10019
Tel: 212-757-6977

Camera Service Center
625 West 54th Street
New York, New York 10019
Tel: 212-757-0906

Cine 60, Inc.
Film Center Building
630 Ninth Avenue
New York, New York 10036
Tel: 212-586-8782

Ferco-Film Equipment Rental
Co.
419 West 54th Street
New York, New York 10019
Tel: 212-581-5474

General Camera
471 Eleventh Avenue
New York, New York 10018
Tel: 212-594-8700

MPCS Communications
    Industries
514 West 57th Street
New York, New York 10019
Tel: 212-586-3690

Mobias Cine, Ltd.
565 Fifth Avenue
New York, New York 10017
Tel: 212-697-8620

Ross-Gaffney, Inc.
21 West 46th Street
New York, New York 10036
Tel: 212-265-2918

Pennsylvania:

Calvin Cinequip, Inc.
1909 Buttonwood Street
Philadelphia, Pennsylvania 19130
Tel: 215-568-6291

O. H. Hirt, Inc.
41 North Eleventh Street
Philadelphia, Pennsylvania 19107
Tel: 215-923-0650

Texas:

K & H Productions
3601 Oak Grove
Dallas, Texas 75204
Tel: 214-526-5268

PSI Film Laboratory, Inc.
3011 Diamond Park Drive
Dallas, Texas 75347
Tel: 214-631-5670

Texas Theatre Supply
915 South Alamo Street
San Antonio, Texas 78205
Tel: 512-222-1002

Utah:

Stockdale & Company, Inc.
200 East First South
Salt Lake City, Utah 84111
Tel: 801-521-3505

Washington:

Aero Marc, Inc.
5518 Empire Way South
Seattle, Washington 98118
Tel: 206-725-1400

Seattle Motion Picture Service
4717 Aurora North
Seattle, Washington 98103
Tel: 206-632-3717

Casting Agencies
& Consultants

Agent contact is required for virtually all casting for Los Angeles producti
organizations, and to only a slightly lesser degree in New York. Act
seeking employment are cautioned to determine each casting agency's poli
by writing prior to telephoning or making a personal visit.

California:

Los Angeles area:

Allied Casting Agency, Inc.
3518 Cahuenga Boulevard
West Hollywood, California
90028
Tel: 213-851-3515

Maxine Anderson & Associates
9172 Sunset Boulevard
Los Angeles, California 90069
Tel: 213-274-9927

Hoyt Bowers & Associates
Twentieth Century–Fox Studios
10201 West Pico Boulevard
Los Angeles, California 90067
Tel: 213-277-2211

Ross Brown Casting
7319 Beverly Boulevard, Suite 10
Los Angeles, California 90036
Tel: 213-938-2575

Ruth Burch
195 South Beverly Drive
Beverly Hills, California 90212
Tel: 213-273-1161

CHN International Agency
7428 Santa Monica Boulevard
Los Angeles, California 90046
Tel: 213-874-8252

Carman Productions, Inc.
15456 Cabrito Road
Van Nuys, California 91406
Tel: 213-873-7370

Casting Services
439 South La Cienega Bouleva
Los Angeles, California 90048
Tel: 213-278-1030

Central Casting Corporation
8480 Beverly Boulevard
Los Angeles, California 90048
Tel: 213-938-2325

Harvey Clermont Casting Servi
780 North Gower Street
Los Angeles, California 90036
Tel: 213-463-0100

Coordinators 2
8113 1/2 Melrose Avenue
Los Angeles, California 90046
Tel: 213-653-6110

Joe Gottfried Management
15456 Cabrito Road
Van Nuys, California 91406
Tel: 213-873-7370
Tel: 213-873-2842

Hollywood Casting Agency
7046 Hollywood Boulevard
Los Angeles, California 90028
Tel: 213-461-9308

Independent Casting, Inc.
1956 North Cahuenga Boulevard
Los Angeles, California 90028
Tel: 213-465-6157

Robert Longenecker Agency
8438 Melrose Place
Los Angeles, California 90069
Tel: 213-653-3770

L. McFadden Studios
1210 1/2 North La Brea Avenue
Los Angeles, California 90038
Tel: 213-272-1544

Native American
    Research/Consultants
526 South Reese Place
Burbank, California 91506
Tel: 213-848-6531

Marvin Paige Casting
8721 Sunset Boulevard, Suite 205
Los Angeles, California 90069
Tel: 213-659-3040

Screen Children's Guild Agency
12444 Ventura Boulevard
Studio City, California 91604
Tel: 213-985-6131

Joe Scully—Casting
1800 North Argyle Avenue
Los Angeles, California 90028
Tel: 213-461-7447

Show Talent International
    Agency
831 North Fairfax Avenue
Los Angeles, California 90046
Tel: 213-653-6701

Lynn Stalmaster & Associates
7466 Beverly Boulevard
Los Angeles, California 90036
Tel: 213-938-6148

Talento
1459 Seward Street
Los Angeles, California 90028
Tel: 213-466-7741

Jack Wolfman Productions
1474 North Kings Road
Los Angeles, California 90069
Tel: 213-656-4787

San Francisco area:

Brebner Agency
1615 Polk Street
San Francisco, California 94109
Tel: 415-775-1802

Florida:

Florida Talent, Inc.
2631 East Oakland Park
    Boulevard
Fort Lauderdale, Florida 33310
Tel: 305-947-1931

McDermott Talent Agency
923 North Golf
Hollywood, Florida 33022
Tel: 305-947-6798

Marion Polan, Inc.
1111 S.E. Seventh Street
Miami, Florida 33101
Tel: 305-379-7526

Talent Enterprises
1603 N.E. 123rd Street
Miami, Florida 33101
Tel: 305-891-1832

Ann Wright, Inc.
2539 South Bayshore Drive
Miami, Florida 33101
Tel: 305-445-2448

Georgia:

Beverly Anderson Associates
710 Peachtree Street, N.E.
Atlanta, Georgia 30308
Tel: 404-881-8758

Susan Orpin
295 West Wieuca Road, N.E.
Atlanta, Georgia 30347
Tel: 404-255-5156

The Phoenix Agency, Inc.
1379 West Peachtree Street
Atlanta, Georgia 30308
Janet Caldwell
Tel: 404-892-1434

Linda Spatz Casting
3079 Lanier Drive
Atlanta, Georgia 31520
Tel: 404-237-1887

Hawaii:

Gregg Kendall and Associates,
Inc.
Ilikai Hotel, Suite 101
1777 Ala Moana Boulevard
Honolulu, Hawaii 96815
Tel: 808-946-9577

Ruth Revere Talent Agency
2708 Laniloa, P.O. Box 3079
Honolulu, Hawaii 96802
Tel: 808-537-3139

St. John Studios of Hawaii
1860 Ala Moana Boulevard
Honolulu, Hawaii 96815
Tel: 808-947-2822

Nevada:

Nevada Motion Picture Service
2025 Paradise Road
Las Vegas, Nevada 89105
Tel: 702-734-0975

New Mexico:

Chaparral Casting & Services,
Inc.
928 Avenida Manana, N.E.
Albuquerque, New Mexico 87110
Tel: 505-266-0460
Carmen Martinez, President

Cinema Services of New Mexico
712 Sundown Place, S.E.
Albuquerque, New Mexico 87108
Tel: 505-255-7003
Jeanne Swain, President

New York:

All-Arts Talent Casting Agency
200 West 54th Street
New York, New York 10019
Tel: 212-582-4933

Beckwith Casting Company
39 West 55th Street
New York, New York 10019
Riccardo Bertoni
Tel: 212-765-4251

Carter on a Shoestring
160 West 95th Street
New York, New York 10025
Kit Carter
Tel: 212-864-3147

Cast-away! Casting Service
6 East 39th Street
New York, New York 10016
Sue Hessel
Jane Iredale
Tel: 212-684-3821

Casting Group, Inc.
1650 Broadway
New York, New York 10019
Bill Williams
Thomas Fiorello
Marty Richards
Gil Champion
Tel: 212-581-8762

Casting People, Inc.
175 East 62nd Street
New York, New York 10021
Tel: 212-838-6300

Central Casting Corporation
200 West 54th Street
New York, New York 10019
Tel: 212-582-4933

Barbara Claman, Inc.
200 West 57th Street
New York, New York 10019
Tel: 212-757-8130

Sylvia Fay
71 Park Avenue
New York, New York 10016
Tel: 212-889-2626

Beverly G. Kenny & Associates
Beverly Kenny
304 East 45th Street
New York, New York 10017
Tel: 212-685-1608

Vic Ramos Casting
130 East 70th Street
New York, New York 10021
Tel: 212-734-7235

Pat Sweeney
310 West Eleventh Street
New York, New York 10014
Tel: 212-582-4240

Talent Services Associates, Inc.
418 Park Avenue South
New York, New York 10016
Tel: 212-889-8650

Estelle Tepper
1650 Broadway
New York, New York 10019
Tel: 212-581-6205

Joy Weber Casting
317 West 89th Street
New York, New York 10024
Tel: 212-362-3922

Bill Williams, Jr.
1650 Broadway
New York, New York 10019
Tel: 212-581-6205

Geri Windsor & Associates
  Casting, Ltd.
1650 Broadway
New York, New York 10019
Tel: 212-586-4282

Texas:

The Casting Company
7034 Irongate Lane
Dallas, Texas 75214
Tel: 214-272-6069

Washington:

Oscar Productions, Inc.
1122 26th Avenue South
Seattle, Washington 98144
Tel: 206-324-9440

Catering

While catering services are widely available, catering operations for motion picture productions require specialized equipment, including mobile kitchens for location work. Also, movie schedules and union agreements require food preparation and serving at odd hours when conventional catering services may not operate.

Arizona:

Western Mobile Food Service
609 West Rillito
Tucson, Arizona 85703
Tel: 602-792-3877

California:

A A and M Catering Service
4177 Buckingham Road
Los Angeles, California 90008
Tel: 213-295-3988

A. L. Catering Company, Inc.
14507 Sylvan Street
Van Nuys, California 91404
Tel: 213-345-5471

Budd Catering Company
5353 West Third Street
Los Angeles, California 90020
Tel: 213-934-1822

Cabaret Party Catering
9348 Santa Monica Boulevard,
    Suite 101
Beverly Hills, California 90210
Tel: 213-278-4700

Carin's Catering
15423 Chatsworth Street
Mission Hills, California 91341
Tel: 213-846-7247

The Casserole
414 North La Cienega Boulevard
Los Angeles, California 90048
Tel: 213-655-7054

The Casserole
300 South Flower
Orange, California 92668
Tel: 714-532-6564

The Casserole
2841 Canon Street
San Diego, California 92106
Tel: 714-223-7109

Ralph Green Motion Picture
    Catering
1514 Flower Street
Glendale, California 91201
Tel: 213-243-1514

Rolly Harper Catering
7782 San Fernando Road
Sun Valley, California 91352
Tel: 213-875-1958

Hi-Butch
9055 Woodman Avenue
Pacoima, California 91331
Tel: 213-892-4391

King Swede Motion Picture
Catering
3001 West Magnolia Boulevard
Burbank, California 91505
Tel: 213-846-7247

Luau Restaurant
421 North Rodeo Drive
Beverly Hills, California 90210
Tel: 213-272-8484

Madera Catering
563 Los Angeles Street
Simi, California 93065
Tel: 805-527-0787

Ed Michaelson Catering
Company
9324 San Fernando Road
Sun Valley, California 91352
Tel: 213-875-2620

Monte's Party Pantry
3610 Multiview Drive
Los Angeles, California 90068
Tel: 213-851-3610

Universal Catering
4329 Lankershim Boulevard
North Hollywood, California
91602
Tel: 213-761-8314

Weston's Party Foods
9163 Sunset Boulevard
West Hollywood, California
90069
Tel: 213-274-9228

Connecticut:

Skandia Restaurant & Caterers
East Pembroke Road
Danbury, Connecticut 06810
Tel: 203-748-4188

Nevada:

Bonnie Springs Old Nevada
830 East Sahara Avenue, Suite 1
Las Vegas, Nevada 89105
Tel: 702-732-2115

New Jersey:

Roberto's
379 Washington Avenue
Hillsdale, New Jersey 07642
Tel: 201-666-1055

New York:
New York City:

Bronxdale Delicatessen, Inc.
210 West 231st Street
Bronx, New York 10463
Tel: 212-546-9694
Tel: 212-796-3083

Demyan Caterers
730 Van Duzer Street
Staten Island, New York 10304
Tel: 212-448-7337

The Director's
212 East Ninth Street
New York, New York 10003
Tel: 212-475-5350

Color Corrections

California:

Ray Johnson
5555 Sunset Boulevard
Los Angeles, California 90028
Tel: 213-465-4108

New York:

Lance Studios
151 West 46th Street
New York, New York 10036
Tel: 212-586-4233

National Studios
209 West 40th Street
New York, New York 10018
Tel: 212-695-0550

Unigraphic, Inc.
592 Fifth Avenue
New York, New York 10021
Tel: 212-757-9220

Color Processes

California:

Acme Film Laboratories, Inc.
1161 North Highland Avenue
Los Angeles, California 90028
Tel: 213-464-7471

De Luxe General, Inc.
1546 North Argyle Avenue
Los Angeles, California 90038
Tel: 213-462-6171

General Aniline and Film
  Corporation
626 Imperial Highway
LaHabre, California 90631
Tel: 213-625-1672

Technicolor, Inc.
6311 Romaine Street
Los Angeles, California 90028
Tel: 213-467-1101

New York:

Bebell, Inc.
416 West 45th Street
New York, New York 10036
Tel: 212-245-8900

Cineffects Color Laboratories,
  Inc.
115 West 45th Street
New York, New York 10036
Tel: 212-581-4730

Criterion Film Laboratories
415 West 55th Street
New York, New York 10019
Tel: 212-265-2180

De Luxe General, Inc.
321 West 44th Street
New York, New York 10036
Tel: 212-247-3220

Finest Color Laboratory, Inc.
130 West 42nd Street
New York, New York 10036
Tel: 212-239-4655

Guffanti Film Laboratories, In
630 Ninth Avenue
New York, New York 10036
Tel: 212-265-5530

Manchester Color Laboratories,
  Inc.
533 West 47th Street
New York, New York 10036
Tel: 212-765-3135

Movielab Color Corporation
619 West 54th Street
New York, New York 10019
Tel: 212-586-0360

Pic Color Corporation
25 West 45th Street
New York, New York 10036
Tel: 212-757-4220

TVC Laboratories, Inc.
311 West 43rd Street
New York, New York 10036
Tel: 212-586-5090

Technicolor, Inc.
342 Madison Avenue
New York, New York 10016
Tel: 212-661-4833

Consultants

Private motion picture consultants offer a variety of services, typical among them the obtaining of shooting permits, budget preparation and consultation, location, and prop assistance. See also "Locations & Location Assistance" and, for governmental assistance available, "Film Commissions."

California:

Boasberg/Goldstein, Inc.
9056 Santa Monica Boulevard
Los Angeles, California 90069

Native American
  Research/Consultants
526 South Reese Place
Burbank, California 91506
Tel: 213-848-6531

Colorado:

Jackson R. Cravens
1624 Iroquois Road
Pueblo, Colorado 81001
Tel: 303-344-9294

New York:

Milt Goodman
58 West 58th Street
New York, New York 10019
Tel: 212-758-3261

Oblio Motion Picture Consultants
238 West Fourteenth Street
New York, New York 10011
Tel: 212-929-7316

Costumes

See also the listings under "Wardrobe."

California:

A-Cinema Costumers of
Hollywood
1773 Cahuenga Boulevard
Los Angeles, California 90028
Tel: 213-464-9894

Frank Acuna
8212 Sunset Boulevard
Los Angeles, California 90046
Tel: 213-656-1413

Adele's of Hollywood
5059 Hollywood Boulevard
Los Angeles, California 90038
Tel: 213-662-2231

Asiatic Rentals
678 North Spring Street
Los Angeles, California 90038
Tel: 213-628-9086

Berman's Costume Company
1040 North Las Palmas Avenue
Los Angeles, California 90038
Tel: 213-466-6454

D'Arcy
4720 1/4 Woodman Avenue
Sherman Oaks, California 91403
Tel: 213-783-5133

Darjon Leather and Suede
14727 1/4 Oxnard
Van Nuys, California 91401
Tel: 213-785-7402

Hollywood Fancy Feathers
512 South Broadway
Los Angeles, California 90013
Tel: 213-625-8453

House of Uniforms
334 North Beverly Drive
Beverly Hills, California 902
Tel: 213-272-1721

IC Costume Rentals
6121 Santa Monica Boulevard
Los Angeles, California 90038
Tel: 213-496-2056

International Costume Compa
8316 Melrose Avenue
Los Angeles, California 90069
Tel: 213-653-2446

Krofft Enterprises, Inc.
11347 Vanowen Street
North Hollywood, California
91603
Tel: 213-877-3361

Moro Landis Productions
10960 Ventura Boulevard
North Hollywood, California
91604
Tel: 213-761-9510

Meyers Costume Company
1753 Cahuenga Boulevard
Los Angeles, California 90028
Tel: 213-465-6589

Don Post Studios
811 Milford
Glendale, California 91203
Tel: 213-245-4134

San Diego Costume Company
1041 Seventh Avenue
San Diego, California 92101
Tel: 714-232-0745

Tuxedo Center
7360 Sunset Boulevard
Los Angeles, California 90046
Tel: 213-874-4200

Florida:

ABC Costume Shop
185 N.E. 59th Street
Miami, Florida 33101
Tel: 305-757-3492

Dixon Costume Shop
1828 Biscayne Boulevard
Miami, Florida 33101
Tel: 305-374-8366

Illinois:

Fritz & Schoultz & Co.
15 West Hubbard Street
Chicago, Illinois 60610
Tel: 312-644-4024

Marcella
2048 West Lawrence Avenue
Chicago, Illinois 60625
Tel: 312-878-1723

New York Costume Company
10 West Hubbard Street
Chicago, Illinois 60610
Tel: 312-644-6644

New York:

Animal Costume Company
236 West 55th Street
New York, New York 10019
Tel: 212-245-5199

Mme. Berthe
1600 Broadway
New York, New York 10019
Tel: 212-757-4170

Brooks–Van Horn Costume
    Company
117 West Seventeenth Street
New York, New York 10011
Tel: 212-989-8000

Chenko Studio
108 West 45th Street
New York, New York 10017
Tel: 212-582-1646

De Masi Costumes
785 Eighth Avenue
New York, New York 10036
Tel: 212-489-9439

Ray Diffen Stage Clothes
121 West Seventeenth Street
New York, New York 10011
Tel: 212-675-2634

Eaves Costume Company, Inc.
151 West 46th Street
New York, New York 10036
Tel: 212-757-3730

Mme. Karinska
20 West 57th Street
New York, New York 10019
Tel: 212-247-3341

Critics

The two principal critics' groups are based in New York: the Nation Society of Film Critics and the New York Film Critics Circle. A degree overlap exists between memberships in the two organizations. Newspap critics who are not members of either organization can be located in *Editor Publisher Year Book,* published annually by The Editor & Publisher Co., In 850 Third Avenue, New York, New York 10022; Telephone: 212-752-70£ In smaller cities the critic's chair is normally occupied by the entertainme editor.

NATIONAL SOCIETY OF FILM CRITICS

California:

Charles Champlin
Los Angeles Times
Times Mirror Square
Los Angeles, California 90053
Tel: 213-625-2345

D.C.:

Hollis Alpert
American Film, The American
    Film Institute
The John F. Kennedy Center for
    the Performing Arts
Washington, D.C. 20566
Tel: 202-833-9300

Gary Arnold
Washington Post
1150 Fifteenth Street, N.W.
Washington, D.C. 20005
Tel: 202-223-6000

Illinois:

Roger Ebert
Chicago Sun-Times
Field Enterprises, Inc.,
    Newspaper Div.
401 North Wabash Avenue
Chicago, Illinois 60611
Tel: 312-321-2640

Bruce Williamson
Playboy Magazine
Playboy Building
919 North Michigan Avenue
Chicago, Illinois 60611
Tel: 312-751-8000

Massachusetts:

Stuart Byron, a critic for
The Boston Phoenix
Boston, Massachusetts 02215
Tel: 617-536-5390

New York:

Joy Gould Boyum
The Wall Street Journal
22 Cortlandt Street
New York, New York 10007
Tel: 212-285-5000

Vincent Canby
The New York Times
229 West 43rd Street
New York, New York 10036
Tel: 212-556-1234

Jay Cocks
Time Magazine
Time & Life Building
1271 Avenue of the Americas
New York, New York 10020
Tel: 212-586-1212

Judith Crist
Saturday Review/World
    Magazine
488 Madison Avenue
New York, New York 10022
Tel: 212-751-7900

David Denby
Harper's Magazine
2 Park Avenue
New York, New York 10016
Tel: 212-686-8710

Bernard Drew
Gannett News Service
Broad and Exchange Streets
Rochester, New York 14614
Tel: 716-232-7100

Joseph Gelmis
Newsday
550 Stewart Avenue
Garden City, New York 11550
Tel: 516-741-1234

Penelope Gilliatt
The New Yorker
25 West 43rd Street
New York, New York 10036
Tel: 212-695-1414

Roger Greenspun
Penthouse Magazine
909 Third Avenue
New York, New York 10022
Tel: 212-593-3301

Molly Haskell
The Village Voice
80 University Place
New York, New York 10003
Tel: 212-924-4669

Pauline Kael
The New Yorker
25 West 43rd Street
New York, New York 10036
Tel: 212-695-1414

Michael Korda
Glamour Magazine
350 Madison Avenue
New York, New York 10017
Tel: 212-692-5500

Jon Landau
Rolling Stone
78 East 56th Street
New York, New York 10022
Tel: 212-486-9560

Andrew Sarris
The Village Voice
80 University Place
New York, New York 10003
Tel: 212-924-4669

Richard Schickel
Time Magazine
Time & Life Building
1271 Avenue of the Americas
New York, New York 10020
Tel: 212-586-1212

Paul Zimmerman
Newsweek Magazine
444 Madison Avenue
New York, New York 10022
Tel: 212-350-2000

NEW YORK FILM CRITICS CIRCLE

D.C.:

Hollis Alpert
American Film
The American Film Institute
The John F. Kennedy Center for
  the Performing Arts
Washington, D.C. 20566
Tel: 202-833-9300

New York:

Joy Gould Boyum
The Wall Street Journal
22 Cortlandt Street
New York, New York 10007
Tel: 212-285-5000

Vincent Canby
The New York Times
229 West 43rd Street
New York, New York 10036
Tel: 212-556-1234

Kathleen Carroll
New York Daily News
220 East 42nd Street
New York, New York 10017
Tel: 212-682-1234

Jay Cocks
Time Magazine
Time & Life Building
1271 Avenue of the Americas
New York, New York 10020
Tel: 212-586-1212

Judith Crist
Saturday Review/World
  Magazine
488 Madison Avenue
New York, New York 10022
Tel: 212-751-7900

Bernard Drew
Gannett News Service
Broad and Exchange Streets
Rochester, New York 14614
Tel: 716-232-7100

Joseph Gelmis
Newsday
550 Stewart Avenue
Garden City, New York 11550
Tel: 516-741-1234

Penelope Gilliatt
The New Yorker
25 West 43rd Street
New York, New York 10036
Tel: 212-695-1414

Roger Greenspun
Penthouse Magazine
909 Third Avenue
New York, New York 10022
Tel: 212-593-3301

Ann Guarino
New York Daily News
220 East 42nd Street
New York, New York 10017
Tel: 212-682-1234

Molly Haskell
The Village Voice
80 University Place
New York, New York 10003
Tel: 212-924-4669

Frances Herridge
The New York Post
210 South Street
New York, New York 10002
Tel: 212-349-5000

Pauline Kael
The New Yorker
25 West 43rd Street
New York, New York 10036
Tel: 212-695-1414

Howard Kissel
Women's Wear Daily
7 East Twelfth Street
New York, New York 10003
Tel: 212-741-4000

Robert Salmaggi
Group W
90 Park Avenue
New York, New York 10016
Tel: 212-983-6500

Andrew Sarris
The Village Voice
80 University Place
New York, New York 10003
Tel: 212-924-4669

Richard Schickel
Time Magazine
Time & Life Building
1271 Avenue of the Americas
New York, New York 10020
Tel: 212-586-1212

Frances Taylor
Long Island Press
168th Street & Jamaica Avenue
Jamaica, New York 11432
Tel: 212-658-1234

Howard Thompson
The New York Times
229 West 43rd Street
New York, New York 10036
Tel: 212-556-1234

A. H. Weiler
The New York Times
229 West 43rd Street
New York, New York 10036
Tel: 212-556-1234

Archer Winsten
The New York Post
210 South Street
New York, New York 10002
Tel: 212-349-5000

William Wolf
Cue Magazine
20 West 43rd Street
New York, New York 10036
Tel: 212-563-7170

Paul D. Zimmerman
Newsweek
444 Madison Avenue
New York, New York 10022
Tel: 212-350-2000

Cutting Rooms

See also "Editing Services."

California:

De Luxe General, Inc.
1546 North Argyle Avenue
Los Angeles, California 90038
Tel: 213-462-6171

F&B/Ceco Editing Center
7051 Santa Monica Boulevard
Los Angeles, California 90038
Tel: 213-466-9361

Horizontal Editing Studios
6253 Hollywood Boulevard
Los Angeles, California 90028
Tel: 213-461-4643

Movielab Film Laboratories, Inc.
6823 Santa Monica Boulevard
Los Angeles, California 90038
Tel: 213-469-5981

Preview House
7655 West Sunset Boulevard
Los Angeles, California 90046
Tel: 213-876-6600

Trans-American Video, Inc.
1541 North Vine Street
Los Angeles, California 90028
Tel: 213-466-2141

District of Columbia:

Capital Film Laboratories
470 E Street, S.W.
Washington, D.C. 20024
Tel: 202-347-1717

Koster Film Facilities, Inc.
1017 New Jersey Avenue, S.E.
Washington, D.C. 20003
Tel: 202-544-4410

New York:

1600 Feature Rentals, Inc.
1600 Broadway
New York, New York 10019
Tel: 212-246-6350

A-1 Reverse-O-Lab
345 West 44th Street
New York, New York 10036
Tel: 212-581-0868

Leonard Anderson Associates,
Inc.
45 West 38th Street
New York, New York 10018
Tel: 212-695-8718

Animated Productions, Inc.
1600 Broadway
New York, New York 10019
Tel: 212-265-2942

Audio Transfers, Inc.
254 West 54th Street
New York, New York 10019
Tel: 212-265-6225

The Camera Mart
456 West 55th Street
New York, New York 10019
Tel: 212-757-6977

Cinema Arts Associates, Inc.
333 West 52nd Street
New York, New York 10019
Tel: 212-246-2860

Criterion Film Laboratories, Inc.
415 West 55th Street
New York, New York 10019
Tel: 212-265-2180

De Luxe General, Inc.
321 West 44th Street
New York, New York 10036
Tel: 212-247-3220

William Greaves Productions
1776 Broadway
New York, New York 10019
Tel: 212-586-7710

Image Sound Studio
1619 Broadway
New York, New York 10019
Tel: 212-765-2840

Movielab Film Laboratories, Inc.
619 West 54th Street
New York, New York 10019
Tel: 212-586-0360

Preview Theatre, Inc.
1600 Broadway
New York, New York 10019
Tel: 212-246-0865

Ross-Gaffney, Inc.
21 West 46th Street
New York, New York 10036
Tel: 212-582-3744

Trilogy Films, Inc.
630 Ninth Avenue
New York, New York 10036
Tel: 212-765-1284

Robert Van Dyke, Inc.
158 West 13th Street
New York, New York 10011
Tel: 212-741-2989

Distributors

Included are distributors of features, shorts, and documentaries intended for theatrical release. At the end of this category appears a listing of distributors who handle X-rated films.

FILMS, THEATRICAL RELEASE

Alaska:

Alaska Pictures, Inc.
Box 937
Juneau, Alaska 99801
Tel: 907-789-9431

Fred G. Kohli Motion Picture
 Service, Inc.
Box 2079
Anchorage, Alaska 99501
Tel: 907-272-7623

Pictures, Inc.
811 Eighth Avenue
Anchorage, Alaska 99501
Tel: 907-279-1515

Arizona:

Arizona Theatre Service
2211 West Roosevelt
Phoenix, Arizona 85009
Tel: 602-253-8615

Film Transport Company
2211 West Roosevelt
Phoenix, Arizona 85009
Tel: 602-253-8615

Films Distributors
3107 East Sells Drive
Phoenix, Arizona 85016
Tel: 602-955-9063

RSVP Releasing Corporation
14445 73rd Street
Scottsdale, Arizona 85254
Tel: 602-948-7091

View Tone Film Systems
 Company
2250 North Sixteenth Street
Phoenix, Arizona 85014
Tel: 602-254-5770

California:
Los Angeles area:

AV-ED Films
7934 Santa Monica Boulevard
Los Angeles, California 90046
Tel: 213-654-9550

Abbey Theatrical Films
9399 Wilshire Boulevard
Beverly Hills, California 90210
Tel: 213-274-8646

Able Film Company
4330 Tujunga
North Hollywood, California
  91603
Tel: 213-877-5216

Allied Artists Pictures, Inc.
291 South La Cienega Boulevard,
  Suite 207
Beverly Hills, California 90211
Tel: 213-657-8270

Allstar Films, Inc.
1535 North Las Palmas Avenue
Los Angeles, California 90038
Tel: 213-466-3596

The American Film Theatre, Inc.
Box 900
Beverly Hills, California 90213
Tel: 213-277-2211

American International Pictures
9033 Wilshire Boulevard
Beverly Hills, California 90211
Tel: 213-278-8118

American International Pictures
  Export Co.
9033 Wilshire Boulevard
Beverly Hills, California 90211
Tel: 213-278-8118

American National Enterprises
1801 Avenue of the Stars
Los Angeles, California 90067
Tel: 213-553-4419

Amerikana Film Company
6725 Sunset Boulevard
Los Angeles, California 90028
Tel: 213-464-3131

Apostolof Film Production &
  S.C.A. Dist.
6430 Sunset Boulevard, Suite 714
Los Angeles, California 90028
Tel: 213-462-6971

Art Films International, Inc.
941 North La Cienega Boulevard
Los Angeles, California 90069
Tel: 213-876-8610

Artisan Releasing Corporation
9200 Sunset Boulevard, Suite 616
Los Angeles, California 90069
Tel: 213-278-2670

Association-Sterling Films, Inc.
7833 San Fernando Road
Sun Valley, California 91352
Tel: 213-875-3242

Avco-Embassy Pictures
10850 Wilshire Boulevard
Los Angeles, California 90028
Tel: 213-879-9600

Azteca Films, Inc.
555 North La Brea Avenue
Los Angeles, California 90036
Tel: 213-938-2413

BCA International
719 Gower Street
Los Angeles, California 90038
Tel: 213-462-5950

Bedford Productions
Twentieth Century–Fox
10201 West Pico Boulevard
West Los Angeles, California
  90035
Tel: 213-277-2211

Belair International Pictures
1640 North Gardner Street
Los Angeles, California 90046
Tel: 213-876-4403

Bernard Productions, Inc.
5150 Wilshire Boulevard
Los Angeles, California 90036
Tel: 213-938-5181

Bernhard Films
321 South Beverly Drive
Beverly Hills, California 90212
Tel: 213-277-6161

Beverly Pictures, Inc.
9952 Santa Monica Boulevard
Beverly Hills, California 90212
Tel: 213-277-8849

Billy Jack Enterprises, Inc.
9336 West Washington Boulevard
Culver City, California 90230
Tel: 213-559-5310

Seymour Borde & Associates
292 South La Cienega Boulevard
Beverly Hills, California 90211
Tel: 213-652-6785

Stephen Bosustow Productions
1649 Eleventh Street
Santa Monica, California 90404
Tel: 213-394-0218

Box Office International Film
Distributors
4774 Melrose Avenue
Los Angeles, California 90029
Tel: 213-660-1770

Brut Productions, Inc.
Burbank Studios
4000 Warner Boulevard
Burbank, California 91522
Tel: 213-843-6000

Bryanston Distributors, Inc.
177 South Beverly Drive
Beverly Hills, California 90212
Tel: 213-273-1262

Buena Vista Distribution
Company, Inc.
1139 Grand Central Avenue
Glendale, California 91201
Tel: 213-240-7600

CFA, Inc.
680 Beach Street
San Francisco, California 94109
Tel: 415-885-5700

Canyon Film Group
6200 Sunset Boulevard, Suite 206
Los Angeles, California 90028
Tel: 213-462-4011

Capital Productions, Inc.
8447 Wilshire Boulevard
Beverly Hills, California 90211
Tel: 213-655-0801

Carlyle Films, Ltd.
6430 Sunset Boulevard, Suite
1502
Los Angeles, California 90028
Tel: 213-466-0864

Cartoon Distributors Corporation
8827 Olympic Boulevard
Beverly Hills, California 90211
Tel: 213-652-8050

Cathedral Films, Inc.
2921 West Alameda
Burbank, California 91503
Tel: 213-848-6637

Cavalcade Pictures, Inc.
959 North Fairfax Avenue
Los Angeles, California 90046
Tel: 213-654-4144

Cinema 5 Distributing Company
9255 West Sunset Boulevard
Los Angeles, California 90069
Tel: 213-274-8928

Cinema "35" Center, Inc.
850 Colorado Boulevard
Los Angeles, California 90041
Tel: 213-255-1296

Cinema National Corporation
9056 Santa Monica Boulevard,
   Suite 200
Los Angeles, California 90069
Tel: 213-274-0128

Cinema Pictures, Inc.
10212 Noble Avenue
Mission Hills, California 91340
Tel: 213-892-6797

Cinemation Industries
9200 Sunset Boulevard, Suite 625
Los Angeles, California 90069
Tel: 213-273-7770

Cinerama Releasing, Inc.
292 South La Cienega Boulevard
Beverly Hills, California 90211
Tel: 213-659-2150

Columbia Pictures Corporation
8671 Wilshire Boulevard
Beverly Hills, California 90211
Tel: 213-657-6410

Continental Distributing, Inc.
8444 Wilshire Boulevard
Beverly Hills, California 90211
Tel: 213-653-3231

Counselor Films
8816 Sunset Boulevard
Los Angeles, California 90069
Tel: 213-659-5720

Crest Film Distributors, Inc.
1979 South Vermont
Los Angeles, California 90007
Tel: 213-733-1123

Crown International Pictures,
   Inc.
292 South La Cienega Boulevard
Beverly Hills, California 90211
Tel: 213-657-6700

Dart Enterprises
5421 Santa Monica Boulevard
Los Angeles, California 90038
Tel: 213-464-9283

Donald A. Davis Productions,
   Inc.
705 North Cole Avenue
Los Angeles, California 90038
Tel: 213-469-6256

Dimension Pictures, Inc.
9000 Sunset Boulevard, Suite 715
Los Angeles, California 90069
Tel: 213-278-6844

Duque Films, Inc.
1213 North Highland Avenue
Los Angeles, California 90028
Tel: 213-466-2491

Echo Film Services
1040 North Las Palmas Avenue
Los Angeles, California 90069
Tel: 213-469-2707

Ellman Film Enterprises, Inc.
8201 Beverly Boulevard
Los Angeles, California 90048
Tel: 213-655-8200

Embassy Pictures Corporation
1928 South Vermont Avenue
Los Angeles, California 90007
Tel: 213-734-8487

Emerson Film Enterprises, Inc.
6922 Hollywood Boulevard
Los Angeles, California 90028
Tel: 213-461-3001

Entertainment Corporation of
    America
554 South San Vicente
Los Angeles, California 90048
Tel: 213-653-9040

Entertainment Ventures, Inc.
1654 Cordova Street
Los Angeles, California 90007
Tel: 213-731-7236

Eve Productions, Inc.
7080 Hollywood Boulevard
Los Angeles, California 90028
Tel: 213-466-7791

Excelsior Distributing
    Corporation
400 South Beverly Drive
Beverly Hills, California 90212
Tel: 213-277-7444

Exhibitor's Service, Inc.
292 South La Cienega Boulevard
Beverly Hills, California 90211
Tel: 213-657-6040

Famous Players International
    Corporation
1210 North Wetherly Drive West
Los Angeles, California 90069
Tel: 213-275-8221

Fanfare Film Corporation
7966 Beverly Boulevard
Los Angeles, California 90048
Tel: 213-658-6434

Far West Films
250 South La Cienega Boulevard
Beverly Hills, California 90211
Tel: 213-659-5161

Favorite Films of California, Inc.
292 South La Cienega Boulevard
Beverly Hills, California 90211
Tel: 213-657-6700

Film Service Distributing
    Corporation
6327 Santa Monica Boulevard
Los Angeles, California 90038

Filmmakers International
    Releasing Company
844 Wilshire Boulevard
Beverly Hills, California 90211
Tel: 213-655-2968

Films, Inc.
5625 Hollywood Boulevard
Los Angeles, California 90028
Tel: 213-466-5481

Fine Productions
6311 Yucca Street
Los Angeles, California 90028
Tel: 213-462-1133

General Film Corporation
839 North Highland Avenue
Los Angeles, California 90038
Tel: 213-469-5321

Gilboy, Inc.
8536 National Boulevard
Culver City, California 90230
Tel: 213-559-2722

Gillman Film Corporation
2365 Westwood Boulevard
Los Angeles, California 90064
Tel: 213-475-8473

Gold-Key Entertainment
855 North Cahuenga Boulevard
Los Angeles, California 90038
Tel: 213-466-9741

Gold Star Pictures
1706 South Beverly Glen
  Boulevard
Los Angeles, California 90024
Tel: 213-277-2186

Goldstone Films of Los Angeles
8444 Wilshire Boulevard
Beverly Hills, California 90211
Tel: 213-653-3231

Great Empire Films
7046 Hollywood Boulevard
Los Angeles, California 90028
Tel: 213-469-2117

HMS Distributing
11130 McCormick
North Hollywood, California
  91601
Tel: 213-769-3061

Hallmark of Hollywood, Inc.
9000 Sunset Boulevard
Los Angeles, California 90069
Tel: 213-274-4040

Jack H. Harris Enterprises
9229 Sunset Boulevard
Los Angeles, California 90069
Tel: 213-278-7812

Hollywood Cinemart
7046 Hollywood Boulevard
Los Angeles, California 90028
Tel: 213-469-2117

Hollywood International Film
  Corporation of America
1044 South Hill Street
Los Angeles, California 90015
Tel: 213-749-2067

Hollywood Star Pictures, Inc.
922 North Vine Street, Suite 205
Los Angeles, California 90038
Tel: 213-463-1316

Hunza Enterprises
8440 Sunset Boulevard
Los Angeles, California 90069
Tel: 213-654-9500

Iae Distributing
1800 North Highland Avenue,
  Suite 507
Los Angeles, California 90028
Tel: 213-461-3811

Idalene Corporation
6515 Sunset Boulevard
Los Angeles, California 90028
Tel: 213-461-1950

Importadora, Inc.
8942 Burton Way
Beverly Hills, California 90212
Tel: 213-276-2149

Independent Artists Productions
P.O. Box 5165
Sherman Oaks, California 91403
Tel: 213-463-4811

Indepix Releasing, Inc.
9000 Sunset Boulevard, Suite 411
Los Angeles, California 90069
Tel: 213-274-6628

Inter-Ocean Films, Ltd.
270 North Canon Drive
Beverly Hills, California 90212
Tel: 213-273-7505

International Amusement
  Corporation
291 South La Cienega Boulevard
Beverly Hills, California 90211
Tel: 213-659-6252

International Cinema
  Corporation
11969 Ventura Boulevard
Studio City, California 91604
Tel: 213-980-0426

International Pictures
  Corporation
1040 North Las Palmas Avenue
Los Angeles, California 90038
Tel: 213-462-6741

International Producers
  Corporation
2609 West Olive Avenue
Burbank, California 91505
Tel: 213-851-0466

Irvmar Productions, Inc.
16603 Ventura Boulevard
Encino, California 91316
Tel: 213-788-9151

Jaguar Pictures Company
Columbia Pictures Corporation
1438 North Gower Street
Los Angeles, California 90028
Tel: 213-462-3111

Jem Film Distributing
  Corporation
1664 Cordova
Los Angeles, California 90007
Tel: 213-731-8748

Al Kolitz Film Distributors
291 South La Cienega Boulevard
Beverly Hills, California 90211
Tel: 213-657-6720

Kriton Productions
7906 Santa Monica Boulevard
Los Angeles, California 90046
Tel: 213-656-5964

R. Kronenberg and Associates
8530 Wilshire Boulevard
Beverly Hills, California 90211
Tel: 213-652-5350

LF Film Distributors
9229 Sunset Boulevard, Suite 422
Los Angeles, California 90069
Tel: 213-271-1664

L-T Films
9200 Sunset Boulevard, Suite
1008
Los Angeles, California 90069
Tel: 213-273-3054

Mark Lester Pictures
1737 Nichols Canyon Road
Los Angeles, California 90046
Tel: 213-876-8560

Magna Pictures Corporation
8444 Wilshire Boulevard
Beverly Hills, California 90211
Tel: 213-273-8640

Majestic International
8949 Sunset Boulevard
Los Angeles, California 90069
Tel: 213-278-4657

Manson Distributing Corporation
9145 Sunset Boulevard, Suite 106
Los Angeles, California 90069
Tel: 213-273-8640

Master Films Distributors, Inc.
10880 Wilshire Boulevard, Suite
604
Los Angeles, California 90029
Tel: 213-475-6841

Medford Film Corporation
6528 West Sunset Boulevard
Los Angeles, California 90028
Tel: 213-461-3529

Media Cinema Corporation
6528 West Sunset Boulevard
Los Angeles, California 90028
Tel: 213-461-3771

Merrick International Films
870 North Vine Street
Los Angeles, California 90038
Tel: 213-462-8444

Metromedia, Inc.
8544 Sunset Boulevard
Los Angeles, California 90069
Tel: 213-657-6290

Moonstone Productions
1061 North Spaulding Avenue
Los Angeles, California 90046
Tel: 213-654-0890

Multi-Pix Ltd.
1220 Sunset Plaza Drive
Los Angeles, California 90069
Tel: 213-652-3223

Mutual General Film
Corporation
9399 Wilshire Boulevard, Suite
110
Beverly Hills, California 90210
Tel: 213-274-8646

National General Pictures
Corporation
8421 Wilshire Boulevard
Beverly Hills, California 90211
Tel: 213-653-7500

National Screen Service
Corporation
2001 South La Cienega Boulevard
Los Angeles, California 90211
Tel: 213-836-1505

National Telefilm Associates, Inc.
12636 Beatrice Street
Los Angeles, California 90066
Tel: 213-390-3663

New World Pictures
8831 Sunset Boulevard
Los Angeles, California 90069
Tel: 213-657-2201

Noble Productions, Inc.
1615 South Crest Drive
Los Angeles, California 90035
Tel: 213-552-2934

Okasis Films International, Inc.
1725 North Ivar, Suite 101
Los Angeles, California 90028
Tel: 213-466-7791

Olympic International
  Distributing Company
1505 North Vine Street
Los Angeles, California 90028
Tel: 213-462-7211

Paradigm Film Distribution
1356 North Genesee Avenue
Los Angeles, California 90046
Tel: 213-461-5762

Paramount Film Distributing
  Corporation
291 South La Cienega Boulevard
Beverly Hills, California 90211
Tel: 213-657-7200

Preferred Enterprises
8303 Melrose Avenue
Los Angeles, California 90069
Tel: 213-653-6696

Producers Distribution
  Corporation
6350 De Longpre Avenue
Los Angeles, California 90028
Tel: 213-466-5776

Producers Film Center
948 North Sycamore Avenue
Los Angeles, California 90038
Tel: 213-851-1122

RBC Films
933 North La Brea Avenue
Los Angeles, California 90038
Tel: 213-874-5050

Realart Pictures
3084 Motor Avenue
Los Angeles, California 90064
Tel: 213-836-6627

Republic Pictures, Inc.
8530 Wilshire Boulevard
Beverly Hills, California 90211
Tel: 213-655-7701

Riviera Productions
6610 Selma Avenue
Los Angeles, California 90028
Tel: 213-462-8585

Romatt Releasing Company
1800 North Highland Avenue,
  Suite 507
Los Angeles, California 90028
Tel: 213-461-3811

Herbert Rosener Company
205 North Canon Drive
Beverly Hills, California 90212
Tel: 213-272-6705

Royal Russian Studios, Inc.
1470 East Mountain Street
Glendale, California 91207
Tel: 213-243-3953

SCA Distributors
6430 Sunset Boulevard, Suite 714
Los Angeles, California 90028
Tel: 213-462-6971

Carl Schaefer Enterprises
3320 Bennett Drive
Los Angeles, California 90068
Tel: 213-874-2324

Joseph M. Schenck Enterprises,
   Inc.
190 North Canon Drive
Beverly Hills, California 90212
Tel: 213-274-8407

Seaberg Film Distributing, Inc.
9465 Wilshire Boulevard
Beverly Hills, California 90212
Tel: 213-274-6864

Sebastian International Pictures,
   Inc.
32107 Lindero Canyon Road
Westlake Village, California
   91361
Tel: 213-889-3148

Shermart Distribution Company
209 North Rexford Drive
Beverly Hills, California 90210
Tel: 213-272-2879

Shochiku Films of America
4417 West Adams Boulevard
Los Angeles, California 90016
Tel: 213-733-8181

Standard Club Productions
3084 Motor Avenue
Los Angeles, California 90064
Tel: 213-838-2145

Straightley Films Ltd.
Box 1951
Beverly Hills, California 90213
Tel: 213-466-7807

Sun International Productions,
   Inc.
11071 Massachusetts Avenue
Los Angeles, California 90025
Tel: 213-478-4034

Sunset International Releasing,
   Inc.
8222 West Third Street
Los Angeles, California 90048
Tel: 213-653-5200

Taylor-Laughlin Distributing
   Company
9336 West Washington Boulevard
Culver City, California 90230
Tel: 213-559-5310

Threshold Films
2025 North Highland Avenue
Los Angeles, California 90068
Tel: 213-874-8413

Toho International, Inc.
834 South La Brea Avenue
Los Angeles, California 90036
Tel: 213-933-5877

Tower Film Company
8400 West Sunset Boulevard
Los Angeles, California 90069
Tel: 213-654-4414

Trans-America Film Corporation
1680 North Vine Street
Los Angeles, California 90028
Tel: 213-466-7575

Transvue Pictures Corporation
14724 Ventura Boulevard, Suite
  909
Sherman Oaks, California 91403
Tel: 213-990-5600

Twentieth Century–Fox Film
  Corporation
291 South La Cienega Boulevard
Beverly Hills, California 90211
Tel: 213-657-6000

UPA Productions of America
4440 Lakeside Drive
Burbank, California 91505
Tel: 213-849-6666

United Artists Exchange
291 South La Cienega Boulevard,
  Suite 310
Beverly Hills, California 90211
Tel: 213-657-7000

United Producers Releasing
  Organization
8310 Beverly Boulevard
Los Angeles, California 90048
Tel: 213-653-2430

United World Films, Inc.
1025 North Highland Avenue
Los Angeles, California 90038
Tel: 213-465-5136

Universal Film Exchanges, Inc.
2001 South Vermont Avenue
Los Angeles, California 90007
Tel: 213-731-2151

Universal Marion Corporation
8400 Sunset Boulevard
Los Angeles, California 90069
Tel: 213-654-4414

Video-Medic Company
10500 Otsego
North Hollywood, California
  91603
Tel: 213-985-9940

The Vidtronics Company, Inc.
855 North Cahuenga Boulevard
Los Angeles, California 90038
Tel: 213-466-9741

Warner Bros. Pictures
  Distributing Corp.
291 South La Cienega Boulevard
Beverly Hills, California 90211
Tel: 213-657-0401

Adrian Weiss Productions
186 North Canon Drive
Beverly Hills, California 90210
Tel: 213-274-9991

West Bay Distributors, Inc.
2473 Crestview Drive
Los Angeles, California 90046
Tel: 213-651-4330

Western International, Inc.
111 North Hudson
Los Angeles, California 90038
Tel: 213-462-0477

Winters-Rosen, Inc.
9110 Sunset Boulevard
Los Angeles, California 90069
Tel: 213-274-6681

World Entertainment
  Corporation
12636 Beatrice Street
Los Angeles, California 90066
Tel: 213-390-3663

World Film Sales, Inc.
9489 Dayton Way, Suite 209
Beverly Hills, California 90210
Tel: 213-273-0622

World Wide Film Distributors
11130 McCormick Street
North Hollywood, California
  91601
Tel: 213-769-3061

World Wide Pictures
2520 West Olive
Burbank, California 91510
Tel: 213-843-1300

Wrather Corporation
270 North Canon Drive
Beverly Hills, California 90210
Tel: 213-278-8521

Yukon Pictures, Inc.
826 North Cole Avenue
Los Angeles, California 90038
Tel: 213-462-0701

San Francisco area:

Allied Artists Productions, Inc.
988 Market Street
San Francisco, California 94102
Tel: 415-441-7767

Avco Embassy Pictures
988 Market Street
San Francisco, California 94102
Tel: 415-776-9665

Buena Vista Film Distribution
  Company, Inc.
680 Beach Street
San Francisco, California 94109
Tel: 415-673-1215

CFA, Inc.
680 Beach Street
San Francisco, California 94109
Tel: 415-885-5700

Cardinal Films
988 Market Street
San Francisco, California 94102
Tel: 415-776-2848

Cinema Financial of America,
  Inc.
680 Beach Street
San Francisco, California 94109
Tel: 415-885-5700

Cinerama Releasing Corporation
1806 Union Street
San Francisco, California 94123
Tel: 415-563-4900

Columbia Pictures Corporation
988 Market Street, Suite 800
San Francisco, California 94102
Tel: 415-771-2525

Emerson Film Enterprises, Inc.
333 Golden Gate Avenue
San Francisco, California 94102
Tel: 415-431-6772

Favorite Films of California, Inc.
255 Hyde Street
San Francisco, California 94102
Tel: 415-776-4409

James Flocker Enterprises, Inc.
3080 La Selva
San Mateo, California 94403
Tel: 415-349-8000

Four Star Excelsior
230 Hyde Street
San Francisco, California 91402
Tel: 415-673-0478

Goldstone Films of California,
Inc.
988 Market Street
San Francisco, California 94102
Tel: 415-673-1855

Lippert, Inc.
544 Golden Gate Avenue
San Francisco, California 94102
Tel: 415-771-5900

Modern Talking Picture Service
16 Spear Street
San Francicso, California 94105
Tel: 415-982-1712

Pacific Film Enterprises
988 Market Street
San Francisco, California 94102
Tel: 415-441-2474

Paramount Pictures, Inc.
1390 Market Street
San Francisco, California 94102
Tel: 415-474-3517

Scope III
988 Market Street
San Francisco, California 94102
Tel: 415-775-4480

Tricontinental Film Center, Inc.
Box 4430
Berkeley, California 94704
Tel: 415-548-3204

Twentieth Century–Fox Film
Corporation
645 Larkin Street
San Francisco, California 94109
Tel: 415-775-1600

United Artists Corporation
544 Golden Gate Avenue
San Francisco, California 94102
Tel: 415-861-2751

Universal Film Exchange
129 Hyde Street
San Francisco, California 94102
Tel: 415-776-3600

Vision Quest, Inc.
389 Ethel Avenue
Mill Valley, California 94941
Tel: 415-388-9094

Warner Bros. Pictures
Distributing Corporation
544 Golden Gate Avenue
San Francisco, California 94102
Tel: 415-474-5938

Colorado:

American International Pictures
2145 Broadway
Denver, Colorado 80205
Tel: 303-825-2263

Azteca Films, Inc.
2147 Broadway
Denver, Colorado 80205

Buena Vista Distribution
Company, Inc.
88 Steele, Suite 301
Denver, Colorado 80206
Tel: 303-321-1200

Columbia Pictures Industries
1860 Lincoln, Suite 250
Denver, Colorado 80203
Tel: 303-534-6341

Favorite Films of California, Inc.
1860 Lincoln, Suite 416
Denver, Colorado 80203
Tel: 303-623-1221

National General Pictures
Corporation
88 Steele
Denver, Colorado 80206
Tel: 303-399-2292

Paramount Pictures Corporation
560 West 53rd Place
Denver, Colorado 80216
Tel: 303-534-8246

Twentieth Century–Fox Film
Corporation
Lincoln Tower Building, Suite
407
1860 Lincoln
Denver, Colorado 80203
Tel: 303-825-5331

United Artists Corporation
1860 Lincoln Street
Denver, Colorado 80203
Tel: 303-825-2325

Universal Film Exchange, Inc.
801 21st Street
Denver, Colorado 80205
Tel: 303-623-3281

Warner Bros. Distributing
Corporation
Lincoln Tower Building, Suite
1146
1860 Lincoln
Denver, Colorado 80203
Tel: 303-534-6178

Connecticut:

Hurlock Cine-World, Inc.
13 Arcadia Road
Old Greenwich, Connecticut
06870
Tel: 203-637-4319

New Haven Film Service, Inc.
90 Woodmont Road
New Haven, Connecticut 06516
Tel: 203-878-1465

District of Columbia:

Allied Artists Pictures
1620 Eye Street, N.W.
Washington, D.C. 20006
Tel: 202-785-0040

American International Pictures
1217 H Street, N.W.
Washington, D.C. 20005
Tel: 202-347-2442

Buena Vista Distribution
Company, Inc.
1100 Vermont Avenue, N.W.,
Room 1006
Washington, D.C. 20005
Tel: 202-296-7730

Columbia Pictures Corporation
711 Fourth Street, N.W.
Washington, D.C. 20001
Tel: 202-628-4035

Modern Talking Picture Service,
Inc.
2000 L Street, N.W.
Washington, D.C. 20036
Tel: 202-293-1222

Twentieth Century–Fox Film
Corporation
1156 Fifteenth Street, N.W., Suite
701
Washington, D.C. 20005
Tel: 202-223-6320

United Artists Corporation
5530 Wisconsin Avenue, N.W.
Washington, D.C. 20015
Tel: 202-652-6658

Universal Film Exchanges, Inc.
227 H Street, N.W.
Washington, D.C. 20001
Tel: 202-638-4141

Warner Bros. Pictures
Distributing Corporation
1141 K Street, N.W., Suite 420
Washington, D.C. 20005
Tel: 202-628-4035

Florida:
  Jacksonville:

American International Pictures
200 Guaranty Life Building
Jacksonville, Florida 32202
Tel: 904-356-5737

Buena Vista Film Distribution
Company, Inc.
Seaboard Coastline Building
Jacksonville, Florida 32201
Tel: 904-355-0741

Columbia Pictures Corporation
11 North Ocean Street
Jacksonville, Florida 32202
Tel: 904-353-5501

General Film Productions
128 East Forsyth Street
Jacksonville, Florida 32202
Tel: 904-358-3641

Independent Film Exchange
128 East Forsyth Street
Jacksonville, Florida 32202
Tel: 904-356-1475

Paramount Film Distributing
Corporation
128 East Forsyth Street
Jacksonville, Florida 32202
Tel: 904-356-3961

United Artists, Inc.
21 West Church Street
Jacksonville, Florida 32202
Tel: 904-353-4476

Miami:

Cinetel International, Inc.
1735 N.W. Seventh Street
Miami, Florida 33101
Tel: 305-643-0250

Euro-Films of the Americas, Inc.
1735 N.W. Seventh Street
Miami, Florida 33101
Tel: 305-643-0250

Film Gems, Inc.
14875 N.E. Twentieth Avenue
Miami, Florida 33101
Tel: 305-944-2981

Ideal Pictures Co.
55 N.E. Thirteenth Street
Miami, Florida 33101
Tel: 305-374-8173

Studio Center, Inc.
14875 N.E. Twentieth Avenue
North Miami, Florida 33161
Tel: 305-944-2911

Warner Bros. Distributing Corp.
1065 N.E. 125th Street
North Miami, Florida 33160
Tel: 305-891-4511

Bert Williams Motion Picture
  Productions and Distributors,
  Inc.
1414 N.E. 183rd Street
North Miami Beach, Florida
  33160
Tel: 305-947-5252

Georgia:

Alliance International
161 Spring Street, N.W.
Atlanta, Georgia 30303
Tel: 404-524-7579

Allied Artists Pictures
  Corporation
Atlanta Film Building, Suite 822
161 Spring Street, N.W.
Atlanta, Georgia 30303
Tel: 404-525-7653

American International Pictures
193 Walton Street, N.W.
Atlanta, Georgia 30303
Tel: 404-688-9845

American National
3070 Presidential Drive
Atlanta, Georgia 30340
Tel: 404-451-7861

Association-Sterling Films
5797 New Peachtree Road
Atlanta, Georgia 30340
Tel: 404-458-6251

Atco Gibraltar Corporation
161 Spring Street, N.W.
Atlanta, Georgia 30303
Tel: 404-688-3031

Atlanta Film Service
161 Spring Street, N.W.
Atlanta, Georgia 30303
Tel: 404-524-5380

Avco Embassy Pictures
Atlanta Film Building
161 Spring Street, N.W., Suite
  620
Atlanta, Georgia 30303
Tel: 404-523-1711

Buena Vista Film Distribution
  Company
503 Walton Building
87 Walton Street, N.W.
Atlanta, Georgia 30303
Tel: 404-525-4647

Centrum International Film
  Corporation
3958 Peachtree Road, N.E., Suite
  303
Atlanta, Georgia 30319
Tel: 404-233-4484

Chappell Releasing Company
2814 New Spring Road
Atlanta, Georgia 30339
Tel: 404-432-3361

Cinerama Releasing Corporation
136 Marietta Street, N.W.
Atlanta, Georgia 30303
Tel: 404-524-5481

Clark Film Releasing Company
Atlanta Film Building, Suite 711
161 Spring Street, N.W.
Atlanta, Georgia 30303
Tel: 404-524-6588

Columbia Pictures Industries
195 Luckie Street, N.W.
Atlanta, Georgia 30303
Tel: 404-521-1524

Film Ventures International
2351 Adams Drive, N.W.
Atlanta, Georgia 30318
Tel: 404-352-3850

General Film Distributing
3950 Peachtree Road, N.E.
Atlanta, Georgia 30319
Tel: 404-577-1542

Independent Film Distributors,
  Inc.
161 Spring Street, N.E.
Atlanta, Georgia 30303
Tel: 404-524-7579

Major Film Distributors, Inc.
161 Spring Street, N.W.
Atlanta, Georgia 30303
Tel: 404-321-5973

Paramount Pictures Corporation
Life of Georgia Tower
Atlanta, Georgia 30308
Tel: 404-873-3141

Sun International Productions
3550 Broad Street
Atlanta, Georgia 30341
Tel: 404-458-0237

Twentieth Century–Fox Film
  Corp.
197 Walton Street, N.W.
Atlanta, Georgia 30303
Tel: 404-523-3722

United Artists Corporation
186 Luckie Street, N.W.
Atlanta, Georgia 30303
Tel: 404-522-6386

Universal Film Exchange
205 Walton Street, N.W.
Atlanta, Georgia 30303
Tel: 404-523-5081

Hawaii:

Hawaii Nichibel Film Company, Inc.
728 Ninth Avenue
Honolulu, Hawaii 96816
Tel: 808-737-3455

Pacific Motion Picture Company, Ltd.
1190 Nuuanu Avenue
Honolulu, Hawaii 96817
Tel: 808-538-1035

Royal Development Company, Ltd.
1370 South Beretania Street
Honolulu, Hawaii 96814
Tel: 808-537-6365

Shochiku Films
1387 North Beretania Street
Honolulu, Hawaii 96817
Tel: 808-733-8181

Illinois:

Allied Artists Pictures
203 North Wabash Avenue
Chicago, Illinois 60601
Tel: 312-782-8634

American International Pictures
32 West Randolph Street
Chicago, Illinois 60601
Tel: 312-332-4755

Avco-Embassy Pictures Corporation
32 West Randolph Street
Chicago, Illinois 60601
Tel: 312-236-7902

Azteca Films, Inc.
1233 South Wabash Avenue
Chicago, Illinois 60605
Tel: 312-922-6186

Buena Vista Distribution Company, Inc.
203 North Wabash Avenue
Chicago, Illinois 60601
Tel: 312-641-6970

Cinemation
32 West Randolph Street, Suite 2000
Chicago, Illinois 60601
Tel: 312-641-2565

Cinerama Releasing Corporation
203 North Wabash Avenue
Chicago, Illinois 60601
Tel: 312-782-1238

Columbia Pictures Corporation
550 West Jackson Boulevard
Chicago, Illinois 60606
Tel: 312-726-6050

Paramount Pictures Corporation
550 West Jackson Boulevard
Chicago, Illinois 60606
Tel: 312-263-4574

Twentieth Century–Fox Film Corporation
550 West Jackson Boulevard
Chicago, Illinois 60606
Tel: 312-372-1584

United Artists Corporation
203 North Wabash Avenue
Chicago, Illinois 60601
Tel: 312-236-7390

Universal Film Exchange, Inc.
425 North Michigan Avenue
Chicago, Illinois 60601
Tel: 312-822-0513

Warner Bros. Distributing
    Corporation
550 West Jackson Boulevard
Chicago, Illinois 60606
Tel: 312-726-1658

Indiana:

American International Pictures
411 Illinois Building
Indianapolis, Indiana 46204
Tel: 317-634-4952

Avco Embassy Pictures
3969 Meadows Drive
Indianapolis, Indiana 46205
Tel: 317-546-6375

Buena Vista Distribution
    Company, Inc.
3000 Meadows Parkway
Indianapolis, Indiana 46205
Tel: 317-545-7236

Paramount Pictures, Inc.
428 Illinois Building
Indianapolis, Indiana 46204
Tel: 317-634-7563

Twentieth Century–Fox Film
    Corporation
3919 Meadows Drive
Indianapolis, Indiana 46205
Tel: 317-545-6625

United Artists Corporation
4000 Meadows Drive, Suite 111
Indianapolis, Indiana 64205
Tel: 317-545-2244

Iowa:

National Screen Service
    Corporation
1005 High Street
Des Moines, Iowa 52804
Tel: 515-244-3911

Paramount Film Distributing
    Corporation
513 Thirteenth Street
Des Moines, Iowa 52803
Tel: 515-288-3638

Producers Distributing Company
1219 Paramount Building
Des Moines, Iowa 50309
Tel: 515-282-5157

Twentieth Century–Fox Film
    Corporation
1216 High Street
Des Moines, Iowa 52804
Tel: 515-244-4281

United Artists Corporation
1213 Grand Avenue
Des Moines, Iowa 50309
Tel: 515-283-0481

Massachusetts:

Allied Artists Pictures
    Corporation
824 Statler Building
Boston, Massachusetts 02178
Tel: 617-357-5621

154

Motion Picture Market Place

American International Pictures
46 Church Street
Boston, Massachusetts 02116
Tel: 617-542-0677

Association-Sterling Films
410 Great Road
Littleton, Massachusetts 01460
Tel: 617-486-3518

Avco-Embassy Pictures
Corporation
20 Winchester Street
Boston, Massachusetts 02116
Tel: 617-482-3325

Buena Vista Distribution
Company, Inc.
Park Square Building
Boston, Massachusetts 02109
Tel: 617-426-9360

Campus Film Service
458 Statler Office Building
Boston, Massachusetts 02109
Tel: 617-542-6068

Cinema 5 Ltd.
920 Park Square Building
Boston, Massachusetts 02109
Tel: 617-357-5065

Cinema Film Buying Inc.
430 Park Square
Boston, Massachusetts 02109
Tel: 617-482-9717

Cinemation Industries Inc.
31 St. James Avenue
Boston, Massachusetts 02109
Tel: 617-423-1934

Cinerama Releasing Corporation
1130 Park Square Building
Boston, Massachusetts 02116
Tel: 617-542-7057

Columbia Pictures Corporation
45 Church Street
Boston, Massachusetts 02116
Tel: 617-426-8980

Davis Film Distributors
925 Statler Building
Boston, Massachusetts 02109
Tel: 617-426-0717

Films, Inc.
161 Massachusetts Avenue
Boston, Massachusetts 02115
Tel: 617-536-1663

Fitzgerald Motion Picture
Service, Inc.
176 Newbury Street
Boston, Massachusetts 02109
Tel: 617-266-2512

G. G. Communications, Inc.
910 Statler Office Building
Boston, Massachusetts 02109
Tel: 617-542-9633

Ellis Gordon Films
614 Statler Building
Boston, Massachusetts 02178
Tel: 617-426-5900

Hallmark Releasing Corporation
308 Boylston Street
Boston, Massachusetts 02146
Tel: 617-267-9763

New England Motion Picture Co.
260 Tremont Street
Boston, Massachusetts 02109
Tel: 617-482-9025

Paramount Pictures Corporation
350 Park Square Building
Boston, Massachusetts 02109
Tel: 617-426-1070

Jud Parker Films, Inc.
31 St. James Avenue
Boston, Massachusetts 02109
Tel: 617-542-0744

Twentieth Century–Fox Film
  Corporation
260 Tremont Street
Boston, Massachusetts 02109
Tel: 617-426-2180

United Artists Corporation
Park Square Building
31 St. James Avenue
Boston, Massachusetts 02116
Tel: 617-426-6540

Universal Film Exchanges, Inc.
60 Church Street
Boston, Massachusetts 02116
Tel: 617-426-8760

University Cinema Associates,
  Inc.
1001 Massachusetts Avenue
Cambridge, Massachusetts 02138
Tel: 617-868-3604

Warner Bros. Pictures
  Distributing Corporation
6 St. James Avenue
Boston, Massachusetts 02116
Tel: 617-482-3290

Michigan:

Allied Artists Pictures
23300 Greenfield Road
Detroit, Michigan 48237
Tel: 313-968-0800

American International Pictures
23300 Greenfield Road
Oak Park, Michigan 48237
Tel: 313-968-7777

Avco-Embassy Pictures
2111 Woodward Avenue
Detroit, Michigan 48201
Tel: 313-962-0737

Buena Vista Distribution Co., Inc.
23300 Greenfield Road
Oak Park, Michigan 48237
Tel: 313-566-1357

Columbia Pictures Corporation
24100 Southfield Road
Southfield, Michigan 48075
Tel: 313-557-2150

Gail Film Distributors
16300 West Nine Mile Road
Southfield, Michigan 48075
Tel: 313-557-5024

Paramount Pictures Corporation
23300 Greenfield Road
Oak Park, Michigan 48237
Tel: 313-968-8137

Twentieth Century–Fox Films
17000 West Eight Mile Road
Southfield, Michigan 48075
Tel: 313-444-5160

United Artists Corporation
24100 Southfield Road
Southfield, Michigan 48075
Tel: 313-557-5770

Universal Film Exchange
436 West Columbia Avenue
Detroit, Michigan 48201
Tel: 313-961-2141

Warner Bros. Distributing
  Corporation
20820 Greenfield Road
Oak Park, Michigan 48237
Tel: 313-564-5826

Minnesota:

American International Pictures
1000 Currie Avenue
Minneapolis, Minnesota 55403
Tel: 612-333-8293

Avco Embassy Pictures
  Corporation, Inc.
1104 Currie Avenue
Minneapolis, Minnesota 55403
Tel: 612-339-2729

Buena Vista Distribution
  Company, Inc.
100 North Seventh Street
Minneapolis, Minnesota 55403
Tel: 612-336-8607

Cinerama Releasing Corporation
704 Hennepin Avenue
Minneapolis, Minnesota 55403
Tel: 612-336-8631

Columbia Pictures Corporation
523 Marquette Avenue
Minneapolis, Minnesota 55401
Tel: 612-333-6227

Paramount Pictures Corporation
1104 Currie Avenue
Minneapolis, Minnesota 55403
Tel: 612-333-0537

United Artists Corporation
704 Hennepin Avenue
Minneapolis, Minnesota 55403
Tel: 612-333-7275

Universal Film Exchanges, Inc.
1113 Currie Avenue
Minneapolis, Minnesota 55403
Tel: 612-333-5334

Warner Bros. Distributing
  Corporation
704 Hennepin Avenue
Minneapolis, Minnesota 55403
Tel: 612-333-3281

Missouri:
Kansas City:

Allied Artists
110 West Eighteenth Street
Kansas City, Missouri 64108
Tel: 816-842-4221

American-International Pictures
1703 Wyandotte Street
Kansas City, Missouri 64108
Tel: 816-421-2324

Buena Vista Distribution
   Company, Inc.
4210 Johnson Drive
Kansas City, Missouri 64141
Tel: 816-362-9500

Columbia Pictures Corporation
3130 Broadway
Kansas City, Missouri 64111
Tel: 816-561-3021

Sun International Productions
25 East Twelfth Street
Kansas City, Missouri 64152
Tel: 816-471-0415

Twentieth Century–Fox Film
   Corporation
1703 Wyandotte Street
Kansas City, Missouri 64108
Tel: 816-421-7253

United Artists Corporation
1703 Wyandotte Street
Kansas City, Missouri 64108
Tel: 816-471-1123

Warner Bros. Distributing
   Corporation
1703 Wyandotte Street
Kansas City, Missouri 64108
Tel: 816-421-4645

St. Louis:

American International Pictures
539 North Grand Avenue
St. Louis, Missouri 63103
Tel: 314-553-8344

Avco-Embassy Pictures
539 North Grand Avenue
St. Louis, Missouri 63103
Tel: 314-533-8344

Buena Vista Distribution
   Company, Inc.
539 North Grand Avenue
St. Louis, Missouri 63103
Tel: 314-539-1159

National Screen Service
1001 Hanley Industrial Court
St. Louis, Missouri 63114
Tel: 314-968-1730

Paramount Pictures Corporation
539 North Grand Avenue
St. Louis, Missouri 63103
Tel: 314-652-3680

United Artists Corporation
539 North Grand Avenue
St. Louis, Missouri 63103
Tel: 314-553-0346

New York:
New York City:

AFT Distributing Corporation
1350 Avenue of the Americas
New York, New York 10019
Tel: 212-489-8820

Abkco Industries, Inc.
1700 Broadway
New York, New York 10019
Tel: 212-582-5533

Adelphia Pictures Corporation
160 Third Avenue
New York, New York 10003
Tel: 212-228-1452

Allied Artists Pictures
  Corporation
15 Columbus Circle
New York, New York 10023
Tel: 212-541-9200

Altura Films International, Inc.
225 East 46th Street
New York, New York 10017
Tel: 212-753-5443

The American Film Theatre, Inc.
1350 Avenue of the Americas
New York, New York 10019
Tel: 212-489-8820

American International Pictures
  Export Corporation
165 West 46th Street
New York, New York 10036
Tel: 212-489-8100

American International Pictures,
  Inc.
165 West 46th Street
New York, New York 10036
Tel: 212-489-8100

Aquarius Releasing, Inc.
Selwyn Theatre Building
229 West 42nd Street
New York, New York 10019
Tel: 212-787-6208

Artkino Pictures, Inc.
165 West 46th Street, Suite 915
New York, New York 10036
Tel: 212-245-6570

Artscope, Ltd.
310 West 53rd Street
New York, New York 10019
Tel: 212-265-7420

Audubon Films
850 Seventh Avenue
New York, New York 10019
Tel: 212-586-4913

Avco Embassy Pictures
  Corporation
1301 Avenue of the Americas
New York, New York 10019
Tel: 212-956-5500

Azteca Films, Inc.
132 West 43rd Street
New York, New York 10036
Tel: 212-695-4740

Joseph Brenner Associates, Inc.
570 Seventh Avenue
New York, New York 10018
Tel: 212-354-6070

Brut Productions, Inc.
1345 Sixth Avenue
New York, New York 10019
Tel: 212-581-3114

Bryanston Distributors, Inc.
630 Ninth Avenue
New York, New York 10036
Tel: 212-581-5240

Buena Vista Distribution
  Company, Inc.
477 Madison Avenue
New York, New York 10022
Tel: 212-593-8900

Joseph Burstyn, Inc.
100 West 57th Street
New York, New York 10019
Tel: 212-245-1750

Cambist Films, Inc.
850 Seventh Avenue
New York, New York 10019
Tel: 212-586–5810

The Cannon Releasing
  Corporation
405 Park Avenue
New York, New York 10022
Tel: 212-759-5700

Casolaro Film Distributing
  Company
132 Lafayette Street
New York, New York 10013
Tel: 212-966-2112

Centaur Releasing Corporation
165 West 46th Street
New York, New York 10036
Tel: 212-581-4980

Chancellor Films, Inc.
200 West 57th Street
New York, New York 10019
Tel: 212-246-4940

Cinecom Corporation
165 West 46th Street
New York, New York 10036
Tel: 212-265-8610

Cinema 5, Ltd.
595 Madison Avenue
New York, New York 10022
Tel: 212-421-5555

Cinemation Industries, Inc.
1350 Avenue of the Americas
New York, New York 10019
Tel: 212-765-3430

Cinerama Releasing Corporation
1290 Avenue of the Americas
New York, New York 10019
Tel: 212-581-5858

Classic Entertainment
  Corporation
445 Park Avenue
New York, New York 10022
Tel: 212-765-1059

Columbia Pictures Industries, Inc.
165 West 46th Street
New York, New York 10036
Tel: 212-246-0900

Continental Film Distributing
241 East 34th Street
New York, New York 10016
Tel: 212-683-6300

Crystal Pictures, Inc.
1560 Broadway, Room 414
New York, New York 10036
Tel: 212-757-5130

EDP Films, Inc.
600 Madison Avenue
New York, New York 10022
Tel: 212-758-4777

EMI Film Distributors, Inc.
1370 Avenue of the Americas
New York, New York 10019
Tel: 212-757-7470

Empire Films, Inc.
22 East 40th Street
New York, New York 10016
Tel: 212-532-7027

Filmmakers Cooperative
175 Lexington Avenue
New York, New York 10016
Tel: 212-889-3820

Fine Arts Films, Inc.
1501 Broadway
New York, New York 10036
Tel: 212-279-6734

Globe Pictures, Inc.
37 West 57th Street
New York, New York 10019
Tel: 212-751-6040

Goldstone Film Enterprises
1546 Broadway
New York, New York 10036
Tel: 212-246-4662

Grove Press Films
53 East Eleventh Street
New York, New York 10014
Tel: 212-677-2400

Harrington Film Distributing
  Corporation
165 West 46th Street
New York, New York 10036
Tel: 212-575-5959

Hemisphere Pictures, Inc.
445 Park Avenue, Suite 1405
New York, New York 10022
Tel: 212-759-8707

Independent-International Pictures
  Corporation
165 West 46th Street
New York, New York 10036
Tel: 212-869-9333

International Film Exchange,
  Ltd.
159 West 53rd Street
New York, New York 10019
Tel: 212-582-4318

Kelly-Jordan Enterprises, Inc.
342 Madison Avenue
New York, New York 10017
Tel: 212-682-1720

Levitt-Pickman Films, Inc.
505 Park Avenue
New York, New York 10022
Tel: 212-832-8842

Madison World Film Company
310 East 44th Street
New York, New York 10017
Tel: 212-687-1950

Magna Pictures Corporation
1700 Broadway
New York, New York 10019
Tel: 212-765-2800

Howard Mahler Films, Inc.
509 Madison Avenue, Suite 1206
New York, New York 10022
Tel: 212-832-1021

Maron Films Ltd.
888 Seventh Avenue
New York, New York 10019
Tel: 212-586-2656

Marvin Films, Inc.
1501 Broadway
New York, New York 10036
Tel: 212-354-5700

Monarch Releasing Corporation
330 West 58th Street
New York, New York 10019
Tel: 212-757-3635

Movies En Route, Inc.
1540 Broadway
New York, New York 10036
Tel: 212-245-5175

National Film Service, Inc.
800 Second Avenue
New York, New York 10017
Tel: 212-867-2492

New Line Cinema
121 University Place
New York, New York 10003
Tel: 212-674-7460

New Yorker Films
43 West 61st Street
New York, New York 10023
Tel: 212-247-6110

Pacemaker Pictures, Inc.
1501 Broadway
New York, New York 10036
Tel: 212-563-0875

Paragon Pictures
40 West 57th Street
New York, New York 10019
Tel: 212-541-6770

Paramount Film Distributing
Corporation
1 Gulf & Western Plaza
New York, New York 10023
Tel: 212-333-4600

Peacock Releasing Corporation
333 West 52nd Street
New York, New York 10019
Tel: 212-541-5770

Principal Film Exchange, Inc.
630 Ninth Avenue
New York, New York 10036
Tel: 212-246-6660

Productions Unlimited, Inc.
40 West 57th Street
New York, New York 10019
Tel: 212-541-6770

Walter Reade Organization, Inc.
241 East 34th Street
New York, New York 10016
Tel: 212-683-6300

Republic Pictures International
Corporation
655 Madison Avenue, Suite 1201
New York, New York 10021
Tel: 212-838-8813

Sands Film Company, Inc.
1955 Merrick Road
Merrick, New York 11566
Tel: 212-895-3996

Scotia American Productions
600 Madison Avenue
New York, New York 10022
Tel: 212-758-4775

Shochiku Films of America, Inc.
551 Fifth Avenue
New York, New York 10017
Tel: 212-697-6146

Silverstein International
    Corporation
200 West 57th Street
New York, New York 10019
Tel: 212-541-6620

Times Film Corporation
144 West 57th Street
New York, New York 10019
Tel: 212-757-6980

Toho International (USA) Inc.
1501 Broadway, Suite 2005
New York, New York 10036
Tel: 212-563-5258

Trans-America Film Corporation
888 Seventh Avenue
New York, New York 10019
Tel: 212-582-7232

Twentieth Century–Fox Film
    Corporation
1345 Avenue of the Americas
New York, New York 10019
Tel: 212-397-8500

Unique Films
165 West 46th Street
New York, New York 10036
Tel: 212-575-9532

Unisphere Releasing Corporation
165 West 46th Street
New York, New York 10036
Tel: 212-575-5959

United Artists Corporation
729 Seventh Avenue
New York, New York 10019
Tel: 212-245-6000

Universal Film Exchange of New
    York
630 Ninth Avenue
New York, New York 10036
Tel: 212-246-4747

Universal Film Exchanges, Inc.
445 Park Avenue
New York, New York 10022
Tel: 212-759-7500

Warner Bros. Distributing
    Corporation
75 Rockefeller Plaza
New York, New York 10020
Tel: 212-484-8000

North Carolina:

Allied Artists Pictures
    Corporation
320 South Tryon Street
Charlotte, North Carolina 28202
Tel: 704-333-9261

American International Pictures
    Exchange
311 South Church Street
Charlotte, North Carolina 28202
Tel: 704-335-5512

Buena Vista Distribution
    Company, Inc.
221 South Church Street
Charlotte, North Carolina 28202
Tel: 704-333-8491

Cinema Film Distributing
222 South Church Street
Charlotte, North Carolina 28202
Tel: 704-332-8539

Cinemation Industries
221 South Church Street
Charlotte, North Carolina 28202
Tel: 704-372-1037

Columbia Pictures Corporation
226 South Church Street
Charlotte, North Carolina 28202
Tel: 704-332-2156

International Amusement
  Corporation
222 South Church Street
Charlotte, North Carolina 28202
Tel: 704-332-4163

Paramount Film Distributing
  Corporation
222 South Church Street
Charlotte, North Carolina 28202
Tel: 704-332-5101

Premier Pictures
221 South Church Street
Charlotte, North Carolina 28202
Tel: 704-332-5101

Pyramid Films
221 South Church Street
Charlotte, North Carolina 28202
Tel: 704-333-2894

Twentieth Century–Fox Film
  Corporation
308 South Church Street
Charlotte, North Carolina 28202
Tel: 704-332-7101

United Artists Corporation
221 West Third Street
Charlotte, North Carolina 28202
Tel: 704-332-5507

Universal Film Exchange, Inc.
313 South Church Street
Charlotte, North Carolina 28202
Tel: 704-332-3159

Variety Films Company
221 South Church Street
Charlotte, North Carolina 28202
Tel: 704-333-0369

Warner Bros. Pictures
330 South Tryon Street
Charlotte, North Carolina 28202
Tel: 704-376-5611

Ohio:
Cincinnati:

American International Pictures
35 East Seventh Street
Cincinnati, Ohio 45202
Tel: 513-621-6443

Buena Vista Distribution
  Company, Inc.
617 Vine Street
Cincinnati, Ohio 45202
Tel: 513-721-4766

Paramount Pictures Corporation
35 East Seventh Street
Cincinnati, Ohio 45202
Tel: 513-241-6150

Twentieth Century–Fox Film
  Corporation
617 Vine Street
Cincinnati, Ohio 45202
Tel: 513-241-6460

United Artists Corporation
35 East Seventh Street
Cincinnati, Ohio 45202
Tel: 513-241-1546

Universal Film Exchanges, Inc.
1628 Central Parkway
Cincinnati, Ohio 45214
Tel: 513-421-3820

Warner Bros. Pictures
  Distributing Corporation
1014 Vine Street
Cincinnati, Ohio 45202

Cleveland:

Allied Artists Pictures
2108 Payne Avenue
Cleveland, Ohio 44114
Tel: 216-861-0390

American International Pictures
Film Building
Cleveland, Ohio 44114
Tel: 216-621-9376

Avco-Embassy Pictures
  Corporation
19201 Villaview
Cleveland, Ohio 44119
Tel: 216-531-5360

Cinerama Releasing
2108 Payne Avenue
Cleveland, Ohio 44114
Tel: 216-696-3606

Columbia Pictures Corporation
Film Exchange Building
2108 Payne Avenue
Cleveland, Ohio 44114
Tel: 216-241-3545

Twentieth Century–Fox Film
  Corporation
2108 Payne Avenue
Cleveland, Ohio 44114
Tel: 216-861-2257

Universal Film Exchange, Inc.
1721 Superior Avenue
Cleveland, Ohio 44114
Tel: 216-771-0413

Warner Bros. Pictures
  Distributing Corporation
19201-B Villaview
Cleveland, Ohio 44119
Tel: 216-486-6700

Pennsylvania:
Philadelphia:

Allied Artists Pictures
1612 Market Street
Philadelphia, Pennsylvania 19103
Tel: 215-563-8082

American Film Company
1329 Vine Street
Philadelphia, Pennsylvania 19107
Tel: 215-922-1800

American International Pictures
1612 Market Street
Philadelphia, Pennsylvania 19103
Tel: 215-568-6684

Avco-Embassy Pictures
Corporation
303 North Thirteenth Street
Philadelphia, Pennsylvania 19107
Tel: 215-561-0335

Buena Vista Film Distribution
Co., Inc.
1612 Market Street
Philadelphia, Pennsylvania 19103
Tel: 215-567-0845

Columbia Pictures Corporation
1612 Market Street
Philadelphia, Pennsylvania 19103
Tel: 215-568-3889

Lopert Pictures Corporation
Fox Building
Philadelphia, Pennsylvania 19103
Tel: 215-563-9500

Paramount Pictures Corporation
Fox Building
Philadelphia, Pennsylvania 19103
Tel: 215-567-3672

Twentieth Century–Fox Film
Corporation
Fox Building
Philadelphia, Pennsylvania 19103
Tel: 215-568-7030

United Artists Corporation
Fox Building
Philadelphia, Pennsylvania 19103
Tel: 215-563-9500

Warner Bros. Pictures
Distributing Corporation
Sixteenth and Market Streets
Philadelphia, Pennsylvania 19139
Tel: 215-563-9530

Pittsburgh:

American International Pictures
415 Van Braam Street
Pittsburgh, Pennsylvania 15219
Tel: 412-281-1630

Buena Vista Film Distribution
Company, Inc.
Fulton Building
107 Sixth Street
Pittsburgh, Pennsylvania 15229
Tel: 412-281-9911

Paramount Pictures Corporation
Fulton Building
107 Sixth Street
Pittsburgh, Pennsylvania 15229
Tel: 412-281-9270

United Artists Corporation
Fulton Building
107 Sixth Street
Pittsburgh, Pennsylvania 15229
Tel: 412-471-8960

Wheeler Film Company
107 Sixth Street
Pittsburgh, Pennsylvania 15229
Tel: 412-471-8225

Tennessee:

American International Pictures
399 South Second
Memphis, Tennessee 38103
Tel: 901-526-8328

United Artists Corporation
1437 Central Avenue
Memphis, Tennessee 38104
Tel: 901-527-3836

Universal Film Exchanges, Inc.
138 Huling Street
Memphis, Tennessee 38103
Tel: 901-526-4161

Texas:

Allied Artists
640 A Merchandise Building
Dallas, Texas 75201
Tel: 214-747-1658

American International Pictures
2011 Jackson Street
Dallas, Texas 75201
Tel: 214-748-4964

American National Enterprises
11422 Harry Hines Boulevard
Dallas, Texas 75229
Tel: 214-243-5171

Avco-Embassy Pictures
1712 Commerce Street
Dallas, Texas 75201
Tel: 214-748-7249

Buena Vista Distribution
   Company, Inc.
1504 Tower Petroleum Building
1907 Elm Street
Dallas, Texas 75201
Tel: 214-748-5306

Cinemation
500 South Ervay Building, Suite
   617B
Dallas, Texas 75201
Tel: 214-741-6284

Cinerama Releasing Corporation
500 South Ervay Building
Dallas, Texas 75201
Tel: 214-747-3175

Columbia Pictures Industries
1900 Young Street
Dallas, Texas 75201
Tel: 214-741-3541

Charles M. Conner Productions
4713 Braeburn Drive
Bellaire, Texas 77401
Tel: 713-668-9900

Dal-Art Films
2017 Young Street
Dallas, Texas 75201
Tel: 214-748-8342

Dimension General–Erie
   Distributing
10830 North Central Expressway
Dallas, Texas 72531
Tel: 214-692-7744

Films, Inc.
1414 Dragon Street
Dallas, Texas 75207
Tel: 214-741-4071

Major Film Distributors
1907 Elm Street
Dallas, Texas 75201
Tel: 214-744-4069

Mulberry Square Releasing, Inc.
10300 North Central Expressway
  #120
Dallas, Texas 75231
Tel: 214-369-0513

Paramount Pictures Corporation
401 North Pearl Expressway
Dallas, Texas 75201
Tel: 214-741-5565

Sack Amusement Enterprises
1710 Jackson Street
Dallas, Texas 75201
Tel: 214-742-9445

Starline Pictures
500 South Ervay Street
Dallas, Texas 75201
Tel: 214-748-5709

Sun International Productions
11422 Harry Hines Boulevard
Dallas, Texas 75229
Tel: 214-243-2401

Twentieth Century–Fox Pictures
  Corp.
1400 South Griffin
Dallas, Texas 75215
Tel: 214-748-7221

United Artists Corporation
Mercantile Continental Building
Dallas, Texas 75247
Tel: 214-742-6174

Universal Film Exchanges, Inc.
810 South St. Paul Street
Dallas, Texas 75201
Tel: 214-741-3164

Variety Film Distributors
4308 North Central Expressway
Dallas, Texas 75206
Tel: 214-827-7800

Warner Bros. Distributing
  Corporation
10830 North Central
Dallas, Texas 72531
Tel: 214-691-6101

Utah:

Ambassador Releasing, Inc.
355 East 2100 South
Salt Lake City, Utah 84115
Tel: 801-487-4287

American Cinema, Inc.
555 East Fourth South
Salt Lake City, Utah 84102
Tel: 801-521-8161

American National Enterprises,
  Inc.
556 East Second South
Salt Lake City, Utah 84102
Tel: 801-521-9400

Washington:

American International Pictures
2401 Second Avenue
Seattle, Washington 98121
Tel: 206-622-0660

Buena Vista Distribution
Company, Inc.
2419 Second Avenue
Seattle, Washington 98121
Tel: 206-624-0186

Favorite Films of California, Inc.
2318 Second Avenue, Second
Floor
Seattle, Washington 98121
Tel: 206-624-6234

Paramount Pictures Corporation
2312 Second Avenue
Seattle, Washington 98121
Tel: 206-622-4287

Parnell Film Distribution, Inc.
2318 Second Avenue
Seattle, Washington 98121
Tel: 206-622-0246

Seattle National Film Services
900 Maynard Avenue, South
Seattle, Washington 98134
Tel: 206-682-6685

Twentieth Century–Fox Film
Corporation
2421 Second Avenue
Seattle, Washington 98121
Tel: 206-623-7815

United Artists Corporation
975 John Street
Seattle, Washington 98109
Tel: 206-622-3788

Universal Film Exchange, Inc.
2401 Second Avenue
Seattle, Washington 98121
Tel: 206-623-6823

Warner Bros. Distributing
Corporation
2704 Second Avenue
Seattle, Washington 98121
Tel: 206-622-0046

Wisconsin:

American International Pictures
212 West Wisconsin Avenue
Milwaukee, Wisconsin 53203
Tel: 414-273-3887

Buena Vista Distribution
Company, Inc.
212 West Wisconsin Avenue
Milwaukee, Wisconsin 53203
Tel: 414-273-5111

Milwaukee Film Center, Inc.
333 North 25th Street
Milwaukee, Wisconsin 53233
Tel: 414-344-0300

Theatres Service Company
9235 West Capitol Drive
Milwaukee, Wisconsin 53222
Tel: 414-271-6529

United Artists Corporation
212 West Wisconsin Avenue
Milwaukee, Wisconsin 53203
Tel: 414-271-6529

X-Rated Films

The Motion Picture Association of America's X rating is awarded for
on-screen violence, for sexual athletics, and for language the MPAA Ratings
Board deems objectionable. The inclusion of an individual or business
organization here does not connote the association with filmed material that
some members of the community would consider pornography. The X rating
may likewise be self-imposed by the distributor without submitting the film
for official rating by MPAA.

California:
   Los Angeles area:

A G Enterprises
7766 Santa Monica Boulevard
Los Angeles, California 90046
Tel: 213-654-9158

Apostolof Film Productions, Inc.
Stephen C. Apostolof
6430 Sunset Boulevard
Los Angeles, California 90028
Tel: 213-462-6971

Art Films International
941 North La Cienega Boulevard
Los Angeles, California 90069
Tel: 213-876-8610

Box Office International Films
Harry Novak
4774 Melrose Avenue
Los Angeles, California 90029
Tel: 213-660-1770

Dan Cady
8235 Santa Monica Boulevard
Los Angeles, California 90046
Tel: 213-828-7577

Donald A. Davis Productions,
   Inc.
705 North Cole Avenue
Los Angeles, California 90038
Tel: 213-469-6256

Entertainment Ventures, Inc.
1654 Cordova Street
Los Angeles, California 90007
Tel: 213-731-7236

Essex Pictures Company
1617 El Centro
Los Angeles, California 90028

Films International, Inc.
P.O. Box 3748
Los Angeles, California 90028
Tel: 213-466-7791

Freeway Film Corporation
1662 Cordova Street
Los Angeles, California 90007
Tel: 213-731-8373

Goldstone Films
8444 Wilshire Boulevard
Beverly Hills, California 90211
Tel: 213-653-3231

Cinema Dynamics
1505 Vine Street
Los Angeles, California 90028
Tel: 213-469-3434

Hollywood International Film
  Corporation of America
1044 South Hill Street
Los Angeles, California 90015
Tel: 213-749-2067

JAACOV Productions
6605 Hollywood Boulevard, Suite
  211
Los Angeles, California 90028
Tel: 213-465-4444

Key Films
1344 North Hayworth
Los Angeles, California 90046
Tel: 213-874-7355

Pacific Distribution Company
Murray Perlstein
8560 Sunset Boulevard
Los Angeles, California 90069

Phoenix International Films
1658 Cordova Street
Los Angeles, California 90007
Tel: 213-734-2062

Plymouth Distributors
1800 North Highland Avenue
Los Angeles, California 90028
Tel: 213-461-2868

Pyramid Entertainment
8235 Santa Monica Boulevard
Los Angeles, California 90046
Tel: 213-828-7577

Rm Films International, Inc.
1725 North Ivar, Suite 101
Los Angeles, California 90028
Tel: 213-466-7791

Reliable T.S. Company
P.O. Box 8093
Van Nuys, California 91409
Tel: 213-788-5585

Stu Segall & Associates
8564 Melrose Avenue
Los Angeles, California 90069
Tel: 213-657-6901

Sunset International Releasing,
  Inc.
8222 West Third Street
Los Angeles, California 90048
Tel: 213-653-3020

United Theatrical Amusement
1664 1/2 Cordova Street
Los Angeles, California 90007
Tel: 213-732-7742

San Francisco area:

Alex DeRenzy
1 Highland Avenue
San Rafael, California 94901

IRMI Films Corporation
328 Coral Ridge Drive
Pacifica, California 94044

KTVK, Ltd.
90 Golden Gate Avenue
San Francisco, California 94012

Mitchell Brothers Film Group
895 O'Farrell Street
San Francisco, California 94109
Tel: 415-441-1930
Tel: 212-541-5136 (New York)

Georgia:

Jack Vaughn Productions
161 Spring Street, N.W.
Atlanta, Georgia 30303
Tel: 404-523-7531

Illinois:

Brian Distributing Company
32 West Randolph Street
Chicago, Illinois 60601
Tel: 312-332-1739

Kaplan-Continental
203 North Wabash Avenue
Chicago, Illinois 60601
Tel: 312-782-8413

Maryland:

Associated Pictures Corporation
19 West Mt. Royal Avenue
Baltimore, Maryland 21201
Tel: 301-385-0600

Massachusetts:

Ellis Gordon Films
614 Statler Office Building
Boston, Massachusetts 02116
Tel: 617-426-5900

Michigan:

Gail Films
16300 West Nine Mile Road
Southfield, Michigan 48075
Art Weisberg
Tel: 313-557-5024

Missouri:

Thomas Film Distributing, Inc.
110 West Eighteenth Street
Kansas City, Missouri 64108
John Shipp

New Jersey:

Plymouth Distributors
P.O. Box 542
Old Bridge, New Jersey 08857
Tel: 201-679-4141

New York:
Buffalo:

Frontier Amusement
505 Pearl Street
Buffalo, New York 14202
Tel: 716-854-6752

New York City:

Amero Brothers, Inc.
165 West 46th Street, Suite 305
New York, New York 10036
Tel: 212-575-7919

Aquarius Film Releasing, Inc.
229 West 42nd Street
New York, New York 10036
Tel: 212-787-6208

Audubon Films
850 Seventh Avenue
New York, New York 10019
Tel: 212-586-4913

Brobinyak, Inc.
250 West 57th Street, Suite 2101
New York, New York 10019

Cambist Films, Inc.
850 Seventh Avenue
New York, New York 10019
Lee Hessel
Tel: 212-586-5810

Catalyst Films
850 Seventh Avenue
New York, New York 10019
Tel: 212-586-4913

Chancellor Films, Inc.
200 West 57th Street, Suite 1207
New York, New York 10019
Tel: 212-246-4940

Jack Deveau
240 West 73rd Street
New York, New York 10023
Tel: 212-787-1260

Distribpix, Inc.
432 West 54th Street
New York, New York 10019
Tel: 212-489-8130

Hand-in-Hand Films, Inc.
1697 Broadway
New York, New York 10019
Tel: 212-582-2372

Horizon Pictures, Inc.
711 Fifth Avenue
New York, New York 10022
Tel: 212-421-6810

Inish Kae, Ltd.
2 West 45th Street
New York, New York 10036
Tel: 212-575-1892

LAC Film Distributors
60-14 67th Avenue
Ridgewood, New York 11227
Tel: 212-386-6524

Marvin Films, Inc.
1650 Broadway
New York, New York 10036
Tel: 212-354-5700

Mature Pictures Corporation
630 Ninth Avenue
New York, New York 10036
Tel: 212-541-7860

William Mishkin Motion
    Pictures, Inc.
1501 Broadway
New York, New York 10036
Tel: 212-736-0266

P R P
P.O. Box 329
Canal Street Station
New York, New York 10013

The Parmit Company
250 West 57th Street, Suite 2101
New York, New York 10019

c/o Savage Enterprises
Armond Peters
435 West 57th Street
New York, New York 10019
Tel: 212-757-9697

Stu Segall & Associates
1600 Broadway, Suite 611
New York, New York 10019
Tel: 212-582-4910

Saliva Films
A Division of New Line Cinema
  Corp.
121 University Place
New York, New York 10003
Tel: 212-674-7460

A. L. Shackleton Films, Inc.
330 West 58th Street, Suite 14N
New York, New York 10019
Tel: 212-757-3635

Times Film Corporation
144 West 57th Street
New York, New York 10019
Tel: 212-757-6980
Jean Goldwurm, President

Variety Films, Inc.
630 Ninth Avenue
New York, New York 10036
Tel: 212-757-3512
Les Baker, President

North Carolina:

Charlotte Booking & Film
  Distributing Services
230 South Tryon Street, Suite
  1025
Charlotte, North Carolina 28232
Tel: 704-376-5569

Galaxy Films
222 South Church Street
Charlotte, North Carolina 28201
Tel: 704-372-6747

International Amusement
  Corporation
4325 Glenwood Avenue
Raleigh, North Carolina 27612

Pyramid Pictures, Inc.
230 South Tryon Street, Suite
  1070
Charlotte, North Carolina 28202
Tel: 704-333-2894

Variety Films
221 South Church Street
Charlotte, North Carolina 28201
Tel: 704-333-0369

Ohio:

Ed Salzberg, Inc.
35 East Seventh Street
Cincinnati, Ohio 45202
Tel: 513-241-3671

Pennsylvania:

G. Schuyler Beattie
106 Ivy Wood Lane
Radnor, Pennsylvania 19087
Tel: 215-688-1145

John Glaus Agency
462 Woodrift Lane
Pittsburgh, Pennsylvania 15219
Tel: 412-653-5493

Tennessee:

Contemporary Films Distributors
831 South Cooper Street
Memphis, Tennessee 38104
Carl R. Carter, Principal
William Mallozzi, Principal
Jerry Ponticelle, Principal
Tel: 901-278-7342

Texas:

Film Booking Office
500 South Ervay, Suite 603B
Dallas, Texas 75201
Tel: 214-744-3165

Goldstone Films of Texas
500 South Ervay Street
Dallas, Texas 75201
Tel: 214-742-4869

Sack Amusement Enterprises
1710 Jackson Street
Dallas, Texas 75201
Tel: 214-742-9445

Dubbing

California:

Los Angeles area:

Cinesound
915 North Highland Avenue
Los Angeles, California 90038
Tel: 213-464-1155

Consolidated Film Industries
959 North Seward Street
Los Angeles, California 90038
Tel: 213-462-3161

Craig Corporation
12140 Bellflower
Compton, California 90224
Tel: 213-537-1233

Edit-Rite, Inc.
1213 North Highland Avenue
Los Angeles, California 90038
Tel: 213-465-6117

Film Technology Company, Inc.
6900 Santa Monica Boulevard
Los Angeles, California 90038
Tel: 213-465-4908

Glen Glenn Sound Company
6624 Romaine Street
Los Angeles, California 90038
Tel: 213-469-7221

San Francisco area:

James Flocker Enterprises, Inc.
3080 La Selva
San Mateo, California 94403
Tel: 415-349-8000

New York:

New York City:

Aquarius Transfer
12 East 46th Street
New York, New York 10017
Tel: 212-581-0123

Image Sounds Studios, Inc.
1619 Broadway
New York, New York 10019
Tel: 212-581-6717

Magno Recording Studios, Inc.
212 West 48th Street
New York, New York 10036
Tel: 212-757-8855

National Film Center
232 East 46th Street
New York, New York 10017
Tel: 212-757-6440

National Recording Studios, Inc.
730 Fifth Avenue
New York, New York 10019
Tel: 212-757-6440

Ross-Gaffney, Inc.
21 West 46th Street
New York, New York 10036
Tel: 212-582-3744

The Sound Shop, Inc.
304 East 44th Street
New York, New York 10017
Tel: 212-757-9800

Titan Productions, Inc.
1600 Broadway
New York, New York 10019
Tel: 212-757-7129

Trans-Audio, Inc.
254 West 54th Street
New York, New York 10019
Tel: 212-265-6225

Editing Equipment

California:

Los Angeles area:

Ametron/American Electrical
  Supply, Inc.
1200 North Vine Street
Los Angeles, California 90038
Tel: 213-466-4321

Chet Baker Rentals
605 North La Brea Avenue
Los Angeles, California 90036
Tel: 213-935-8611

Birns & Sawyer, Inc.
1026 North Highland
Los Angeles, California 90038
Tel: 213-466-8211

Boden Sales Company
6137 St. Clair Street
North Hollywood, California
  91606
Tel: 213-763-9059

R. B. Chenoweth Films
1860 East North Hills Drive
La Habre, California 90631
Tel: 213-861-9909

Christy's Editorial Film Supply
2920 West Magnolia Boulevard
Burbank, California 91505
Tel: 213-845-1755

Cinema Arts-Crafts
914 North Fairfax
Los Angeles, California 90046
Tel: 213-654-0502

Hal Dinnes Productions
6314 La Mirada Avenue
Los Angeles, California 90038
Tel: 213-467-7146

Erro Film Service
6069 Sunset Boulevard
Los Angeles, California 90028
Tel: 213-467-3039

F&B/Ceco of California, Inc.
F&B/Ceco Editing Center
7051 Santa Monica Boulevard
Los Angeles, California 90038
Tel: 213-466-9361

Filmkraft Services
6850 Lexington Avenue
Los Angeles, California 90038
Tel: 213-464-7746

Alan Gordon Enterprises, Inc.
1430 North Cahuenga Boulevard
Los Angeles, California 90028
Tel: 213-466-3561

Alan Gordon Enterprises, Inc.
5362 North Cahuenga Boulevard
North Hollywood, California
  91601
Tel: 213-985-5500

Hollywood Film Company
956 Seward Street
Los Angeles, California 90038
Tel: 213-462-3284

Horizontal Editing Studios
6253 Hollywood Boulevard
Los Angeles, California 90028
Tel: 213-461-4643

J & R Film Company
905 North Cole Avenue
Los Angeles, California 90038
Tel: 213-467-3107

Roy Law Enterprises
3407 West Olive Street
Burbank, California 91505
Tel: 213-846-7740

Leonetti Cine Rentals
5609 Sunset Boulevard
Los Angeles, California 90028
Tel: 213-469-2987

Magnasync-Movieola
1001 North Highland
Los Angeles, California 90038
Tel: 213-466-5233

Magnasync-Movieola
5539 Riverton Avenue
North Hollywood, California
    91601
Tel: 213-877-2791

Maier Hancock Industries
13212 Raymer Street
North Hollywood, California
    91605
Tel: 213-764-0280

Metro Kalver, Inc.
8927 West Exposition Boulevard
Los Angeles, California 90034
Tel: 213-870-1602

Movie Tech
6518 Santa Monica Boulevard
Los Angeles, California 90038
Tel: 213-467-8491

Jack Pill & Associates
6370 Santa Monica Boulevard
Los Angeles, California 90038
Tel: 213-466-5391

SOS/Photo-Cine-Optics, Inc.
7051 Santa Monica Boulevard
Los Angeles, California 90038
Tel: 213-466-9361

Tech-Camera Rentals
6370 Santa Monica Boulevard
Los Angeles, California 90038
Tel: 213-466-5391

San Francisco area:

American Zoetrope Film Facility
827 Folsom Street
San Francisco, California 94107
Tel: 415-989-0600

Leo Diner Films
322-350 Golden Gate
San Francisco, California 94102
Tel: 415-775-3664

Ferco
363 Brannan Street
San Francisco, California 94107
Tel: 415-957-1787

Snazelle Films, Inc.
155 Fell Street
San Francisco, California 94102
Tel: 415-431-5490

Sound Genesis, Inc.
445 Bryant Street
San Francisco, California 94107
Tel: 415-391-8776

Hawaii:

Pacific Instrumentation
5388 Papai Street
Honolulu, Hawaii 96821
Tel: 808-373-1287

Nevada:

K-B Cine Supply
Box 12611
Las Vegas, Nevada 89112
Tel: 702-451-5290

Rugar Electronics
4515 Industrial Road
Las Vegas, Nevada 89103
Tel: 702-736-4331

New York:
New York City:

Cinergy Corporation
33 West 94th Street
New York, New York 10028
Tel: 212-222-2644

Editing Machine, Inc.
630 Ninth Avenue
New York, New York 10036
Tel: 212-757-5420

Ferco
419 West 54th Street
New York, New York 10019
Tel: 212-581-5474

Motion Picture Enterprises
Tarrytown, New York 10591
Tel: 212-245-0969

Preview Theatre
1600 Broadway
New York, New York 10019
Tel: 212-741-2989

Texas:

Automated Commercial Training
Systems, Inc.
9817 Westpark
Houston, Texas 77042
Tel: 713-783-1380

De Alberich & Associates
5907 Star Lane
Houston, Texas 77027
Tel: 713-783-0210

Piccadilly Films International
Company, Inc.
1802 N.E. Loop 410, Gold Carpet
Suite
San Antonio, Texas 78246
Tel: 512-824-3548

Utah:

Stockdale and Company, Inc.
200 East First South
Salt Lake City, Utah 84111
Tel: 801-521-3505

Washington:

Northwest Sound and Production
  Service
129 First Street, West
Seattle, Washington 98121
Tel: 206-282-4766

Pal Productions, Inc.
10003 Lenora Street
Seattle, Washington 98121
Tel: 206-682-1339

Rarig Film Center
200 West Mercer
Seattle, Washington 98119
Tel: 206-284-2650

Editing Facilities

California:
Los Angeles area:

Anchor Productions
4455 Los Feliz Boulevard
Los Angeles, California 90027
Tel: 213-661-2640

Aquarius Films
906 North Poinsettia Place
West Hollywood, California
90046
Tel: 213-656-0050

Astrofilm Service
932 North La Brea Avenue
Los Angeles, California 90038
Tel: 213-851-1673

R. B. Chenoweth Films
1860 East North Hills Drive
La Habra, California 90631
Tel: 213-691-1652

Creative Film Arts
7070 Waring Avenue
Los Angeles, California 90038
Tel: 213-933-8495

Hal Dennis Productions
6314 La Mirada Avenue
Los Angeles, California 90038
Tel: 213-467-7146

Edit-Rite, Inc.
1213 North Highland Avenue
Los Angeles, California 90038
Tel: 213-465-6117

Editing Film Center
956 North Seward Street
Los Angeles, California 90038
Tel: 213-462-3284

F&B/Ceco of California, Inc.
F&B/Ceco Editing Center
7051 Santa Monica Boulevard
Los Angeles, California 90038
Tel: 213-466-9361

Filmkraft Services
6850 Lexington Avenue
Los Angeles, California 90038
Tel: 213-464-7746

Foto-Kem Industries, Inc.
3215 Cahuenga Boulevard West
Los Angeles, California 90028
Tel: 213-876-8100

Samuel Goldwyn Studios
1041 North Formosa Avenue
Los Angeles, California 90046
Tel: 213-851-1234

Horizontal Editing Studios
6233 Hollywood Boulevard
Los Angeles, California 90028
Tel: 213-461-4643

Image Films, Inc.
8563 Beverly Boulevard
Los Angeles, California 90048
Tel: 213-657-5141

Kaleidoscope Films, Ltd.
6345 Fountain Avenue
Los Angeles, California 90028
Tel: 213-465-1151

Kriton Production
7906 Santa Monica Boulevard
Los Angeles, California 90046
Tel: 213-656-5964

Lion's Gate Films
1334 Westwood Boulevard
Los Angeles, California 90024
Tel: 213-475-4987

Lori Productions, Inc.
6087 Sunset Boulevard
Los Angeles, California 90028
Tel: 213-466-7567

Major Independent Film
  Productions, Inc.
1207 North Western Avenue
Los Angeles, California 90029
Tel: 213-461-2721

Metro-Goldwyn-Mayer, Inc.
10202 West Washington
  Boulevard
Culver City, California 90230
Tel: 213-836-3000

Movie Tech
6518 Santa Monica Boulevard
Los Angeles, California 90038
Tel: 213-467-8491

The Petersen Company
1330 North Vine Street
Los Angeles, California 90028
Tel: 213-466-9351

Post Production Center
1213 North Highland Avenue
Los Angeles, California 90038
Tel: 213-465-6117

SOS/Photo-Cine-Optics, Inc.
7051 Santa Monica Boulevard
Los Angeles, California 90038
Tel: 213-466-9361

Soundco
932-C North La Brea Avenue
Los Angeles, California 90038
Tel: 213-851-1622

Don Stern Productions
3623 Cahuenga Boulevard
Los Angeles, California 90068
Tel: 213-851-3673

Translations Unlimited
1150 West Olive Avenue
Burbank, California 91506
Tel: 213-849-3144

Water Barrel Productions, Inc.
901 Westbourne Drive
Los Angeles, California 90069
Tel: 213-659-5313

West Ho Films
3611 Cahuenga Boulevard West
Los Angeles, California 90068
Tel: 213-851-4277

Wollin Production Services, Inc.
666 North Robertson Boulevard
Los Angeles, California 90069
Tel: 213-659-0175

Sacramento area:

Glynis Films
955 Venture Court
Sacramento, California 95825
Tel: 916-967-4943

San Diego area:

Cal Photo Motion Picture Lab
3494 Pickett Street
San Diego, California 92110
Tel: 714-297-1621

The Odyssey Corporation
1333 Camino Del Rio South
San Diego, California 92108
Tel: 714-291-6830

San Francisco area:

American Zoetrope Inc.
American Zoetrope Film
    Facilities
827 Folsom Street
San Francisco, California 94107
Tel: 415-989-0600

Bonanza Films
The Embarcadero
222 Agriculture Building
San Francisco, California 94105
Tel: 415-956-5600

Leo Diner Films
332-350 Golden Gate
San Francisco, California 94102
Tel: 415-775-3664

James Flecker Enterprises, Inc.
3080 La Selva
San Mateo, California 94403
Tel: 415-349-8000

Manifest Production Service
308 Eleventh Street
San Francisco, California 94102
Tel: 415-626-5596

Medion, Inc.
12309 Polk Street
San Francisco, California 94109
Tel: 415-776-3440

J. C. Morgan Film Productions
World Trade Center
San Francisco, California 94111
Tel: 415-392-5271

Snazelle Films, Inc.
155 Fell Street
San Francisco, California 94102
Tel: 415-431-5490

Sound Genesis, Inc.
445 Bryant Street
San Francisco, California 94107
Tel: 415-391-8776

The Sound Service
55 Stevenson Street
San Francisco, California 94105
Tel: 415-433-3674

Colorado:

Cinema Services
Box 398
Eldorado Springs, Colorado
    80025
Tel: 303-433-4913

Florida:

Cinema City Studios
6015 Highway 301 North
Tampa, Florida 33610
Tel: 813-621-4731

Reela Film Laboratories, Inc.
65 N.W. Third Street
Miami, Florida 33101
Tel: 305-377-2611

Satellite Film, Inc.
10780 Kendale South Boulevard
Miami, Florida 33101
Tel: 305-274-0384

Studio Center, Inc.
148 N.E. Twentieth Avenue
North Miami, Florida 33161
Tel: 305-944-2911

Warren Sound Studios
35 N.E. 62nd Street
Miami, Florida 33101
Tel: 305-754-9539

Woroner Films, Inc.
1995 N.E. 150th Street
North Miami, Florida 33161
Tel: 305-945-5465

Georgia:

A F E R
1846 Briarwood Road, N.E.
Atlanta, Georgia 30329
Tel: 404-633-4101

AND, Inc.
1428-B Mason Street, N.E.
Atlanta, Georgia 30324
Tel: 404-876-1033

The Cutting Room
761 Peachtree Street
Atlanta, Georgia 30308
Tel: 404-872-7404

Avrum Fine
428 161 Spring Street, N.W.
Atlanta, Georgia 30303
Tel: 404-523-4669

Lanco Sound, Inc.
3486 West Hospital Road
Atlanta, Georgia 30341
Tel: 404-457-1244

The Studio Center
445 Bishop Street
Atlanta, Georgia 30318
Tel: 404-874-2252

Hawaii:

Hawaii Production Center
1534 Kapiolani Boulevard
Honolulu, Hawaii 96814
Tel: 808-941-3011

Spectrum Motion Pictures
2962 East Manoa Road
Honolulu, Hawaii 96822
Tel: 808-988-7122

Idaho:

Tri/Media Communications
8200 Preece Drive
Boise, Idaho 83705
Tel: 208-376-4088

Illinois:

Academy Film Productions, Inc.
123 West Chestnut Street
Chicago, Illinois 60610
Tel: 312-642-5877

William Birch & Associates
161 East Grand Avenue
Chicago, Illinois 60611
Tel: 312-527-2135

Chicago Postproduction, Inc.
540 North Lake Shore Drive
Chicago, Illinois 60611
Tel: 312-644-4090

Cine-Graff Motion Pictures
515 West Oakdale Avenue
Chicago, Illinois 60657
Tel: 312-327-9200

Cinema Processors, Inc.
211 East Grand Avenue
Chicago, Illinois 60611
Tel: 312-642-6453

George W. Colburn Laboratory,
   Inc.
164 North Wacker Drive
Chicago, Illinois 60606
Tel: 312-332-6286

Conformer Services
201 West Euclid Avenue
Arlington Heights, Illinois 60004
Tel: 312-253-0153

Douglas Film Industries
10 West Kinzie Street
Chicago, Illinois 60610
Tel: 312-664-7455

Edit/Chicago
600 North McClurg Court
Chicago, Illinois 60611
Tel: 312-787-9100

Editors' Choice
444 North Wabash Avenue
Chicago, Illinois 60611
Tel: 312-644-5311

Film Conformers, Inc.
222 West Huron Street
Chicago, Illinois 60610
Tel: 312-266-9300

First Cut, Ltd.
1932 North Larrabee Street
Chicago, Illinois 60614
Tel: 312-943-5058

John Fogelson, Inc.
100 East Ohio Street
Chicago, Illinois 60611
Tel: 312-787-8090

Hollywood Film Company
211 East Grand Avenue
Chicago, Illinois 60611
Tel: 312-644-1940

Jack Lieb Productions, Inc.
1230 West Washington Boulevard
Chicago, Illinois 60607
Tel: 312-666-1220

Glen McGowan & Son
161 East Grand Avenue
Chicago, Illinois 60611
Tel: 312-943-7742

Fred A. Niles Communication
    Centers, Inc.
1058 West Washington Boulevard
Chicago, Illinois 60607
Tel: 312-738-4181

Optimus, Inc.
625 North Michigan Avenue
Chicago, Illinois 60611
Tel: 312-321-0880

The Reel Thing
520 North Michigan Avenue
Chicago, Illinois 60611
Tel: 312-321-9166

Will Shaw & Associates
3 East Huron Street
Chicago, Illinois 60611
Tel: 312-787-0110

Studio Seven P.S.
615 North Wabash Avenue
Chicago, Illinois 60611
Tel: 312-337-7171

Don Tait Enterprises, Inc.
161 East Grand Avenue
Chicago, Illinois 60611
Tel: 312-642-3986

Massachusetts:

Ballantine Films, Inc.
115 Newbury Street
Boston, Massachusetts 02106
Tel: 617-267-2160

Film Associates
421 Broadway
Cambridge, Massachusetts 02138
Tel: 617-492-1062

The Film Group, Inc.
2400 Massachusetts Avenue
Cambridge, Massachusetts 02138
Tel: 617-354-5695

Nevada:

K-B Productions
Box 12611
Las Vegas, Nevada 89112
Tel: 702-451-5290

New York:

Editing Gallery, Inc.
211 East 51st Street
New York, New York 10022
Tel: 212-371-9224

Editors Corner
150 East 52nd Street
New York, New York 10022
Tel: 212-688-4334

Editors Hideaway
595 Madison Avenue
New York, New York 10022
Tel: 212-759-1105

Editors Scene, Inc.
41 East 42nd Street
New York, New York 10017
Tel: 212-682-5181

Film Equipment Rental
  Company
419 West 54th Street
New York, New York 10019
Tel: 212-581-5474

Film-Rite, Inc.
35 West 45th Street
New York, New York 10036
Tel: 212-246-0131

Film Tech, Inc.
49 West 45th Street
New York, New York 10036
Tel: 212-245-1881
Milton Siegel, President

Kaleidoscope Films Limited
353 West 57th Street
New York, New York 10019
Tel: 212-265-2377

Ross-Gaffney, Inc.
21 West 46th Street
New York, New York 10036
Tel: 212-582-3744

Texas:

A-V Corporation
2518 North Boulevard
Houston, Texas 77006
Tel: 713-523-6701

Dale Berry & Associates, Inc.
9001 E R L Thornton Freeway
Dallas, Texas 75228
Tel: 214-324-0409

Cine Services, Inc.
3109 East Randol Mill Road
Arlington, Texas 76011
Tel: 817-265-9581

Piccadilly Films International
  Company Limited
1802 N.E. Loop 410, Gold Carpet
  Suite
San Antonio, Texas 78246
Tel: 512-824-3548

Utah:

Stockdale and Company, Inc.
200 East First South
Salt Lake City, Utah 84111
Tel: 801-521-3505

Washington:

JRB Motion Graphics
3323 Ninth Avenue West
Seattle, Washington 98119
Tel: 206-284-0834

Know Productions, Inc.
1003 Lenora Street
Seattle, Washington 98121
Tel: 206-682-6931

Pal Productions, Inc.
1003 Lenora Street
Seattle, Washington 98121
Tel: 206-682-1339

Rarig Film Center
200 West Mercer
Seattle, Washington 98119
Tel: 206-284-2650

Editing Services

California:
Los Angeles area:

Akkad International Productions, Inc.
8730 Sunset Boulevard
Los Angeles, California 90069
Tel: 213-657-7670

Anchor Productions Ltd.
4455 Los Feliz Boulevard
Los Angeles, California 90027
Tel: 213-661-2640

Aquarius Films
906 North Poinsettia Place
West Hollywood, California 90046
Tel: 213-656-0050

Artisan Releasing Corporation
9200 Sunset Boulevard
Los Angeles, California 90069
Tel: 213-278-2670

Astrofilm Service
932 North La Brea Avenue
Los Angeles, California 90038
Tel: 213-851-1673

August Film Continuity Service
7923 Hollywood Boulevard
Los Angeles, California 90046
Tel: 213-874-1310

Centre Films, Inc.
1103 North El Centro Avenue
Los Angeles, California 90038
Tel: 213-466-5123

Lee Chaney & Associates
6362 Hollywood Boulevard
Los Angeles, California 90028
Tel: 213-464-5333

R. B. Chenoweth Films
1860 East North Hills Drive
La Habra, California 90631
Tel: 213-691-1652

Cine Group
8560 Sunset Boulevard
Los Angeles, California 90069
Tel: 213-652-4800

Collier's Editorial Service, Inc.
514 North Avenue
La Puente, California 91746
Tel: 213-464-8440

Communications Group West
6335 Homewood Avenue
Los Angeles, California 90028
Tel: 213-461-4024

Complete Negative Service
6007 Waring Avenue
Los Angeles, California 90038
Tel: 213-463-7753

Consolidated Films Industries
959 Seward Street
Los Angeles, California 90038
Tel: 213-462-3161

Cornerstone Productions
6087 Sunset Boulevard
Los Angeles, California 90028
Tel: 213-462-0071

Craig Productions
1546 North Argyle Avenue
Los Angeles, California 90028
Tel: 213-462-6171

Creative Film Arts
7070 Waring Avenue
Los Angeles, California 90038
Tel: 213-933-8495

Cut
3625 Regal Place
Los Angeles, California 90068
Tel: 213-876-0336

Hal Dennis Productions
6314 La Mirada Avenue
Los Angeles, California 90038
Tel: 213-467-7146

Echo Film Services
1040 North Las Palmas Avenue
Los Angeles, California 90038
Tel: 213-469-2707

Edit International
6725 Sunset Boulevard
Los Angeles, California 90028
Tel: 213-463-1121

Edit-Rite, Inc.
1213 North Highland Avenue
Los Angeles, California 90038
Tel: 213-465-6117

Edit West
6335 Homewood Avenue
Los Angeles, California 90028
Tel: 213-463-0220

Richard Einfeld
1512 North Las Palmas Avenue
Los Angeles, California 90028
Tel: 213-461-3731

F-M Motion Picture Service
733 North Highland Avenue
Los Angeles, California 90038
Tel: 213-937-1622

F & D Film Cutting Service
   Company
959 Seward Street
Los Angeles, California 90004
Tel: 213-467-8652

The Film Place
6521 Homewood Avenue
Los Angeles, California 90028
Tel: 213-464-0116

Film Technology Company, Inc.
6900 Santa Monica Boulevard
Los Angeles, California 90038
Tel: 213-465-4908

Filmic Editorial Service
3215 Cahuenga Boulevard West
Los Angeles, California 90068
Tel: 213-851-3700

Filmkraft Services
6850 Lexington Avenue
Los Angeles, California 90038
Tel: 213-464-7746

Finishing Filmhouse
931 North Cole, Suite 204
Los Angeles, California 90038
Tel: 213-466-1681

Foto-Kem Industries, Inc.
3215 Cahuenga Boulevard West
Los Angeles, California 90028
Tel: 213-876-8100

Samuel Goldwyn Studios
1041 North Formosa Avenue
Los Angeles, California 90046
Tel: 213-851-1234

Hank Gotzenberg, Inc.
1617 North El Centro, Suite 14
Los Angeles, California 90028
Tel: 213-467-5690

Group One Productions
3255 Cahuenga Boulevard
Los Angeles, California 90068
Tel: 213-876-3300

Horizontal Editing Studios
6253 Hollywood Boulevard
Los Angeles, California 90028
Tel: 213-461-4643

Image Films, Inc.
8563 Beverly Boulevard
Los Angeles, California 90048
Tel: 213-657-5141

Imagivision, Inc.
1585 Crossroads of the World
Los Angeles, California 90028
Tel: 213-461-8263

Independent Producers Service
7370 Melrose Avenue
Los Angeles, California 90046
Tel: 213-655-3599

J & J Film Service, Inc.
6324 Santa Monica Boulevard
Los Angeles, California 90038
Tel: 213-469-2954

Jahol Film Editorial
8300 Santa Monica Boulevard,
    Suite 3A
Los Angeles, California 90210
Tel: 213-654-2890

Frank Jones Associates
1150 West Olive Avenue
Burbank, California 91506
Tel: 213-843-2031

Kaleidoscope Films Ltd.
6345 Fountain Avenue
Los Angeles, California 90028
Tel: 213-465-1151

Kriton Productions
7906 Santa Monica Boulevard
Los Angeles, California 90046
Tel: 213-656-5964

L. J. G. Productions
1600 North Western Avenue
Los Angeles, California 90027
Tel: 213-469-3692

Lori Productions, Inc.
6087 Sunset Boulevard
Los Angeles, California 90028
Tel: 213-466-7567

Major Independent Film
    Productions, Inc.
1207 North Western Avenue
Los Angeles, California 90029
Tel: 213-461-2721

Metro-Goldwyn-Mayer, Inc.
10202 West Washington
    Boulevard
Culver City, California 90230
Tel: 213-836-3000

Mirage Film Production
6335 Homewood Avenue
Los Angeles, California 90028
Tel: 213-465-8130

Moustache Productions
9017 Harratt Street
Los Angeles, California 90069
Tel: 213-464-5161

Movie Tech
6518 Santa Monica Boulevard
Los Angeles, California 90038
Tel: 213-467-8491

Nemours Productions, Inc.
3518 West Cahuenga Boulevard
Los Angeles, California 90068
Tel: 213-851-3660

Paragon Films
7325 Santa Monica Boulevard
Los Angeles, California 90046
Tel: 213-851-0488

The Petersen Company
1330 North Vine Street
Los Angeles, California 90028
Tel: 213-466-9351

The Picture Company
729 North Seward Avenue
Los Angeles, California 90038
Tel: 213-467-2683

Post Production Center
1213 North Highland Avenue
Los Angeles, California 90038
Tel: 213-465-6117

Post Time Editorial, Inc.
1777 North Vine Street, Suite 409
Los Angeles, California 90028
Tel: 213-462-6968

Producers Film Center
948 North Sycamore Avenue
Los Angeles, California 90038
Tel: 213-851-1122

Producers Film Services, Inc.
1041 North Formosa Avenue
Los Angeles, California 90046
Tel: 213-851-2030

Production House West
6671 Sunset Boulevard
Los Angeles, California 90028
Tel: 213-462-2378

Productions West, Inc.
1134 North Highland Avenue
Los Angeles, California 90038
Tel: 213-464-0169

Glen Roland Films
8543 Clifton Way
Beverly Hills, California 90211
Tel: 213-271-0533

Ronald S. Sexton
729 North Seward Street
Los Angeles, California 90038
Tel: 213-467-2683

Jack Spear Production Company
3215 Cahuenga Boulevard
Los Angeles, California 90068
Tel: 213-851-4123

Don Stern Productions
3623 Cahuenga Boulevard West
Los Angeles, California 90068
Tel: 213-851-3673

Suffilm, Inc.
959 North Seward Street
Los Angeles, California 90038
Tel: 213-463-1458

Teleprint of Los Angeles, Inc.
6043 Hollywood Boulevard
Los Angeles, California 90028
Tel: 213-464-7221

Translations Unlimited
1150 West Olive Avenue
Burbank, California 91506
Tel: 213-849-3144

Universal City Studios
100 Universal City Plaza
Universal City, California 91608
Tel: 213-985-4321

Water Barrel Productions, Inc.
901 Westbourne Drive
Los Angeles, California 90069
Tel: 213-659-5313

Jerry Webb and Associates
1238 North Highland Avenue
Los Angeles, California 90038
Tel: 213-469-6226

West Ho Films, Inc.
3611 Cahuenga Boulevard West
Los Angeles, California 90068
Tel: 213-851-4277

Wollin Production Services, Inc.
666 North Robertson Boulevard
Los Angeles, California 90069
Tel: 213-659-0175

San Diego area:

The Odyssey Corporation
1333 Camino Del Rio South
San Diego, California 92108
Tel: 714-291-6830

San Francisco area:

American Zoetrope, Inc.
American Zoetrope Film Facility
827 Folsom Street
San Francisco, California 94107
Tel: 415-989-0600

Furman Films
3466 21st Street
San Francisco, California 94110
Tel: 415-282-1300

Manifest Production Service
308 Eleventh Street
San Francisco, California 94102
Tel: 415-626-5596

Medion, Inc.
1239 Polk Street
San Francisco, California 94109
Tel: 415-776-3440

J. C. Morgan Film Productions
World Trade Center
San Francisco, California 94111
Tel: 415-392-5271

Motion Picture Service Company
125 Hyde Street
San Francisco, California 94102
Tel: 415-673-9162

W. A. Palmer Films
611 Howard Street
San Francisco, California 94105
Tel: 415-986-5961

Snazelle Films, Inc.
155 Fell Street
San Francisco, California 94102
Tel: 415-431-5490

Sound Genesis, Inc.
445 Bryant Street
San Francisco, California 94107
Tel: 415-391-8776

Studio 16, Inc.
2135 Powell Street
San Francisco, California 94133
Tel: 415-982-2097

Colorado:

Cinema Service
Box 398
Eldorado Springs, Colorado
    80025
Tel: 303-443-4913

E. K. Edwards & Son, Inc.
2120 South Holly
Denver, Colorado 80222
Tel: 303-757-5130

District of Columbia:

Byron Motion Pictures, Inc.
65 K Street, N.E.
Washington, D.C. 20002
Tel: 202-783-2700

TW II Productions
1611 Connecticut Avenue, N.W.
Suite 1
Washington, D.C. 20009
Tel: 202-265-4433

Florida:

Post Productions Services
3808 San Nicholas Street
Tampa, Florida 33609
Tel: 813-253-0402

Georgia:

Avrum Fine
161 Spring Street, N.W.
Atlanta, Georgia 30303
Tel: 404-523-1846
Tel: 404-631-3856

Hawaii:

David Cornwell Productions, Inc.
1358 Kapiolani Boulevard
Honolulu, Hawaii 96814
Tel: 808-949-7000

The House of Eric Productions
1760 Ala Moana Boulevard
Waikiki, Hawaii 96815
Tel: 808-533-3877

Spectrum Motion Pictures
2962 East Manoa Road
Honolulu, Hawaii 96822
Tel: 808-988-7122

Illinois:

Clasky!
305 Ashland
Evanston, Illinois 60602
Tel: 312-869-6282

Edit/Chicago Inc.
600 North McClurg Court
Chicago, Illinois 60611
Tel: 312-787-9100

Editing Et Cetera
5116 North Cicero Avenue
Chicago, Illinois 60630
Tel: 312-283-1140

Editors' Choice
444 North Wabash Avenue
Chicago, Illinois 60611
Tel: 312-644-5311

The Film Conformers, Inc.
222 West Huron Street
Chicago, Illinois 60610
Tel: 312-266-9300

First Cut Limited
1932 North Larrabee Street
Chicago, Illinois 60614
Tel: 312-943-5058

John Fogelson, Inc.
100 East Ohio Street
Chicago, Illinois 60611
Tel: 312-787-8090

Barbara Kaplan
400 North Michigan Avenue
Chicago, Illinois 60611
Tel: 312-943-2649

Glen McGowan & Son, Ltd.
161 East Grand Avenue
Chicago, Illinois 60611
Tel: 312-943-7742

My Sister's Cutting Room
746 West Belden Avenue, 2nd
floor
Chicago, Illinois 60614
Tel: 312-871-2090

Optimus, Inc.
625 North Michigan Avenue
Chicago, Illinois 60611
Tel: 312-321-0880

The Reel Thing
520 North Michigan Avenue,
Room 810
Chicago, Illinois 60611
Tel: 312-321-9166

Swan Editorial Service
469 East Ohio Street
Chicago, Illinois 60611
Tel: 312-542-6230

Nevada:

Nevada Motion Picture Service
2025 Paradise Road
Las Vegas, Nevada 89105
Tel: 702-734-0975

Specialties Design and
Manufacture
3429 Encina Drive
Las Vegas, Nevada 89121
Tel: 702-451-5290

New York:

Al Cine Services
3 East 57th Street
New York, New York 10022
Tel: 212-752-1087

Allegro Film Service
201 West 52nd Street
New York, New York 10019
Tel: 212-586-3057

Ani-Live Film Service, Inc.
45 West 45th Street
New York, New York 10036
Tel: 212-247-1800

Animated Products, Inc.
1600 Broadway
New York City, New York 10019
Tel: 212-265-2942

Armand Film Services, Inc.
120 West 44th Street
New York, New York 10036
Tel: 212-581-3866

Barnor Film Service
120 East 56th Street, Suite 1530
New York, New York 10022
Tel: 212-832-7333

Jerry Bender Editorial
26 East 36th Street
New York, New York 10016
Tel: 212-686-7407

Flo Califano
2 West 45th Street
New York, New York 10036
Tel: 212-867-7256

B. Canarick's Company, Ltd.
50 East 42nd Street
New York, New York 10017
Tel: 212-972-1015

Chung Group, Inc.
17 East 48th Street
New York, New York 10017
Tel: 212-832-0530

Cine Metric, Inc.
2 West 45th Street
New York, New York 10036
Tel: 212-869-8670

Cine Top, Inc.
1600 Broadway
New York, New York 10019
Tel: 212-582-4848

Cinema Arts Associates
333 West 52nd Street
New York, New York 10019
Tel: 212-246-2860

Consolidated Film Industries
15 Columbus Circle
New York, New York 10023
Tel: 212-581-1090

Cutting Board Editorial Service,
   Inc.
310 East 44th Street
New York, New York 10017
Tel: 212-661-5640

DJM Films, Inc.
4 East 46th Street
New York, New York 10017
Tel: 212-687-0111

Jeff Dell Film Service
10 East 53rd Street
New York, New York 10022
Tel: 212-371-7915

Double Image, Inc.
16 West 46th Street
New York, New York 10036
Tel: 212-582-4781

Duffex, Inc.
30 East 40th Street
New York, New York 10016
Tel: 212-889-5265

E.A.F. Editorial Services, Inc.
30 East 40th Street
New York, New York 10016
Tel: 212-679-7150

Editeam, Inc.
369 Lexington Avenue
New York, New York 10017
Tel: 212-986-9327

Editing Concepts
214 East 50th Street
New York, New York 10022
Tel: 212-980-3340

The Editor Gramaglia, Inc.
15 East 48th Street
New York, New York 10017
Tel: 212-838-1134

Edna & Friends, Inc.
35 West 45th Street
New York, New York 10036
Tel: 212-765-9849

Film Billders, Inc.
30 East 40th Street
New York, New York 10016
Tel: 212-683-4004

Film Boutique, Inc.
14 East 52nd Street
New York, New York 10022
Tel: 212-371-8690

Film Snip, Inc.
30 East 40th Street
New York, New York 10016
Tel: 212-683-0341

Fotosonic, Inc.
15 West 46th Street
New York, New York 10036
Tel: 212-586-0355

Si Fried Productions
49 West 45th Street
New York, New York 10036
Tel: 212-757-4424

John Horvath, Inc.
150 East 42nd Street
New York, New York 10022
Tel: 212-751-2022

Howal/Gellman Film Associates
302 East 41st Street
New York, New York 10017
Tel: 212-687-4646

J. G. Films, Inc.
245 West 55th Street
New York, New York 10019
Tel: 212-265-0862

Robert Jubin Ltd.
120 East 56th Street
New York, New York 10022
Tel: 212-832-1075

Jupiter Editorial Service
45 West 45th Street
New York City, New York 10036
Tel: 212-764-0182

Kaleidoscope Films Ltd.
353 West 57th Street
New York, New York 10019
Tel: 212-265-2377

Kenco Films, Inc.
619 West 54th Street
New York City, New York 10019
Tel: 212-867-9590

Bill King Editorial Services
18 West 45th Street
New York City, New York 10036
Tel: 212-986-5707

Lebowitz Films, Inc.
147 East 50th Street
New York City, New York 10022
Tel: 212-725-1490

Jim Lenkowsky
1619 Broadway
New York City, New York 10019
Tel: 212-581-9520

Leshaw Film Service, Inc.
150 East 52nd Street
New York, New York 10022
Tel: 212-751-8833

M.H.P. Filmbox, Inc.
116 East 38th Street
New York, New York 10016
Tel: 212-725-5990

M.K.R. Films, Inc.
300 West 55th Street
New York, New York 10019
Tel: 212-265-4878

Magus Editing
216 East 49th Street
New York, New York 10017
Tel: 212-371-1255

Leonard Mandelbaum, Inc.
25 West 45th Street
New York, New York 10036
Tel: 212-575-1995

Meridian Film Editorial Service,
  Inc.
45 West 45th Street
New York, New York 10036
Tel: 212-581-3434

Montage Film Services, Inc.
152 West 42nd Street
New York, New York 10036
Tel: 212-279-0808

P.A.T. Film Services
630 Ninth Avenue
New York, New York 10036
Tel: 212-247-0900

PDR Productions, Inc.
747 Third Avenue
New York, New York 10017
Tel: 212-755-9019

Henry Paticoff Editorial Service
33 West 54th Street
New York, New York 10019
Tel: 212-757-1335

Pelco Editorial, Inc.
8 West 40th Street
New York, New York 10018
Tel: 212-868-0935

The Prime Cut, Inc.
243 East 49th Street
New York, New York 10017
Tel: 212-753-0834

Print Service International
1414 Avenue of the Americas
New York, New York 10019
Tel: 212-751-7004

Projected Film
45 West 45th Street
New York, New York 10036
Tel: 212-581-1030

Irving Rathner
1600 Broadway
New York, New York 10019
Tel: 212-757-4240

Rolini Films
145 East 52nd Street
New York, New York 10022
Tel: 212-832-7176

STB Editorial Service, Inc.
95 Madison Avenue
New York, New York 10016
Tel: 212-686-7925

Sandpiper Editorial Service, Inc.
305 East 46th Street
New York, New York 10017
Tel: 212-754-0766

Laurence Solomon Film Group
1619 Broadway
New York, New York 10019
Tel: 212-582-6246

Lou Somerstein
21 West 46th Street
New York, New York 10036
Tel: 212-582-9153

Spectrum Associates, Inc.
536 West 29th Street
New York, New York 10001
Tel: 212-524-6266

Leo Steiner
15 West 46th Street
New York, New York 10036
Tel: 212-586-0355

Suski/Fallick East
49 West 45th Street
New York, New York 10036
Tel: 212-581-0018

Oregon:

Forde Motion Picture Labs
2153 N.E. Sandy Boulevard
Portland, Oregon 97232
Tel: 503-234-0553

Texas:

A-V Corporation
2518 North Boulevard
Houston, Texas 77006
Tel: 713-523-6701

Automated Commercial Training
  Systems, Inc.
9817 Westpark
Houston, Texas 77042
Tel: 713-783-1380

Cine Services, Inc.
3109 East Randol Mill Road
Arlington, Texas 76011
Tel: 817-265-9581

Houston Film Co-op, Inc.
Box 58932
Houston, Texas 77058
Tel: 713-482-7960

Piccadilly Films International
  Company, Ltd.
1802 N.E. Loop 410, Gold Carpet
  Suite
San Antonio, Texas 78246
Tel: 512-824-3548

Utah:

Stockdale and Company Inc.
200 East First Street South
Salt Lake City, Utah 84111
Tel: 801-521-3505

Washington:

Forde Motion Picture Labs
306 Fairview Avenue North
Seattle, Washington 98109
Tel: 206-682-2510

Gardner/Marlow/Maes Corporation
Seattle Tower, Penthouse
Seattle, Washington 98101
Tel: 206-624-9090

JRB Motion Graphics
3323 Ninth Avenue West
Seattle, Washington 98119
Tel: 206-284-0834

Multi-Media Productions
1200 Stuart Street
Seattle, Washington 98101
Tel: 206-624-8390

Northwest Sound and Production
   Service
129 First Street West
Seattle, Washington 98121
Tel: 206-282-4766

Pal Productions, Inc.
1003 Lenora Street
Seattle, Washington 98121
Tel: 206-682-1339

Effects
(Film & Photographic)

See also the listings under "Special Effects."

California:

Howard A. Anderson Company
5451 Marathon Street
Los Angeles, California 90038
Tel: 213-463-0100
Ext: 2001

Anicam
6331 Homewood Avenue
Los Angeles, California 90028
Tel: 213-465-4114

Bob Beck & Associates
1538 Cassil Place
Los Angeles, California 90038
Tel: 213-462-7093

Braverman Productions, Inc.
8961 Sunset Boulevard
Los Angeles, California 90069
Tel: 213-656-7214

Butler-Glouner
1438 North Gower
Los Angeles, California 90052
Tel: 213-462-3111

Cinefx/Acme Lab., Inc.
1161 North Highland
Los Angeles, California 90038
Tel: 213-464-7474

Cinema Research
6860 Lexington Avenue
Los Angeles, California 90028
Tel: 213-461-3235

Cineservice of Hollywood
1459 North Seward Street
Los Angeles, California 90038
Tel: 213-463-3178

Complete Film Service
932 North La Brea Avenue
Los Angeles, California 90038
Tel: 213-654-7100

Consolidated Film Industries
959 North Seward Street
Los Angeles, California 90038
Tel: 213-462-3161

Richard Einfeld Productions
1512 North Las Palmas Avenu
Los Angeles, California 90038
Tel: 213-461-3731

Film Effects of Hollywood
1140 North Citrus
Los Angeles, California 90038
Tel: 213-469-5808

Filmagic
6362 Hollywood Boulevard
Los Angeles, California 90028
Tel: 213-464-5333

Hogan-Lee Images
12849 Magnolia Boulevard
North Hollywood, California
91607
Tel: 213-980-3566

Imagic, Inc.
845 North Highland Avenue
Los Angeles, California 90038
Tel: 213-461-3744

Ray Mercer & Company
4241 Normal Avenue
Los Angeles, California 90029
Tel: 213-663-9331

Modern Film Effects
725 North Highland Avenue
Los Angeles, California 90030
Tel: 213-938-2155

National Screen Service
7026 Santa Monica Boulevard
Los Angeles, California 90210
Tel: 213-466-5111

Opticals West
7026 Santa Monica Boulevard
Los Angeles, California 90038
Tel: 213-466-5111

Pacific Title Studio
6350 Santa Monica Boulevard
Los Angeles, California 90210
Tel: 213-464-0121
Paramount Studios

Phot-Effex
3701 Oak Street
Burbank, California 91505
Tel: 213-849-6959

Westheimer Company
736 North Seward Street
Los Angeles, California 90038
Tel: 213-466-8271

New York:

Lester Berghan & Associates, Inc.
8 East Twelfth Street
New York, New York 10003
Tel: 212-924-3632

Cineffects, Inc.
115 West 45th Street
New York, New York 10036
Tel: 212-246-0950

Cinopticals, Inc.
501 Madison Avenue
New York, New York 10022
Tel: 212-935-0087

Du-Art Color Corporation
245 West 55th Street
New York, New York 10019
Tel: 212-757-4580

Film Opticals, Inc.
421 West 54th Street
New York, New York 10019
Tel: 212-757-7120

National Screen Service
Corporation
1600 Broadway
New York, New York 10019
Tel: 212-246-5700

National Studios
209 West 40th Street
New York, New York 10018
Tel: 212-695-0550

The Optical House, Inc.
25 West 45th Street
New York, New York 10036
Tel: 212-757-7840

Rainbow Film Effects, Inc.
45 West 45th Street
New York, New York 10036
Tel: 212-247-1676

Electrical Equipment

See also the listings under "Lighting Equipment."

California:

Acey Decy Equipment Co.
1123 North McCadden Place
Los Angeles, California 90038
Tel: 213-464-0201

Beckett Equipment Rentals
1025 North McCadden Place
Los Angeles, California 90038
Tel: 213-465-7141

Berkey Colortran Rental
1007 Isabel Street
Burbank, California 91502
Tel: 213-843-1200

R. L. Bevington, Inc.
650 North Bronson
Los Angeles, California 90004
Tel: 213-466-7778

Leonetti Cine Rentals
5609 West Sunset Boulevard
Los Angeles, California 90028
Tel: 213-469-2987

Lloyd-Davies Enterprises
1021 North McCadden Place
Los Angeles, California 90038
Tel: 213-462-1206

Mole-Richardson Company
937 North Sycamore
Los Angeles, California 90038
Tel: 213-654-3660

Morgan Rents
1123 North Lillian Way
Los Angeles, California 90038
Tel: 213-469-2704

Florida:

Film Equipment Rentals, Inc.
19812 N.E. Twelfth Place
North Miami, Florida 33162
Tel: 305-891-2703

New York:

Camera Mart, Inc.
456 West 55th Street
New York, New York 10019
Tel: 212-757-6977

F&B/Ceco, Inc.
315 West 43rd Street
New York, New York 10036
Tel: 212-586-1420

Film Equipment Rental
  Company
419 West 54th Street
New York, New York 10019
Tel: 212-581-5474

Equipment Rental

The suppliers included here offer a wide range of motion picture–related equipment for rental. See also "Camera Equipment, Sales & Rentals" under the heading Camera Equipment.

Arizona:

ABC Theatrical Rentals & Sales
825 North Seventh Street
Phoenix, Arizona 85006
Tel: 602-258-5204

Arizona Theatre Equipment &
Supply Co., Inc.
1410 East Washington
Phoenix, Arizona 85034
Tel: 602-254-0215

Audio Visual Center
5030 East Broadway
Tucson, Arizona 85711
Tel: 602-325-1515

Az-Tech Graphics
607 West Washington
Phoenix, Arizona 85004
Tel: 602-258-7731

Az-Tech Graphics
1520 East Broadway
Tucson, Arizona 85719
Tel: 602-624-8393

Camera World
7252 First Avenue
Scottsdale, Arizona 85251
Tel: 602-945-6692

Howard's Audio Visual
Equipment
1105 East Broadway
Tucson, Arizona 85719
Tel: 602-624-3821

Hughes-Calihan Corporation
415 East University Boulevard
Tucson, Arizona 85705
Tel: 602-623-0351

Movie Center
2505 East Thomas Road
Phoenix, Arizona 85016
Tel: 602-957-1860

Stage Sound
224 West University Drive
Phoenix, Arizona 85027
Tel: 602-967-9441

Studio Rentals, Inc., of Arizona
2321 East University Drive
Phoenix, Arizona 85034
Tel: 602-244-0361

Universal Audio Corporation
33 East McDowell Road
Phoenix, Arizona 85004
Tel: 602-257-1810

Western Mobile Equipment
   Corporation
609 West Rillito
Tucson, Arizona 85703
Tel: 602-792-3877

Zonar Corporation
2922 West Weldon
Phoenix, Arizona 85017
Tel: 602-264-2100

California:
Los Angeles area:

F&B/Ceco/SOS
7051 Santa Monica Boulevard
Los Angeles, California 90038
Tel: 213-466-9361

Movieola /Magnasync Corp.
1429 Ivar
Los Angeles, California 90028
Tel: 213-466-5233

Producers Equipment Center
5428 Satsuma
North Hollywood, California
   91603
Tel: 213-877-2179

San Francisco area:

American Zoetrope Film Facility
827 Folsom Street
San Francisco, California 94107
Tel: 415-989-0600

Cinerent West Inc.
155 Fell Street
San Francisco, California 94102
Tel: 415-864-4644

Ferco
363 Brannan Street
San Francisco, California 94102
Tel: 415-957-1787

Phelps & Kopp Company
991 Tennessee Street
San Francisco, California 94107
Tel: 415-285-1900

Colorado:

Entertainment Four Studios
1630 Chambers Road
Aurora, Colorado 80010
Tel: 303-341-5600

Western Cine
321 South Pearl Street
Denver, Colorado 80209
Tel: 303-744-1017

Florida:

Aberbach's of Miami Beach
441 Arthur Godfrey Road
Miami Beach, Florida 33139
Tel: 305-532-5446

Atlantic Photo Supplies Co. Inc.
8011 N.E. Second Avenue
Miami, Florida 33101
Tel: 305-757-7848

Cine Technical, Inc.
7330 N.E. Fourth Court
Miami, Florida 33101
Tel: 305-754-2611

Cinetel
14875 N.E. Twentieth Avenue
North Miami, Florida 33161
Tel: 305-947-4037

Film Equipment Rentals, Inc.
103 N.E. 79th Street
Miami, Florida 33101
Tel: 305-891-2703

Grove Stagecraft, Inc.
7101 N.E. Sixth Court
Miami, Florida 33101
Tel: 305-759-1842

Ideal Pictures Company
55 N.E. Thirteenth Street
Miami, Florida 33101
Tel: 305-374-8173

Image Devices, Inc.
811 N.W. Eleventh Street
Miami, Florida 33101
Tel: 305-751-1818

Moviemobile
103 N.E. 29th Street
Miami, Florida 33101
Tel: 305-891-2703

National Theatre Supply Division
of National Screen Service
14819 N.E. Twentieth Avenue
North Miami, Florida 33161
Tel: 305-947-0088

Southern Photo Technical
Service, Inc.
2737 N.W. 75th Street
Miami, Florida 33101
Tel: 305-693-3540

Spire Audio-Visual Co.
24 N.W. 36th Street
Miami, Florida 33101
Tel: 305-576-5736

Studio Center, Inc.
14875 N.E. Twentieth Avenue
North Miami, Florida 33161
Tel: 305-944-2911

Tyler Camera Systems
7330 N.E. Fourth Court
Miami, Florida 33101
Tel: 305-757-5988

Georgia:

A F E R
1846 Briarwood Road, N.E.
Atlanta, Georgia 30329
Tel: 404-633-4101

Cine Associates
3486 West Hospital Road
Atlanta, Georgia 30341
Tel: 404-457-1244

Cinevision
206 Fourteenth Street
Atlanta, Georgia 30304
Tel: 404-875-5616

Production Services Atlanta
2060 Peachtree Industrial Court
Atlanta, Georgia 30341
Tel: 404-451-4624

Bob Segars Lighting
781 Miami Circle
Atlanta, Georgia 30324
Tel: 404-633-5674

Bob Storer
2863 Mobry Lane, N.E.
Atlanta, Georgia 30319
Tel: 404-237-7642

Smith & Friends
Box 11594, Northside Station
Atlanta, Georgia 30305
Tel: 404-266-8717

Spratlin Brothers Stage Lighting
5700 Mallory Road
Red Oak, Georgia 30272
Tel: 404-964-2495

The Studio Center
445 Bishop Street
Atlanta, Georgia 30318
Tel: 404-874-2252

Winnebago
2650 North Decatur Road
Decatur, Georgia 30030
Tel: 404-292-2489

Massachusetts:

Film Associates
421 Broadway
Cambridge, Massachusetts 02138
Tel: 617-492-1062

Fitzgerald Motion Picture
 Service, Inc.
176 Newbury Street
Boston, Massachusetts 02106
Tel: 617-266-2512

Major Theatre Equipment
 Corporation
44 Winchester Street
Boston, Massachusetts 02106
Tel: 617-542-0445

New Mexico:

Acme Camera Repair
2117 San Mateo Boulevard, N.E.
Albuquerque, New Mexico 87110
Tel: 505-255-9831

Bandelier Films, Inc.
2001 Gold Avenue, S.E.
Albuquerque, New Mexico 87106
Tel: 505-242-2679

Biotechnica
Madrid Highway
Santa Fe, New Mexico 87501
Tel: 505-982-1431

Brooks Photo
401 Edith Boulevard, N.E.
Albuquerque, New Mexico 87102
Tel: 505-247-0189

The Camera Shop
109 East San Francisco
Santa Fe, New Mexico 87501
Tel: 505-983-6591

Casa de Cameras
8712 Gutierrez Road, N.E.
Albuquerque, New Mexico 87111
Tel: 505-299-5000

Decol's Inc.
1218 Seventeenth Street
Los Alamos, New Mexico 87544
Tel: 505-662-3091

Gibson Products Company
109 Adams, S.E.
Albuquerque, New Mexico 87108
Tel: 505-268-6466

Hanna & Hanna
218 Central Avenue, S.W.
Albuquerque, New Mexico 87101
Tel: 505-243-6126

Manzano Laboratories
4401 Lead Avenue, S.W.
Albuquerque, New Mexico 87102
Tel: 505-265-7511

Fred Patton Productions
418 1/2 Montezuma
Santa Fe, New Mexico 87501
Tel: 505-982-2504

New York:

The Camera Mart, Inc.
456 West 55th Street
New York, New York 10019
Tel: 212-757-6977
Samuel Hyman, President

Festivals

Only the American film festivals concentrating on feature films are included here. A directory of film and television festivals on a worldwide basis has been published by Back Stage, 165 West 46th Street, New York, New York 10036.

Of the American festivals included in this category, only the New York, Los Angeles, and San Francisco festivals are approved by the International Federation of Film Producers Associations. The Virgin Islands Film Festival is recognized by the International Festival Association.

ATLANTA INTERNATIONAL FILM FESTIVAL

Atlanta International Film
    Festival
J. Hunter Todd, Director &
    Founder
Drawer 13258K
Atlanta, Georgia 30324
Tel: 404-394-6225
Tel: 404-688-4000

After seven years of residence in Atlanta, the International Film Festival transferred its principal activities to the Virgin Islands. According to festival founder and director, J. Hunter Todd, "The Atlanta event will continue on a limited, reduced basis, following the Virgin Islands Film Festival by several weeks as a noncompetitive, invitational screening that will feature winners of the Virgin Islands Festival. The new Virgin Islands Film Festival will gain all major film market activities, the awards competition, and filmmaker participation during the ten-day No-vember event to be held in St. Thomas." The Atlanta festival, as its Virgin Islands counterpart, will screen films in six major categories: features, shorts, documentaries, experimental films, and two television categories.

CHICAGO INTERNATIONAL FILM FESTIVAL

Chicago International Film
    Festival
Michael J. Kutza, Jr., Director
12 East Grand Avenue
Chicago, Illinois 60611
Tel: 312-644-3400
Cable: CINEFEST/Chicago

The Chicago International Film Festival is a year-round, nonprofit, nongovernmental cultural and educational corporation formed to encourage the art form of film. The festival, a competitive event, is held annually in the fall. The festival award, the Hugo, is presented in ten major categories: feature film, documentary, short subject, student film, entertainment film for children, tel-

210

evision production, business and industrial, television commercial, theatrical commercial, and filmstrips. These ten categories are further divided into eighty-four subcategories. Further information concerning dates, entry fees, and requirements may be obtained from the festival director, Michael J. Kutza, Jr.

NEW YORK FILM FESTIVAL

New York Film Festival
Ms. Joanne Koch, Administrative Director
The Film Society of Lincoln Center
1865 Broadway
New York, New York 10023
Tel: 212-765-5100
Ext: 311

The New York Film Festival is a principal activity of the Film Society of Lincoln Center. Other Film Society activities include the sponsoring of a New Directors/New Films program at the Museum of Modern Art, "Movies in the Parks," and a Film-in-Education Program.

Martin E. Segal is president of the Film Society of Lincoln Center. Richard Roud is director of the New York Film Festival, and Joanne Koch is administrative director of the society.

The New York Film Festival is presented each fall, usually in September-October. The festival is noncompetitive. There are no prizes or entry fees, and selection is based on artistic excellence from films produced within a specified period (roughly the twelve-month period preceding the festival opening date), with certain exceptions. The annual

cutoff dates and the necessary application forms can be obtained from the Film Society of Lincoln Center. The completed application must accompany the submitted film.

THE LOS ANGELES INTERNATIONAL FILM EXPOSITION (FILMEX)

The Los Angeles International Film Exposition (Filmex)
Gary Essert, Director
Filmex Headquarters
P.O. Box 1739
Hollywood, California 90028
Tel: 213-846-5530
Cable: ROSEBUD/Los Angeles

Filmex is a nonprofit cultural organization founded in 1971. The fourteen-day annual exposition, held in the spring, is dedicated to presenting films not ordinarily available to the people of Los Angeles. The purpose of Filmex is to originate and coordinate special programs that illuminate the art of film. Filmex accomplishes this through the presentation of an annual film exposition of international scope and through several related activities.

Filmex is a noncompetitive, annual event, open to the general public, under the patronage of private sponsors and organizational grants. Principal screenings are held at a major motion picture theater. Each film is presented once; however, the director reserves the right to schedule a second public screening if deemed appropriate. Filmex is accredited by the International Federation of Film Producers Associations and is subject to its regulations.

Films may be new or vintage, of any length, and produced in any gauge or format. New films in current U.S. distribution are ineligible.

Films are chosen by the Filmex Selection Committee and staff. Additional information and application forms may be obtained from Gary Essert, director, or Gary Abrahams, associate director.

PHILADELPHIA INTERNATIONAL FILM FESTIVAL

Philadelphia International Film
   Festival
Ralph Moore, Director
Ninth and Walnut Streets
Philadelphia, Pennsylvania 19107
Tel: 215-629-0700
Cable: PHILMFEST

The Philadelphia International Film Festival presents motion pictures of short and feature length that exemplify the vitality of contemporary world cinema.

The festival's home is the Walnut Street Theatre, one of the United States' oldest performing arts centers. It is a nonprofit organization and a member of the Greater Philadelphia Cultural Alliance, the sponsoring body of the Philadelphia Festival, of which the Philadelphia International Film Festival is an integral part.

Works are exhibited in the film festival by invitation from the Selection Panel, and each film is honored with the Festival Award. All festival showings are open to the general public at the Walnut Street Theatre or other scheduled, publicly announced locations.

Films in languages other than English must have English subtitles and be available in 16mm or 35mm, preferably with optical soundtracks. Publicity material, complete credit listings, and 8 × 10 glossy stills should accompany prints when they are sent for consideration.

The cost of transporting films to the Selection Panel and to the festival is borne by the entrant on an insured, prepaid basis. All films will be covered by insurance while under the festival's care and will be returned by the least expensive means, unless other arrangements are made with the festival beforehand.

Only the finest care will be given to all films, but the festival, its management, or its Selection Panel cannot assume liability for damage to prints from normal use.

It is suggested that films from outside the United States be entered through a U.S. representative or diplomatic channels, thus avoiding delay and additional expense. In the case of works sent directly from abroad to Philadelphia, the following information must be in the festival's hands before shipment is made: (1) Title of the film and English translation. (2) Gauge of stock and running time. (3) Length of film in linear feet. (4) Number of reels and total weight. (5) Value in U.S. dollars. A copy of this declaration must be attached to the film itself and the shipment must be addressed to:

The Director

Philadelphia International Film Festival

Ninth and Walnut Streets

Philadelphia, Pennsylvania 19107 USA

"Notify Charles Kurz Company"

SAN FRANCISCO INTERNATIONAL FILM FESTIVAL

San Francisco International Film
Festival
Lorena Cantrell, Associate
Director
1409 Bush Street
San Francisco, California 94109
Tel: 415-928-8333
Cable: Filmfest San Francisco
USA

The San Francisco International
Film Festival is an annual event held
in October featuring the exhibition of
international films and presentation
of special in-person tributes honoring
actors, directors, producers, cinematographers and writers. The festival is
noncompetitive for features and
shorts, but competitive in two categories: television and film as communication.

The San Francisco International
Film Festival is organized as a non-
profit corporation. Festival officials
are: George Gund, Chairman;
Claude Jarman, Vice-Chairman;
Lorena Cantrell, Associate Director,
Programming-Administration; Mark
Chase, Associate Director, Program-
ming-Publicity; Martin Rubin, As-
sociate Director, Tributary Programs.

TELLURIDE FILM FESTIVAL

Telluride Film Festival
Stella Hartwig Pence, Denver
Coordinator
1228 Fifteenth Street
Denver, Colorado 80202
Tel: 303-222-3653

The Telluride Film Festival is a
three-day annual event presented in
early September in Telluride, Colo
rado. The First Annual Telluride
Film Festival, held in 1974, attracted
considerable nationwide attention because of the personal appearances of
Francis Ford Coppola, Gloria Swanson, and Leni Riefenstahl. Telluride
is a noncompetition festival and no
awards are presented. The film selection committee consists of the festival's three directors: James Card,
Tom Luddy, and Bill Pence. Films
are screened in the restored Sheridan
Opera House, capacity 250, in Telluride, a resuscitated ghost town.

USA FILM FESTIVAL

USA Film Festival
Ms. Mary K. MacFarland,
Assistant Director/Coproducer
P.O. Box 3105
Dallas, Texas 75275
Tel: 214-692-2979

The USA Film Festival, held annually in the spring, features a week of premieres of the best American films of the year, shorts, and features, as selected by a panel of leading American film critics. The festival, which presents no awards, restricts its offerings to films directed by directors of American citizenship. Either the producer, director, or star is present onstage with a critic for audience discussions following every screening. All films, except the annual Great Director's Retrospective, are either world or regional premieres. Other festival events that occur throughout the year include Great Actor, Producer, or Screenwriter Retrospectives, and a Children's Film Festival. The festival, which operates as a nonprofit corporation, is staffed by Dr. G. William Jones, Director; Mary K. MacFarland, Coproducer/Associate Director; Nancy A. Willen, Coproducer/Publicity Director.

THE VIRGIN ISLANDS FILM FESTIVAL

The Virgin Islands Film Festival
J. Hunter Todd, Founder &
    President
St. Thomas, Virgin Islands 00801
Tel: 809-774-3050
Cable: PARADISE/USVI

The International Film Festival, founded by J. Hunter Todd and headquartered for seven years in Atlanta, shifted its base of operations during 1975 to the U.S. Virgin Islands. Sponsorship of the renamed festival, the Virgin Islands Festival, is by the Virgin Islands Film Society, a nonprofit corporation. The festival is planned as an annual, competitive event and film market to be held in November, uniting film professionals from North, Central and South America. Film competition is divided into six major categories: features, shorts, documentaries, experimental films, and two television categories. Subcategories in each major area detail all types of film and tape production. Special categories will be formed for students, super 8mm, and independent films. Coordination for the festival is supplied by the Film Promotion Office of the Virgin Islands Department of Commerce. Further information and application blanks may be obtained from the director.

Film Commissions

Surveyed here are the film production assistance facilities and personnel of fifty states, Puerto Rico, the U.S. Virgin Islands, and the two American ci maintaining film offices, New York and San Francisco. As of press ti sixteen states plus the Virgin Islands operate film assistance offices, a legislation creating film commissions is pending in another handful of sta Considerable informal assistance is available in quite a few other states, indicated below. Approximately 35% of all films produced in the Uni States are produced outside California.

In addition to the production assistance available from the offic governmental sources included in this category, certain private organizati and individuals provide similar services. See "Locations & Locat Assistance."

Alabama:

Alabama Development Office
Doug Benton, Director, Publicity
and Information
State Highway Building, Room
403
Montgomery, Alabama 36104
Tel: 205-269-7171

Alabama has no formal film assistance program or office. Information
and assistance is supplied on an ad
hoc basis by the Alabama Development Office.

Alaska:

Alaska Division of Tourism
Rick Kiefer, Travel Information
Officer
Pouch E
Juneau, Alaska 99811
Tel: 907-465-2010

Alaska has no formal film as
tance program at present, but L
tenant Governor Lowell Thomas,
who has a professional backgroun(
motion picture production, is in
ested in instituting a program.

Arizona:

Office of Economic Planning a
Development
Fred Graham, Motion Picture
Development Coordinator
1645 West Jefferson, Room 4
Phoenix, Arizona 85007
Tel: 602-271-5011

Arizona has an active mot
picture coordination office as a sect
of the Office of Economic Plann
and Development. Arizona claim:
ranks third, following California a
New York, in terms of American f
production in recent months. T
state publishes a film kit and provi
producers with answers to spec
questions upon request.

Arkansas:

Department of Parks and
  Tourism
Max Love, Assistance Travel
  Director
State Capitol
Little Rock, Arkansas 72201
Tel: 501-371-1121

Arkansas does not maintain a
formal film assistance staff. Members
of the Arkansas Department of Parks
and Tourism have in the past been
available in advisory capacities to
producers interested in Arkansas locations.

California:

President, Board of Public Works
Sol M. Marcus, Commissioner
Room 368, City Hall
200 North Spring Street
Los Angeles, California 90012
Tel: 213-485-3371

The City of Los Angeles has joined
with motion picture industry members based in the metropolitan area to
form the Los Angeles Film Development Committee to assist producers
filming locally.

San Francisco Convention &
  Visitors Bureau
Louise B. Miller, Marketing
  Coordinator
1390 Market Street
San Francisco, California 94102
Tel: 415-626-5500

San Francisco has an official
motion picture coordinator headquartered on the staff of the San Francisco
Convention & Visitors Bureau. The
bureau has published *Location: San
Francisco, The Film-Makers Handbook,* a
comprehensive guide to filmmaking
in the Bay Area. In addition to the
listing of suppliers, technicians, and
production adjuncts, details are included on permits required for location shooting on all public land in the
area and in public institutions.

California State Department of
  Commerce
Motion Picture Development
  Council
Frederick A. Ricci, Manager,
  Division of Business and
  Industry Development
1400 Tenth Street
Sacramento, California 95814
Tel: 916-445-2008

Surprisingly, California had no
formal motion picture development
program until 1974. The Motion
Picture Development Council was
created by the 1974 legislature as part
of a bill establishing a motion picture
development unit in the Division of
Economic Development. As yet the
council has not produced a state
directory or film kit. Organizations
and individuals seeking assistance
within the state should contact the
council. As noted below, the city of
Los Angeles maintains a one-stop
permit office to expedite the obtaining
of necessary shooting permits within
the city.

Colorado:

Governor's Motion Picture and
Television Advisory
Commission
Karol W. Smith, Director
600 State Capitol Annex
Denver, Colorado 80203
Tel: 303-892-2205

The Colorado Motion Picture and
Television Advisory Commission has
been active since 1969. It has produced a 52-page manual that contains a community profile section and
a special services section. The community profile section contains a
breakdown by community or location,
area contact, transportation, hotels,
motels, restaurants, catering services,
equipment, and unique features of
each area. The special services section
contains information on inter- and
intrastate transportation, special
equipment and props, guilds and
unions, film services, special towns
and streets, studios and production
companies, and talent agencies available in the state. Also contained in the
manual are listings for brochures on
the state and in-state directories. This
manual is available to all motion
picture and television production
companies and independent filmmakers upon request.

The commission likewise provides
location assistance, transportation arrangements, and maintains a comprehensive photo file.

Connecticut:

Connecticut Department of
Commerce
Hugo T. Saglio, Chief,
Communications Services
210 Washington Street
Hartford, Connecticut 06106
Tel: 203-566-5456

A bill to establish a Connecticut
motion picture commission to promote local film production has been
introduced, but the commission has
not been created as of press time.
Pending the organization of a formal
film assistance program, interested
parties should contact the Department of Commerce.

Delaware:

Delaware State Visitors Service
Donald R. Mathewson, Visitors
Information Officer
45 The Green
Dover, Delaware 19901
Tel: 302-678-4254

Delaware has no formal film assistance office and information requests
are handled by the State Visitor
Service.

Florida:

Bureau of Marketing
Development
Ben Harris, Administrator,
Motion Picture and TV
Services
Room 530 VA
107 West Gaines Street
Tallahassee, Florida 32304
Tel: 904-488-5507

Florida is a new member of the
group of states active in film production assistance with the formation of a
Motion Picture and TV Services
office. The office has produced two
comprehensive directories: *Regulations
Directory,* which concentrates on per-
mit-granting authorities within the
state, and *Directory of the Florida Motion
Picture and Television Industry.* The latter

directory pinpoints the craftsmen, suppliers, and professionals in the Florida motion picture industry. Copies of both directories are available from the Bureau of Marketing Development.

Georgia:

Georgia Department of
    Community Development
Ed Spivia, Director, Public
    Relations
P.O. Box 38097
Atlanta, Georgia 30334
Tel: 404-656-3552

Georgia is very active in film production coordination. Among the services available from film coordinator Ed Spivia's office are: in-state transportation, photography, liaison, coordination, permits, chamber of commerce assistance, accommodations, and weather information. The Georgia film office produces an impressive film kit that includes a talent and services directory.

Hawaii:

Department of Planning and
    Economic Development
Hideto Kono, Director
P.O. Box 2359
Honolulu, Hawaii 96804
Tel: 808-548-3033

Hawaii does not have a formal film production assistance program but encourages film production in the islands. Information requests should be directed to the Economic Development Division of the state government in Honolulu.

Idaho:

Division of Tourism & Industrial
    Development
Lloyd D. Howe, Administrator
Capitol Building
Boise, Idaho 83720
Tel: 208-384-2470

Idaho does not have a formal program for encouraging the filming of motion pictures locally but does have staff available to assist in location scouting. Requests for information should be routed to the Division of Tourism & Industrial Development.

Illinois:

Illinois Film Services
Richard M. Holtzman, Director
205 West Wacker Drive, Suite
    1100
Chicago, Illinois 60606
Tel: 312-793-3600

Illinois Film Services is the film production assistance office for the state. It publishes a comprehensive directory of service organizations, suppliers, and film industry professionals. Copies of the directory are available from the Illinois Film Services office in Chicago.

Indiana:

Indiana Department of
    Commerce
Walter J. Schuchmann, Director
332 State House
Indianapolis, Indiana 46204
Tel: 317-633-4450

Indiana has no film production assistance program. Inquiries should be directed to the Department of Commerce.

Iowa:

Iowa Development Commission
Phil Morgan, Public Information
   Supervisor
250 Jewett Building
Des Moines, Iowa 50309
Tel: 515-281-3251

As the state's chief promotion agency, the Iowa Development Commission acts as production liaison in the absence of a formal film assistance program.

Kansas:

George Mathews, Director of
   Tourism
State Office Building
Topeka, Kansas 66612
Tel: 913-296-3481

The state of Kansas does not maintain a special office to provide assistance in motion picture production. The contact within the state is the director of tourism.

Kentucky:

Department of Public
   Information
W. L. Knight, Director,
   Advertising and Travel
   Promotion
Capitol Annex Building
Frankfort, Kentucky 40601
Tel: 502-564-4930

In the absence of a Kentucky film assistance office, the travel division processes information requests and lends assistance to filmmakers.

Louisiana:

Louisiana Film Commission
Nick Pollacia, Jr., Director
Box 44185, Capitol Station
Baton Rouge, Louisiana 70804
Tel: 504-389-5371

The Louisiana Film Commission was formed in 1974 as a division of the Department of Commerce and Industry. The commission, in addition to providing answers to specific questions about filming in Louisiana, has compiled a directory of Louisiana suppliers, service organizations and film professionals.

Maine:

Maine Department of Commerce
   and Industry
Paul J. Fournier, Publicity
   Representative, Promotion
   Division
State Capitol
Augusta, Maine 04330
Tel: 207-289-2656

The state of Maine cooperates with filmmakers informally through the Department of Commerce and Industry, but maintains no staff for the purpose of offering full-time production assistance.

Maryland:

Maryland Department of
    Economic & Community
    Development
William A. Pate, Director
2525 Riva Road
Annapolis, Maryland 21401
Tel: 301-267-5265

Maryland has no film production assistance office and information requests should be directed to the Department of Economic & Community Development.

Massachusetts:

Department of Commerce and
    Development
Ernest A. Lucci, Deputy
    Commissioner, Division of
    Vacation/Tourism
Leverett Saltonstall Building,
    Government Center
100 Cambridge Street
Boston, Massachusetts 02202
Tel: 617-727-3221

Massachusetts has no official film assistance staff or facility and assistance to filmmakers is provided by the Vacation/Tourism Division of the Department of Commerce and Development.

Michigan:

Office of Economic Expansion
David E. Sanger, Industrial
    Representative, Industrial
    Development Division
Law Building
Lansing, Michigan 48913
Tel: 517-373-3530

No state office exists in Michigan for the express purpose of assisting filmmaking operations, but three private, nonprofit organizations have been formed to foster film production. The Industrial Development Division of the Office of Economic Expansion is the state office presently coordinating liaison between organizations and filmmakers.

Minnesota:

Department of Economic
    Development
David K. Cummings, Director,
    Publicity & Promotion Division
480 Cedar Street
St. Paul, Minnesota 55101
Tel: 612-296-5021

The Department of Economic Development is anxious to provide help to visiting filmmakers but maintains no special office for film production assistance. The Publicity and Promotion Director of the Department of Economic Development is the person to call.

Mississippi:

Mississippi Film Commission
Charles W. Allen, Director
2000 Walter Sillers Building
Jackson, Mississippi 39205
Tel: 601-354-6711

The Mississippi Film Commission is the official state agency charged with assisting filmmakers. The commission can provide assistance with scouting locations, housing, government, and expediting permits.

Missouri:

Division of Commerce and
Industrial Development
Dave Eppelsheimer, Research
Associate
P.O. Box 118
Jefferson City, Missouri 65101
Tel: 314-751-4241

Missouri advises that it has "exquisite beauty and historic sites, but alas no program for assistance in motion picture production other than supplying information." The Division of Commerce and Industrial Development, which supplies the information, is most helpful.

Montana:

Department of Highways
Scott Warden, Montana Motion
 Picture Coordinator
Helena, Montana 59601
Tel: 406-449-2654

In Los Angeles:
Patrick Mathews
2400 West Silver Lake Drive
Los Angeles, California 90039
Tel: 213-665-2429

Montana has become active in soliciting film production and, in addition to having a Motion Picture Coordinator attached to the Travel Promotion Unit, has produced a comprehensive *Motion Picture & Television Location Manual*. Montana also maintains a Motion Picture Location Coordinator in Los Angeles. The Los Angeles coordinator contacts producers whose scripts could be shot in Montana, and shows them a pres-

entation of Montana scenics and facilities. He then sends the script to Montana where the film office shoot photos and matches them to scenes in the script. The film office acquire local contacts, motel rates, weather information, air facilities, catering and other information for the producer. If the production team visit the state for scouting, transportation and personal assistance is provided by the office. Scott Warden is the very efficient coordinator of the film location division.

Nebraska:

Department of Economic
 Development
Don A. Atwater, Public
 Information Director
Box 94666, State Capitol
Lincoln, Nebraska 68509
Tel: 402-477-8984

While Nebraska does not have a state film commission, the governor has designated the Department of Economic Development to act in his behalf in accommodating motion picture companies and film producers. The Public Information Director of that department is the local contact.

Nevada:

Motion Picture Division
Department of Economic
 Development
Carson City, Nevada 89701
Tel: 702-882-7478

In Las Vegas:
Las Vegas News Bureau
Convention Center
3150 Paradise Road
Las Vegas, Nevada 89109
Tel: 702-735-3611

Nevada maintains a Motion Picture Division within the Department of Economic Development in the state capitol as well as an adjunct office in Las Vegas.

New Hampshire:

New Hampshire Office of
    Industrial Development
Paul H. Guilderson, Director
P.O. Box 856, State House Annex
Concord, New Hampshire 03301
Tel: 603-271-2591

Film production coordination in New Hampshire is handled by the Office of Industrial Development.

New Jersey:

Division of Economic
    Development
Thomas A. Kelly, Director
P.O. Box 2766
Trenton, New Jersey 08625
Tel: 609-292-7757

New Jersey has no film production assistance program and inquiries should be directed to the Division of Economic Development.

New Mexico:

New Mexico Motion Picture
    Industry Commission
Howard A. Rubin, Director
1050 Old Pecos Trail
Santa Fe, New Mexico 87501
Tel: 505-827-2889

In Los Angeles:
Fred Banker Associates
3467 Wrightwood Drive
Studio City, California 91604
Tel: 213-877-0691

The New Mexico Motion Picture Industry Commission maintains offices both in Santa Fe and Los Angeles, and publishes a New Mexico location and services manual. The most recent statistics available indicate productions with total budgets of about $20,000,000 have been filmed in New Mexico during the last two years.

New York:

Department of Commerce
Stanley Freedgood, Deputy
    Commissioner, Division of
    Public Information
99 Washington Avenue
Albany, New York 12245
Tel: 518-474-1141

Motion picture production assistance outside New York City is centered in the Division of Public Information, which has no separate staff or funding for aiding filmmakers, but does maintain a location identification file. The Department of Commerce, of which the Division of Public Information is a part, has been designated to act as liaison between producers and state agencies, such as state parks and institutions, whose facilities producers might wish to use.

City of New York

Walter Wood, Director, Office for
  Motion Pictures and Television
415 Madison Avenue
New York, New York 10017
Tel: 212-593-8970

After an eleven-month hiatus following the departure of Mayor Lindsay, Mayor Beame in December, 1974 appointed Walter Wood as director of the city's Office for Motion Pictures and Television. At the same time Mayor Beame unveiled a Mayor's Advisory Council on Motion Pictures and Television comprising thirty members. New York City's one-stop film office handles the issuance of permits and is adept at troubleshooting production problems that arise with the thirty-odd motion picture unions in the city.

North Carolina:

Department of Natural and
  Economic Resources
Ms. Barbara Clifton, Special
  Projects Coordinator, Travel
  and Promotion Division
P.O. Box 27687
Raleigh, North Carolina 27611
Tel: 919-829-4171

The Special Projects Coordinator of the Travel and Promotion Division has the responsibility to assist motion picture production in North Carolina. Interested film companies are supplied possible location sites and general information. If the company then decides to film in North Carolina, the coordinator provides local contacts and expedites the granting of permits within state agencies.

North Dakota:

Business and Industrial
  Development Department
Bruce Bartch, Director
State Office Building
Bismarck, North Dakota 58501
Tel: 701-224-2810

North Dakota has no formal film assistance program, and requests for information should be directed to the Business and Industrial Development Department.

Ohio:

Department of Economic and
  Community Development
Ms. Sunny Hersh, Advertising
  Bureau
State Office Tower
30 East Broad Street
Columbus, Ohio 43215
Tel: 614-466-2480

The Advertising Bureau of the Department of Economic and Community Development handles state coordination with filmmakers, including location assistance and permissions from government agencies and local organizations.

Oklahoma:

Oklahoma Tourism & Recreation
  Commission
Tom Gray, Manager, Special
  Projects
500 Will Rogers Building
Oklahoma City, Oklahoma 73105
Tel: 405-521-3981

or: Lieutenant Governor
George Nigh

Tel: 405-521-2161

Oklahoma does not have a staff designated to work full-time on motion picture production assistance. Under a 1971 law, however, the Tourism Promotion Division of the Tourism & Recreation Department was instructed to promote, encourage, and assist motion picture production business within the state. The department has published a production booklet containing location data and a comprehensive policy statement on motion picture production.

Oregon:

Oregon State Economic
  Development Division
Edward J. Whelan, Director
Loyalty Building, Ninth Floor
317 S.W. Alder Street
Portland, Oregon 97204
Tel: 503-229-5535

Oregon has no film office and requests for assistance should be directed to the State Economic Development Division.

Continental Operations Branch
Economic Development
  Administration
Carlos A. Molina, Industrial
  Representative, Commonwealth
  of Puerto Rico
1290 Avenue of the Americas
New York, New York 10019
Tel: 212-245-1200

Legislation to create a Puerto Rican Institute of Cinematographic Arts and Industries to promote filmmaking in Puerto Rico has been introduced in the Commonwealth Legislature. As of press time no action on the proposed legislation had taken place. Pending the creation of the institute, film production assistance will be rendered, as in the past, by the commonwealth's Economic Development Administration.

Pennsylvania:

Pennsylvania Department of
  Commerce
Walter G. Arader, Secretary
South Office Building
Harrisburg, Pennsylvania 17120
Tel: 717-787-3003

Pennsylvania has no film office and requests for assistance and information should be directed to the Department of Commerce.

Rhode Island:

Rhode Island Department of
  Economic Development
James Roberson, Director
One Weybosset Hill
Providence, Rhode Island 02908
Tel: 401-277-2601

Rhode Island has no film office and information requests should be directed to the Department of Economic Development.

South Carolina:

State Development Board
Bob Glover, Associate Director
P.O. Box 927
Columbia, South Carolina 29202
Tel: 803-758-3145

The State Development Board of South Carolina can lend site location assistance and acts as the film production liaison office within the state.

South Dakota:

South Dakota Department of
Economic and Tourism
Development
Bill Honerkamp, State Travel
Director
423 East Capitol
Pierre, South Dakota 57501
Tel: 605-224-3301

As the state travel director wryly puts it, "South Dakota isn't exactly the motion picture capital of the world." The Department of Economic and Tourist Development, however, is equipped to supply limited assistance to filmmakers. The Division of Tourism assists producers in locating sites, personnel, props, and equipment.

Tennessee:

Tourism Development Division
Ms. Martha Boyd, Travel
Industry Specialist
1028 Andrew Jackson State Office
Building
Nashville, Tennessee 37219
Tel: 615-741-3282

Tennessee has compiled and produced a location guide that is available to producers. The state does not maintain a film assistance office, and production assistance is a joint effort of the Industrial Development and Tourism divisions of the Department of Economic and Community Development.

Texas:

Texas Film Commission
Ms. Diane Booker, Director
P.O. Box 12428, Capitol Station
Austin, Texas 78711
Tel: 512-475-3785

With 276,000 square miles of possible locations, it is not surprising that Texas is actively engaged in film production assistance. The Texas Film Commission has compiled a directory of services, suppliers, and professionals located within the state. The commission provides location assistance and maintains an extensive library of Texas towns and landscapes available for previewing. Liaison with state, local, and federal agencies is supplied as well as general assistance in making contacts and obtaining cooperation. The commission's assistant director, Rod Davis, edits their interesting bimonthly newsletter *FILMTEXAS!*

Utah:

Utah Travel Council
Hal Schlueter, Movie/TV
  Coordinator
Council Hall–Capitol Hill
Salt Lake City, Utah 84114
Tel: 801-328-5681

Utah includes a motion picture and television coordinator on the staff of the Utah Travel Council. The state also produces a film kit that includes a location site manual.

Vermont:

Vermont Agency of Development
  and Community Affairs
Tony Egan, Chief of Marketing
  and Travel
Montpelier, Vermont 05602
Tel: 802-828-3236

While the state of Vermont has no individual or office to coordinate motion picture production, the Information/Travel Division of the Agency of Development and Community Affairs serves as liaison between film units and local communities.

Virgin Islands:

U.S. Virgin Islands Department
  of Commerce
Winston deLugo, Director, Film
  Promotion Office
P.O. Box 1692
St. Thomas, Virgin Islands 00801
Tel: 809-774-1331

The U.S. Virgin Islands has been active in film production assistance since the formation of a Film Promotion Office in the Department of Commerce in 1974. The Film Promotion Office is the only one-stop film office in the Caribbean. The office provides production assistance, red-tape cutting, and local contacts. Rental helicopters with Tyler mounts, studio space, and a wide range of equipment and personnel for underwater photography are available. Dawn Blackford is the very capable production coordinator.

Virginia:

Virginia State Travel Service
Robert J. Spiker, Director of
  Audio-Visual Services
6 North Sixth Street
Richmond, Virginia 23219
Tel: 804-770-2051

Virginia has initiated a film production assistance unit in the Richmond office of the Virginia State Travel Service and has published a handsome promotional kit for producers, *Film Production the Virginia Way.* The office of Audio-Visual Services has 10,000 photographs on file, is equipped to provide production services anywhere in Virginia, and can answer specific questions as they arise. In-state transportation and liaison with law enforcement agencies are likewise provided.

Washington:

Department of Commerce &
Economic Development
Hank Pearson, Coordinator,
Motion Picture Bureau
General Administration Building
Olympia, Washington 98504
Tel: 206-753-3065

The Motion Picture Bureau of the Department of Commerce & Economic Development offers a one-stop service for filmmakers. Included are such functions as providing site photos, securing permits, providing a wide range of information, and making available free transportation to potential filming locations.

West Virginia:
Industrial Development Division

West Virginia Department of
Commerce
Christopher L. Potts, Industrial
Representative
State Office Building 6
1900 Washington Street, East
Charleston, West Virginia 25305
Tel: 304-348-2234

West Virginia maintains no film office and liaison is supplied to interested filmmakers by the Industrial Development Division of the West Virginia Department of Commerce

Wisconsin:

Wisconsin Department of
Business Development
William C. Kidd, Secretary
123 West Washington Avenue
Madison, Wisconsin 53702
Tel: 608-266-3222

Wisconsin does not have specific facilities and staff to assist motion picture production in the state, but the Department of Business Development encourages film production and is equipped to supply assistance on an ad hoc basis.

Wyoming:

Wyoming Travel Commission
Randy Wagner, Assistant
Director
2320 Capitol Avenue
Cheyenne, Wyoming 82002
Tel: 307-777-7777

The state of Wyoming has no special agency to attract or financially assist film production companies. The Wyoming Travel Commission has frequently worked with film producers providing the following services: location scouting, landowner permission, state-federal agency coordination, local contacts and casting, and photographic assistance.

Film Libraries

Arcoa International
2727 North Central Avenue
Phoenix, Arizona 85004
Tel: 602-263-6641

Craig Pease Enterprises
P.O. Box 1118
Scottsdale, Arizona 85252
Tel: 602-945-4807

California:
Los Angeles area:

Auto Racing Library
160 North San Jose Drive
Glendora, California 91740
Tel: 213-963-2055

Lem Bailey Color Stock Library
7934 Santa Monica Boulevard
Los Angeles, California 90046
Tel: 213-654-8197

California International
    Productions
6710 Melrose Avenue
Los Angeles, California 90038
Tel: 213-939-1491

Cinema Pictures, Inc.
10212 Noble Avenue
Mission Hills, California 91340
Tel: 213-892-6797

Vincent' Cobb
P.O. Box 5432
Beverly Hills, California 90210
Tel: 213-277-5554

Color Stock Library, Inc.
7934 Santa Monica Boulevard
Los Angeles, California 90046
Tel: 213-654-9550

de Forest Research
5451 Marathon Street
Los Angeles, California 90038
Tel: 213-469-2271

Moe DiSesso Rental Library
13618 Van Nuys Boulevard
Pacoima, California 91331
Tel: 213-899-4905

Larry Dorn Associates/World
    Backgrounds
9145 Sunset Boulevard
Los Angeles, California 90069
Tel: 213-274-7233

Elmer Dyer
711 North La Jolla
Los Angeles, California 90046
Tel: 213-655-5447

Evco Film Library
838 North Seward Street
Los Angeles, California 90038
Tel: 213-464-9252

Film Effects of Hollywood, Inc.
1140 North Citrus Avenue
Los Angeles, California 90038
Tel: 213-469-5808

Films, Inc.
5626 Hollywood Boulevard
Los Angeles, California 90028
Tel: 213-466-5481

Fox Movietonews Library
10201 West Pico Boulevard
Los Angeles, California 90035
Tel: 213-277-2211
Ext: 2851

Hollywood Film Archive
8344 Melrose Avenue
Los Angeles, California 90069
Tel: 213-933-3345

Hollywood Stock Film Library
1041 North Formosa Avenue
Los Angeles, California 90046
Tel: 213-851-2030

Frank Jones Associates
1150 West Olive Street
Burbank, California 91506
Tel: 213-843-2031

Stacy Keach Productions
5216 Laurel Canyon Boulevard
North Hollywood, California
  91607
Tel: 213-877-0472

Cameron McKay Productions
6850 Lexington Avenue
Los Angeles, California 90038
Tel: 213-463-6073

Metro-Goldwyn-Mayer, Inc.
10202 West Washington
  Boulevard
Culver City, California 90230
Tel: 213-836-3000

Lillian Michelson Research
  Library
501 Doheny Road
Beverly Hills, California 90210
Tel: 213-654-7177

Parachuting Associates
5300 Santa Monica Boulevard
Los Angeles, California 90029
Tel: 213-464-7124
Paramount Studios

Pippin Production Associates
3344 Mentone Avenue
Los Angeles, California 90034
Tel: 213-838-6292

Producers Library Service
7325 Santa Monica Boulevard
Los Angeles, California 90046
Tel: 213-851-2201

Q-Ed Productions
2921 West Alameda Boulevard
Burbank, California 91505
Tel: 213-849-2275

Ernest Reshovsky
2419 Claremont Avenue
Los Angeles, California 90027
Tel: 213-651-4220

Glen R. Roland, Jr.
8543 Clifton Way
Beverly Hills, California 90211
Tel: 213-271-0533

Allan Sandler Film Libraries, Inc.
1001 North Poinsettia Place
Los Angeles, California 90028
Tel: 213-876-2021

Sherman-Grinberg Film
  Libraries, Inc.
1040 North McCadden Place
Los Angeles, California 90038
Tel: 213-464-7491

Studio Archives
3950 Laurel Canyon Boulevard
Studio City, California 91604
Tel: 213-345-3500

TWA Film & Television
  Promotions
308 North Rodeo Drive
Beverly Hills, California 90211
Tel: 213-276-1194

Trans-American Film
  Corporation
1680 North Vine Street
Los Angeles, California 90028
Tel: 213-466-7575

United Airlines
626 Wilshire Boulevard
Los Angeles, California 90017
Tel: 213-482-2000

Universal City Studios
100 Universal City Plaza
Universal City, California 91608
Tel: 213-985-4321

Wolfe Worldwide Films
1657 Sawtelle Boulevard
Los Angeles, California 90025
Tel: 213-879-1360

San Francisco area:

Above San Francisco Company
444 Market Street
San Francisco, California 94111
Tel: 415-981-1135

The Cinema Verite Company
115 New Montgomery Street
San Francisco, California 94105
Tel: 415-566-6776

Contemporary Films/McGraw-
  Hill
1714 Stockton Street
San Francisco, California 94133
Tel: 415-362-3115

Media Generalists
69 Clementina Street
San Francisco, California 94105
Tel: 415-433-3337

Modern Talking Picture Service
16 Spear Street
San Francisco, California 94105
Tel: 415-982-1712

San Francisco Newsreel
630 Natoma Street
San Francisco, California 94103
Tel: 415-621-6196

Westcoast Films
25 Lusk Street
San Francisco, California 94107
Tel: 415-362-4700

Hawaii:

Cine-Pic Hawaii
1847 Pacific Heights Road
Honolulu, Hawaii 96813
Tel: 808-533-2677

David Cornwell Productions, Inc.
1358 Kapiolani Boulevard
Honolulu, Hawaii 96814
Tel: 808-949-7000

Film Services of Hawaii, Ltd.
716 Cooke Street
Honolulu, Hawaii 96813
Tel: 808-538-1928

Hawaii State Library
478 South King
Honolulu, Hawaii 96813
Tel: 808-548-2340

Standard Oil Film Library
227 Mokauea
Honolulu, Hawaii 96819
Tel: 808-841-0072

Nebraska:

Modern Sound Pictures, Inc.
1402 Howard Street
Omaha, Nebraska 68102
Tel: 402-341-8476

New York:

American Airlines
633 Third Avenue
New York, New York 10017
Tel: 212-867-1234

Eastern Airlines
10 Rockefeller Plaza
New York, New York 10020
Tel: 212-986-4500

Fotosonic, Inc.
15 West 46th Street
New York, New York 10036
Tel: 212-586-0355

Haberstroh Special Effects
    Studios, Inc.
9 West Nineteenth Street
New York, New York 10003
Tel: 212-255-1827

Hearst Metrotone News
235 East 45th Street
New York, New York 10017
Tel: 212-682-7690

Modern Talking Picture Service,
    Inc.
1212 Avenue of the Americas
New York, New York 10019
Tel: 212-586-5530

Museum of Modern Art Film
    Library
11 West 53rd Street
New York, New York 10019
Tel: 212-245-8900

NBC Films, Inc.
30 Rockefeller Plaza
New York, New York 10020
Tel: 212-247-8300

Charles Ross, Inc.
333 West 52nd Street
New York, New York 10019
Tel: 212-246-5470

Sherman-Grinberg Film
    Libraries, Inc.
630 Ninth Avenue
New York, New York 10036
Tel: 212-765-5170

Stratford International Film
  Searchers, Inc.
250 West 57th Street
New York, New York 10019
Tel: 212-586-3828

Telenews Film Corporation
235 East 45th Street
New York, New York 10017
Tel: 212-682-5600

Trans America Film Corporation
888 Seventh Avenue
New York, New York 10019
Tel: 212-582-7232

UPITN Corporation
460 West 54th Street
New York, New York 10019
Tel: 212-682-0400

Visnews Film Library
30 Rockefeller Plaza
New York, New York 10020
Tel: 212-541-7150

Oklahoma:

Douglas Productions
1300 McGee Drive, Suite 106A
Norman, Oklahoma 73069
Tel: 405-321-1200

Texas:

Piccadilly Films International
  Company, Ltd.
1802 N.E. Loop 410, Gold Carpet
  Suite
San Antonio, Texas 78246
Tel: 512-824-3548

Washington:

Northwoods Studio
Building 7, Suite 104
300 120th Avenue, N.E.
Bellevue, Washington 98005
Tel: 206-454-9470

Seattle Motion Picture Service
4717 Aurora North
Seattle, Washington 98103
Tel: 206-632-3717

Film Repair

Listings in this category include film preservation, treatment, and rejuv nation.

California:

Artisan Releasing Corporation
9200 Sunset Boulevard
Los Angeles, California 90069
Tel: 213-278-2670

C. H. Carleton Company
7608 San Fernando Road
Sun Valley, California 91352
Tel: 213-767-8507

Cine-Chrome Labs
4075 Transport Street
Palo Alto, California 94303
Tel: 415-321-5678

Filmtreat International
  Corporation
730 Salem Street
Glendale, California 91203
Tel: 213-242-2181

Frank Jones Associates
1150 Olive Avenue
Burbank, California 91506
Tel: 213-843-2031

Leonard Film Service
1700 East Walnut Street
Pasadena, California 91106
Tel: 213-681-9950

Peerless Film Processing
  Corporation
829 North Highland Avenue
Los Angeles, California 90038
Tel: 213-466-6341

Permafilm of California, Inc.
137 North La Brea Avenue
Los Angeles, California 90036
Tel: 213-936-1156

Producers Film Center
948 North Sycamore Avenue
Hollywood, California 90038
Tel: 213-851-1122

New Jersey:

Filmlife Inc.
Filmlife Building
141 Moonachie Road
Moonachie, New Jersey 07074
Tel: 201-440-8500

New York:

Filmtreat International
  Corporation
250 West 64th Street
New York, New York 10023
Tel: 212-799-2500

Peerless Film Processing
  Corporation
250 West 64th Street
New York, New York 10023
Tel: 212-799-2500

Utah:

Stockdale and Company, Inc.
200 East First South
Salt Lake City, Utah 84111
Tel: 801-521-3505

Film Shipping

California:

Los Angeles area:

Air Sea Forwarders
10425 South La Cienega
  Boulevard
Los Angeles, California 90045
Tel: 213-776-1611

B & W Film Delivery
1972 West Washington Boulevard
Los Angeles, California 90018
Tel: 213-735-8383

Barnett International Forwarders,
  Inc., of California
8635 Aviation Boulevard
Inglewood, California 90301
Tel: 213-776-1178

Beekay Film Delivery
1972 West Washington Boulevard
Los Angeles, California 90018
Tel: 213-733-0233

Bliss Film Delivery
1120 South Second Street
Alhambra, California 91801
Tel: 213-282-9532

Film Transport Company of
  California
1525 West 23rd Street
Los Angeles, California 90007
Tel: 213-734-4141

Gardner's Delivery Service, Inc
11229 South Prairie
Inglewood, California 90303
Tel: 213-978-9018

Gilboy, Inc.
8536 National Boulevard
Los Angeles, California 90230
Tel: 213-559-2722

Novo International Corporatio
8635 Aviation Boulevard
Inglewood, California 90301
Tel: 213-776-1178

Santa Barbara Special Deliver
1972 West Washington Boulevar
Los Angeles, California 90018
Tel: 213-734-5590

San Francisco area:

Film Messenger Service
215 Golden Gate Avenue
San Francisco, California 9410
Tel: 415-431-4074

NFS Operating Corporation
35 Guy Place
San Francisco, California 9410
Tel: 415-362-2182

Colorado:

Denver Shipping and Inspection
  Bureau
2118 Stout Street
Denver, Colorado 90205
Tel: 303-222-5616

Southwestern Film Service
2118 Stout Street
Denver, Colorado 90205
Tel: 303-244-2287

Connecticut:

New Haven Film Service
90 Woodmont Road
Milford, Connecticut 06460
Tel: 203-878-1465

Rosen Film Delivery System
1890 Dixwell Avenue
Hamden, Connecticut 06514
Tel: 203-288-9161

Florida:

Jacksonville Film Service
2208 West 21st Street
Jacksonville, Florida 32209
Tel: 904-355-5447

Georgia:

Atlanta Film Service
161 Spring Street, N.W.
Atlanta, Georgia 30318
Tel: 404-524-5380

Benton Film Forwarding
  Company
168 Baker Street, N.W.
Atlanta, Georgia 30313
Tel: 404-577-2821

Theatres Service Company
830 Willoughby Way, N.E.
Atlanta, Georgia 30312
Tel: 404-521-0730

Illinois:

Allin Express Service
2101 South Peoria Street
Chicago, Illinois 60608
Tel: 312-666-5407

Clark Service, Inc.
2265 West St. Paul Avenue
Chicago, Illinois 60647
Tel: 312-342-3140

Consolidated Film Delivery
2270 South Archer Avenue
Chicago, Illinois 60616
Tel: 312-326-4120

Emery Airfreight
Chicago O'Hare Airport
Chicago, Illinois 60666
Tel: 312-686-7300

Lavin Brothers Film Delivery
  Service
6328 North Richmond Avenue
Chicago, Illinois 60659
Tel: 312-274-6450

Novo Air Freight
2707 Coyle Avenue
Chicago, Illinois 60645
Tel: 312-593-7300

Standard Trucking Company
2270 Archer Avenue
Chicago, Illinois 60616
Tel: 312-225-1458

Indiana:

Bradford Film Transit Company
718 North Senate Avenue
Indianapolis, Indiana 46202
Tel: 317-636-2800

Feature Film Service, Inc.
4950 Prospect Street
Indianapolis, Indiana 46203
Tel: 317-357-8548

Indiana Transit Service
4300 West Morris Street
Indianapolis, Indiana 46241
Tel: 317-241-9321

States Film Service, Inc.
429 North Senate Avenue
Indianapolis, Indiana 46204
Tel: 317-638-3531

Iowa:

Iowa Film Inspection & Shipping
  Depot
3123 Delaware
Des Moines, Iowa 50313
Tel: 515-265-1469

Iowa Parcel Service, Inc.
3123 Delaware
Des Moines, Iowa 50313
Tel: 515-265-5221

H. W. King Delivery Service
1320 Grand Avenue
Des Moines, Iowa 50309
Tel: 515-243-5269

News Film Agency
2500 South Harwood
Des Moines, Iowa 50312
Tel: 515-428-5181

Louisiana:

Film Inspection Service, Inc.
2411 Edenborn Avenue
Metairie, Louisiana 70001
Tel: 504-833-5552

Novo Air Freight
2411 Edenborn Avenue
Metairie, Louisiana 70001
Tel: 504-837-0922

Schaffer Film Service, Inc.
P.O. Box 9344
Metairie, Louisiana 70004
Tel: 504-833-9670

Massachusetts:

NFS Operating Corporation
621 East First Street
Boston, Massachusetts 02127
Tel: 617-268-6510

Michigan:

Jay G. Trucking Service
9237 Warwick
Detroit, Michigan 48228
Tel: 313-838-5462

Pep Lines Trucking Company
15120 Third
Highland Park, Michigan 48203
Tel: 313-883-3200

Sullivan Film Service
2598 Chalmers
Detroit, Michigan 48215
Tel: 313-821-4713

Minnesota:

Century Motor Freight, Inc.
3245 Fourth Street, S.E.
Minneapolis, Minnesota 55414
Tel: 414-645-9484

Midwest Motor Express
2778 Cleveland Avenue, North
St. Paul, Minnesota 55113
Tel: 414-633-5653

Novo Air Freight, Inc.
701 North Fourth Street
Minneapolis, Minnesota 55401
Tel: 414-336-5341

Pitts Film Service, Inc.
149 Jackson Avenue, North
Hopkins, Minnesota 55343
Tel: 414-938-7290

Missouri:

Central Shipping and Exhibitors
    Film Delivery Service
101 West Tenth Avenue, North
Kansas City, Missouri 64116
Tel: 816-471-0884

Harry Kahan Film Delivery
3974 Page
St. Louis, Missouri 63113
Tel: 314-371-6572

Lewton Film Service, Inc.
12721 San Clemente
St. Louis, Missouri 63111
Tel: 314-739-0717

Nebraska:

Mills Film Transfer
1234 South Ninth Street
Lincoln, Nebraska 68108
Tel: 402-432-1197

Omaha Film Depot
1441 North Eleventh Street
Omaha, Nebraska 68108
Tel: 402-342-6576

Pierce Film Service
512 South Brown Street
Pierce, Nebraska 68767
Tel: 308-329-6365

Rapid Film Service
East Lincoln Highway
Grand Island, Nebraska 68801
Tel: 308-382-4058

New Jersey:

Hudson Film Delivery
Corporation
560 Main Street
Fort Lee, New Jersey 07024
Tel: 201-947-5200

State Film Delivery
560 Main Street
Fort Lee, New Jersey 07024
Tel: 201-947-5200

New York:

Barnett/Novo International
Corporation
425 East 53rd Street
New York, New York 10019
Tel: 212-758-3500

Barnett/Novo International
Corporation
John F. Kennedy International
Airport
New York, New York 11430
Tel: 212-656-5740

Bonded Services Division
733 Third Avenue
New York, New York 10017
Tel: 212-661-7600

Clark Service, Inc.
24 North Third Street
Albany, New York 12204
Tel: 518-434-1289

National Film Carriers, Inc.
800 Second Avenue
New York, New York 10017
Tel: 212-867-2492

Prudential Film Distributors
Corporation
630 Ninth Avenue
New York, New York 10036
Tel: 212-265-6884

Trans-World International, Inc.
767 Fifth Avenue
New York, New York 10022
Tel: 212-832-4760

North Carolina:

Carolina Delivery Service
Company, Inc.
1336 South Graham Street
Charlotte, North Carolina 28203
Tel: 704-333-5196

Carolina Film Service, Inc.
5012 Hovis Road
Charlotte, North Carolina 28201
Tel: 704-394-3129

Observer Transportation
Company
1600 West Independence
Boulevard
Charlotte, North Carolina 28208
Tel: 704-377-5431

Ohio:

Columbus-Cincinnati Trucking
Company
939 North Twentieth Street
Columbus, Ohio 43219
Tel: 614-258-2913

Film Service Company
1717 Logan Street
Cincinnati, Ohio 45210
Tel: 513-241-5986

Five States Film Service, Inc.
421 Bauer Street
Cincinnati, Ohio 45214
Tel: 513-621-4240

Lahmann Film Service Company
214 West Elder Street
Cincinnati, Ohio 45210
Tel: 513-421-2823

States Film Service, Inc.
2336 Payne Avenue
Cleveland, Ohio 44114
Tel: 216-771-3723

Oklahoma:

Magic Empire Express
920 S.W. Second Street
Oklahoma City, Oklahoma 74120
Tel: 405-235-8543

Mistletoe Express Service, Inc.
111 North Harrison
Oklahoma City, Oklahoma 73104
Tel: 405-236-1482

O & A Film Lines
706 West Sheridan
Oklahoma City, Oklahoma 73102
Tel: 405-232-9900

Oregon:

Howard Bell Film Service
907 N.W. Nineteenth Street
Portland, Oregon 97209
Tel: 503-227-2932

Lovett Interstate Theatre Service
935 N.W. Nineteenth Avenue
Portland, Oregon 97209
Tel: 503-224-6108

Portland National Film Service
2369 N.W. Quimby Street
Portland, Oregon 97210
Tel: 503-224-6205

Pennsylvania:

Clark Service, Inc.
829 North 29th Street
Philadelphia, Pennsylvania 19130
Tel: 215-232-3500

Exhibitors Service Company
85 Helen Street
McKees Rocks, Pennsylvania
  15136
Tel: 412-771-5010

Highway Express Lines, Inc.
3200 South Twentieth Street
Philadelphia, Pennsylvania 19145
Tel: 215-336-6060

Kally Express Exhibitors Service
239 Calmar Drive
Verona, Pennsylvania 15147
Tel: 412-731-9018

Pittsburgh Film Service
Nichol Avenue
McKees Rocks, Pennsylvania
  15136
Tel: 412-771-2665

Tennessee:

Film Transit, Inc.
291 Hernando Street
Memphis, Tennessee 38126
Tel: 901-525-6894

Memphis Film Service, Inc.
3931 Homewood Road
Memphis, Tennessee 38118
Tel: 901-365-7550

Texas:

Blue Bonnett Express Agency,
    Inc.
5009 Rusk
Houston, Texas 77023
Tel: 713-923-9101

Central Shipping and Inspection
2500 South Harwood
Dallas, Texas 75201
Tel: 214-421-5411

Film Express Agency
1402 Palmer
Houston, Texas 77003
Tel: 713-225-4170

Film Transfer
1066 West Mockingbird Lane
Dallas, Texas 75235
Tel: 214-637-6690

Texas Film Service
518 South Main Avenue
San Antonio, Texas 78204
Tel: 512-227-9295

Valley Film Service
518 South Main Avenue
San Antonio, Texas 78204
Tel: 512-227-9295

Utah:

NFS Operating Corporation
350 West Sixth Street
Salt Lake City, Utah 84110
Tel: 801-364-7729

Washington:

Inland Northwest Film Service,
    Inc.
2201 Sixth Avenue, South
Seattle, Washington 98148
Tel: 206-682-4766

Local Film Delivery, Inc.
900 Maynard South
Seattle, Washington 98104
Tel: 206-682-6663

National Screen Service
    Corporation
2413 Second Avenue
Seattle, Washington 98121
Tel: 206-624-2882

Northwest Film Service, Inc.
79 South Dearborn Street
Seattle, Washington 98134
Tel: 206-622-0241

Seattle National Film Service
900 Maynard Avenue, South
Seattle, Washington 98104
Tel: 206-682-6685

Wisconsin:

Film Center, Inc.
333 North 25th Street
Milwaukee, Wisconsin 53233
Tel: 414-342-3717

Novo International Air Freight
  Corporation
4930 South Second
Milwaukee, Wisconsin 53207
Tel: 414-482-3200

Film Stock

Included here are suppliers of raw film stock.

California:
Los Angeles area:

Kodak Film Raw Stock Center
7052 Santa Monica Boulevard
Los Angeles, California 90038
Tel: 213-466-7658

Studio Film Exchange, Inc.
11555 Ventura Boulevard
Studio City, California 91604
Tel: 213-985-3303

San Francisco area:

Eastman Kodak Company
9100 Alcosta Boulevard
San Ramon, California 94583
Tel: 415-828-7000

Colorado:

Eastman Kodak Company
Jack T. Billings
Denver, Colorado 80202
Tel: 303-986-4347

New York:

Metropolitan Visual Products
453 West 47th Street
New York, New York 10036
Tel: 212-245-8027

Raw Stock Center
9 East 37th Street
New York, New York 10016
Tel: 212-679-1218

Studio Film Exchange, Inc.
366 West 46th Street
New York, New York 10036
Tel: 212-265-3740

Texas:

Eastman Kodak Company
Jack T. Billings
Dallas, Texas 75221
Tel: 214-351-3221

Film Storage

See also "Film Vaults."

California:

Bekins Film Service Center
1025 North Highland Avenue
Los Angeles, California 90028
Tel: 213-466-9271

Bonded Service, Inc.
8290 Santa Monica Boulevard
Los Angeles, California 90046
Tel: 213-654-7575

Consolidated Film Industries
959 North Seward Street
Los Angeles, California 90028
Tel: 213-462-3161

Evco Refrigerated Film Vaults
838 North Seward Street
Los Angeles, California 90038
Tel: 213-464-9252

Filmtreat International
   Corporation
730 Salem Street
Glendale, California 91203
Tel: 213-242-2181

Hollywood Film Company
956 North Seward Street
Los Angeles, California 90038
Tel: 213-462-3284

Producers Film Center
948 North Sycamore Avenue
Los Angeles, California 90038
Tel: 213-851-1122

Seward Film Vaults
1010 North Seward Street
Los Angeles, California 90038
Tel: 213-464-0141

New York:

Bekins Archival Services, Inc.
619 West 51st Street
New York, New York 10019
Tel: 212-489-7890

Bonded Film Storage
733 Third Avenue
New York, New York 10017
Tel: 212-661-7600

Filmtreat International
   Corporation
250 West 64th Street
New York, New York 10023
Tel: 212-799-2500

Tape-Films, Inc.
619 West 54th Street
New York, New York 10019
Tel: 212-867-9590

Film Transfer

This category includes transfer from film to videotape and videotape to film. Suppliers of one service are not necessarily equipped to handle two-way transfers.

FILM TO VIDEOTAPE

California:

Acme Film Laboratories, Inc.
1161 North Highland Avenue
Los Angeles, California 90038
Tel: 213-464-7471

Audio-Video Craft, Inc.
7710 Melrose Avenue
Los Angeles, California 90046
Tel: 213-655-3511

Cal-Visuals
201 Mason Street, Suite 468
San Francisco, California 94102
Tel: 415-771-5466

Camera Systems International
1033 Byram
Los Angeles, California 90015
Tel: 213-748-8925

Consolidated Film Industries
959 Seward Street
Los Angeles, California 90038
Tel: 213-462-3161

DeLuxe General, Inc.
1546 North Argyle Avenue
Los Angeles, California 90028
Tel: 213-462-6171

Film Technology Company, In
6900 Santa Monica Boulevard
Los Angeles, California 90038
Tel: 213-465-4908

Ocee Ritch Productions
1136 North Las Palmas Aven
Los Angeles, California 90038
Tel: 213-461-9231

Oxford Films
1136 North Las Palmas Aven
Los Angeles, California 90038
Tel: 213-461-9231

Studio Eight
3001 Red Hill, Building Six
Costa Mesa, California 92626
Tel: 714-979-0440

Telaudio Centre
634 South Victory Boulevard
Burbank, California 91502
Tel: 213-849-1433

Video Systems, Inc.
12530 Beatrice Street
Los Angeles, California 90066
Tel: 213-871-0677

Videodetics Corporation
2121 South Manchester Avenue
Anaheim, California 92802
Tel: 714-532-3364

Vidicopy Corporation
South Bay Office Center, Suite
470
1287 Lawrence Station Road
Sunnyvale, California 94086
Tel: 408-734-4370

District of Columbia:

Byron Motion Pictures Inc.
65 K Street, N.E.
Washington, D.C. 20002
Tel: 202-783-2700

Illinois:

Mediatech
824 Busse Highway
Park Ridge, Illinois 60068
Tel: 312-693-8366

Video Tran Inc.
211 East Grand Avenue
Chicago, Illinois 60611
Tel: 312-329-9890

WTTW Recording Services
5440 North St. Louis Avenue
Chicago, Illinois 60625
Tel: 312-583-5000

New York:

De Luxe General, Inc.
630 Ninth Avenue
New York, New York 10036
Tel: 212-489-8800

Image Transform, Inc.
2 West 45th Street
New York, New York 10036
Tel: 212-986-3551

MPCS Communications
  Industries
514 West 57th Street
New York, New York 10019
Tel: 212-586-3690

National Video Center
730 Fifth Avenue
New York, New York 10019
Tel: 212-757-6440

Reeves Cinetel, Inc.
304 East 44th Street
New York, New York 10017
Tel: 212-679-3550

Rombex Productions Corporation
245 West 55th Street
New York, New York 10019
Tel: 212-757-3681

TVR, Inc.
556 West 54th Street
New York, New York 10019
Tel: 212-541-4030

Technicolor, Inc.
342 Madison Avenue
New York, New York 10017
Tel: 212-490-3086

Windsor Total Video
652 First Avenue
New York, New York 10016
Tel: 212-725-8080

Tennessee:

Motion Picture Laboratories, Inc.
781 South Main Street
Memphis, Tennessee 38106
Tel: 901-774-4944

Texas:

Automated Commercial Training
    Systems, Inc.
9817 Westpark
Houston, Texas 77042
Tel: 713-783-1380

Piccadilly Films International
    Company, Ltd.
1802 N.E. Loop 410
Gold Carpet Suite
San Antonio, Texas 78246
Tel: 512-824-3548

VIDEOTAPE TO FILM

California:
Los Angeles area:

Acme Film Laboratories
1161 North Highland Avenue
Los Angeles, California 90038
Tel: 213-464-7471

Ametron/American Electronics
    Supply, Inc.
1200 North Vine Street
Los Angeles, California 90038
Tel: 213-466-4321

Audio Video Craft, Inc.
7710 Melrose Avenue
Los Angeles, California 90046
Tel: 213-655-3511

Cine Group
8560 Sunset Boulevard
Los Angeles, California 90069
Tel: 213-652-4800

Consolidated Film Industries
959 Seward Street
Los Angeles, California 90038
Tel: 213-462-3161

Image Transform, Inc.
4142 Lankershim Boulevard
North Hollywood, California
    91602
Tel: 213-985-7566

Photo & Sound Company
870 Monterey Pass Road
Monterey Park, California 91754
Tel: 213-264-6850

Sony Corporation of America
700 West Artesia Boulevard
Compton, California 90220
Tel: 213-537-4300

Video Tape Mobile
634 South Victory Boulevard
Burbank, California 91502
Tel: 213-849-1433

Video View, Inc.
1617 North El Centro Avenue
Los Angeles, California 90028
Tel: 213-463-4179

The Vidtronics Company, Inc.
855 North Cahuenga Boulevard
Los Angeles, California 90038
Tel: 213-466-9741

San Francisco area:

Cal-Visuals
201 Mason Street, Suite 468
San Francisco, California 94102
Tel: 415-771-5466

Leo Diner Films, Inc.
332-350 Golden Gate Avenue
San Francisco, California 94102
Tel: 415-775-3664

Harry McCune Sound Studio
991 Howard Street
San Francisco, California 94103
Tel: 415-777-2700

W. A. Palmer Films
611 Howard Street
San Francisco, California 94105
Tel: 415-986-5961

Skinner, Hirsch & Kaye
229 Kearny Street
San Francisco, California 94108
Tel: 415-421-7370

Skinner Studio
345 Sutter Street
San Francisco, California 94108
Tel: 415-986-5040

Sony Corporation of America
Crocker Industrial Park
230 West Hill Place
Brisbane, California 94005
Tel: 415-467-4900

Hawaii:

Pacific Instrumentation
5388 Papai Street
Honolulu, Hawaii 96821
Tel: 808-373-1287

Illinois:

Consolidated Film Industries
333 North Michigan Avenue
Chicago, Illinois 60601
Tel: 312-641-0028

New York:

Consolidated Film Industries
15 Columbus Circle
New York, New York 10023
Tel: 212-581-1090

Film Vaults

Locations included here are equipped with security plus the controls for temperature and humidity variables that film storage requires.

California:

Bekins Film Service Center
1025 North Highland Avenue
Los Angeles, California 90038
Tel: 213-466-9271

Editing Film Center
942-946 Seward Street
Los Angeles, California 90038
Tel: 213-462-3284

Evco Refrigerated Film Vaults
838 North Seward Street
Los Angeles, California 90038
Tel: 213-464-9252

Gilboy, Inc.
8536 National Boulevard
Culver City, California 90230
Tel: 213-559-2722

Hollywood Film Company
956 North Seward Street
Los Angeles, California 90038
Tel: 213-462-3284

Seward Film Vaults
1010 North Seward Street
Los Angeles, California 90038
Tel: 213-464-0141

Grip Equipment

See also "Lighting Equipment."

Arizona:

Studio Rentals Incorporated of
  Arizona
2321 East University Drive
Phoenix, Arizona 85034
Tel: 602-252-5848

California:
Los Angeles area:

R. L. Bevington Grip Equipment
650 North Bronson
Los Angeles, California 90004
Tel: 213-466-7778

Birns & Sawyer, Inc.
1026 North Highland Avenue
Los Angeles, California 90038
Tel: 213-466-8211

Cine Group
8560 Sunset Boulevard
Los Angeles, California 90069
Tel: 213-652-4800

Cine-Tran Mobile Studio Systems
4010 Colfax Avenue
Studio City, California 91604
Tel: 213-769-8149

Combo Rentals
813 North California Street
Burbank, California 91505
Tel: 213-846-7678

F&B/CECO of California, Inc.
7051 Santa Monica Boulevard
Los Angeles, California 90038
Tel: 213-466-9361

J. L. Fisher, Inc.
10918 Burbank Boulevard
North Hollywood, California
  91601
Tel: 213-877-8848

Grip-Rite Rentals
140 North Victory Boulevard
Burbank, California 91502
Tel: 213-849-1614

Alex R. Hume
140 North Victory
Burbank, California 91502
Tel: 213-849-1614

Kritton Productions
7906 Santa Monica Boulevard
Los Angeles, California 90046
Tel: 213-656-5964

Leonetti Cine Rentals
5609 Sunset Boulevard
Los Angeles, California 90028
Tel: 213-469-2987

Lloyd-Davies Enterprises
1021 North McCadden Place
Los Angeles, California 90038
Tel: 213-462-1206

Magnasync/Movieola, Inc.
5539 Riverton Avenue
North Hollywood, California
  91601
Tel: 213-877-2791

Matthews Studio Equipment, Inc.
7041 Vineland Avenue
North Hollywood, California
  91605
Tel: 213-938-1802
Tel: 213-875-2444

Metro-Goldwyn-Mayer, Inc.
10202 West Washington
  Boulevard
Culver City, California 90230
Tel: 213-836-3000

Mobile Production Systems
1225 North Vine Street
Los Angeles, California 90038
Tel: 213-465-7141

Mole-Richardson Company
937 North Sycamore Avenue
Los Angeles, California 90038
Tel: 213-851-0111

Motion Picture Equipment
  Corporation
5428 Satsuma Avenue
North Hollywood, California
  91601
Tel: 213-766-4397

PSI-Production Systems, Inc.
1123 North Lillian Way
Los Angeles, California 90038
Tel: 213-469-2704

Jack Pill & Associates
6370 Santa Monica Boulevard
Los Angeles, California 90038
Tel: 213-466-5391

Porta-Crane Company, Inc.
11927 Sherman Road
North Hollywood, California
  91605
Tel: 213-765-9843

Producers Equipment Center
5428 Satsuma Avenue
North Hollywood, California
  91601
Tel: 213-766-4397

Production Systems
1123 North Lillian Way
Los Angeles, California 90038
Tel: 213-469-2704

Michael Shore Grip Rental
4604 Slauson Avenue
Culver City, California 90230
Tel: 213-876-2100

SOS/Photo-Cine-Optics, Inc.
7051 Santa Monica Boulevard
Los Angeles, California 90038
Tel: 213-466-9361

Bob Stindt Camera Dollys
3329 Burton Avenue
Burbank, California 91504
Tel: 213-845-4616

Tech-Camera Rentals
6370 Santa Monica Boulevard
Los Angeles, California 90038
Tel: 213-466-5391

Tuckers
1301 South La Brea Avenue
Los Angeles, California 90019
Tel: 213-937-3955

UPS Studio Rentals
6561 Santa Monica Boulevard
Los Angeles, California 90038
Tel: 213-461-1442

Universal City Studios
100 Universal City Plaza
Universal City, California 91608
Tel: 213-985-4321

San Diego area:

H. J. Anderson Company, Inc.
8937 Camplex Drive
San Diego, California 92123
Tel: 714-565-6984

San Francisco area:

American Zoetrope, Inc.
American Zoetrope Film Facility
827 Folsom Street
San Francisco, California 94107
Tel: 415-989-0600

Brooks Cameras, Inc.
45 Kearny Street
San Francisco, California 94108
Tel: 415-392-1902

Cinema Services Company
325 Corey Way South
San Francisco, California 94080
Tel: 415-761-6058

Cinerent West, Inc.
155 Fell Street
San Francisco, California 94102
Tel: 415-864-4644

Ferco
363 Brannan Street
San Francisco, California 94107
Tel: 415-398-2307

Film Producers Service
34B De Luca Place
San Rafael, California 94901
Tel: 415-456-4551

Manifest Production Service
308 Eleventh Street
San Francisco, California 94102
Tel: 415-626-5596

The Phelps & Kopp Company
991 Tennessee Street
San Francisco, California 94107
Tel: 415-285-1900

Skinner Studio
345 Sutter Street
San Francisco, California 94108
Tel: 415-986-5040

Colorado:

Cinema Services
P.O. Box 398
Eldorado Springs, Colorado
   80025
Tel: 303-443-4913

Western Cine Service, Inc.
312 South Pearl
Denver, Colorado 80209
Tel: 303-744-1017

252

Motion Picture Market Place

Florida:

Film Equipment Rentals, Inc.
19812 N.E. Twelfth Street
North Miami, Florida 33162
Tel: 305-891-2703

Hawaii:

House of Eric Productions
1760 Ala Moana Boulevard
Honolulu, Hawaii 96815
Tel: 808-533-3877

Nevada:

Rugar Electronics
4515 Industrial Road
Las Vegas, Nevada 89103
Tel: 702-736-4331

New York:

Boken, Inc.
349 West 48th Street
New York, New York 10036
Tel: 212-581-5507

The Camera Mart, Inc.
456 West 55th Street
New York, New York 10019
Tel: 212-757-6977

Feature Systems, Inc.
513 West 26th Street
New York, New York 10001
Tel: 212-736-0447

Filmtrucks–New York
512 West 39th Street
New York, New York 10018
Tel: 212-524-8668

Charles Ross, Inc.
333 West 52nd Street
New York, New York 10019
Tel: 212-246-5470

Texas:

Dale Berry and Associates, Inc.
9001 E. R. L. Thornton Freeway
Dallas, Texas 75228
Tel: 214-324-0409

PSI Film Laboratory
3011 Diamond Park Drive
Dallas, Texas 75347
Tel: 214-631-5670

Washington:

W. Brooks Baum Cinema
   Productions
715 First Avenue West
Seattle, Washington 98119
Tel: 206-283-6456

Northwest Sound & Production
129 First Street West
Seattle, Washington 98121
Tel: 206-282-4766

Guilds & Unions

California:

Los Angeles area:

Actors Equity Association
6430 Sunset Boulevard
Los Angeles, California 90028
Tel: 213-462-2334

Affiliated Property Craftsmen
Local 44, IATSE, AF of L
7429 Sunset Boulevard
Los Angeles, California 90046
Tel: 213-876-2320

American Cinema Editors
422 South Western Avenue
Los Angeles, California 90020
Tel: 213-386-1946

American Federation of Guards,
Local No. 1
4157 West Fifth Street, Room 220
Los Angeles, California 90020
Tel: 213-387-3127

American Federation of Labor
and Congress of Industrial
Organizations
2705 West Eighth Street
Los Angeles, California 90005
Tel: 213-387-7281

American Federation of
Musicians, Local 47
817 North Vine Street
Los Angeles, California 90038
Tel: 213-462-2161

American Federation of
Television and Radio Artists
(AFTRA)
1717 North Highland Avenue
Los Angeles, California 90028
Tel: 213-461-8111

American Guild of Authors &
Composers
6331 Hollywood Boulevard
Los Angeles, California 90028
Tel: 213-462-1108

American Guild of Musical
Artists
6430 Sunset Boulevard, Room 603
Los Angeles, California 90028
Tel: 213-461-3714

American Guild of Variety Artists
6331 Hollywood Boulevard, Suite
202
Los Angeles, California 90028
Tel: 213-464-8281

Artists' Managers Guild
7046 Hollywood Boulevard
Los Angeles, California 90028
Tel: 213-465-7107

Association of Film Craftsmen
1800 North Argyle, Suite 501
Los Angeles, California 90028
Tel: 213-462-7484

Broadcast Television Recording
  Engineers, Local 45, IBEW
3518 Cahuenga Boulevard, West,
  Suite 307
Los Angeles, California 90068
Tel: 213-851-5515

Building Service Employees
  International Union, Local
  278, AF of L
740 South Western Avenue
Los Angeles, California 90005
Tel: 213-386-4815

Composers and Lyricists Guild of
  America
6565 Sunset Boulevard, Suite 420
Los Angeles, California 90028
Tel: 213-462-6068

Costume Designers' Guild
11286 Westminster Street
Los Angeles, California 90066
Tel: 213-397-3162

Directors Guild of America, Inc.
7950 Sunset Boulevard
Los Angeles, California 90046
Tel: 213-656-1220

Film Technicians, Local 683,
  IATSE, AF of L
6721 Melrose Avenue
Los Angeles, California 90038
Tel: 213-935-1123

IATSE—International
Photographers,
  Local No. 659
7715 Sunset Boulevard
Los Angeles, California 90046
Gerald Smith, Business
  Representative
Tel: 213-876-0160

IATSE and MPMO
7715 Sunset Boulevard, Suite 210
Los Angeles, California 90046
Tel: 213-876-1600

IBEW, Local 40, AF of L–CIO
3353 Barham Boulevard
Los Angeles, California 90068
Tel: 213-851-4004

International Photographers,
  Local 659, IATSE and
  MPMO
7715 Sunset Boulevard
Los Angeles, California 90046
Tel: 213-876-0160

International Sound Technicians,
  Local 695, IATSE, MPMO,
  AF of L
15840 Ventura Boulevard, Suite
  303
Encino, California 91436
Tel: 213-872-0452

Make-up Artists and Hair Stylists,
IATSE Local 706, and
MPMO of U.S. and Canada
11519 Chandler Boulevard
North Hollywood, California
91604
Tel: 213-984-1700

Motion Picture Costumers,
IATSE, Local 705, MPMO,
AF of L
1427 North La Brea Avenue
Los Angeles, California 90028
Tel: 213-851-0220

Motion Picture Crafts Service,
IATSE, Local 727, AF of L
12754 Ventura Boulevard, Suite
205
North Hollywood, California
91604
Tel: 213-984-2401

Motion Picture Editors Guild,
Local 776, IATSE
7715 Sunset Boulevard, Suite 100
Los Angeles, California 90046
Tel: 213-876-4770

Motion Picture Electricians,
Local 728, IATSE, MPMO,
AF of L–CIO
3400 Barham Boulevard
Los Angeles, California 90068
Tel: 213-851-3300

Motion Picture First Aid
Employees, Local 767, IATSE,
AF of L
1238 Wilson Avenue
Glendale, California 91206
Tel: 213-242-6411

Motion Picture Illustrators and
Matte Artists, Local 790,
IATSE
7715 Sunset Boulevard
Los Angeles, California 90046
Tel: 213-876-2010

Motion Picture Set Painters,
Local 729, IATSE, AF of L
12754 Ventura Boulevard, Suite
207-208
Los Angeles, California
Tel: 213-984-3000

Motion Picture Studio
Cinetechnicians, Local 789,
IATSE, AF of L–CIO
4545 Santa Monica Boulevard
Los Angeles, California 90029
Tel: 213-666-2852

Motion Picture Studio Grips,
Local 80, IATSE, AF of L
6926 Melrose Avenue
Los Angeles, California 90038
Tel: 213-931-1419

Motion Picture Studio
Projectionists, Local 165,
IATSE and MPMO of U.S.
and Canada, Inc.
6640 Sunset Boulevard, Suite 110
Los Angeles, California 90028
Tel: 213-461-2985

Musicians Mutual Protective
Association, Local 47, AF of L
817 North Vine Street
Los Angeles, California 90038
Tel: 213-462-2161

Office Employees International
Union, Local 174, AF of L-
CIO
9056 Santa Monica Boulevard,
    Suite 301
Los Angeles, California 90069
Tel: 213-278-5880

Ornamental Plasterers, Local 755,
    AF of L
7429 Sunset Boulevard, Room 104
Los Angeles, California 90046
Tel: 213-876-3053

Producers Guild of America, Inc.
8201 Beverly Boulevard
Los Angeles, California 90048
Tel: 213-651-0084

The Publicists Guild, Local 818,
    IATSE and MPMO, AF of L
1427 North La Brea Avenue
Los Angeles, California 90028
Tel: 213-851-1600

Scenic and Title Artists, Local
    816, IATSE
7429 Sunset Boulevard
Los Angeles, California 90046
Tel: 213-876-1440

Screen Actors Guild
7750 Sunset Boulevard
Los Angeles, California 90046
Tel: 213-876-3030

Screen Cartoonists Guild
    (Teamsters Local 986)
1616 West Ninth Street
Los Angeles, California 90015
Tel: 213-380-9860

Screen Cartoonists, Local 839,
    IATSE
12441 Ventura Boulevard
Studio City, California 91604
Tel: 213-766-7151

Screen Extras Guild, Inc.
3629 Cahuenga Boulevard, W
Los Angeles, California 90068
Tel: 213-851-4301

Script Supervisors, Local 871,
    IATSE
7715 Sunset Boulevard
Los Angeles, California 90046
Tel: 213-876-4433

Set Designers and Model Maker
    Local 847, IATSE
7715 Sunset Boulevard
Los Angeles, California 90046
Tel: 213-876-3010

Society of Motion Picture Art
    Directors, Local 876, IATS
7715 Sunset Boulevard
Los Angeles, California 90046
Tel: 213-876-4330

Sound Construction, Installation
    & Maintenance Technicians,
    IBEW, Local 40, AF of L–CI
3353 Barham Boulevard
Los Angeles, California 90068
Tel: 213-851-4004

Story Analysts, Local 854, IATS
7715 Sunset Boulevard
Los Angeles, California 90046
Tel: 213-876-1600

Studio Air Conditioning
  Engineers, IBEW, Local 40,
  AF of L–CIO
3353 Barham Boulevard
Los Angeles, California 90068
Tel: 213-851-4004

Studio Teachers, Local 884,
  IATSE
3630 South Dentley
Los Angeles, California 90034
Tel: 213-838-4482

Studio Transportation Drivers,
  Local 399, IBT
4747 Vineland Avenue, Suite 3
North Hollywood, California
  91602
Tel: 213-986-7731

Studio Utility Employees, Local
  724, AF of L
6700 Melrose Avenue
Los Angeles, California 90038
Tel: 213-938-6277

Theatre Projectionists, Local 150
6255 Sunset Boulevard, Suite 606
Los Angeles, California 90028
Tel: 213-461-2928

Theatrical Stage Employees,
  Local 33, IATSE, AF of L
2858 West Eighth Street
Los Angeles, California 90005
Tel: 213-380-1648

Theatrical Wardrobe Attendants,
  Local 768, IATSE
805 South Bradish
Glendora, California 91740
Tel: 213-936-6303

Waitresses and Cafeteria
  Workers, Local 8, AF of
  L–CIO
321 South Bixel Street
Los Angeles, California 90017
Tel: 213-482-9800

Writers Guild of America—West,
  Inc.
8955 Beverly Boulevard
Los Angeles, California 90048
Tel: 213-274-8601

San Diego area:

Screen Actors Guild
3045 Rosecrans, Room 206
San Diego, California 92110
Representative Jackie Walters
Tel: 714-222-3996

Actors' Equity Association
100 Bush Street
San Francisco, California 94104
Tel: 415-986-4060

AFL/CIO, CLC
126 Hyde Street
San Francisco, California 94102
Tel: 415-771-7017

American Federation of
  Television and Radio Artists
  (AFTRA)
100 Bush Street
San Francisco, California 94104
Tel: 415-391-7510
Donald S. Tayer, Executive
  Secretary and Counsel
Jean A. Hughes, Assistant
  Executive Secretary
Lee Warren, Assistant Executive
  Secretary

American Guild of Musical
  Artists (AGMA)
100 Bush Street
San Francisco, California 94104
Tel: 415-986-4060

International Alliance of
  Theatrical Stage Employees
  (IATSE), Local No. 16
230 Jones Street
San Francisco, California 94102
Eddie Powell, Business
  Representative
Tel: 415-441-6401

International Brotherhood of
  Teamsters-Chauffeurs, Local
  No. 265
1269 Howard Street
San Francisco, California 94103
Peter Derenale, Business
  Representative
Tel: 415-861-0323

International Brotherhood of
  Teamsters-Drivers, Local No.
  85
459 Fulton Street
San Francisco, California 94102
Dan Flanigan, Business
  Representative
John Murnin, Business
  Representative
Tel: 415-861-2912

Moving Picture Machine
  Operators Union, Local No.
  162
230 Jones Street, Room 302
San Francisco, California 94102
Henry Meyer, Business Manager
Tel: 415-928-1777

Musicians Union Local 6,
  American Federation of
  Musicians
230 Jones Street
San Francisco, California 941
Tel: 415-775-8118

NABET Local 51 Radio & TV
  Engineers
126 Hyde Street
San Francisco, California 941
Tel: 415-771-5350

National Association of Broadca
  Employees and Technicians
  (NABET) Local No. 532
126 Hyde Street
San Francisco, California 941
Robert Lenihan, Business
  Representative
Tel: 415-771-7017

Screen Actors Guild (SAG)
San Francisco Branch
100 Bush Street
San Francisco, California 941
Tel: 415-391-7510
Donald S. Tayer, Executive
  Secretary
Jean A. Hughes, Assistant
  Executive Secretary

Theatrical Stage Employees'
  Local 16 IATSE
230 Jones Street
San Francisco, California 941(
Tel: 415-441-6400

Theatrical Wardrobe Attendant
  Local 784 IATSE
230 Jones Street
San Francisco, California 941(
Tel: 415-474-6881

Colorado:

AFTRA
Box 154
Wheat Ridge, Colorado 80033
Charles Thomas, Denver
  Representative
Tel: 303-232-3744

IATSE No. 7, Denver Stage
  Hands
1070 Insurance Exchange
  Building
Denver, Colorado 80202
James Carey, Business Agent
Tel: 303-534-2423

IATSE No. 47, Stage Employees
1629 Saratoga Road
Pueblo, Colorado 81001
Normand O. Martin, Business
  Manager
Tel: 303-542-0850
Tel: 303-543-2980

Screen Actors Guild
Denver, Colorado 80202
Berni Kirs
Tel: 303-377-8888

Teamsters Local No. 17
3245 Eliot Street
Denver, Colorado 80211
Temple R. Webb
Tel: 303-433-6497

Teamsters Local No. 146
1426 North Hancock Street
Colorado Springs, Colorado
  80903
Robert D. Menapace
Tel: 303-632-1902

Florida:

AFTRA
6660 Biscayne Boulevard
Miami, Florida 33101
Tel: 305-759-4121

AGVA
350 Lincoln Road
Miami, Florida 33101
Tel: 305-538-2708

Association of Film Craftsmen
13911 N.W. Twentieth Court
Opa Loca, Florida 33054
Tel: 305-681-9808

Directors Guild of America, Inc.
7101 S.W. 139th Street
Miami, Florida 33101
Tel: 305-238-5800

IATSE, Cameramen #666
1007 South Ocean Drive
Hollywood, Florida 33022
Tel: 305-949-6401

Screen Actors Guild
3226 Ponce de Leon Boulevard
Coral Gables, Florida 33134
Melvin B. Karl, Representative
Tel: 305-444-7677

Georgia:

AFTRA/SAG
2288 Peachtree Road, #201
Atlanta, Georgia 30305
Tom Even, Representative
Tel: 404-351-4328

IATSE Local 41
781 Miami Circle
Atlanta, Georgia 30324
Tel: 404-262-7104

Hawaii:

AFL-CIO
925 Bethel
Honolulu, Hawaii 96813
Tel: 808-537-2531

American Federation of TV &
    Radio Artists (AFTRA)
2305 South Beretania
Honolulu, Hawaii 96814
Tel: 808-941-9445

American Guild of Variety Artists
    (AGVA)
Waikiki Biltmore Hotel
Honolulu, Hawaii 96815
Tel: 808-923-7531

Screen Extras Guild
1888-H Kalakaua
Honolulu, Hawaii 96815
Tel: 808-949-1112

Illinois:

Actors' Equity Association
360 North Michigan Avenue,
    Room 1401
Chicago, Illinois 60611
Tel: 312-641-0393

American Federation of
    Television and Radio Artists
307 North Michigan Avenue
Chicago, Illinois 60601
Tel: 312-372-8081

Chicago Federation of Musicians
175 West Washington Boulevard
Chicago, Illinois 60602
Tel: 312-782-0063

Directors Guild of America, Inc.
40 East Oak Street
Chicago, Illinois 60611
Tel: 312-944-6040

IATSE–Local 476 Studio
    Mechanics
327 South La Salle Street
Chicago, Illinois 60604
Tel: 312-922-5215

IATSE–Local 666
327 South La Salle Street
Chicago, Illinois 60604
Tel: 312-341-0966

IATSE–Local 780 Motion Picture
    Lab Technicians & Film
    Editors
327 South La Salle Street
Chicago, Illinois 60604
Tel: 312-922-7105

IBEW–Local 1220
203 North Wabash Avenue
Chicago, Illinois 60611
Tel: 312-332-1908

IPMPI Local 666, Chicago Suite
    1122

International Photographers of
    the Motion Picture Industries
327 South La Salle Street
Chicago, Illinois 60604
Tel: 312-341-0966

Motion Picture Lab Technicians
327 South La Salle Street
Chicago, Illinois 60604
Tel: 312-922-7105

Motion Picture Screen
  Cartoonists
6145 North Milwaukee Avenue
Chicago, Illinois 60646
Tel: 312-631-4444

Motion Picture Studio Mechanics
327 South La Salle Street
Chicago, Illinois 60604
Tel: 312-922-5215

Moving Picture Machine
  Operators
188 West Randolph Street
Chicago, Illinois 60601
Tel: 312-236-4582

NABET, Chicago Local 41
80 East Jackson Boulevard
Chicago, Illinois 60604
Tel: 312-922-2462

National Association of Broadcast
. Employees and Technicians
80 East Jackson Boulevard
Chicago, Illinois 60604
Tel: 312-922-2462

Screen Actors Guild
307 North Michigan Avenue
Chicago, Illinois 60601
Herbert H. Neuer, Representative
Tel: 312-372-8081

Theatrical Wardrobe Attendants
15218 Dante Avenue
Dolton, Illinois 60419
Tel: 312-849-0223

Massachusetts:

Screen Actors Guild
11 Beacon Street, Room 1103
Boston, Massachusetts 02108
Robert M. Segal, Representative
Tel: 617-712-0208

Michigan:

Screen Actors Guild
3200 David Stott Building
Detroit, Michigan 48226
Tomi Thurston, Representative
Tel: 313-963-0269

Nevada:

American Guild of Variety Artists
  (AGVA)
120 East Flamingo Road
Las Vegas, Nevada 89109
Tel: 702-734-8132

IATSE & MPMO Local 720
  AFL/CIO CLC
2923 Industrial Road
Las Vegas, Nevada 89109
Tel: 702-735-6003

Musicians Local 369 AFM
1611 Fremont
Las Vegas, Nevada 89101
Tel: 702-384-9474
Wardrobe Attendants

New York:

AFTRA
1350 Avenue of the Americas
New York, New York 10019
Tel: 212-265-7700

Actors' Equity Association
165 West 46th Street
New York, New York 10036
Tel: 212-757-7660

American Federation of
   Musicians
641 Lexington Avenue
New York, New York 10022
Tel: 212-758-0600

American Federation of
   Musicians, Local 802
261 West 52nd Street
New York, New York 10019
Tel: 212-757-7722

American Guild of Authors and
   Composers
40 West 57th Street
New York, New York 10019
Tel: 212-757-8833

American Guild of Musical
   Artists, Inc.
1841 Broadway
New York, New York 10023
Tel: 212-265-3687

American Guild of Variety Artists
1540 Broadway
New York, New York 10036
Tel: 212-765-0800

Associated Actors and Artists of
   America
165 West 46th Street
New York, New York 10036
Tel: 212-245-8295

Associated Musicians of Greater
   New York
261 West 52nd Street
New York, New York 10019
Tel: 212-757-7722

Association of Theatrical Agents
   & Managers
268 West 47th Street
New York, New York 10036
Tel: 212-582-3750

Authors' Guild, Inc.
234 West 44th Street
New York, New York 10036
Tel: 212-695-4145

The Authors League of America,
   Inc.
234 West 44th Street
New York, New York 10036
Tel: 212-736-4811

Conference of Motion Picture and
   Television Unions
236 West 55th Street
New York, New York 10019
Tel: 212-245-5986

Directors Guild of America, Inc.
110 West 57th Street
New York, New York 10019
Tel: 212-581-0370

The Dramatists Guild, Inc.
234 West 44th Street
New York, New York 10036
Tel: 212-563-2233

Exhibition Employees Union,
Local 829, IATSE
10-38 Jackson Avenue
Long Island City, New York
11101
Tel: 212-361-7395

Film Editors, Local 771
250 West 57th Street
New York, New York 10019
Tel: 212-582-3728

IATSE, Main Office
1270 Avenue of the Americas
New York, New York 10020
Richard Walsh
John Hall
Tel: 212-245-4370

IBTC
577 Ninth Avenue
New York, New York 10036
Tel: 212-524-9328

IPMPI, Local 644
250 West 57th Street
New York, New York 10019
Tel: 212-247-3860

Legitimate Theatre Employees
Local—B183
235 West 46th Street, Room 320
New York, New York 10036
Tel: 212-245-2331
Local 52, IATSE

Make-up Artists and Hair Stylists
230 West 41st Street
New York, New York 10036
Tel: 212-354-6016

Motion Picture Film Editors
630 Ninth Avenue
New York, New York 10036
Tel: 212-582-3728

Motion Picture Lab Technicians
165 West 46th Street
New York, New York 10036
Tel: 212-757-5540

Motion Picture Publicists
1639 Broadway
New York, New York 10019
Tel: 212-586-6385

Motion Picture Studio Mechanics
221 West 57th Street
New York, New York 10019
Tel: 212-765-0741

Moving Picture Machine
Operators Union, Local 306,
IATSE
745 Seventh Avenue
New York, New York 10019
Tel: 212-586-5157

NABET Film & Tape Local 15
165 West 46th Street
New York, New York 10036
Tel: 212-869-0800

National Association of Broadcast
Employees & Technicians
135 West 50th Street
New York, New York 10020
Tel: 212-757-3065

Operating Engineers
132 Fourth Avenue
New York, New York 10003
Tel: 212-473-1700

Photographers, Local 644
250 West 57th Street
New York, New York 10019
Tel: 212-247-3860

Projectionists—IATSE
745 Seventh Avenue
New York, New York 10019
Tel: 212-586-5157

Publicists Guild, Local 818,
    IATSE & MPMO
1270 Avenue of the Americas
New York, New York 10020
Tel: 212-245-4369

Radio & Television Broadcast
    Engineers Union, Local 1212,
    IBEW
230 West 41st Street
New York, New York 10036
Tel: 212-354-6770

Scenic Artists
319 West 48th Street
New York, New York 10036
Tel: 212-246-8023

Screen Actors Guild
551 Fifth Avenue
New York, New York 10017
Tel: 212-687-4623
John T. McGuire, Representative

Screen Cartoonists, Local 841
25 West 43rd Street
New York, New York 10036
Tel: 212-354-6410

Screen Publicists Guild
13 Astor Place
New York, New York 10003
Tel: 212-673-5120

Script Supervisors, Local 161
250 West 57th Street
New York, New York 10019
Elizabeth Savage, Business
    Representative
Tel: 212-245-4562

Stage Directors & Choreographers
1619 Broadway
New York, New York 10019
Tel: 212-246-5118

Studio Mechanics, Local 52
250 West 57th Street
New York, New York 10019
Tel: 212-765-0541

Teamsters, Local 817
577 Ninth Avenue
New York, New York 10036
Tel: 212-524-9328

Theatre, Amusement & Cultural
    Service Employees, Local 54,
    SEIU, AFL-CIO
1650 Broadway
New York, New York 10019
Tel: 212-265-6556

Theatrical Costume Workers
    Union, Division of Local 38,
    ILGWU-AFL-CIO
218 West 40th Street
New York, New York 10017
Tel: 212-565-5100

Theatrical Drivers Union, No.
    817
577 Ninth Avenue
New York, New York 10018
Tel: 212-524-9328

Theatrical Protective Union No. 1
254 West 54th Street
New York, New York 10019
Tel: 212-265-2394

Theatrical Stage Employees
  Union No. 4
66 Court Street, Suite 1407
Brooklyn, New York 11201
Tel: 212-875-9475
Theatrical State Employees,
  IATSE

Theatrical Wardrobe Attendants
1501 Broadway
New York, New York 10036
Tel: 212-221-1717

Treasurers & Ticket Sellers
  Union, No. 751, IATSE
227 West 45th Street
New York, New York 10036
Tel: 212-245-7186

United Scenic Artists
1540 Broadway
New York, New York 10036
Tel: 212-575-5120

Wardrobe Attendants, Local 764
250 West 57th Street
New York, New York 10019
David M. Michaels, Business
  Representative
Tel: 212-582-4910

Writers Guild of America—East,
  Inc.
1212 Avenue of the Americas
New York, New York 10036
Tel: 212-757-3317

Pennsylvania:

Screen Actors Guild
1405 Locust Street, Room 811
Philadelphia, Pennsylvania 19102
W. Melvin Evans, Representative
Tel: 215-545-3150

Texas:

Screen Actors Guild
3220 Lemmon Avenue, Suite 102
Dallas, Texas 75204
Clinta Dayton, Representative
Tel: 214-522-2085

Inserts

Included are suppliers of printed inserts and insert shots.

California:

Los Angeles area:

Howard A. Anderson Company
Paramount Studios
5451 Marathon Street
Los Angeles, California 90038
Tel: 213-463-0100

Angel Arts Design Associates
11729 Kling Street
North Hollywood, California
91607
Tel: 213-763-8023

Bob Beck & Associates
1538 Cassil Place
Los Angeles, California 90028
Tel: 213-462-7093

Cinema Research Corporation
6860 Lexington Avenue
Los Angeles, California 90038
Tel: 213-461-3235

Consolidated Film Industries
959 North Seward Street
Los Angeles, California 90038
Tel: 213-462-3161

Robert Costa Productions
1615 Colorado Boulevard
Los Angeles, California 90041
Tel: 213-255-1841

Craftsman Company
1050 North Cahuenga Boulevard
Los Angeles, California 90028
Tel: 213-469-5594

Creative Film Arts
7070 Waring Avenue
Los Angeles, California 90038
Tel: 213-933-8495

Film Effects of Hollywood, Inc
1140 North Citrus
Los Angeles, California 90038
Tel: 213-469-5808

Earl Hays Press
1121 North Las Palmas Avenue
Los Angeles, California 90038
Tel: 213-466-2495

Ray Mercer & Company
4241 Normal Avenue
Los Angeles, California 90029
Tel: 213-663-9331

Modern Film Effects
725 North Highland Avenue
Los Angeles, California 90038
Tel: 213-938-2155

National Screen Service
Corporation
7026 Santa Monica Boulevard
Los Angeles, California 90038
Tel: 213-466-5111

Opticals West
7026 Santa Monica Boulevard
Los Angeles, California 90038
Tel: 213-466-5111

Photo-Effex
3701 Oak Street
Burbank, California 91505
Tel: 213-849-6959

Van Der Veer Photo Effects
3518 West Cahuenga Boulevard
Los Angeles, California 90068
Tel: 213-851-4333

Westheimer Company
736 North Seward Street
Los Angeles, California 90038
Tel: 213-466-8271

San Francisco area:

W. A. Palmer Films
611 Howard Street
San Francisco, California 94105
Tel: 415-986-5961

Skinner Studio
345 Sutter Street
San Francisco, California 94108
Tel: 415-986-5040

Stop Frame, Inc.
1736 Stockton Street
San Francisco, California 94133
Tel: 415-434-4413

Hawaii:

Cine-Pic Hawaii
1847 Pacific Heights Road
Honolulu, Hawaii 96813
Tel: 808-533-2677

Illinois:

Consolidated Film Industries
333 North Michigan Avenue
Chicago, Illinois 60601
Tel: 312-641-0028

New York:

Consolidated Film Industries
15 Columbus Circle
New York, New York 10023
Tel: 212-581-1090

Laboratories

California:
Los Angeles area:

Acme Film & Videotape Labs, Inc.
1161 North Highland Avenue
Los Angeles, California 90038
Tel: 213-464-7471

Akkad International Productions, Inc.
8730 Sunset Boulevard
Los Angeles, California 90069
Tel: 213-657-7670

American Film Industries, Inc.
1138 North La Brea Avenue
Los Angeles, California 90038
Tel: 213-467-1118

Howard A. Anderson Company
5451 Marathon Street
Los Angeles, California 90038
Tel: 213-463-0100

Audio Visual Headquarters Corporation
515 South Olive Street
Los Angeles, California 90013
Tel: 213-629-3661

C. H. Carleton Company
7608 San Fernando Road
Sun Valley, California 91352
Tel: 213-767-8507

Cine-Craft Film Laboratories
8764 West Beverly Boulevard
Los Angeles, California 90028
Tel: 213-652-7357

Cineservice, Inc.
1459 North Seward Street
Los Angeles, California 90028
Tel: 213-463-3178

Color Reproduction Company
7936 Santa Monica Boulevard
Los Angeles, California 90046
Tel: 213-654-8010

Consolidated Film Industries
959 North Seward Street
Los Angeles, California 90028
Tel: 213-462-3161

Cre-Art Photo Labs, Inc.
6920 Melrose Avenue
Los Angeles, California 90038
Tel: 213-937-3390

Crest National Film Laboratories
1141 North Seward Street
Los Angeles, California 90038
Tel: 213-462-6696

Deluxe General, Inc.
1546 North Argyle Avenue
Los Angeles, California 90028
Tel: 213-462-6171

Deluxe General, Inc.
1377 North Serrano Avenue
Los Angeles, California 90027
Tel: 213-466-8631

Jacques Descent Productions
1676 North Western Avenue
Los Angeles, California 90027
Tel: 213-466-8469

Dymat Valley Film Laboratories
2704 West Olive
Burbank, California 91505
Tel: 213-846-7262

Eastman Kodak Laboratory
1017 North Las Palmas Avenue
Los Angeles, California 90038
Tel: 213-465-7151

Film Effects of Hollywood
1140 North Citrus
Los Angeles, California 90038
Tel: 213-469-5808

The Film House
584 North Larchmont Boulevard
Los Angeles, California 90004
Tel: 213-461-4618

Filmservice Laboratories, Inc.
6327 Santa Monica Boulevard
Los Angeles, California 90038
Tel: 213-464-5141

Flora Color, Inc.
1715 North Mariposa Street
Los Angeles, California 90027
Tel: 213-633-2291

Fotokem Industries, Inc.
3215 Cahuenga Boulevard West
Los Angeles, California 90068
Tel: 213-876-8100

Hollywood Film Enterprises, Inc.
6060 Sunset Boulevard
Los Angeles, California 90028
Tel: 213-464-2181

MGM Laboratories, Inc.
10202 West Washington
  Boulevard
Culver City, California 90230
Tel: 213-836-3000

Hal Mann Laboratories
7070 Santa Monica Boulevard
Los Angeles, California 90038
Tel: 213-466-3231

Metro-Kalvar, Inc.
8927 West Exposition Building
Los Angeles, California 90034
Tel: 213-870-1602

Modern Film Laboratories, Inc.
832 North Cole Avenue
Los Angeles, California 90028
Tel: 213-464-7293

Movielab-Hollywood, Inc.
6823 Santa Monica Boulevard
Los Angeles, California 90038
Tel: 213-469-5981

Newsfilm Laboratories, Inc.
516 North Larchmont Boulevard
Los Angeles, California 90004
Tel: 213-462-8292

Pacific Colorfilm, Inc.
574 North Larchmont Boulevard
Los Angeles, California 90004
Tel: 213-463-6844

Pacific Film Industries
5220 Santa Monica Boulevard
Los Angeles, California 90029
Tel: 213-661-1104

Pacific Title and Art Studio
6350 Santa Monica Boulevard
Los Angeles, California 90038
Tel: 213-464-0121

Peerless Film Processing
  Corporation
829 North Highland
Los Angeles, California 90038
Tel: 213-464-7156

Producers Photographic
  Laboratories
6660 Santa Monica Boulevard
Los Angeles, California 90038
Tel: 213-462-1334

Rainbow Film Laboratories
6520 Santa Monica Building
Los Angeles, California 90008
Tel: 213-469-8976

Reversals Unlimited
6903 Melrose Avenue
Los Angeles, California 90038
Tel: 213-938-3641

SYNC Film Laboratories
1962 Wilcox Avenue
Los Angeles, California 90068
Tel: 213-469-5134

Technicolor, Inc.
6311 Romaine Street
Los Angeles, California 90038
Tel: 213-462-6111

Yale Laboratories
1509 North Gordon Avenue
Los Angeles, California 90028
Tel: 213-464-6181

Palo Alto area:

Cine-Chrome Laboratories, Inc.
4075 Transport Street
Palo Alto, California 94303
Tel: 415-321-5678

San Diego area:

Cal Photo Motion Picture
  Laboratories
3494 Pickett Street
San Diego, California 92110
Tel: 714-297-1621

San Francisco area:

Leo Diner Films, Inc.
332-350 Golden Gate Avenue
San Francisco, California 94102
Tel: 415-775-3664

Golden News Films
1557 Pine Street
San Francisco, California 94109
Tel: 415-776-7484

Highland Laboratories
90 Tehama Street
San Francisco, California 94105
Tel: 415-986-5480

Monaco Laboratories, Inc.
950 Columbus Avenue
San Francisco, California 94133
Tel: 415-673-0511

Motion Picture Service Company
125 Hyde Street
San Francisco, California 94102
Tel: 415-673-9162

Multichrome Laboratories
760 Gough Street
San Francisco, California 94102
Tel: 415-431-6567

Alfred T. Palmer Productions
563 Second Street
San Francisco, California 94107
Tel: 415-392-4449

W. A. Palmer Films, Inc.
611 Howard Street
San Francisco, California 94105
Tel: 415-986-5961

Patterson Films Corporation
125 Hyde Street
San Francisco, California 94102

Sola Photo & Sound
3290 Mission Street
San Francisco, California 94110
Tel: 415-282-6058

Colorado:

Alexander Film Services
3200 North Nevada Avenue
Colorado Springs, Colorado
80907
Tel: 303-471-2150

Rocky Mountain Film Lab
727 South Nome Street
Aurora, Colorado 80012
Tel: 303-366-0312

United Film Industries
1028 Acoma Street
Denver, Colorado 80204
Tel: 303-244-4629

Western Cine Service, Inc.
312 South Pearl
Denver, Colorado 80209
Tel: 303-744-1017

District of Columbia:

Byron Motion Pictures, Inc.
65 K Street, N.E.
Washington, D.C. 20002
Tel: 202-783-2700

Capital Film Laboratories, Inc.
470 E Street, S.W.
Washington, D.C. 20024
Tel: 202-347-1717

Koster Film Facilities, Inc.
1017 New Jersey Avenue, S.E.
Washington, D.C. 20003
Tel: 202-544-4410

Rodgers Film, Inc.
1130 New Hampshire Avenue,
N.W.
Washington, D.C. 20037
Tel: 202-223-4181

Washington Film Laboratories,
Inc.
1042 Wisconsin Avenue, N.W.
Washington, D.C. 20007
Tel: 202-333-1162

Florida:
Jacksonville:

Russell Barton Film Company
4805 Lenox Avenue
Jacksonville, Florida 32205

Robert R. Favorite Productions
305 First Federal Building
Jacksonville, Florida 33202
Tel: 904-353-8155

Lawrence Smith Productions, Inc.
3024 Lenox Avenue
Jacksonville, Florida 32205
Tel: 904-389-1334

Miami:

Capital Film Laboratories, Inc.
1998 N.E. 150th Street
North Miami, Florida 33161
Tel: 305-949-4252

Reela Film Laboratories, Inc.
65 N.E. Third Street
Miami, Florida 33128
Tel: 305-377-2611

Tampa:

Channel 8 Color Lab
905 East Jackson Street
Tampa, Florida 33601
Tel: 813-229-7781

Georgia:

Cinema Processors, Inc.
2156 Faulkner Road
Atlanta, Georgia 30324
Tel: 404-633-1448

Color-Graphic
3184 Roswell Road, N.W.
Atlanta, Georgia 30305
Tel: 404-233-2174

Southern Film Lab., Inc.
2381 John Glenn Drive, Suite 105
Chamblee, Georgia 30341
Tel: 404-458-0026

Hawaii:

Pacific Colorfilm
1534 Kapiolani Boulevard
Honolulu, Hawaii 96809
Tel: 808-941-3011

Illinois:

Astro Color Laboratories, Inc.
61 West Erie Street
Chicago, Illinois 60610
Tel: 312-943-5865

Bell & Howell Company
7100 McCormick Boulevard
Lincolnwood, Illinois 60645
Tel: 312-262-1600

Chilton Film Services
10 West Kinzie Street
Chicago, Illinois 60610
Tel: 312-329-0363

Cinema Processors, Inc.
211 East Grand Avenue
Chicago, Illinois 60611
Tel: 312-642-6453

George W. Colburn Laboratory,
  Inc.
164 North Wacker Drive
Chicago, Illinois 60606
Tel: 312-332-6286

Consolidated Film Industries
333 North Michigan Avenue
Chicago, Illinois 60601
Tel: 312-641-0028

Deluxe General of Illinois
2433 Delta Lane
Elk Grove, Illinois 60007
Tel: 312-569-2250

Douglas Film Industries, Inc.
10 West Kinzie Street
Chicago, Illinois 60610
Tel: 312-664-7455

Eagle Film Laboratory, Inc.
4971 North Elston Avenue
Chicago, Illinois 60630
Tel: 312-282-7161

Eastman Kodak Company
1712 South Prairie Avenue
Chicago, Illinois 60616
Tel: 312-922-9691

Filmack Studios
1327 South Wabash Avenue
Chicago, Illinois 60605
Tel: 312-427-3395

Hollywood Film Company
211 East Grand Avenue
Chicago, Illinois 60611
Tel: 312-644-1940

Image Transform, Inc.
625 North Michigan Avenue
Chicago, Illinois 60611
Tel: 312-337-7222

Mediatech, Inc.
528 North Michigan Avenue
Chicago, Illinois 60611
Tel: 312-644-1314

Superior Bulk Film Company
442 North Wells Street
Chicago, Illinois 60610
Tel: 312-644-4448

Videx Corporation
1920 North Lincoln Avenue
Chicago, Illinois 60614
Tel: 312-266-9811

Visual Effects, Inc.
57 West Grand Avenue
Chicago, Illinois 60610
Tel: 312-642-8441

Indiana:

Filmcraft Laboratories
5323 West 86th Street
Indianapolis, Indiana 46268
Tel: 317-299-7070

Lakeside Laboratory
5929 East Dunes Highway
Gary, Indiana 46403
Tel: 317-731-5600

Louisiana:

Delta Films
327 Market Street
Shreveport, Louisiana 71101
Tel: 318-423-2679

Pan American Films
822 North Rampart Street
New Orleans, Louisiana 70116
Tel: 504-522-5364

Maryland:

Alpha Film Laboratories
P.O. Box 5325
Baltimore, Maryland 21209
Tel: 301-252-4150

National Cine Laboratories
4319 Rhode Island Avenue
Brentwood, Maryland 20036
Tel: 301-779-6800

Quality Film Labs
5800 York Road
Baltimore, Maryland 21212
Tel: 301-435-1212

Massachusetts:

Film Service Laboratory
58-62 Berkeley Street
Boston, Massachusetts 02115
Tel: 617-542-1238

Michigan:

Allied Film Laboratory, Inc.
9930 Greenfield
Detroit, Michigan 48227
Tel: 313-272-3990

Custom Tech
14350 Charlevois
Detroit, Michigan 48233
Tel: 313-822-0550

Detroit Film Laboratory
800 West Fort
Detroit, Michigan 48226
Tel: 313-962-9333

Dynamic Film Service
3028 East Grand Boulevard
Detroit, Michigan 48202
Tel: 313-873-4720

Film Craft Laboratories, Inc.
66 Sibley
Detroit, Michigan 48201
Tel: 313-962-2611

The Jam Handy Organization
2792 East Grand Boulevard
Detroit, Michigan 48211
Tel: 313-845-2450

Producers Color Service
2921 East Grand Boulevard
Detroit, Michigan 48202
Tel: 313-874-1112

Missouri:
Kansas City:

Calvin Laboratories
1105 Truman Road
Kansas City, Missouri 64106
Tel: 816-421-1230

ESO-S Pictures, Inc.
1121 West 47th Street
Kansas City, Missouri 64112
Tel: 816-531-1481

St. Louis:

Cine-Graphic Film Laboratory,
  Inc.
101 North Seventeenth Street
St. Louis, Missouri 63103
Tel: 314-421-5827

Magnetic Film Lab, Inc.
4468 Shaw Avenue
St. Louis, Missouri 63110
Tel: 314-773-4819

Montana:

Photo-Cine Laboratories
Box 515
Billings, Montana 59103
Tel: 406-252-3077

Nebraska:

Cornhusker Film Processing
  Laboratories
1817 Vinton Street
Omaha, Nebraska 68108
Tel: 402-341-4290

New Jersey:

Triangle Labs
20 Commercial Avenue
Fairview, New Jersey 07022
Tel: 201-941-2020

New York:

A-1 Reverse-O-Labs
345 West 44th Street
New York, New York 10036
Tel: 212-581-0868

Accurate Film Labs
145 West 45th Street
New York, New York 10036
Tel: 212-581-5245

Arta Lab, Inc.
723 Seventh Avenue
New York, New York 10019
Tel: 212-586-7556

Azure Film, Inc.
432 West 45th Street
New York, New York 10036
Tel: 212-247-3415

Bebell, Inc.
416 West 45th Street
New York, New York 10036
Tel: 212-245-8900

Berkey Film Processing
77 East Twelfth Street
New York, New York 10003
Tel: 212-475-8700

Capital Film Lab New York, Inc.
1619 Broadway
New York, New York 10019
Tel: 212-541-4540

276

Motion Picture Market Place

Cineffects Color Lab, Inc.
115 West 45th Street
New York, New York 10036
Tel: 212-581-4730

Cinelab Corporation
421 West 54th Street
New York, New York 10019
Tel: 212-765-1670

Consolidated Film Industries
15 Columbus Circle
New York, New York 10023
Tel: 212-581-1090

Control Film Service
421 West 54th Street
New York, New York 10019
Tel: 212-245-1574

Criterion Film Laboratories, Inc.
415 West 55th Street
New York, New York 10019
Tel: 212-265-2180

Deluxe General, Inc.
321 West 44th Street
New York, New York 10036
Tel: 212-247-3220

Deluxe Laboratories
630 Ninth Avenue
New York, New York 10036
Tel: 212-489-8800

Du-Art Film Laboratories
245 West 55th Street
New York, New York 10019
Tel: 212-757-4580

Filmlab, Inc.
126 West 46th Street
New York, New York 10036
Tel: 212-582-2863

Filmstronics Labs
231 West 54th Street
New York, New York 10019
Tel: 212-586-3150

Finast Color Labs, Inc.
130 West 42nd Street
New York, New York 10017
Tel: 212-239-4655

Guffanti Film Laboratories, Inc.
630 Ninth Avenue
New York, New York 10036
Tel: 212-265-5530

Hollywood Film Company
524 West 43rd Street
New York, New York 10036
Tel: 212-563-1546

Huemark Films, Inc.
277 East 44th Street
New York, New York 10017
Tel: 212-986-5066

IBC Color Labs, Inc.
533 West 47th Street
New York, New York 10036
Tel: 212-765-8800

J & D Labs, Inc.
421 West 45th Street
New York, New York 10036
Tel: 212-581-4725

James Color Laboratories, Inc.
1156 Avenue of the Americas
New York, New York 10036
Tel: 212-682-8232

Kin-O-Lux, Inc.
17 West 45th Street
New York, New York 10036
Tel: 212-586-1880

Manhattan Color Laboratories
222 East 44th Street
New York, New York 10017
Tel: 212-661-5610

Media Film Services, Inc.
351 West 52nd Street
New York, New York 10019
Tel: 212-581-4995

Movielab, Inc.
619 West 54th Street
New York, New York 10019
Tel: 212-586-0360

Multicolor Film Labs, Inc.
244 West 49th Street
New York, New York 10019
Tel: 212-247-4770

Precision Film Laboratories
630 Ninth Avenue
New York, New York 10036
Tel: 212-489-8800

Quality Film Laboratories
  Company
619 West 54th Street
New York, New York 10019
Tel: 212-586-4912

Radiant Film Laboratories, Inc.
321 West 44th Street
New York, New York 10036
Tel: 212-582-7310

TVC Laboratories, Inc.
311 West 43rd Street
New York, New York 10036
Tel: 212-586-5090

Technicolor, Inc.
Radiant Division
321 West 44th Street
New York, New York 10036
Tel: 212-582-7310

Top Notch Film Laboratory, Inc.
333 West 52nd Street
New York, New York 10019
Tel: 212-757-5622

North Carolina:

Motion Picture Laboratories, Inc.
Piedmont Division
2517 South Boulevard
Charlotte, North Carolina 28203
Tel: 704-525-5416

Ohio:
Cincinnati:

Cincinnati Film Labs
3705 Lonsdale Street
Cincinnati, Ohio 45227
Tel: 513-271-5540

Film Art, Inc.
2436 Vine Street
Cincinnati, Ohio 45220
Tel: 513-621-4930

Marathon Movie Laboratory
2436 Vine Street
Cincinnati, Ohio 45219
Tel: 513-621-5313

Cleveland:

Filmlab Service
4019 Prospect Avenue
Cleveland, Ohio 44103
Tel: 216-881-4510

Dayton:

Film Associates
4600 South Dixie Avenue
Dayton, Ohio 45439
Tel: 513-292-2164

Oregon:

Evergreen Film Service, Inc.
1658 Willamette
Eugene, Oregon 97401
Tel: 503-686-2183

Forde Motion Picture
  Laboratories
2153 N.E. Sandy Boulevard
Portland, Oregon 97232
Tel: 503-234-0553

King Film Laboratories
1501 S.W. Jefferson Street
Portland, Oregon 97201
Tel: 503-224-8620

Pennsylvania:
Philadelphia:

Color Tech Film Laboratories,
  Inc.
640 North Broad Street
Philadelphia, Pennsylvania 19130
Tel: 215-236-9100

Film Makers of Philadelphia
21 North Tenth Street
Philadelphia, Pennsylvania 19107
Tel: 215-923-5825

News Reel Laboratory
1733 Sansome Street
Philadelphia, Pennsylvania 19103
Tel: 215-746-3892

Pittsburgh:

Motion Picture Film Services, Inc.
209 Ninth Street
Pittsburgh, Pennsylvania 15222
Tel: 412-566-2222

WRS Motion Picture
  Laboratories
210 Semple Street
Pittsburgh, Pennsylvania 15213
Tel: 412-683-6300

South Carolina:

Southeastern Film Company
3604 Main Street
Columbia, South Carolina 29203
Tel: 803-252-3753

Tennessee:

Motion Picture Laboratories, Inc.
781 South Main Street
Memphis, Tennessee 38106
Tel: 901-948-0456

Texas:

A-V Corporation
2518 North Boulevard
Houston, Texas 77006
Tel: 713-523-6701

Dale Berry & Associates, Inc.
9001 ERL Thornton Freeway
Dallas, Texas 75228
Tel: 214-324-0409

Jamieson Film Company
6911 Forest Park Road
Dallas, Texas 75235
Tel: 214-350-1283

Motion Picture Laboratories of
    Dallas, Inc.
3825 Bryan Street
Dallas, Texas 75204
Tel: 214-823-8158

PSI Film Laboratories, Inc.
3011 Diamond Park Drive
Dallas, Texas 75347
Tel: 214-631-5670

The Photographic Laboratories
1926 West Gray
Houston, Texas 77019
Tel: 713-529-5846

Southwest Film Laboratory, Inc.
3024 Fort Worth Avenue
Dallas, Texas 75211
Tel: 214-331-8347

Utah:

Stockdale & Company, Inc.
200 East First South
Salt Lake City, Utah 84111
Tel: 801-521-3505

Washington:

Alpha Cine Laboratories
1001 Lenora
Seattle, Washington 98166
Tel: 206-682-9230

Forde Motion Picture
    Laboratories
306 Fairview Avenue North
Seattle, Washington 98109
Tel: 206-682-2510

Wisconsin:

Central Film Laboratory & Photo
    Supply
1021 North Third Street
Milwaukee, Wisconsin 53203
Tel: 414-272-0606

Lighting Consultants

California:

Los Angeles area:

Academy Lighting Consultants,
Inc.
6777 Hollywood Boulevard
Los Angeles, California 90028
Tel: 213-462-3941

Act Design and Execution
14106 Ventura Boulevard
Sherman Oaks, California 91403
Tel: 213-788-4219

Century Strand, Inc.
3411 West El Segundo Boulevard
Hawthorne, California 90250
Tel: 213-776-4600

Company Theatre
1024 South Robertson Boulevard
Los Angeles, California 90035
Tel: 213-659-0794

George T. Howard & Associates
7046 Hollywood Boulevard
Los Angeles, California 90028
Tel: 213-462-2343

Imero Fiorentino Associates, Inc.
7250 Franklin Avenue
Los Angeles, California 90046
Tel: 213-876-6000

Kilgore Limited/Jim Kilgore
10041 Moorpark Street
North Hollywood, California
91602
Tel: 213-877-4066

Kriton Productions
7906 Santa Monica Boulevard
Los Angeles, California 90046
Tel: 213-656-5964

Los Angeles Stage Lighting
Company, Ltd.
1451 Venice Boulevard
Los Angeles, California 90006
Tel: 213-384-1241

Mole-Richardson Company
937 North Sycamore Avenue
Los Angeles, California 90038
Tel: 213-851-0111

Olesen Company
1535 Ivar Avenue
Los Angeles, California 90028
Tel: 213-465-5194

Glen R. Roland, Jr.
8543 Clifton Way
Beverly Hills, California 9021
Tel: 213-271-0533

Soundesign Engineers
Box 921
Beverly Hills, California 9021
Tel: 213-276-2726

Sun Dance Lighting
7860 Lasaine Avenue
Northridge, California 91324
Tel: 213-343-2434

Telaudio Center
634 South Victory Boulevard
Burbank, California 91502
Tel: 213-849-1433

Palo Alto area:

Century Strand, Inc.
2443 Ash Street
Palo Álto, California 94306
Tel: 415-327-3262

San Diego area:

H. J. Anderson Company
4441 Park Boulevard
San Diego, California 92116
Tel: 714-297-4451

San Francisco area:

Cinema Services Company
325 Corey Way
South San Francisco, California
   94080
Tel: 415-761-6058

Manifest Production Service
308 Eleventh Street
San Francisco, California 94102
Tel: 415-626-5596

Colorado:

Stage Engineer and Supply, Inc.
Box 2002
Colorado Springs, Colorado
   80901
Tel: 303-635-2935

Hawaii:

The House of Eric Productions
1760 Ala Moana Boulevard
Honolulu, Hawaii 96815
Tel: 808-533-3877

Nevada:

Imero Fiorentino Associates, Inc.
2781 South Bronco
Las Vegas, Nevada 89102
Tel: 702-876-6661

Pembrex Theatre Supply
   Company
3519 Algonquin Drive
Las Vegas, Nevada 89109
Tel: 702-735-5278

New York:

Academy Lighting Consultants
444 West 63rd Street
New York, New York 10023
Tel: 212-582-8101

Imero Fiorentino Associates, Inc.
10 West 66th Street
New York, New York 10023
Tel: 212-787-3050

Vega Associates, Inc.
408 West 57th Street
New York, New York 10019
Tel: 212-541-7040

Washington:

Stordahl's Place Productions
3831 34th Avenue West
Seattle, Washington 98199
Tel: 206-285-3022

Lighting Equipment

Arizona:

Southwestern Studio
Carefree, Arizona 85331
Tel: 602-946-3404

Special Events Coordinators, Inc.
3422 West Weldon Avenue
Phoenix, Arizona 85017
Tel: 602-272-1337

Studio Rentals Incorporated of
   Arizona
2321 East University Drive
Phoenix, Arizona 85034
Tel: 602-252-5848

California:
Los Angeles area:

Acey-Decy Equipment Company
3417 North Cahuenga Boulevard
West Los Angeles, California
   90028
Tel: 213-851-3550

Audio Acoustics Engineers
13912 Ponderosa Avenue
Santa Ana, California 92701
Tel: 213-543-5082

Bardwell & McAlister, Inc.
7269 Santa Monica Boulevard
Los Angeles, California 90038
Tel: 213-876-4133

Bates Lighting Company
1215 Bates Avenue
Los Angeles, California 90029
Tel: 213-661-1262

Bob Beck & Associates
1538 Cassil Place
Los Angeles, California 90028
Tel: 213-462-7093

Beckett Motion Picture
   Equipment
1025 North McCadden Place
Los Angeles, California 90038
Tel: 213-465-7141

Berkey-Colortran, Inc.
1015 Chestnut Street
Burbank, California 91403
Tel: 213-843-1200

Birns & Sawyer, Inc.
1026 North Highland Avenue
Los Angeles, California 90038
Tel: 213-466-8211

Century Strand, Inc.
3411 West El Segundo Boulevar
Hawthorne, California 90250
Tel: 213-679-0624

Cine Group
8560 Sunset Boulevard
Los Angeles, California 90069
Tel: 213-652-4800

Cinema Productions Corporation
2037 Granville Avenue
Los Angeles, California 90025
Tel: 213-478-0711

Colortran Industries
1015 Chestnut Street
Burbank, California 91502
Tel: 213-843-1200

F. W. Corbett Productions
1835 Third Avenue
Los Angeles, California 90019
Tel: 213-733-5251

F&B/Ceco of California, Inc.
7051 Santa Monica Boulevard
Los Angeles, California 90038
Tel: 213-466-9361

John P. Filbert Company
1100 Flower Street
Glendale, California 91201
Tel: 213-247-6550

Alan Gordon Enterprises, Inc.
1430 North Cahuenga Boulevard
Los Angeles, California 90028
Tel: 213-466-3561

Alan Gordon Enterprises, Inc.
5362 North Cahuenga Boulevard
North Hollywood, California
  91601
Tel: 213-985-5500

Hollywood Camera Company
5405 Cahuenga Boulevard
North Hollywood, California
  91601
Tel: 213-466-1318

James Studio Neon Company
752 North Cahuenga Boulevard
Los Angeles, California 90038
Tel: 213-467-8000

Kliegl Brothers Western
  Corporation
13400 Saticoy Street, No. 12
North Hollywood, California
  91605
Tel: 213-764-9990

Kriton Productions
7906 Santa Monica Boulevard
Los Angeles, California 90046
Tel: 213-656-5964

Leonetti Cine Rentals
5609 Sunset Boulevard
Los Angeles, California 90028
Tel: 213-469-2987

Lloyd-Davies Enterprises
1021 North McCadden Place
Los Angeles, California 90038
Tel: 213-462-1206

Los Angeles Stage Lighting
  Company, Ltd.
1451 Venice Boulevard
Los Angeles, California 90006
Tel: 213-384-1241

Roy Low Enterprises
3407 West Olive Street
Burbank, California 91505
Tel: 213-846-7740

Matrix Image
6622 Variel Avenue
Canoga Park, California 91303
Tel: 213-883-6622

Metro-Goldwyn-Mayer, Inc.
10202 West Washington
  Boulevard
Culver City, California 90230
Tel: 213-836-3000

Mobile Production Systems
1225 North Vine Street
Los Angeles, California 90038
Tel: 213-465-7141

Mole-Richardson Company
937 North Sycamore Avenue
Los Angeles, California 90038
Tel: 213-851-0111

Movie Tech
6518 Santa Monica Boulevard
Los Angeles, California 90038
Tel: 213-467-8491

Olesen Company
1535 Ivar Avenue
Los Angeles, California 90028
Tel: 213-465-5194

PSI-Production Systems, Inc.
1123 North Lillian Way
Los Angeles, California 90038
Tel: 213-469-2704

Jack Pill & Associates
6370 Santa Monica Boulevard
Los Angeles, California 90038
Tel: 213-466-3238

Glen R. Roland, Jr.
8543 Clifton Way
Beverly Hills, California 90211
Tel: 213-271-0533

SOS Photo-Cine-Optics, Inc.
7051 Santa Monica Boulevard
Los Angeles, California 90038
Tel: 213-466-9361

Tech-Camera Rentals, Inc.
6370 Santa Monica Boulevard
Los Angeles, California 90038
Tel: 213-466-5391

Frank Tucker Studio Lighting
1301 South La Brea Avenue
Los Angeles, California 90019
Tel: 213-937-3955

UPS Studio Rentals
6561 Santa Monica Boulevard
Los Angeles, California 90038
Tel: 213-461-1442

Universal City Studios
100 Universal City Plaza
Universal City, California 91608
Tel: 213-985-4321

Videodetics Corporation
2121 South Manchester Avenue
Anaheim, California 92802
Tel: 714-532-3364

Palo Alto area:

Century Strand Inc.
2443 Ash Street
Palo Alto, California 94306
Tel: 415-327-3262

San Diego area:

H. J. Anderson Company, Inc.
4441 Park Boulevard
San Diego, California 92116
Tel: 714-297-4451

Multi Image Productions, Inc.
8170 Ronson Road
San Diego, California 92111
Tel: 714-560-8385

San Francisco area:

American Zoetrope, Inc.
American Zoetrope Film Facility
827 Folsom Street
San Francisco, California 94107
Tel: 416-989-0600

Brooks Cameras, Inc.
45 Kearny Street
San Francisco, California 94108
Tel: 415-392-1902

Cinema Services Company
325 Corey Way
South San Francisco, California
94080
Tel: 415-761-6058

Ferco
363 Brannan Street
San Francisco, California 94107
Tel: 415-957-1787

Adolph Gasser, Inc.
5733 Geary Boulevard
San Francisco, California 92421
Tel: 415-751-0145

Holzmueller Corporation
360 Sixth Street
San Francisco, California 94103
Tel: 415-861-2050

Manifest Production Services
308 Eleventh Street
San Francisco, California 94102
Tel: 415-626-5596

The Phelps & Kopp Company
991 Tennessee Street
San Francisco, California 94107
Tel: 415-285-1900

Skinner Studio
345 Sutter Street
San Francisco, California 94108
Tel: 415-986-5040

Colorado:

Cinema Services
Box 398
Eldorado Springs, Colorado
80025
Tel: 303-443-4913

Stage Engineer and Supply, Inc.
Box 2002
Colorado Springs, Colorado
80901
Tel: 303-635-2935

Western Cine Service, Inc.
312 South Pearl Street
Denver, Colorado 80209
Tel: 303-744-1017

Florida:

Stage Equipment & Lighting
12231 N.E. Thirteenth Court
North Miami, Florida 33161
Tel: 305-891-2010

Hawaii:

Attco
2805 Koapaka
Honolulu, Hawaii 96814
Tel: 808-841-0991

The House of Eric Productions
1760 Ala Moana Boulevard
Waikiki, Hawaii 96815
Tel: 808-533-3877

Pacific Instrumentation
5388 Papai Street
Honolulu, Hawaii 96821
Tel: 808-373-1287

Illinois:

Grand Stage Lighting Company
630 West Lake Street
Chicago, Illinois 60606
Tel: 312-332-5611

Helix Ltd.
679 North Orleans Street
Chicago, Illinois 60654
Tel: 312-944-4400

Studio Lighting Company
2212 North Halsted Street
Chicago, Illinois 60614
Tel: 312-327-2800

Maryland:

R & R Lighting Company, Inc
622 Mississippi Avenue
Silver Spring, Maryland 20910
Tel: 301-589-9025

Massachusetts:

Dekko Film Productions, Inc.
126 Dartmouth Street
Boston, Massachusetts 02106
Tel: 617-536-6160

Film Associates
421 Broadway
Cambridge, Massachusetts 02138
Tel: 617-492-1062

Michigan:

Jack Frost
234 Piquette
Detroit, Michigan 48202
Tel: 313-873-8030

Nevada:

Nevada Lite-Rite, Inc.
2332 South Highland Drive
Las Vegas, Nevada 89102

Pembrex Theatre Supply
  Company
3519 Algonquin Drive
Las Vegas, Nevada 89109
Tel: 702-735-5278

New York:

Berkey-Colortran, Inc.
842 Broadway
New York, New York 10003
Tel: 212-475-8700

Boken, Inc.
349 West 48th Street
New York, New York 10036
Tel: 212-581-5626

Camera Mart, Inc.
456 West 55th Street
New York, New York 10019
Tel: 212-757-6977

Thomas Cestare, Inc.
131 North Cottage Street
Valley Stream, New York 11580
Tel: 516-561-2065

Clipstrip-Bubbelight, Inc.
349 West 48th Street
New York, New York 10036
Tel: 212-581-5515

F&B/Ceco, Inc.
315 West 43rd Street
New York, New York 10036
Tel: 212-486-1420

Feature Systems, Inc.
513 West 26th Street
New York, New York 10001
Tel: 212-736-0447

Filmtrucks, New York
512 West 39th Street
New York, New York 10018
Tel: 212-524-8668

Charles Ross, Inc.
333 West 52nd Street
New York, New York 10019
Tel: 212-246-5470

Times Square Theatrical &
   Studio Supply Corporation
318 West 47th Street
New York, New York 10036
Tel: 212-245-4155

Pennsylvania:

Aladdin Stage Lighting
510 South Street
Philadelphia, Pennsylvania 19105
Tel: 215-923-1036

Texas:

Dale Berry & Associates, Inc.
9001 E R L Thornton Freeway
Dallas, Texas 75228
Tel: 214-324-0409

Performing Arts Supply
   Company, Inc.
5734 Green Ash
Houston, Texas 77036
Tel: 713-667-8101

Utah:

Stockdale & Company, Inc.
200 East First South
Salt Lake City, Utah 84111
Tel: 801-521-3505

Washington:

Aero Marc, Inc.
5518 Empire Way South
Seattle, Washington 98118
Tel: 206-725-1400

Brooks W. Baum Cinema
    Productions
715 First Avenue West
Seattle, Washington 98119
Tel: 206-283-6456

Display & Stage Lighting
2410 First Avenue
Seattle, Washington 98121
Tel: 206-622-7850

Northwest Sound & Production
129 First Street, West
Seattle, Washington 98121
Tel: 206-282-4766

Stordahl's Place Productions
3831 34th Avenue West
Seattle, Washington 98199
Tel: 206-285-3022

Locations &
Location Assistance

Included here are the sources of nongovernmental assistance with location scouting. State and city offices involved in film production assistance, including location work, are listed under "Film Commissions."

Arizona:

Apacheland Movie Ranch and
   Studio
Apache Junction, Arizona 85220
Tel: 602-946-1780

Bradshaw Location Service
Box 195
Sedona, Arizona 86336
Tel: 602-282-7385

Old Tucson Studio
Tucson Mountain Park
201 South Kinney Road
Tucson, Arizona 85705
Tel: 602-792-3100

California:
   Los Angeles area:

Act Design and Execution
14106 Ventura Boulevard
Sherman Oaks, California 91403
Tel: 213-788-4219

Argus Productions International
1438 Davies Drive
Beverly Hills, California 90210
Tel: 213-274-2891

Bell Ranch
2517 West Grand Avenue
Alhambra, California 91801
Tel: 213-281-2728

Columbia Pictures Ranch
4000 Warner Boulevard
Burbank, California 91505
Tel: 213-843-7280

Coordinators 2
8113 1/2 Melrose
Los Angeles, California 90046
Tel: 213-653-6110

Film Locations International
Marina Del Ray, California
   90291
Tel: 213-821-8500

Rolly Harper, Inc.
7782 San Fernando Road
Sun Valley, California 91352
Tel: 213-768-1644

Hope Town Movie Ranch
1601 Kuehnr Drive
Santa Susana, California 93063
Tel: 805-526-1147

Iverson Ranch
P.O. Box 306
Chatsworth, California 91331
Tel: 213-341-1970

Motion Picture Location Service
2517 West Grand
Alhambra, California 91801
Tel: 213-281-2728

Pacific Films, Inc.
Box 5055
Sherman Oaks, California 91413
Tel: 213-769-7404

Production Assistance
11627 Oxnard
North Hollywood, California
    91606
Tel: 213-769-2200

Ridgerose Company
800 North Seward Street
Los Angeles, California 90038
Tel: 213-466-4271

Searchlighters Location Service
1223 North Larrabee Street
Los Angeles, California 90069
Tel: 213-652-2056

Wonderland West
Santa Susana Pass Road
Chatsworth, California 91311
Tel: 213-882-9966

San Francisco area:

The Phelps & Kopp Company
991 Tennessee Street
San Francisco, California 94107
Tel: 415-285-1900

Snazelle Films, Inc.
155 Fell Street
San Francisco, California 94102
Tel: 415-431-5490

Colorado:

Cinema Services
P.O. Box 398
Eldorado Springs, Colorado
    80025
Tel: 303-443-4913

Kenneth A. Meyer Film
    Productions
2181 South Grape
Denver, Colorado 80222
Tel: 303-758-2534

Florida:

Cinema City Studios, Inc.
6015 Highway 301 North
Tampa, Florida 33610
Tel: 813-621-4731

Hawaii:

Allison-Donnellan Productions,
    Inc.
832 Halekauwila Street
Honolulu, Hawaii 96813
Tel: 808-537-4115

Louisiana:

DiMaggio Associates
411 Frenchmen Street
New Orleans, Louisiana 70116
Tel: 504-945-2025

Nevada:

Bonnie Springs Old Nevada
830 East Sahara Avenue, Suite 1
Las Vegas, Nevada 89105
Tel: 707-732-2115

New York:

Locations, Inc.
Box 75
Oyster Bay, L.I., New York 11771
Tel: 516-922-0250

Texas:

Century Studios, Inc.
4519 Maple Avenue
Dallas, Texas 75219
Tel: 214-522-3310

Happy Shahan's Alamo Village
P.O. Box 528
Brackettville, Texas 78832
Tel: 512-563-2580

Washington:

W. Brooks Baum Cinema
   Production
715 First Avenue West
Seattle, Washington 98119
Tel: 206-283-6456

JRB Motion Graphics
3323 Ninth Avenue
West Seattle, Washington 98119
Tel: 206-284-0834

Major Studios

In the good old days all the major motion picture companies maintaine studio facilities. With changing economics part of that valuable real estate now occupied by condominiums, and many major production compani don't operate studios. Listed here are the principal existing Hollywoo studios and their operating personnel. Not included are major companies i terms of gross sales, such as American-International and Billy Jac Enterprises, which don't maintain studios.

California:

Burbank Studios
4000 Warner Boulevard
Burbank, California 91522
Tel: 213-843-6000
Department Heads:
Robert Hagel, President
Gary Paster, Studio Executive
Seymour Yack, Accounting
Terry Dunne, Time Office
Edward Medman, Business
  Affairs, Labor Relations,
  Vice-President
Herman David, Plant Operations
Jack Froelich, Technical Services
Herb Cheek, Operations Services
Roy Regan, Personnel
Norma Smith, Telephone
Alex Bryce, Electrical
  Maintenance
Everett Olson, Construction
Jack Belyeu, Transportation
Edmundo Gonzalez, Still
  Laboratory
Frank Decker, Mail and Graphics
Lou Rentz, Plumbing
Sid Loranger, Special Effects
Bill Widmayer, Camera
Rudy Frank, Camera Machine

Larry Comstock, Grip
Hal Landaker, Production/Soun
Murray Schaffer, Post Productio
  Service
Al Green, Post Production/Soun
Jim Bailey, Projection
Charles Swan, First Aid
Bud Hanes, Purchasing/Stores
Ted Goldstone, Labor/Utility
Max Frankel, Property
Bob Ayers, Greens
George Centi, Staff
Bob Taylor, Drapery
John Reeves, Security
Mike Michaelnan, Paint/Sceni
Ben Lane, Makeup/Hair
Jack Delaney, Wardrobe
Harry Kemm, Art
Ray Carter, Set Lighting
Jim Winfree, Record Recordin
Dick Smith, Prop Shop

Walt Disney Productions
500 South Buena Vista Street
Burbank, California 91521
Tel: 213-849-3411
Corporate Officers:
Donn B. Tatum, Chairman of the
  Board and Chief Executive
  Officer

E. Cardon Walker, President and
Chief Operating Officer
William H. Anderson,
Vice-President–Production
and Studio Operations
Michael L. Bagnall,
Vice-President–Finance
Ronald J. Cayo,
Vice-President–Business Affairs
Roy E. Disney,
Vice-President–16mm
Production
Vincent H. Jefferds,
Vice-President–Marketing–
Consumer Products Division
Lawrence E. Tryon,
Vice-President and
Treasurer
Ronald W. Miller,
Vice-President–
Executive Producer
Richard T. Morrow,
Vice-President–General
Counsel
Richard A. Nunis,
Vice-President–Operations—
Disneyland and Walt Disney
World
James L. Stewart,
Vice-President–Corporate
Relations
and Assistant to the President
George A. Sullivan,
Vice-President–
Tax Administration
Alberto F. Trevino, Jr.,
Vice-President–Real Estate
Frank Waldheim, Vice-President
and Eastern Counsel
Bruce F. Johnson, Controller
Luther R. Marr, Secretary–Legal
Leland L. Kirk, Assistant
Secretary–Treasurer

Donald A. Escen, Assistant
Treasurer and Assistant
Controller
Douglas E. Houck, Assistant
Controller
Donald E. Trucker, Assistant
Controller

General Service Studios
1040 North Las Palmas Avenue
Los Angeles, California 90038
Tel: 213-469-9011
James Nasser, President
Theodore Nasser, Secretary
Henry Nasser, Treasurer
Charles S. Concklin, Comptroller
Sally Ragsdale, Assistant
Secretary

Samuel Goldwyn Productions,
Studio Division
1041 North Formosa Avenue
Los Angeles, California 90046
Tel: 213-851-1234
Jack P. Foreman, General
Manager
Donald Daves, Assistant General
Manager
Leonard A. Johnson, Controller
Harry (Jim) Crawford, Manager
Producer Services
Donald Rogers, Sound
Department Head
Norman Tucker, Head
Projectionist
William Blaylock, Purchasing
Agent
Walter Reiher, Studio Controller
Edward Freibert, Time Keeper
George Jackisch, Drapery
Department Head
Tom Seehof, Sales Manager

Metro-Goldwyn-Mayer Studio
10202 West Washington
Boulevard
Culver City, California 90230
Tel: 213-836-3000
Fred Benninger, Chairman,
Board of Directors
Kirk Kerkorian, Vice-Chairman
and Chief Executive Officer
Frank E. Rosenfelt, President and
Chief Operations Officer
Barrie K. Brunet, Executive
Vice-President
James D. Aljian, Senior
Vice-President–Finance
Daniel Melnick, Senior
Vice-President–Theatrical
Production
Harris Katleman,
Senior-President–Television
Byron Shapiro, Vice-
President–Domestic Distribution
Frank I. Davis,
Vice-President–Business Affairs
John P. Beronio, Treasurer
Robert A. Harrison, Controller
Bernard Segelin, Secretary
Benjamin B. Kahane, Assistant
Secretary
Roger L. Mayer, Assistant
Secretary
Kenneth A. Wagner, Assistant
Controller

Production Executives:
Lindsley Parsons, Jr., Division
Vice-President, Production
Operations
Roger L. Mayer, General
Manager, Studio
Jack Dunning, Post-Production
Supervisor
Lewis Rachmil, Production
Executive, Features

Les Frends, Director of
Administration–Television

**Production Department Heads
and Key Personnel:**
Dale Hutchinson, Production
Manager
Steve Cerveny, Electrical
Jack Dunning, Editing
Freeman Davies, Post-Production
Assistant
Harry Lojewski, Music
Lorey Yzuel, Construction
James Fasbender, Production
Estimating
Ray Manheimer, National
Publicity Manager
Carl D. Bennett, Story Editor
Lyle Burbridge, Sound
Norman Kaphan, Still
Laboratory
Hugh Feeley, Transportation
Ted Hatfield, National
Advertising Coordinator

Department Heads:
Robert L. King, Director of
Marketing Services, Motion
Pictures and Television
Tom A. Jones, Publicity Director
Robert Moore, Director of Art
and Advertising
Barney Rogers, Property
Chuck Keehne, Wardrobe
Robert Schiffer, Makeup
Herbert B. Taylor, Sound
Supervisor
Bob Gibeaut, Studio Manager
John Mansbridge, Art and Set
Decoration
Bob Jackman, Music
Karl Karpe, Transportation
Art Cruickshank, Special Effects
Frank Paris, Story Department
Marcus Robertson, Electrical

Gerald Moon, Chief Police
Donald E. Tucker, Accounting
Edward Hansen, Animation
Marvin Schnall, Casting
Paul Devenport, Purchasing
Dick Grills, Camera
Earl Weldon, Editing

Paramount Pictures Corporation
202 North Canon Drive
Beverly Hills, California 90210
Tel: 213-463-0100
Barry Diller, Chairman and Chief
  Executive Officer
Arthur R. Barron, Executive
  Vice-President
D. Barry Reardon,
  Vice-President–Sales
  Administration
Arthur N. Ryan,
  Vice-President–Production
  Administration
Charles O. Glenn,
  Vice-President–Marketing
Norman Weitman, Senior
  Vice-President in charge of
  Domestic Distribution
Gordon Weaver, Vice-
  President–Publicity
Bob Goodfried, Vice-President in
  charge of West Coast and
  Studio Publicity
Robin French, Vice-President for
  Production
Lindsley Parsons, Jr.,
  Vice-President–Executive
  Production
  Manager
Harold Bud Austin, Executive
  Vice-President of Paramount
  Television
Bruce Lansbury, Senior
  Vice-President of Creative

Affairs for Paramount
Television
Eugene Frank, Vice-
  President–West Coast Counsel
  for Paramount Pictures
Walter Josiah, Vice-
  President–Chief Resident
  Counsel
Norman Flicker, Vice
  President–East Coast
  Production
Al Lo Presti, Vice-President in
  Charge of Worldwide
  Technical Facilities
Richard P. Schonland, Director,
  Industrial Relations
Tony Hoffman, National Director
  of Field Advertising and
  Publicity
Richard J. Winters, Director
  National Advertising, Publicity
  and Promotion for Paramount
  Television
Burt Solomon, Director of
  Publicity
Sid Eisenberg, National
  Advertising Manager

Screen Gems, Inc.
Colgems Square
Burbank, California 91505
Tel: 213-843-6000
Executives:
John H. Mitchell, President
Art Frankel, Vice-President,
  Programming
Edward Masket, Vice-President
  in Charge of Administration
Seymour Friedman,
  Vice-President and Executive
  Production Manager
Lawrence Werner, Vice-President
  and Post-Production Manager

Henry Colman, Vice-President,
Current Programs
Renee Valente, Vice-President,
Talent
James Johnson, Vice-President,
West Coast Studio;
Administrator and Controller
of West Coast Operations,
Columbia Pictures Industries,
Inc.
Richard Kerns, Vice-President
EUE/Screen Gems, West
Coast
Al Simon, Director, Tape
Operations
Paul Stager, Studio Counsel
Doug Duitsman, Director of
Studio Publicity and
Promotion
Joe Goodson, Director, Program
Development
Allan Rice, Director of Business
Affairs
Richard Campbell, Western
Division Sales Manager
William Hart, Vice-President in
Charge of Syndication Sales
Norman Horowitz,
Vice-President and General
Manager, International
Herb Lazarus, Vice-President,
International Sales
Walter Kaufman, Vice-President,
Legal and Business Affairs,
International

Studio Center–Facility of CBS,
Inc.
4024 Radford Avenue
Studio City, California 91604
Tel: 213-763-8411
Tel: 213-877-2761

Executives:
Robert Norvet, Vice-President
Edward Denault, Production
Manager
James Rhodes, Plant Manager
Bruce Lowry, Controller
Department Heads:
Morton Stevens, Music
Eliot Bliss, Sound
Cosmas Bolger, Editorial
Al Heschong, Art
Paul Wurtzel, Construction
Albert Ellena, Paint
Tom Long, Grip
Bill Rosson, Plant Maintenance
R. Chaldu, Electric
Warren Welch, Property
Pierre Beauvais, Drapery
Frank Delmar, Wardrobe
George Lane, Makeup
Bud Thompson, Transportation
James Sater, Camera
Earl Wroten, Estimating
Betty Taylor, Accounting
Dean Henning, Payroll
Anise Kreuscher, Telephone
Marion Anderson, Hospital

Twentieth Century–Fox Film
Corporation
Box 900
Beverly Hills, California 90213
Studio: 10201 West Pico
Boulevard
Los Angeles, California 90035
Tel: 213-277-2211
Corporate Officers:
Dennis C. Stanfill, Chairman of
the Board and Chief Executive
Officer
Bernard Barron, Vice-President,
Studio Operations

E. A. Bowen, Vice-President and
Treasurer

Jerome Edwards, Vice-President
and General Counsel

Jack Haley, Jr., Vice-President,
Television

William J. Immerman,
Vice-President, Business
Affairs

Jay Kanter, Vice-President,
Production

Alan Ladd, Jr., Vice-President,
Worldwide Production

John P. Meehan, Vice-President
and Controller

Burton J. Morrison,
Vice-President, Entertainment
Group Controller

Peter S. Myers, Vice-President,
Domestic Distribution

David Raphel, Vice-President,
Foreign Distribution

Jonas Rosenfield, Jr.,
Vice-President, Advertising,
Publicity and Promotion

David Y. Handelman, Secretary

E. Lyle Marshall, Assistant
Treasurer

Subsidiary and Division Officers:

Herbert N. Eiseman, President,
Twentieth Century Music
Corporation

Robert T. Kreiman, President,
DeLuxe General Inc.

Royce J. Moodabe, Managing
Director, Amalgamated
Theatres Ltd.

Russ Regan, President, Twentieth
Century Records

Donald E. Swartz, President and
General Manager, KMSP-TV

John Mostyn, General Manager,
Hoyts Theatres Ltd.

Lewis N. Wolff, President,
Twentieth Century–Fox
Realty & Development
Company

Universal City Studios
100 Universal City Plaza
Universal City, California 91608
Tel: 213-985-4321

Studio Executives:

Gordon B. Forbes, Studio
Operations Manager

Marshall Green, Executive
Production Manager

Joseph James, Post Production

G. Clark Ramsey,
Publicity-Advertising

Gareth Hughes, Labor
Relations–Personnel

Joseph DiMuro, Law

Harry Garfield, Music

Richard M. Birnie, Production
Manager

Hilton Green, Production
Manager

Department Heads:

William DeCinces, Art, Property,
Technical

William Edwards, Camera

William Batlines, Casting

Ralph Winters, Casting

Franz Vander Velden,
Commissary

Virgil Summers, Construction
Superintendent

William Hornbeck, Editorial

Richard Belding, Editorial

William Miner, Electric-
Mechanical Maintenance

Ray Shackelford, Electric-Stage

Jack Rush, Film Library

Robert Aldrich, Grip

June Loos, Hospital

William Vanden Bossche,
  Insurance
Nick Marcellino, Makeup-
  Hairdressing
Wallace Woodworth, Paint
Hugh Jenkins, Purchasing
R. Andrew Lee, Research
James P. Nye, Security
Richard Stumpf, Sound
Roland Chiniquy, Special Effects
Michael Ludmer, Story
Ralph Woodworth, Studio
  Services
James Elkin, Title and Optical
Brad Metcalfe, Transportation
Vincent Dee, Wardrobe

Warner Brothers, Inc.
4000 Warner Boulevard
Burbank, California 91522
Tel: 213-843-6000

Warner Brothers, Inc.
75 Rockefeller Plaza
New York, New York 10019
Tel: 212-484-8000

Ted Ashley, Cochairman of the
  Board
Frank Wells, Cochairman of the
  Board and Chief Operating
  Officer
John Calley, President and
  Executive in Charge of
  Worldwide Production
Bob Solo, Executive
  Vice-President, Production
Leo Greenfield, Vice-President,
  Domestic Sales
Myron Karlin, Vice-President,
  Foreign Sales
Richard Lederer, Vice-President,
  Advertising and Publicity

Joe Hyams, Vice-President,
  Publicity
Charles Greenlaw, Executive
  Vice-President for Worldwide
  Management
Jack Freedman, Vice-President,
  Business Affairs
Gerald Leider, Executive
  Vice-President, Foreign
  Production
Sidney Kiwitt, Vice-President
Larry Leshansky, Vice-President
Ralph Peterson, Vice-President
Ed Silvers, Vice-President
Stanley Belkin, Assistant
  Secretary
Allan B. Ecker, Assistant
  Secretary
Martin A. Fischer, Assistant
  Secretary
Henry M. Heymann, Assistant
  Secretary
Peter D. Knecht, Assistant
  Secretary
Norman K. Samick, Assistant
  Secretary
Bernard Sorkin, Assistant
  Secretary
Marvin Walden, Assistant
  Secretary
Ralph Peterson, Treasurer
Henry Cole, Assistant Treasurer
Edward Romano, Assistant
  Treasurer
Walter Solomon, Assistant
  Treasurer
Solomon M. Weiss, Assistant
  Treasurer
Sidney Ganis, Director of
  Advertising
Ernie Grossman, National
  Director of Publicity &
  Promotion

George Nelson, Eastern Publicity
Director
William A. Latham, Western
Publicity Director
Robert Dorfman, Eastern
Advertising Director
Leo Wilder, Director of Field
Exploitation Activities
David Judson, Cooperative
Advertising Director
Vincent Tubbs, Press Director of
Community Relations

New York:

Columbia Pictures Industries, Inc.
711 Fifth Avenue
New York, New York 10022
Tel: 212-751-4400

Executive Officers:
Leo Jaffe, Chairman of the Board
David Begelman, President
Seymour H. Malamed, Executive
Vice-President, Administration
Peter Guber, Executive
Vice-President, World Film
Production
Charles M. Powell, Executive
Vice-President
John H. Mitchell, Executive
Vice-President
Joseph A. Fischer, Financial
Vice-President and Treasurer
Burton Marcus, Vice-President,
General Counsel and Secretary
Allen Adler, Vice-President,
Corporate Development
Patrick M. Mellilo, Controller

Makeup Supplies

California:

Los Angeles area:

Ball Beauty Supplies
416 North Fairfax
Los Angeles, California 90036
Tel: 213-655-2330

John Chambers Studio, Inc.
7850 Willis Avenue
Van Nuys, California 91402
Tel: 213-988-0123

Christina's
1023 North La Brea Avenue
Los Angeles, California 90038
Tel: 213-340-0357

Columbia Drug Company
6098 Sunset Boulevard
Los Angeles, California 90028
Tel: 213-464-7555

Max Factor & Company
1666 North Highland Avenue
Los Angeles, California 90028
Tel: 213-462-6131

Frends Beauty Supply Company
5202 Laurel Canyon Boulevard
North Hollywood, California
   91607
Tel: 213-877-4828

Invincible Sales Corporation
2303 West Ninth Street
Los Angeles, California 90006
Tel: 213-383-1685

Mercury Beauty Supply
337 South Western Avenue
Los Angeles, California 90038
Tel: 213-383-1285

Norcostco, Inc.
15976 East Francisquito Avenu
La Puente, California 91744
Tel: 213-968-6459

Ben Nye Corporation
11571 Santa Monica Bouleva
Los Angeles, California 90025

Olesen Company
1535 Ivar Avenue
Los Angeles, California 90028
Tel: 213-465-5194

Rainbow Beauty Supply
7323 Beverly Boulevard
Los Angeles, California 90052
Tel: 213-936-2191

Schwabs
401 North Bedford Drive
Beverly Hills, California 9021
Tel: 213-271-5721

Schwabs
435 North Bedford Drive
Beverly Hills, California 9021
Tel: 213-275-4505

Schwabs
8024 Sunset Boulevard
Los Angeles, California 90046
Tel: 213-656-1212

Schwabs
9201 Sunset Boulevard
Los Angeles, California 90069
Tel: 213-273-5111

Jack Sperling Beauty Supply
13639 Vanowen Street
Van Nuys, California 91405
Tel: 213-781-6300

San Diego area:

H. J. Anderson Company, Inc.
8937 Complex Drive
San Diego, California 92123
Tel: 714-565-6984

San Diego Costume Company
7899 Clairemont Mesa Boulevard
San Diego, California 92111
Tel: 714-232-0745

San Francisco area:

Dance Art Company
222 Powell Street
San Francisco, California 94102
Tel: 415-392-4912

Encore Theatrical Supply
    Company
5929 MacArthur Boulevard
Oakland, California 94605
Tel: 415-568-1881

Lewin Drug Company
500 Geary Street
San Francisco, California 94102
Tel: 415-673-1818

Bob Mandell's Costume Shop
834 Mission Street
San Francisco, California 94103
Tel: 415-391-0811

Colorado:

Colorado Costume Company
2100 Broadway
Denver, Colorado 80205
Tel: 303-825-6874

University Park Pharmacy
Evans and University
Denver, Colorado 80210
Tel: 303-722-4781

Florida:

Benson Hotel Pharmacy
1201 Lincoln Road
Miami, Florida 33101
Tel: 305-531-6427

Gables Beauty Supply
2529 Ponce De Leon
Coral Gables, Florida 33134
Tel: 305-446-6654

Hawaii:

The Dance Studio
3280 Pauma Place
Honolulu, Hawaii 96822
Tel: 808-988-4637

Illinois:

Advance Theatrical
125 North Wabash Avenue
Chicago, Illinois 60611
Tel: 312-772-7150

Syd Simons, Inc.
2 East Oak Street
Chicago, Illinois 60611
Tel: 312-943-2333

Nevada:

Universal Models
3661 South Maryland Parkway
Las Vegas, Nevada 89109
Tel: 702-732-2499

Williams Costume Company, Inc.
226 North Third Street
Las Vegas, Nevada 89101
Tel: 702-384-1384

New York:

Margo Bergmann, Inc.
599 Eleventh Avenue
New York, New York 10036
Tel: 212-246-5930

Tom Fields Associates, Inc.
601 West 26th Street
New York, New York 10001
Tel: 212-691-2260

Bob Kelly Cosmetics
151 West 46th Street
New York, New York 10036
Tel: 212-245-2237

Make-Up Center, Ltd.
150 West 55th Street
New York, New York 10019
Tel: 212-977-9494

Mehron, Inc.
325 West 37th Street
New York, New York 10018
Tel: 212-524-1133

Zauder Brothers, Inc.
902 Broadway
New York, New York 10011
Tel: 212-228-2600

Texas:

Dale Berry and Associates, Inc
9001 ERL Thornton Freeway
Dallas, Texas 75228
Tel: 214-324-0409

Elbee Company
821 West Commerce
San Antonio, Texas 78207
Tel: 512-223-4561

Performing Arts Supply
    Company, Inc.
5734 Green Ash
Houston, Texas 77036
Tel: 713-667-8101

Southern Importers
4825 San Jacinto Street
Houston, Texas 77004
Tel: 713-524-8236

Washington:

Display and Costume Supply, Inc
202 Bell Street
Seattle, Washington 98121
Tel: 206-624-4810

Manuscript Services

Typing and manuscript services are widely available. Those listed here are familiar with the format requirements for screenplays, shooting scripts, and related motion picture documents.

California:

Barbara's Place
9255 Sunset Boulevard
Los Angeles, California 90069
Tel: 213-273-1015

Ed Leavitt & Company
7382-7384 Melrose Avenue
Los Angeles, California 90046
Tel: 213-655-2750

Mimi O'Graph Co., Inc.
10824 Ventura Boulevard
North Hollywood, California
91604
Tel: 213-877-0977

Wright-O
1771 North Cahuenga Boulevard
Los Angeles, California 90028
Tel: 213-463-1131

New York:

ABC Manuscript & Steno Service
30 Rockefeller Plaza
New York, New York 10020
Tel: 212-247-6671

Author Aid Associates
340 East 52nd Street
New York, New York 10022
Tel: 212-758-4213

Empire State Secretarial Service,
Inc.
350 Fifth Avenue
New York, New York 10016
Tel: 212-736-8072

Professional Editing & Typing
Services
410 East Twentieth Street
New York, New York 10003
Tel: 212-477-0615

Florida:

Cinema Script Services
18831 N.W. 24th Avenue
Miami, Florida 33101
Tel: 305-624-0277

Music: Effects, Scoring & Production

California:
Los Angeles area:

Artisan Releasing Corporation
9200 Sunset, Suite 616
Los Angeles, California 90069
Tel: 213-278-2670

Auspex Music
12188 Laurel Terrace Drive
Studio City, California 91604
Tel: 213-877-1078

Barnum Entertainment
    Enterprises, Inc.
12023 Rhode Island Avenue
Los Angeles, California 90025
Tel: 213-466-6129

Bernard Productions, Inc.
5150 Wilshire Boulevard
Los Angeles, California 90036
Tel: 213-938-5181

Braverman Productions
8961 Sunset Boulevard
Los Angeles, California 90069
Tel: 213-278-5444

Carman Productions, Inc.
15456 Cabrito Road
Van Nuys, California 91406
Tel: 213-873-7370

Jules Chaikin Music Services
12188 Laurel Terrace Drive
Studio City, California 91604
Tel: 213-877-1078

Chicory Music, Inc.
6362 Hollywood Boulevard
Los Angeles, California 90028
Tel: 213-469-8149

Creative Composers & Associal
11360 Dona Doretea Drive
Studio City, California 91604
Tel: 213-656-7060

Dore Records, Inc.
1608 North Argyle
Los Angeles, California 90028
Tel: 213-462-6608

Richard Einfeld Productions
1512 North Las Palmas Aven
Los Angeles, California 90038
Tel: 213-461-3731

El Dorado Recording Studio
1717 North Vine Street
Los Angeles, California 90028
Tel: 213-467-6151

The Establishment, Inc.
9000 Sunset Boulevard
Los Angeles, California 90069
Tel: 213-274-9483

Fidelity Recording Studio
6315 Yucca Street
Los Angeles, California 90028
Tel: 213-464-6277

Ernie Freeman Enterprises
6255 Sunset Drive
Los Angeles, California 90027
Tel: 213-466-3261

Futura Music, Inc.
1717 North Highland Avenue,
　　Room 902
Los Angeles, California 90028
Tel: 213-465-5500

Garrett Music Enterprises
6255 Sunset, Suite 1019
Los Angeles, California 90028
Tel: 213-467-2181

General Music Corporation
6410 Willoughby
Los Angeles, California 90052
Tel: 213-462-0715

Gordon/Casady, Inc.
6671 Sunset, Suite 1591
Los Angeles, California 90046
Tel: 213-466-3444

Larry Greene Productions
1151 Sunset Hills Road
Los Angeles, California 90069
Tel: 213-273-0643

Merv Griffin Productions
1735 North Vine Street
Los Angeles, California 90028
Tel: 213-461-4701

Group One Productions, Inc.
3255 Cahuenga Boulevard
Los Angeles, California 90068
Tel: 213-876-3300

Heller Corporation
1606 North Highland Avenue
Los Angeles, California 90028
Tel: 213-466-7765

Hollywood Film Associates
2025 North Highland Avenue
Los Angeles, California 90068
Tel: 213-874-8413

Image Films, Inc.
8563 Beverly Boulevard
Los Angeles, California 90048
Tel: 213-657-5141

Jalmia Enterprises
2715 Jalmia Drive
Los Angeles, California 90046
Tel: 213-874-3349

Stacy Keach Productions
5216 Laurel Canyon Boulevard
North Hollywood, California
　　91607
Tel: 213-877-0472

Doug Moody Productions
Mystic Music Centre
6277 Selma Avenue
Los Angeles, California 90028
Tel: 213-464-9667

Music Industries
1513 North Cahuenga Boulevard
Los Angeles, California 90028
Tel: 213-465-0082

Musical Services–Pacific Music
1305-1309 North Highland
   Avenue
Los Angeles, California 90028
Tel: 213-463-5888

Next Stage Productions
1031 North La Brea Avenue
Los Angeles, California 90038
Tel: 213-851-0304

Eddie Norton Music Service, Inc.
729 North Seward Street
Los Angeles, California 90038
Tel: 213-462-2728

Parasound, Inc.
2825 Hyans Street
Los Angeles, California 90026
Tel: 213-462-3311

Don Perry Enterprises, Inc.
8961 Sunset Boulevard
Los Angeles, California 90069
Tel: 213-278-8961

The Petersen Company
1330 North Vine Street
Los Angeles, California 90028
Tel: 213-466-9351

The Production Company, Inc.
8612 West Pico Boulevard
Los Angeles, California 90035
Tel: 213-659-3940

Production House West
6671 Sunset Boulevard
Los Angeles, California 90028
Tel: 213-462-2378

Roger Music, Inc.
449 South Beverly Drive
Beverly Hills, California 9021.
Tel: 213-553-8789

Song Power
6922 Hollywood Boulevard
Los Angeles, California 90028
Tel: 213-461-4941

Sound City, Inc.
15456 Cabrito Road
Van Nuys, California 91406
Tel: 213-787-3722

Synchrofilm, Inc.
1213 North Highland Avenue
Los Angeles, California 90028
Tel: 213-466-2491

R. Michael Terr Productions
2473 Crestview Drive
Los Angeles, California 90046
Tel: 213-654-7506

Triplex Productions, Inc.
9000 Sunset Boulevard
Los Angeles, California 90069
Tel: 213-274-9483

Turnstyle Music
9207 Alden Drive
Beverly Hills, California 9021(
Tel: 213-276-6795

San Francisco area:

Stephen Baffrey Productions
2774 Jackson Street
San Francisco, California 94115
Tel: 415-921-3607

The Coppola Company
916 Kearny Street
San Francisco, California 94111
Tel: 415-788-7500

Furman Films
3466 21st Street
San Francisco, California 94110
Tel: 415-282-1300

Imagination, Inc.
443 Jackson Street
San Francisco, California 94111
Tel: 415-435-5480

Pre-Dawn Enterprises, Inc.
501 Litho Street
Sausalito, California 94965
Tel: 415-332-5160

Sound Genesis, Inc.
445 Bryant Street
San Francisco, California 94107
Tel: 415-391-8776

The Sound Service
55 Stevenson Street
San Francisco, California 94105
Tel: 415-433-3674

Georgia:

AND, Inc.
1428-B Mason Street, N.E.
Atlanta, Georgia 30324
Tel: 404-876-1033

John Barbe
5055 High Point Road, N.E.
Atlanta, Georgia 30305
Tel: 404-255-2278

Doppler Enterprises, Inc.
417 Peachtree Street, N.E.
Atlanta, Georgia 30308
Tel: 404-873-6941

Kintel Corporation
1200 Spring Street
Atlanta, Georgia 30308
Tel: 404-874-3668

Tim McCabe Productions
230 Peachtree Street

Hawaii:

Cine-Pic Hawaii
1847 Pacific Heights Road
Honolulu, Hawaii 96813
Tel: 808-533-2677

The House of Eric Productions
1760 Ala Moana Boulevard
Waikiki, Hawaii 96815
Tel: 808-533-3877
Atlanta, Georgia 30363
Tel: 404-688-2124

Trolly Productions
3759 Main Street
College Park, Georgia 30337
Tel: 404-768-0057

Tunesmith
3108-A Buford Highway, N.E.
Atlanta, Georgia 30329
Tel: 404-292-7406

New York:

Aquarius Transfer
12 East 46th Street
New York, New York 10017
Tel: 212-581-0123

Aries Sound International
245 East 63rd Street
New York, New York 10021
Tel: 212-838-4940

Emil Ascher, Inc.
666 Fifth Avenue
New York, New York 10019
Tel: 212-581-4504

Channel Sound/Manne
45 West 45th Street
New York, New York 10036
Tel: 212-586-4311

Correlli-Jacobs Film Music, Inc.
25 West 45th Street
New York, New York 10036
Tel: 212-586-6673

Duffex, Inc.
30 East 40th Street
New York, New York 10036
Tel: 212-889-5265

Filmsounds, Inc.
128 East 41st Street
New York, New York 10017
Tel: 212-867-0330

Music for Films, Inc.
49 West 45th Street
New York, New York 10036
Tel: 212-247-3577

Music House, Inc.
16 East 48th Street
New York, New York 10017
Tel: 212-758-7773

Musicues Corporation
1156 Avenue of the Americas
New York, New York 10036
Tel: 212-757-3641

Picture Scores, Inc.
115 West 45th Street
New York, New York 10036
Tel: 212-586-1845

Dan Pinsky, Inc.
21 West 46th Street
New York, New York 10036
Tel: 212-869-3318

Pisces Music, Inc.
12 East 46th Street
New York, New York 10017
Tel: 212-697-7247

Ross-Gaffney, Inc.
21 West 46th Street
New York, New York 10036
Tel: 212-697-7247

Thomas J. Valentino, Inc.
151 West 46th Street
New York, New York 10036
Tel: 212-246-4675

Texas:

Ralph Stachon & Associates, Inc
1322 Inwood Road
Dallas, Texas 75247
Tel: 214-638-6231

Washington:

Gardner/Marlow/Maes Corporation
Seattle Tower, Penthouse
Seattle, Washington 98101
Tel: 206-624-9090

Music Libraries

California:

Los Angeles area:

Buzzy's Recording Services
8719 Santa Monica Boulevard
Los Angeles, California 90069
Tel: 213-659-5444

Capitol Records Music
  Production
1750 North Vine Street
Los Angeles, California 90028
Tel: 213-462-6252

Carman Productions, Inc.
15456 Cabrito Road
Van Nuys, California 91406
Tel: 213-873-7370

Chappell & Company, Inc.
1530 North Gower Street
Los Angeles, California 90028
Tel: 213-467-5181

Cinesound
915 North Highland Avenue
Los Angeles, California 90038
Tel: 213-464-1155

Richard Einfeld, Inc.
1512 North Las Palmas Avenue
Los Angeles, California 90028
Tel: 213-461-3731

F–M Motion Picture Services
733 North Highland Avenue
Los Angeles, California 90038
Tel: 213-937-1622

Film Technology Company, I
6900 Santa Monica Boulevar
Los Angeles, California 90038
Tel: 213-465-4908

General Music Corporation
6410 Willoughby Avenue
Los Angeles, California 90038
Tel: 213-462-0715

Instant Music
5325 Sunset Boulevard
Los Angeles, California 90027
Tel: 213-665-8020

Music Industries
1513 North Cahuenga Bouleva
Los Angeles, California 90028
Tel: 213-465-0082

Mystic Sound Studio Library
Mystic Music Centre
6277 Selma Avenue
Los Angeles, California 90028
Tel: 213-464-9667

The Petersen Company
1330 North Vine Street
Los Angeles, California 90028
Tel: 213-466-9351

Quality Sound, Inc.
5625 Melrose Avenue
Los Angeles, California 90038
Tel: 213-467-7154

Regent Recorded Music, Inc.
6464 Sunset Boulevard, Room 515
Los Angeles, California 90028
Tel: 213-463-6869

Riviera Productions
6610 Selma Avenue
Los Angeles, California 90028
Tel: 213-462-8585

Sound City, Inc.
15456 Cabrito Road
Van Nuys, California 91406
Tel: 213-787-3722

Southern Library of Recorded
   Music
6922 Hollywood Boulevard
Los Angeles, California 90028
Tel: 213-469-1667

R. Michael Terr Productions
2473 Crestview Drive
Los Angeles, California 90046
Tel: 213-654-7506

West Bay Distributors
2473 Crestview Drive
Los Angeles, California 90046
Tel: 213-654-7506

San Francisco area:

Coast Recorders, Inc.
829 Folsom Street
San Francisco, California 94107
Tel: 415-397-7676

W. A. Palmer Films
611 Howard Street
San Francisco, California 94105
Tel: 415-986-5961

Parasound, Inc.
680 Beach Street, Room 495
San Francisco, California 94109
Tel: 415-776-2808

The Sound Service
55 Stevenson Street
San Francisco, California 94105
Tel: 415-443-3674

Studio 16, Inc.
2135 Powell Street
San Francisco, California 94133
Tel: 415-982-2097

Colorado:

Western Cine Service
312 South Pearl Street
Denver, Colorado 80209
Tel: 303-744-1017

New York:

Chappell Music Library
810 Seventh Avenue
New York, New York 10019
Tel: 212-977-7213

DeWolfe Music Library
25 West 45th Street
New York, New York 10036
Tel: 212-586-6673

Sam Fox Film Rights, Inc.
62 Cooper Square
New York, New York 10003
Tel: 212-777-3353

M.S.T.S. Music, Inc.   **Washington:**
1600 Broadway
New York, New York 10019   JRB Motion Graphics
Tel: 212-246-4687   3323 Ninth Avenue West
                                  Seattle, Washington 98119
                                  Tel: 206-284-0834

Opticals & Optical Effects

California:

Howard A. Anderson Company
5451 Marathon Street
Los Angeles, California 90038
Tel: 213-463-0100

Cinefx
1161 North Highland Avenue
Los Angeles, California 90038
Tel: 213-464-7474

Consolidated Film Industries
959 North Seward Street
Los Angeles, California 90038
Tel: 213-462-3161

Film Effects of Hollywood, Inc.
1140 North Citrus
Los Angeles, California 90038
Tel: 213-469-5808

Ray Mercer & Company
4241 Normal Avenue
Los Angeles, California 90029
Tel: 213-663-9331

Metro-Goldwyn-Mayer, Inc.
10202 West Washington
  Boulevard
Culver City, California 90230
Tel: 213-836-3000

The Optical House
3499 West Cahuenga Boulevard
Los Angeles, California 90028
Tel: 213-851-5303

Opticals West
7026 Santa Monica Boulevard
Los Angeles, California 90038
Tel: 213-466-5111

Pacific Title & Art Studio
6350 Santa Monica Boulevard
Los Angeles, California 90038
Tel: 213-464-0121
Paramount Studios

The Westheimer Company
736 North Seward Street
Los Angeles, California 90038
Tel: 213-466-8271

Florida:

Florida Optical House Inc.
338 N.E. 35th Terrace
Miami, Florida 33137
Tel: 305-576-5300

Illinois:

Consolidated Film Industries
333 North Michigan Avenue
Chicago, Illinois 60601
Tel: 312-641-0028

New York:

Animated Products, Inc.
1600 Broadway
New York, New York 10019
Tel: 212-265-2942

B & O
619 West 54th Street
New York, New York 10019
Tel: 212-246-9390

Cinopticals, Inc.
501 Madison Avenue
New York, New York 10022
Tel: 212-935-0087

Computer Opticals, Inc.
2 West 45th Street
New York, New York 10036
Tel: 212-869-0170

Consolidated Film Industries
15 Columbus Circle
New York, New York 10023
Tel: 212-581-1090

Directors Group, Inc.
410 East 54th Street
New York, New York 10022
Tel: 212-759-8995

EFX Unlimited, Inc.
321 West 44th Street
New York, New York 10036
Tel: 212-541-9220

Exceptional Opticals, Inc.
17 East 45th Street
New York, New York 10017
Tel: 212-972-4760

Film Opticals, Inc.
421 West 54th Street
New York, New York 10022
Tel: 212-757-7120

The Film Place, Inc.
35 West 45th Street
New York, New York 10036
Tel: 212-757-9225

I. F. Studios, Inc.
328 East 44th Street
New York, New York 10017
Tel: 212-683-4747

Mini-Effects
19 West 44th Street
New York, New York 10036
Tel: 212-869-0370

The Optical House
25 West 45th Street
New York, New York 10036
Tel: 212-757-7840

Optimum Effects, Inc.
20 East 46th Street
New York, New York 10017
Tel: 212-697-2683

Professional Opticals, Inc.
20 East 46th Street
New York, New York 10017
Tel: 212-682-1757

Rainbow Film Effects, Inc.
45 West 45th Street
New York, New York 10035
Tel: 212-247-1676

Select Effects, Inc.
2 West 45th Street
New York, New York 10036
Tel: 212-869-3988

Technical Film Studio
333 West 52nd Street
New York, New York 10019
Tel: 212-245-9186

Tri-Pix Film Service, Inc.
49 West 45th Street
New York, New York 10036
Tel: 212-582-0650

World Effects, Inc.
20 East 46th Street
New York, New York 10017
Tel: 212-687-7070

Personal Managers

In the complex hierarchy of stardom, personal managers assume responsibility of career guidance, while the agent's function becor principally that of booking the client.

California:

Aarons Enterprises
9145 Sunset Boulevard
Los Angeles, California 90069
Tel: 213-278-7620

Altobelli, Cohen & Hennessey
10050 Cielo Drive
Beverly Hills, California 90210
Tel: 213-274-4510

American Variety International
9220 Sunset Boulevard
Los Angeles, California 90069
Tel: 213-273-3060

Sanford Arnoff
15910 Ventura Boulevard
Encino, California 91316
Tel: 213-981-0044

Artists Entertainment Complex
1100 North Alta Loma Road
Los Angeles, California 90069
Tel: 213-657-3390

BNB Associates
9454 Wilshire Boulevard
Beverly Hills, California 90212
Tel: 213-273-7020

Robert Baker
1560 North La Brea Avenue
Los Angeles, California 90028
Tel: 213-464-0411

Clyde Baldscheen & Associat
P.O. Box 356
Woodland Hills, California 91:
Tel: 213-346-6100

Geoffrey Barr
800 Tortuoso Way
Los Angeles, California 9002
Tel: 213-476-3165

Art Benson
1560 North La Brea Avenue
Los Angeles, California 90028
Tel: 213-464-0411

Gary Blye Enterprises
8746 Sunset Boulevard
Los Angeles, California 9006
Tel: 213-657-8740

Bernie Brillstein Company, I
144 South Beverly Drive
Beverly Hills, California 90:
Tel: 213-275-6135

Tedd Brookes
1155 North La Cienega
   Boulevard
Los Angeles, California 90069
Tel: 213-659-4740

Al Bruno Associates
104 Wilshire Boulevard
Los Angeles, California 9002
Tel: 213-475-0608

Ruth Burch Personal
  Management
195 South Beverly Drive
Beverly Hills, California 90210
Tel: 213-273-1161

Burke & Sheils Enterprises
9229 Sunset Boulevard
Los Angeles, California 90069
Tel: 213-273-7000

C. Wilson Brenton
14827 Ventura Boulevard
Sherman Oaks, California 91403
Tel: 213-986-8862

Gail Cabot Management
6640 Sunset Boulevard
Los Angeles, California 90028
Tel: 213-466-5181

Paul Cantor Enterprises, Ltd.
144 South Beverly Drive
Beverly Hills, California 90212
Tel: 213-274-9222

Chicory Management
6362 Hollywood Boulevard
Los Angeles, California 90028
Tel: 213-469-8149

Herb Cohen Management
5831 Sunset Boulevard
Los Angeles, California 90028
Tel: 213-461-3267

Harry Colomby
315 South Crescent Drive
Beverly Hills, California 90212
Tel: 213-553-0646

Compass Management
211 South Beverly Drive
Beverly Hills, California 90212
Tel: 213-271-5122

Ron De Blasio
9000 Sunset Boulevard
Los Angeles, California 90069
Tel: 213-273-2304

James Fitzgerald Enterprises, Inc.
9255 Sunset Boulevard
Los Angeles, California 90069
Tel: 213-275-5251

Robert Fitzpatrick Corporation
9000 Sunset Boulevard
Los Angeles, California 90069
Tel: 213-272-7772

Bill Franklin
9071 Wonderland Park Avenue
Los Angeles, California 90046
Tel: 213-650-1160

Gai Talent Management, Inc.
1474 North Kings Road
Los Angeles, California 90069
Tel: 213-656-4787

The Geffen-Roberts Company
9120 Sunset Boulevard
Los Angeles, California 90069
Tel: 213-278-0881

Phillip B. Gittelman
1012 North Hammond Street
Los Angeles, California 90069
Tel: 213-276-3880

Sid Gold
1155 North La Cienega
  Boulevard
Los Angeles, California 90069
Tel: 213-657-6486

B H Goldberg
8450 De Longpre Avenue
Los Angeles, California 90069
Tel: 213-657-2249

Gerald Gordon Enterprises
1451 North Las Palmas Avenue
Los Angeles, California 90028
Tel: 213-463-1845

Marc Gordon Productions
1022 North Palm Avenue
Los Angeles, California 90069
Tel: 213-659-0055

Joe Gottfried–Carmen
  Productions
15456 Cabrito Road
Van Nuys, California 91406
Tel: 213-873-7370
GR Management

Leonard Grainger
793 Linda Flora Drive
Los Angeles, California 90049
Tel: 213-472-1805

Leonard Grant & Associates
9000 Sunset Boulevard
Los Angeles, California 90069
Tel: 213-274-9483

The Great American Amusement
  Company
1050 Coral Drive
Los Angeles, California 90069
Tel: 213-278-3900

Don Gregory
9200 Sunset Boulevard
Los Angeles, California 90069
Tel: 213-278-2866

Gregory/Thomas, Ltd.
9229 Sunset Boulevard
Los Angeles, California 90069
Tel: 213-273-6715

Greif-Garris Management
8467 Beverly Boulevard
Los Angeles, California 90048
Tel: 213-653-4780

James William Guercio
  Enterprises, Inc.
8600 Melrose Avenue
Los Angeles, California 90069
Tel: 213-659-1301

Halcyon Management
  Productions, Inc.
9056 Santa Monica Boulevard
Los Angeles, California 90210
Tel: 213-275-5365

Heffernan Management
1407 Valley Heart Drive
Burbank, California 91506
Tel: 213-849-6771

Heller, Seymour & Associates
9220 Sunset Boulevard
Los Angeles, California 90069
Tel: 213-273-3060

Howard Hinderstein
18809 Paseo Nuevo Drive
Tarzana, California 91356
Tel: 213-881-1213

Hyland-Chandler Agency
9100 Sunset Boulevard
Los Angeles, California 90069
Tel: 213-271-8188

J B Productions
9908 Santa Monica Boulevard
Beverly Hills, California 90212
Tel: 213-277-3881

Katz-Gallin-Leffler Enterprises
9255 Sunset Boulevard
Los Angeles, California 90069
Tel: 213-273-4210

Ken Kragen & Friends
451 North Canon Drive
Beverly Hills, California 90210
Tel: 213-273-5011

Richard Kravitt Management
8711 West Olympic Boulevard
Los Angeles, California 90035
Tel: 213-652-2805

Russ Larson Management
650 North Bronson
Los Angeles, California 90028
Tel: 213-461-3141

Olga Lee
Hotel Sunset Marquis
1200 North Alta Loma
Los Angeles, California 90069
Tel: 213-657-1333

Jerry Levy
9056 Santa Monica Boulevard
Los Angeles, California 90069
Tel: 213-275-5366

John Levy Enterprises
8467 Beverly Boulevard
Los Angeles, California 90048
Tel: 213-651-0783

Milton Lewis
140 South Lasky Drive
Beverly Hills, California 90212
Tel: 213-271-2145

Richard O. Linke Associates, Inc.
4405 Riverside Drive
Burbank, California 91505
Tel: 213-843-6900

William Loeb Management, Inc.
233 South Beverly Drive
Beverly Hills, California 90212
Tel: 213-273-3570

Ace London
1622 North Fairfax
Los Angeles, California 90069
Tel: 213-469-3636

Sam J. Lutz Artists Personal
    Management
1626 North Vine Street
Los Angeles, California 90028
Tel: 213-469-1993

Lee Magid, Inc.
5750 Melrose Avenue
Los Angeles, California 90038
Tel: 213-463-2353

Management Three, Ltd.
400 South Beverly Drive
Beverly Hills, California 90212
Tel: 213-277-9633

Marino Management
1901 Avenue of the Stars
Los Angeles, California 90067
Tel: 213-980-1552

Sy Marsh, Ltd.
9000 Sunset Boulevard
Los Angeles, California 90069
Tel: 213-273-8554

Mike Merrick Enterprises
9000 Sunset Boulevard
Los Angeles, California 90069
Tel: 213-278-1211

Arnold Mills & Associates
8721 Sunset Boulevard
Los Angeles, California 90069
Tel: 213-657-2024

Mark Mordoh
9200 Sunset Boulevard
Los Angeles, California 90069
Tel: 213-273-3394

Multi-Media Management
6464 Sunset Boulevard
Los Angeles, California 90028
Tel: 213-466-6321

Noga Enterprises
P.O. Box 350
Beverly Hills, California 90213
Tel: 213-271-9179

Rose Pichinson
144 South Beverly Drive
Beverly Hills, California 90212
Tel: 213-553-4432

Pines Devin, Ltd.
8039 Mulholland Drive
Los Angeles, California 90046
Tel: 213-654-7400

Julian Portman Agency
1680 North Vine Street
Los Angeles, California 90028
Tel: 213-463-8154

Peter Rachtman
1050 Carol Drive
Los Angeles, California 90069
Tel: 213-278-3900

Jess Rand Associates
9460 Wilshire Boulevard
Beverly Hills, California 90212
Tel: 213-275-6000

Frank Ray Enterprises
222 North Canon Drive
Beverly Hills, California 90210
Tel: 213-276-6205

Regency Artists, Ltd.
9200 Sunset Boulevard
Los Angeles, California 90069
Tel: 213-273-7103

Bernie Rich
2254 Gloaming Way
Beverly Hills, California 90210
Tel: 213-274-8513

Bert Rogal Artists Management
1114 North Gardner Street
Los Angeles, California 90046
Tel: 213-876-5511

Glenn Rose & Associates
1100 Alta Loma Road
Los Angeles, California 90069
Tel: 213-657-2390

Bette Rosenthal
9220 Sunset Boulevard
Los Angeles, California 90069
Tel: 213-273-3060

Ross & Steinman
8721 Sunset Boulevard
Los Angeles, California 90069
Tel: 213-652-7177

Art Rush, Inc.
10221 Riverside Drive
North Hollywood, California
  91602
Tel: 213-985-3033

Samuels Artists & Productions,
  Ltd.
9046 Sunset Boulevard
Los Angeles, California 90069
Tel: 213-278-5050

Nick Sevano
9220 Sunset Boulevard
Los Angeles, California 90069
Tel: 213-273-3590

Shapiro & West Management
141 El Camino Drive
Beverly Hills, California 90212
Tel: 213-278-8896

Mel Shayne Enterprises
9229 Sunset Boulevard
Los Angeles, California 90069
Tel: 213-276-4149

Thomas P. Sheils
9229 Sunset Boulevard
Los Angeles, California 90069
Tel: 213-273-7070

Edward Sherman
9930 Robbins Drive
Beverly Hills, California 90212
Tel: 213-553-8746

Joseph S. Shribman
449 South Beverly Drive
Beverly Hills, California 90212
Tel: 213-553-8787

Bill Siddons
8512 Santa Monica Boulevard
Los Angeles, California 90069
Tel: 213-659-1667

Roy Silver
8756 Holloway Drive
Los Angeles, California 90069
Tel: 213-659-4830

Cliffie Stone Productions
6255 Sunset Boulevard
Los Angeles, California 90028
Tel: 213-462-6933

Norton Styne Company
148 South Beverly Drive
Beverly Hills, California 90212
Tel: 213-274-9475

Skip Taylor Productions
6331 Hollywood Boulevard
Los Angeles, California 90028
Tel: 213-466-4159

Larry Thompson
9255 Sunset Boulevard
Los Angeles, California 90069
Tel: 213-273-4660

Mimi Weber Management
9738 Arby Drive
Beverly Hills, California 90210
Tel: 213-278-8440

William A. Weems, Associates
170 North Robertson Boulevard
Beverly Hills, California 90211
Tel: 213-659-3612

Williams & Price
8831 Sunset Boulevard
Los Angeles, California 90069
Tel: 213-657-4521

Howard Wolf
8890 Evanview Drive
Los Angeles, California 90064
Tel: 213-657-8030

Gene Yusem & Associates
9000 Sunset Boulevard
Los Angeles, California 90069
Tel: 213-278-1314

Stanford Zucker & Associates
9350 Wilshire Boulevard
Beverly Hills, California 90212
Tel: 213-274-6703

New York:

4-F International
153A East 30th Street
New York, New York 10016
Tel: 212-725-8381

Roger Ailes
888 Seventh Avenue
New York, New York 10019
Tel: 212-765-3022

Buddy Allen
65 West 55th Street
New York, New York 10019
Tel: 212-581-8988

Artists Entertainment Complex
641 Lexington Avenue
New York, New York 10022
Tel: 212-421-3760

Artists Management
165 West 66th Street
New York, New York 10023
Tel: 212-799-6091

Ascola-Kay Enterprises
315 West 57th Street
New York, New York 10019
Tel: 212-245-6460

Bandana Enterprises
Dee Anthony
1060 Park Avenue
New York, New York 10028
Tel: 212-348-8133

Tino Barzie
15 Central Park West
New York, New York 10023
Tel: 212-586-1015

Murray Becker
133 Fifth Avenue
New York, New York 10003
Tel: 212-475-7100

Jack Beekman
445 Park Avenue
New York, New York 10022
Tel: 212-371-3300

Harvey Bellovin
410 East 64th Street
New York, New York 10021
Tel: 212-752-5181

Berger, Ross & Steinman
15 Central Park West
New York, New York 10023
Tel: 212-751-2156

Sam Berk
35 West 53rd Street
New York, New York 10019
Tel: 212-265-1984

Bobby Bernard
1414 Avenue of the Americas
New York, New York 10019
Tel: 212-753-9843

Sid Bernstein
136 East 55th Street
New York, New York 10022
Tel: 212-752-1563

Bernie Block
1005 Second Avenue
New York, New York 10022
Tel: 212-838-0087

Jackie Bright
850 Seventh Avenue
New York, New York 10019
Tel: 212-247-2930

Frank Campana
850 Seventh Avenue
New York, New York 10019
Tel: 212-489-0555

Robert Coe
433 East 56th Street
New York, New York 10022
Tel: 212-753-1506

David Cogan
350 Fifth Avenue
New York, New York 10001
Tel: 212-594-3335

Cutler-Korman
200 West 57th Street
New York, New York 10019
Tel: 212-586-6363

William Danielle
105 East 63rd Street
New York, New York 10021
Tel: 212-371-4575

Keller Davis
165 West 46th Street
New York, New York 10036
Tel: 212-541-8740

Peter Dean
161 West 54th Street
New York, New York 10019
Tel: 212-265-0789

David DeSilva
225 East 57th Street
New York, New York 10022
Tel: 212-759-8180

Lenny Ditson
162 West 56th Street
New York, New York 10019
Tel: 212-581-8922

Harvey Elkin
118 West 57th Street
New York, New York 10019
Tel: 212-489-1591

Martin Erlichman
677 Fifth Avenue
New York, New York 10022
Tel: 212-421-6110

Phil Farrell
850 Seventh Avenue
New York, New York 10019
Tel: 212-757-4140

Mike Gendel
200 West 57th Street
New York, New York 10019
Tel: 212-245-2915

Walter Gould
866 Third Avenue
New York, New York 10022
Tel: 212-752-3920

Lloyd Greenfield
1 Rockefeller Plaza
New York, New York 10020
Tel: 212-245-8130

Ken Greengrass
595 Madison Avenue
New York, New York 10022
Tel: 212-421-8415

Al Grossman
75 East 55th Street
New York, New York 10022
Tel: 212-751-7030

Allen Herman
25 Central Park West
New York, New York 10023
Tel: 212-265-6565

Joe Higgins
100 West 57th Street
New York, New York 10019
Tel: 212-247-5216

David Hocker
667 Madison Avenue
New York, New York 10021
Tel: 212-751-3669

Val Irving
114 East 61st Street
New York, New York 10021
Tel: 212-755-8932

David Jonas
101 West 57th Street
New York, New York 10019
Tel: 212-247-5150

Murray Kane
7 West 96th Street
New York, New York 10025
Tel: 212-749-6440

Jerry Katz
527 Madison Avenue
New York, New York 10022
Tel: 212-752-0850

Raymond Katz
300 East 57th Street
New York, New York 10022
Tel: 212-582-4900

Helen Keane
49 East 96th Street
New York, New York 10028
Tel: 212-722-2921

Romy Kister
445 Park Avenue
New York, New York 10022
Tel: 212-486-1951

Kay Korwin
40 West 55th Street
New York, New York 10019
Tel: 212-581-1840

Joe Lauer
275 Central Park West
New York, New York 10024
Tel: 212-873-0192

Phil Lawrence
595 Madison Avenue
New York, New York 10022
Tel: 212-421-8415

Morty R. Lefkoe
59 West 71st Street
New York, New York 10023
Tel: 212-724-1949

Harold Leventhal
250 West 57th Street
New York, New York 10019
Tel: 212-586-6553

John Levy
119 West 57th Street
New York, New York 10019
Tel: 212-245-2488

Marty Litke Management, Inc.
119 West 57th Street
New York, New York 10019
Tel: 212-765-0960

Management Three, Ltd.
136 East 55th Street
New York, New York 10022
Tel: 212-752-1563

John Marotta
125 Seventh Avenue South
New York, New York 10014
Tel: 212-675-4078

Marshall Management
315 West 57th Street
New York, New York 10019
Tel: 212-581-9744

Arthur Miller
1501 Broadway
New York, New York 10036
Tel: 212-565-5056

Arthur Mills
47 West 68th Street
New York, New York 10023
Tel: 212-787-1066

Esther Navarro
39 West 55th Street
New York, New York 10019
Tel: 212-765-6323

Buster Newman
165 West End Avenue
New York, New York 10023
Tel: 212-787-9168

Susan Pimsleur Musical Artists
119 West 57th Street
New York, New York 10019
Tel: 212-586-2747

Charles Prentiss
330 Fifth Avenue
New York, New York 10003
Tel: 212-986-0280

Gerald Purcell
133 Fifth Avenue
New York, New York 10003
Tel: 212-475-7100

Jack Rael
Plaza Hotel
New York, New York 10019
Tel: 212-752-9626

Joseph Rapp
1650 Broadway
New York, New York 10019
Tel: 212-581-6162

Robert Rehbock
207 East 62nd Street
New York, New York 10021
Tel: 212-421-6226

Rollins & Joffe, Inc.
130 West 57th Street
New York, New York 10019
Tel: 212-582-1940

Harry Romm
400 East 56th Street
New York, New York 10022
Tel: 212-752-2411

Arlyne Rothberg
196 East 75th Street
New York, New York 10021
Tel: 212-988-7400

Shelley Rothman
15 Central Park West
New York, New York 10023
Tel: 212-246-2180

Dick Rubin
200 West 57th Street
New York, New York 10019
Tel: 212-245-7810

Phil Schapiro
221 West 57th Street
New York, New York 10019
Tel: 212-581-6830

George Scheck
161 West 54th Street
New York, New York 10019
Tel: 212-586-6767

Robert Schwaid
10 West 66th Street
New York, New York 10023
Tel: 212-757-5200

Norman Schwartz
112 East 61st Street
New York, New York 10021
Tel: 212-755-5629

Don Seat
39 West 55th Street
New York, New York 10019
Tel: 212-581-4144

Jack Segal
850 Seventh Avenue
New York, New York 10019
Tel: 212-265-7489

Gunther Sernau
405 East 54th Street
New York, New York 10022
Tel: 212-355-2553

Russ Sobey
677 West End Avenue
New York, New York 10025
Tel: 212-749-4417

Kuno Sponholz
350 West 55th Street
New York, New York 10019
Tel: 212-265-3777

Laura Springer
65 Central Park West
New York, New York 10023
Tel: 212-724-3517

The Stigwood Organization
135 Central Park West
New York, New York 10023
Tel: 212-595-6655

Stix & Gude
30 Rockefeller Plaza
New York, New York 10020
Tel: 212-247-2690

Richard Towers
1 Rockefeller Plaza
New York, New York 10020
Tel: 212-489-9188

Paul Tush
75 East 55th Street
New York, New York 10022
Tel: 212-752-8181

Richard Voigts
160 West End Avenue
New York, New York 10023
Tel: 212-787-3772

Jerry Weintraub
136 East 55th Street
New York, New York 10022
Tel: 212-752-1563

Alfred F. Zega
2211 Broadway
New York, New York 10024
Tel: 212-877-1529

Producers &
Production Companies

The principal active American producers and production companies ar
presented in this category. Not included are production companies formed fc
the express purpose of producing only one picture, a frequent busines
practice.

Alaska:

Alaska Film Studios
943 Westbury Drive, Box 4-406
Anchorage, Alaska 99509
Tel: 907-279-3112

Alaska Pictures, Inc.
Box 937
Juneau, Alaska 99801
Tel: 907-789-9431

Cinema Alaska Productions
P.O. Box 646
Juneau, Alaska 99801
Tel: 907-586-2249

Films North
203 West Fifteenth Avenue
Anchorage, Alaska 99501
Tel: 907-277-8834

Pictures, Inc.
811 Eighth Avenue
Anchorage, Alaska 99501
Tel: 907-279-1515

Arizona:

AR Films
3830 North Seventh Street
Phoenix, Arizona 85014
Tel: 602-277-4732

Arcoa International
2727 North Central Avenue
Phoenix, Arizona 85004
Tel: 602-263-6641

Aztec Film Productions
2307 East Broadway
Tucson, Arizona 85719
Tel: 602-623-4389

Canyon Films
834 North Seventh Avenue
Phoenix, Arizona 85006
Tel: 602-252-1718

Cave Creek Enterprises
32825 North Scottsdale Road
Cave Creek, Arizona 85331
Tel: 602-488-9281

Marshall L. Faber Productions
6412 East Desert Cove
Scottsdale, Arizona 85254
Tel: 602-948-8086

Frasier Productions
33 East McDowell Road
Phoenix, Arizona 85018
Tel: 602-271-9882

Steve Irwin Productions
40 East Thomas Road
Phoenix, Arizona 85012
Tel: 602-263-9071

H. E. Knox Production, Inc.
10234 North 58th Place
Scottsdale, Arizona 85253
Tel: 602-498-3469

Hank Ludwins & Associates
7335 Sixth Avenue
Scottsdale, Arizona 85251
Tel: 602-949-1495

Ray Manley Film Productions,
    Inc.
238 South Tucson Boulevard
Tucson, Arizona 85716
Tel: 602-623-0307

Old Tucson Productions
201 South Kinney Road
Tucson, Arizona 85705
Tel: 602-792-3100

Craig Pease Enterprises
Box 1118
Scottsdale, Arizona 85252
Tel: 602-945-4807

J. W. Raymond Film Productions
1702 North 44th Street
Phoenix, Arizona 85008
Tel: 602-275-9111

Southwestern Productions, Inc.
P.O. Box 1014
Carefree, Arizona 85331
Tel: 602-946-3404

Swartwout Film Productions
6736 East Avalon Drive
Scottsdale, Arizona 85252
Tel: 602-945-8496

Sync Productions
530 East Mariposa
Phoenix, Arizona 85012
Tel: 602-274-9240

Viva Productions, Inc.
14445 North 73rd Street
Scottsdale, Arizona 85260
Tel: 602-948-7090

Chuck Winter Productions
4127 East Indian School Road
Scottsdale, Arizona 85251
Tel: 602-957-1340

Zodiac Productions, Inc.
2020 East Camelback Road
Phoenix, Arizona 85018
Tel: 602-955-6403

California:
Los Angeles area:

A & M Productions
1416 North La Brea Avenue
Los Angeles, California 90028
Tel: 213-461-9931

ABC Pictures Corporation
1313 North Vine Street
Los Angeles, California 90028
Tel: 213-663-3311

AJL Productions
3531 Royal Woods Drive
Sherman Oaks, California 91403
Tel: 213-784-2132

Ablidon Enterprises, Inc.
13063 Ventura Boulevard
Studio City, California 91604
Tel: 213-981-7575

Acrobat Films
Gerald Ayres
Colgems Square
Burbank, California 91505
Tel: 213-843-6000

Acrobat Productions
4000 Warner Boulevard
Burbank, California 91505
Tel: 213-843-6000

Horst Ahlberg Studio
1117 North Wilcox Place
Los Angeles, California 90038
Tel: 213-462-0731

The Aldrich Company
606 North Larchmont Boulevard
Los Angeles, California 90004
Tel: 213-462-6511

Alemann Films
1021 San Pascual Avenue
Los Angeles, California 90076
Tel: 213-256-0868

Alfra Productions, Inc.
10202 West Washington
  Boulevard
Culver City, California 90230
Tel: 213-870-3311

Irwin Allen Productions
The Producers' Building
  Twentieth Century–Fox
  Studios
Box 900
Beverly Hills, California 90213
Tel: 213-277-2211

Allied Artists Pictures
  Corporation
291 South La Cienega Boulevard
Beverly Hills, California 90211
Tel: 213-657-8270

The Alpha Corporation
13063 Ventura Boulevard
North Hollywood, California
  91604
Tel: 213-788-5750

Sam Altonian Productions
10826 Morrison Street
North Hollywood, California
  91601
Tel: 213-761-1312

American International Pictures
9033 Wilshire Boulevard
Beverly Hills, California 90211
Tel: 213-278-8118

American Productions, Inc.
1654 North Ivar Street
Los Angeles, California 90028
Tel: 213-461-3661

AmeriEuro Pictures Corporation
9336 West Washington Boulevard
Culver City, California 90230
Tel: 213-559-5633

Howard A. Anderson Company
5451 Marathon Street
Los Angeles, California 90038
Tel: 213-463-0100

Anglofilms, Ltd.
9100 Sunset, Suite 200
Los Angeles, California 90069
Tel: 213-273-4470

Animation Filmakers Corporation
444 North Larchmont Boulevard
Los Angeles, California 90004
Tel: 213-463-3116

Animedia
13107 Ventura Boulevard
Studio City, California 91604
Tel: 213-981-6540

Anjul Productions, Inc.
9201 Wilshire Boulevard
Beverly Hills, California 90210
Tel: 213-271-2183

Apocalypse Corporation
6758 Franklin Place
Los Angeles, California 90028
Tel: 213-461-4373

Apostolof Film Productions, Inc.
6430 West Sunset Boulevard
Los Angeles, California 90028
Tel: 213-462-6971

Argus Productions International
1438 Davies Drive
Beverly Hills, California 90210
Tel: 213-274-2891

Artists Entertainment Complex
1100 North Alta Loma Road
Los Angeles, California 90069
Tel: 213-657-3390

Arwin Productions, Inc.
4024 Radford Avenue
North Hollywood, California
    91604
Tel: 213-877-2761

Ashton-Kochmann Productions
8440 Melrose Avenue
Los Angeles, California 90069
Tel: 213-653-6870

Associated Film Enterprises
9255 Sunset Boulevard
Los Angeles, California 90069
Tel: 213-283-5844

Atlantis Productions, Inc.
850 Thousand Oaks
Thousand Oaks, California 91360
Tel: 805-495-2790

The Jack Atlas Organization
1069 Lillian Way
Los Angeles, California 90038
Tel: 213-461-8246

Atticus Corporation
1041 North Formosa Avenue
Los Angeles, California 90046
Tel: 213-851-1234

Avanti Films, Inc.
8271 Melrose Avenue
Los Angeles, California 90046
Tel: 213-651-5060

Avanza Productions, Inc.
1459 Seward Street
Los Angeles, California 90028
Tel: 213-466-7783

Avco-Embassy Pictures
  Corporation
10850 Wilshire Boulevard
Los Angeles, California 90024
Tel: 213-879-9600

Avery/Lindquist Productions
820 North La Brea Avenue
Los Angeles, California 90038
Tel: 213-462-6751

Avis Films, Incorporated
904 East Palm Avenue
Burbank, California 91501
Tel: 213-848-1666

Avnet-Carroll Productions
2001 North Curson Avenue
Los Angeles, California 90046
Tel: 213-876-4449

Avondale Productions
9336 West Washington Boulevard
Culver City, California 90230
Tel: 213-559-5310

B & B Productions
1313 North Vine Street
Los Angeles, California 90028
Tel: 213-461-3388

BBS Productions, Inc.
933 North La Brea Avenue
Los Angeles, California 90038
Tel: 213-874-5050

Bago Productions, Ltd.
1040 North Las Palmas Avenue
Los Angeles, California 90038
Tel: 213-466-6449

Lem Bailey Productions
7934 Santa Monica Boulevard
Los Angeles, California 90046
Tel: 213-654-9550

Bakshi-Krantz Animation, Inc.
6725 Sunset Boulevard
Los Angeles, California 90028
Tel: 213-461-4242

Lucille Ball Productions
100 Universal City Plaza
Universal City, California 91608
Tel: 213-985-4321

Bob Banner Associates, Inc.
132 South Rodeo Drive
Beverly Hills, California 90212
Tel: 213-273-6923

Bob Barker Productions, Inc.
9201 Wilshire Boulevard
Beverly Hills, California 90210
Tel: 213-271-2183

Barnaby Productions
816 North La Cienega Boulevard
Los Angeles, California 90069
Tel: 213-657-6150

Slim Barnard Enterprises
6000 Sunset Boulevard
Los Angeles, California 90028
Tel: 213-462-7344

Arthur Barr Productions, Inc.
1029 North Allen Avenue
Pasadena, California 91104
Tel: 213-797-4702

Jack Barry Productions, Inc.
7966 Beverly Boulevard
Los Angeles, California 90048
Tel: 213-655-4751

Hall Bartlett Films, Inc.
9200 Sunset Boulevard, Suite 908
Los Angeles, California 90069
Tel: 213-278-8883

Sy Bartlett Productions, Inc.
9101 St. Ives Drive
Los Angeles, California 90069
Tel: 213-273-0833

Saul Bass & Associates
7039 Sunset Boulevard
Los Angeles, California 90028
Tel: 213-466-9701

Batjac Productions, Inc.
5451 Marathon Avenue
Los Angeles, California 90038
Tel: 213-463-0100

Bedford Productions
10201 West Pico Boulevard
Los Angeles, California 90035
Tel: 213-277-2211

Belair International Pictures
1640 North Gardner Street
Los Angeles, California 90046
Tel: 213-876-4403

Dave Bell Associates, Inc.
1011 North Cole Street
Los Angeles, California 90038
Tel: 213-466-6301

Belsam Productions, Inc.
352 South Oakhurst Drive
Beverly Hills, California 90212
Tel: 213-271-8417

Tony Benedict Productions
13701 Riverside Drive
Sherman Oaks, California 91403
Tel: 213-981-5577

John B. Bennett Film
    Productions, Inc.
1100 North Alta Loma Road,
    Suite 608
Los Angeles, California 90069
Tel: 213-657-3390

Berberus Productions, Inc.
839 North Highland Avenue
Los Angeles, California 90038
Tel: 213-469-3237

Bernard Productions, Inc.
5150 Wilshire Boulevard
Los Angeles, California 90036
Tel: 213-938-5181

Harvey Bernhard Enterprises
4076 Admiralty Way, Suite 610
Marina Del Rey, California
    90291
Tel: 213-822-1560

Cal Bernstein Productions
722 North Seward Street
Los Angeles, California 90038
Tel: 213-461-3737

Billy Jack Enterprises, Inc.
9336 West Washington Boulevard
Culver City, California 90230
Tel: 213-559-5310

Joey Bishop Enterprises
9454 Wilshire Boulevard
Beverly Hills, California 90212
Tel: 213-273-3777

Black, Mitchell & Wentz
1605 Cahuenga Boulevard
Los Angeles, California 90028
Tel: 213-463-4891

Blanc Communications
  Corporation
9454 Wilshire Boulevard, Room
  305
Beverly Hills, California 90212
Tel: 213-278-2600

Blatty-Friedkin Productions
4000 Warner Boulevard
Burbank, California 91505
Tel: 213-843-6000

Blye/Bearde Productions, Inc.
7800 Beverly Boulevard
Los Angeles, California 90038
Tel: 213-651-2345

Blythe-Truckee Film Productions
6305 Yucca Street
Los Angeles, California 90028
Tel: 213-461-4313

Boardwalk Productions
5150 Wilshire Boulevard, Suite
  505
Los Angeles, California 90036
Tel: 213-938-0109

Bogdanovich Productions
4000 Warner Boulevard
Burbank, California 91522
Tel: 213-843-6000

Boots & Saddles Pictures
  Company
1578 Queens Road
Los Angeles, California 90069
Tel: 213-656-0200

Stephen Bosustow Productions
1649 Eleventh Street
Santa Monica, California 90404
Tel: 213-394-0218

Boxoffice International Pictures
4774 Melrose Avenue
Los Angeles, California 90029
Tel: 213-660-1700

Braverman Productions, Inc.
8961 Sunset Boulevard
Los Angeles, California 90069
Tel: 213-278-5444

Jerry Bresler Productions
10440 Bainbridge Avenue
Los Angeles, California 90024
Tel: 213-279-2908

Bridge Productions, Inc.
9000 Sunset Boulevard
Los Angeles, California 90069
Tel: 213-274-9483

Brien Productions, Inc.
9777 Wilshire Boulevard
Beverly Hills, California 90212
Tel: 213-278-1500

Frederick Brisson Productions
615 South Flower Street
Los Angeles, California 90017
Tel: 213-625-2121

Jack Broder Productions, Inc.
3084 Motor Avenue
Los Angeles, California 90064
Tel: 213-838-2145

Mel Brooks Productions
4000 Warner Boulevard
Burbank, California 91522
Tel: 213-843-6000

William Brose Productions
3168 Oakshire Drive
Los Angeles, California 90068
Tel: 213-851-5822

Bruce Brown Films
24581 Del Prado, Box 714
Dana Point, California 92629
Tel: 213-496-9373

Howard C. Brown Productions
1156 North Highland Avenue
Los Angeles, California 90038
Tel: 213-462-7435

Brut Productions, Inc.
Burbank Studios
4000 Warner Boulevard
Burbank, California 91522
Tel: 213-843-6000

Bryanston Pictures
177 South Beverly Drive
Beverly Hills, California 90212
Tel: 213-273-1262

The Bryna Company
141 El Camino Drive
Beverly Hills, California 90212
Tel: 213-274-5294

H. Werner Buck Enterprises
142 South Fairfax Avenue
Los Angeles, California 90036
Tel: 213-937-4030

Buckmace Productions, Inc.
9454 Wilshire Boulevard
Beverly Hills, California 90212
Tel: 213-273-7020

Zev Bufman Productions
100 Universal City Plaza
Universal City, California 91608
Tel: 213-985-4321

Bur-Walt Productions, Inc.
6366 Santa Monica Boulevard
Los Angeles, California 90038
Tel: 213-464-3127

Burgood, Inc.
7800 Beverly Boulevard
Los Angeles, California 90036
Tel: 213-651-2345

Bill Burrund Productions, Inc.
1100 South La Brea Avenue
Los Angeles, California 90019
Tel: 213-937-0300

Caruth C. Byrd Productions
Goldwyn Studios
1041 North Formosa Avenue
Los Angeles, California 90046
Tel: 213-851-1234

C-G Productions, Inc.
3630 Riverside Drive
Burbank, California 91505
Tel: 213-849-2471

CMC Pictures, Corporation
4063 Radford Avenue, Suite 109
Studio City, California 91604
Tel: 213-985-7175

Sid Caesar Productions
9200 Sunset Boulevard
Los Angeles, California 90069
Tel: 213-276-1014

Cagney Productions, Inc.
6777 Hollywood Boulevard,
Room 501
Los Angeles, California 90028
Tel: 213-464-3783

California International
Productions
6710 Melrose Avenue
Los Angeles, California 90038
Tel: 213-939-1491

Caloric Productions
9000 Sunset Boulevard
Los Angeles, California 90069
Tel: 213-274-8518

Fred Calvert Productions
5352 Laurel Boulevard
North Hollywood, California
91607
Tel: 213-985-1414

Capital Productions, Inc.
8447 Wilshire Boulevard
Beverly Hills, California 90211
Tel: 213-655-0801

Capra/S.C. Productions
1041 North Formosa Avenue
Los Angeles, California 90046
Tel: 213-851-1234

Carlyle Films Ltd.
6430 Sunset Boulevard
Los Angeles, California 90028
Tel: 213-466-0864

Carman Productions, Inc.
15456 Cabrito Road
Van Nuys, California 91406
Tel: 213-873-7370

Carousel Productions of
California
7038 Whitaker Avenue
Van Nuys, California 91406
Tel: 213-785-2010

Carson & Paramount Productions
5451 Marathon Street
Los Angeles, California 90038
Tel: 213-463-0100

Cartridge Film Productions
3408 West Victory Boulevard
Burbank, California 91505
Tel: 213-845-4900

Cascade Pictures of California,
Inc.
6601 Romaine Street
Los Angeles, California 90038
Tel: 213-463-2121

Cathedral Films, Inc.
2921 West Alameda Avenue
Burbank, California 91505
Tel: 213-848-6637

Cavalcade Pictures, Inc.
959 North Fairfax Avenue
Los Angeles, California 90046
Tel: 213-654-4144

Cave Creek Enterprises
4024 Radford Avenue
Studio City, California 91604
Tel: 213-763-8411

Centaur Films
9200 Sunset Boulevard
Los Angeles, California 90069
Tel: 213-273-7150

Centre Films, Inc.
1103 North El Centro Avenue
Los Angeles, California 90038
Tel: 213-466-5123

Cerberus Productions
839 Highland Avenue
Los Angeles, California 90038
Tel: 213-469-5321

Chartoff-Winkler Productions,
   Inc.
4000 Warner Boulevard
Burbank, California 91522
Tel: 213-843-6000

R. B. Chenoweth Films
1860 East North Hills Drive
La Habra, California 90631
Tel: 213-691-1652

Cherokee Productions
1880 Century Park East, Suite
   708
Los Angeles, California 90067
Tel: 213-277-3304

Churchill Films
662 North Robertson Boulevard
Los Angeles, California 90069
Tel: 213-657-5110

Cine Group
8560 Sunset Boulevard
Los Angeles, California 90069
Tel: 213-652-4800

Cine-Magic Productions
7644 Hampton Avenue
West Hollywood, California
   90046
Tel: 213-876-2939

Cine-Tel Productions
6325 Santa Monica Boulevard
Los Angeles, California 90038
Tel: 213-465-3376

Cinema "35" Center, Inc.
850 Colorado Boulevard
Los Angeles, California 90041
Tel: 213-255-1296

Cinema Center Films
4024 Radford Avenue
North Hollywood, California
   91604
Tel: 213-763-8411

Cinema Independent Artists, Ltd.
3215 Cahuenga Boulevard West
Los Angeles, California 90068
Tel: 213-851-3700

Cinema Pictures, Inc.
10212 Noble Avenue
Mission Hills, California 91340
Tel: 213-892-6797

Cinema Video Communications
1040 North Las Palmas Avenue
Los Angeles, California 90038
Tel: 213-466-8643

Cinemobile Systems
8560 Sunset Boulevard
Los Angeles, California 90069
Tel: 213-652-4800

Cinepak-Entervolve Productions
4024 Radford Avenue
Studio City, California 91604
Tel: 213-763-8411

Cinerama, Inc.
141 South Robertson Boulevard
Los Angeles, California 90048
Tel: 213-659-2150

Bob Clampett Productions, Inc.
729 Seward Street
Los Angeles, California 90038
Tel: 213-466-0264

Dick Clark Enterprises
9125 Sunset Boulevard
Los Angeles, California 90069
Tel: 213-278-0311

Herman Cohen Productions, Inc.
650 North Bronson Avenue
Los Angeles, California 90004
Tel: 213-466-3111

Tom Cole Productions
5451 Laurel Canyon Boulevard
North Hollywood, California
  91607
Tel: 213-766-4284

Columbia Pictures Industries
Colgems Square
Burbank, California 91505
Tel: 213-843-6000

Computer Image Corporation
1888 Century Park East
Los Angeles, California 90067
Tel: 213-533-8902

Chuck Connors Productions
15130 Ventura Boulevard
Sherman Oaks, California 91403
Tel: 213-466-2464

Continental Productions
10850 Riverside Drive
North Hollywood, California
  91602
Tel: 213-980-1565

Corday Productions, Inc.
Colgems Square
Burbank, California 91505
Tel: 213-843-6000

Cornerstone Productions
6087 Sunset Boulevard
Los Angeles, California 90028
Tel: 213-462-0071

Coronet International Films
12841 Martha Ann Drive
Los Angeles, California 90720
Tel: 213-598-4260

The Pierre Cossette Company
258 South Beverly Drive
Beverly Hills, California 90212
Tel: 213-278-3366

Douglas S. Cramer & Company
Colgems Square
Burbank, California 91505
Tel: 213-843-6000

Creative Entertainment, Ltd.
1888 Century Park East, Suite
1612
Los Angeles, California 90067
Tel: 213-552-2151

Creative Film Associates
953 North Highland Avenue
Los Angeles, California 90038
Tel: 213-466-2191

Marc Creighton Productions
4112 West Jefferson Boulevard
Los Angeles, California 90016
Tel: 213-888-9070

Bing Crosby Productions, Inc.
5451 Marathon Street
Los Angeles, California 90038
Tel: 213-463-0100

Crown International Pictures
292 South La Cienega Boulevard
Beverly Hills, California 90211
Tel: 213-657-6700

Cally Curtis Company
1111 Las Palmas Avenue
Los Angeles, California 90038
Tel: 213-467-1101

Custom Productions
5530 Cahuenga Boulevard
North Hollywood, California
91601
Tel: 213-877-2557

D & S Cineworld Productions,
Inc.
Box 5705
Sherman Oaks, California 91403
Tel: 213-889-2397

Danree Productions
1606 Vista Del Mar Avenue
Los Angeles, California 90028
Tel: 213-469-9111

D'Antoni-Weitz Productions
Box 900
10201 West Pico Boulevard
Beverly Hills, California 90213
Tel: 213-277-2211

Darr-Don, Inc.
4024 Radford Avenue
Studio City, California 91604
Tel: 213-763-8411

Saul David Productions, Inc.
10202 North Washington
Boulevard
Culver City, California 90230
Tel: 213-836-7314

Sammy Davis Enterprises
9000 Sunset Boulevard
Los Angeles, California 90069
Tel: 213-273-8554

Donald A. Davis Productions,
Inc.
705 North Cole Avenue
Los Angeles, California 90038
Tel: 213-469-6256

Day Productions
1016 North Fairview Street
Burbank, California 91505
Tel: 213-848-1462

Dena Pictures, Inc.
8746 Sunset Boulevard
Los Angeles, California 90069
Tel: 213-657-8942

Dick Denove Productions, Inc.
8533 Sunset Boulevard
Los Angeles, California 90069
Tel: 213-657-0708

De Patie–Frelong Enterprises,
Inc.
6859 Hayvenhurst Avenue
Van Nuys, California 91406
Tel: 213-873-7451

Destiny Productions Limited
P.O. Box 2389
Los Angeles, California 90028
Tel: 213-276-2063

Devlin/Gittes Productions
1601 North Beverly Drive
Beverly Hills, California 90210
Tel: 213-654-3313

Jerry Dexter Productions, Inc.
9538 Brighton Way
Beverly Hills, California 90213
Tel: 213-271-6147

P. Diamond Enterprises, Inc.
7715 Sunset Boulevard, Suite 300
Los Angeles, California 90046
Tel: 213-874-1512

Dimension Films
733 North La Brea Avenue
Los Angeles, California 90038
Tel: 213-937-3506

Dimension Pictures, Inc.
9000 Sunset Boulevard, Suite 715
Los Angeles, California 90069
Tel: 213-278-6844

Directions Unlimited Film
Corporation
247 South Beverly Drive
Beverly Hills, California 90212
Tel: 213-274-5319

Walt Disney Productions
500 South Buena Vista Street
Burbank, California 91503
Tel: 213-845-3141

Documentaries International
1923 Empire Avenue
Burbank, California 91504
Tel: 213-845-3928

Documentary Productions, Inc.
6087 Sunset Boulevard
Los Angeles, California 90028
Tel: 213-465-7092

Donlee Productions
100 Universal City Plaza
Universal City, California 91608
Tel: 213-985-4321

James Doolittle
2700 North Vermont Avenue
Los Angeles, California 90027
Tel: 213-666-6000

Harry Dorsey & Associates
1103 Glendon Avenue
Los Angeles, California 90024
Tel: 213-270-4101

Doty-Dayton Productions
4741 Laurel Canyon Boulevard,
    Suite 202
North Hollywood, California
    91607
Tel: 213-980-7202

Dougfair Corporation
6922 Hollywood Boulevard, Suite
    503
Los Angeles, California 90028
Tel: 213-465-6164

Jack Douglas Organization
8833 Sunset Boulevard
Los Angeles, California 90069
Tel: 213-655-7790

Dove Films
722 North Seward Street
Los Angeles, California 90038
Tel: 213-461-3737

Dramatic Features, Inc.
4024 Radford Avenue
Studio City, California 91604
Tel: 213-763-8411

Driftwood Productions
30 Driftwood
Marina Del Ray, California
    90291
Tel: 213-392-2415

Dudley Productions Ltd.
308 North Rodeo Drive
Beverly Hills, California 90210
Tel: 213-273-5891

Dundee Productions, Inc.
6223 Selma Avenue
Los Angeles, California 90028
Tel: 213-467-5168

Cal Dunn Studios
1040 North Las Palmas Avenue
Los Angeles, California 90038
Tel: 213-469-9011

Dynacom Productions
665 North Lillian Way
Los Angeles, California 90004
Tel: 213-780-2890

Charles Eastman Productions
6685 Sunset Boulevard
Los Angeles, California 90027
Tel: 213-464-3606

Christopher Eaton & Associates
6305 Yucca Street
Los Angeles, California 90028
Tel: 212-461-4313

Echo Productions
1040 North Las Palmas Avenue
Los Angeles, California 90038
Tel: 213-469-2707

Edprod Pictures, Inc.
1680 North Vine Street, Suite
1210
Los Angeles, California 90028
Tel: 213-466-7327

George Edwards Productions
1040 North Formosa Avenue
Los Angeles, California 90028
Tel: 213-851-1234

Ralph Edwards Productions
1717 North Highland Avenue
Los Angeles, California 90028
Tel: 213-463-8121

Richard Einfeld, Inc.
1512 North Las Palmas Avenue
Los Angeles, California 90028
Tel: 213-461-3731

El Cerrito Productions
4000 Warner Boulevard
Burbank, California 91522
Tel: 213-843-6000

The Elliott Concern
932 North La Brea Avenue
Los Angeles, California 90038
Tel: 213-874-9400

Embroya Productions
6430 Sunset Boulevard
Los Angeles, California 90028
Tel: 213-465-3317

Ray Engel Productions
11627 Oxnard Street
North Hollywood, California
91606
Tel: 213-769-2200

Entertainment Corporation of
America
554 South San Vicente
Los Angeles, California 90048
Tel: 213-653-9040

Entertainment Enterprises
1680 Vine Street, Suite 519
Los Angeles, California 90028
Tel: 213-462-6001

Entertainment Media, Ltd.
999 North Doheny Drive
Los Angeles, California 90069
Tel: 213-275-4456

Entertainment Ventures, Inc.
1654 Cordova Street
Los Angeles, California 90007
Tel: 213-731-7236

The Establishment, Inc.
9000 Sunset Boulevard
Los Angeles, California 90069
Tel: 213-274-9483

Eue/Screen Gems
3701 West Oak Street
Burbank, California 91505
Tel: 213-843-3221

Art Evans Productions, Inc.
1136 North Las Palmas Avenue
Los Angeles, California 90038
Tel: 213-461-9231

Robert Evans Productions
Twentieth Century–Fox Studios
Box 900
Beverly Hills, California 90213
Tel: 213-277-2211

Eve Productions Incorporated
7080 Hollywood Boulevard, Suite
415
Los Angeles, California 90028
Tel: 213-466-7791

Everglades Productions, Inc.
1041 North Formosa Avenue
Los Angeles, California 90046
Tel: 213-851-1234

F-M Production
733 North Highland Avenue
Los Angeles, California 90038
Tel: 213-937-1622

FMC Productions
3249 Tareco Drive
Los Angeles, California 90068
Tel: 213-851-4665

FRSCO Productions, Ltd.
General Service Studios
1040 North Las Palmas Avenue
Los Angeles, California 90038
Tel: 213-876-7600

Jerry Fairbanks Productions of
California
826 North Cole Avenue
Los Angeles, California 90038
Tel: 213-462-1101

Falcon Studios
5526 Hollywood Boulevard
Los Angeles, California 90028
Tel: 213-462-9356

Family Films
5823 Santa Monica Boulevard
Los Angeles, California 90038
Tel: 213-462-2243

Famous Players International
Corporation
1210 North Wetherly Drive West
Los Angeles, California 90069
Tel: 213-275-8221

Fanfare Corporation
9000 Sunset Boulevard
Los Angeles, California 90069
Tel: 213-272-9262

Favorite Films of California
292 South La Cienega Boulevard
Beverly Hills, California 90211
Tel: 213-657-6700

Don Fedderson Productions, Inc.
4024 Radford Avenue
Studio City, California 91604
Tel: 213-763-8411

Fidelity Films, Inc.
6315 Yucca Street
Los Angeles, California 90028
Tel: 213-464-6277

Film Communicators
5451 Laurel Canyon
North Hollywood, California
91607
Tel: 213-766-3747

The Film Factory
1610 Argyle Avenue
Los Angeles, California 90028
Tel: 213-461-3881

Film Group
1717 North Highland Avenue
Los Angeles, California 90028
Tel: 213-469-7922

Film Guarantors
8619 Sunset Boulevard
Los Angeles, California 90069
Tel: 213-652-4800

Film Investment Corporation
186 North Canon Drive, Suite 110
Beverly Hills, California 90210
Tel: 213-274-9991

Film Technology Company, Inc.
6900 Santa Monica Boulevard
Los Angeles, California 90038
Tel: 213-465-4908

Filmagic
6362 Hollywood Boulevard
Los Angeles, California 90028
Tel: 213-464-5333

Filmakers Group
100 Universal City Plaza
Universal City, California 91608
Tel: 213-985-4321

Filmation Associates
18107 Sherman Way
Reseda, California 91335
Tel: 213-345-7414

Filmfair, Incorporated
10900 Ventura Boulevard
Studio City, California 91604
Tel: 213-877-3191

Filmline Production Associates,
Inc.
1467 Tamarind Avenue
Los Angeles, California 90028
Tel: 213-466-8667

Films/West Incorporated
518 North La Cienega Boulevar
Los Angeles, California 90048
Tel: 213-659-0024

Filmways Motion Pictures, In
1800 Century Park East, Suite
300
Los Angeles, California 90067
Tel: 213-552-1133

Fine Arts Films, Inc.
11632 Ventura Boulevard
Studio City, California 91604
Tel: 213-980-3034

Edward Finney Productions
1578 Queens Road
Los Angeles, California 90069
Tel: 213-874-0840

First Artists Production
Company, Ltd.
4000 Warner Boulevard
Burbank, California 91522
Tel: 213-843-6000

First Team Productions
932 La Brea Avenue
Los Angeles, California 90038
Tel: 213-876-4900

Flagg Films, Inc.
11071 Ventura Boulevard
Studio City, California 91604
Tel: 213-985-5050

Focus of California, Inc.
1042 North Cole
Los Angeles, California 90038
Tel: 213-462-2353

Format Productions, Inc.
12754 Ventura Boulevard
Studio City, California 91604
Tel: 213-769-3610

Formosa Productions, Inc.
1041 North Formosa Avenue
Los Angeles, California 90046
Tel: 213-851-1234

Fortune Films
12435 Oxnard Street
North Hollywood, California
    91606
Tel: 213-980-1106

Forward Films
1041 North Formosa Avenue
Los Angeles, California 90046
Tel: 213-851-1234

Foster-Brower Productions
4000 Warner Boulevard
Burbank, California 91522
Tel: 213-843-6000

David Foster Productions
8447 Wilshire Boulevard, Suite
    302
Beverly Hills, California 90211
Tel: 213-651-0230

Four Leaf Productions, Inc.
10201 West Pico Boulevard
Los Angeles, California 90064
Tel: 213-277-2211

Four Star International, Inc.
400 South Beverly Drive
Beverly Hills, California 90212
Tel: 213-277-7444

George Fox Corporation
6500 Barton Avenue
Los Angeles, California 90038
Tel: 213-464-2242

Mel Frank Productions
4000 Warner Boulevard
Burbank, California 91522
Tel: 213-843-6000

John Frankenheimer Productions
9171 Wilshire Boulevard
Beverly Hills, California 90210
Tel: 213-274-9911

Frankovich Productions, Inc.
1438 North Gower Street
Los Angeles, California 90038
Tel: 213-462-3111

Freberg, Ltd.
8720 Sunset Boulevard
Los Angeles, California 90069
Tel: 213-657-6550

Leonard Freeman Productions
4024 Radford Avenue
North Hollywood, California
    91604
Tel: 213-763-8411

Ed Friendly Productions
450 North Roxbury Drive
Beverly Hills, California 90210
Tel: 213-275-1193

Robert Fryer Productions
4000 Warner Boulevard
Burbank, California 91522
Tel: 213-843-6000

G. N. Productions
Gabor Nagy
1019 North Cole Avenue
Los Angeles, California 90038
Tel: 213-463-5693

Greg Garrison Productions
3630 Riverside Drive
Burbank, California 91505
Tel: 213-849-2471

Gemini Productions, Inc.
1717 North Highland Avenue
Los Angeles, California 90028
Tel: 213-463-3184

General Film Corporation
839 North Highland Avenue
Los Angeles, California 90038
Tel: 213-469-5321

Geoffrey Productions, Inc.
9201 Wilshire Boulevard
Beverly Hills, California 90210
Tel: 213-271-2183

David Gerber Productions
10201 West Pico Boulevard
Los Angeles, California 90064
Tel: 213-277-2211

Glenco Productions
7800 Beverly Boulevard
Los Angeles, California 90036
Tel: 213-651-2345

William Goetz Productions
11661 San Vicente, Suite 707
Los Angeles, California 90049
Tel: 213-826-4558

Gold-Key Entertainment
855 North Cahuenga Boulevar
Los Angeles, California 90038
Tel: 213-466-9741

Samuel Goldwyn, Jr.,
    Productions, Inc.
1041 North Formosa Avenue
Los Angeles, California 90046
Tel: 213-851-1234

Good Grief Productions
4000 Warner Boulevard
Burbank, California 91522
Tel: 213-843-6000

Mark Good Productions
4000 Warner Boulevard
Burbank, California 91505
Tel: 213-843-6000

Goodshow Corporation
9201 Wilshire Boulevard
Beverly Hills, California 90210
Tel: 213-274-8858

Alex Gordon Productions
360 North Orange Drive
Los Angeles, California 90036
Tel: 213-936-1874

Cliff Gould Project
4000 Warner Boulevard
Burbank, California 91505
Tel: 213-843-6000

Robert M. Gowa
1129 1/2 North Tamarind
    Avenue
Los Angeles, California 90038
Tel: 213-466-5561

Leonard Grant Productions
9000 Sunset Boulevard
Los Angeles, California 90069
Tel: 213-274-9483

Irving Granz Productions
451 North Canon Drive
Beverly Hills, California 90210
Tel: 213-274-9139

Graphic Films Corporation
3341 Cahuenga Boulevard
Los Angeles, California 90068
Tel: 213-851-4100

Great Empire Films
7046 Hollywood Boulevard
Los Angeles, California 90028
Tel: 213-469-2117

Greif-Garris Organization
8467 Beverly Boulevard
Los Angeles, California 90048
Tel: 213-653-4780

Abner J. Greshler Productions,
    Inc.
8400 Sunset Boulevard
Los Angeles, California 90069
Tel: 213-654-5960

Merv Griffin Productions
1735 North Vine Street
Los Angeles, California 90028
Tel: 213-461-4701

Gerry Gross Productions
5800 Sunset Boulevard
Los Angeles, California 90028
Tel: 213-469-3181

Group One Productions, Inc.
3255 Cahuenga Boulevard
Los Angeles, California 90068
Tel: 213-876-3300

Grundkoff-Linson
4000 Warner Boulevard
Burbank, California 91522
Tel: 213-843-6000

Guadaloupe Productions
1715 North Fairfax
Los Angeles, California 90046
Tel: 213-876-9721

Lew Guinn Productions
1600 North Western Avenue
Los Angeles, California 90027
Tel: 213-469-3692

Gus Productions, Inc.
5150 Wilshire Boulevard, Suite
    505
Los Angeles, California 90036
Tel: 213-938-0109

The Haboush Company
6611 Santa Monica Boulevard
Los Angeles, California 90038
Tel: 213-466-4111

Halcyon Productions, Inc.
9056 Santa Monica Boulevard
Beverly Hills, California 90210
Tel: 213-275-5366

Jack Haley, Jr., Productions
1443 Devlin
Los Angeles, California 90069
Tel: 213-276-2726

Hammerlock Productions
6671 Sunset Boulevard, Suite
1514
Los Angeles, California 90028
Tel: 213-462-2378

Handel Film Corporation
8730 Sunset Boulevard
Los Angeles, California 90069
Tel: 213-657-8990

Hanna-Barbera Productions
3400 Cahuenga Boulevard West
Los Angeles, California 90068
Tel: 213-851-5000

Harlequin Productions
5630 Woodman Avenue
Van Nuys, California 91401
Tel: 213-463-6841

Denny Harris Incorporated of
California
12166 West Olympic Boulevard
Los Angeles, California 90064
Tel: 213-826-6565

Jack H. Harris Enterprises
9229 Sunset Boulevard
Los Angeles, California 90069
Tel: 213-278-7812

James Harris Productions
248 1/2 South Lasky Drive
Beverly Hills, California 90212
Tel: 213-273-4270

Harris-Tuchman Productions,
Inc.
751 North Highland Avenue
Los Angeles, California 90038
Tel: 213-936-7189

Paul Harrison Productions
9255 Sunset Boulevard
Los Angeles, California 90069
Tel: 213-654-2354

Joe Hartsfield & Associates
CBS Studio Center
4024 Radford Avenue
North Hollywood, California
91604
Tel: 213-763-8411

Hatos-Hall Productions
6725 Sunset Boulevard
Los Angeles, California 90028
Tel: 213-469-7181

Don Henderson Motion Picture
Co.
4808 Bonvue Avenue
Los Angeles, California 90027
Tel: 213-666-6021

John J. Hennessy Motion Pictures
900 Palm Avenue
South Pasadena, California 91030
Tel: 213-682-2353

Bob Henry Productions
4425 Lakeside Drive
Burbank, California 91505
Tel: 213-985-9711

Alfred Higgins Productions
9100 Sunset Boulevard
Los Angeles, California 90069
Tel: 213-878-0330

Hill-Daves Productions
15300 Ventura Boulevard
Sherman Oaks, California 91403
Tel: 213-788-3595

Hill Production Service, Inc.
835 North Seward Street
Los Angeles, California 90038
Tel: 213-463-0311

Herbert Hirschman Productions
519 North Palm Drive
Beverly Hills, California 90210
Tel: 213-276-0653

Alfred Hitchcock Productions
100 Universal City Plaza
Universal City, California 91608
Tel: 213-985-4321

Hob, Inc.
132 South Rodeo Drive
Beverly Hills, California 90212
Tel: 213-278-6700

Hodges Productions
4000 Warner Boulevard
Burbank, California 91522
Tel: 213-843-6000

Hogan-Lee Images
12849 Magnolia Avenue
North Hollywood, California
    91607
Tel: 213-980-3566

Hollywood Animators
7401 Sunset Boulevard
Los Angeles, California 90046
Tel: 213-876-1190

Hollywood Continental Films,
    Inc.
1532 North Cahuenga Boulevard
Los Angeles, California 90028
Tel: 213-466-1637

Hollywood Film Associates
2025 North Highland Avenue
Los Angeles, California 90068
Tel: 213-874-8413

Hope Enterprises, Inc.
9229 Sunset Boulevard
Los Angeles, California 90069
Tel: 213-271-7231

Hughes Productions
7000 Romaine Street
Los Angeles, California 90038
Tel: 213-654-2500

Ross Hunter Productions
The Burbank Studios
4000 Warner Boulevard
Burbank, California 91522
Tel: 213-843-6000

Ilson-Chambers Productions
4000 Warner Boulevard
Burbank, California 91522
Tel: 213-843-6000

Image Films, Inc.
8563 Beverly Boulevard
Los Angeles, California 90048
Tel: 213-657-5141

Independent Artists Productions
Box 5165
Sherman Oaks, California 91403
Tel: 213-463-4811

Independent Producers Service
7370 Melrose Avenue
Los Angeles, California 90046
Tel: 213-655-3599

International Cinema
Corporation
11969 Ventura Boulevard
Studio City, California 91604
Tel: 213-980-0426

International Film Enterprises
8440 Sunset Boulevard
Los Angeles, California 90069
Tel: 213-654-9500

International Medifilms
3491 West Cahuenga Boulevard
Los Angeles, California 90028
Tel: 213-851-4555

International Pictures
Corporation
1040 North Las Palmas Avenue
Los Angeles, California 90038
Tel: 213-462-6741

International Producers
Corporation
2609 West Olive Avenue
Burbank, California 91505
Tel: 213-851-0466

International Producers Services
3518 Cahuenga Boulevard West
Los Angeles, California 90068
Tel: 213-851-3595

Intro-Media Productions
9000 Sunset Boulevard
Los Angeles, California 90069
Tel: 213-477-7579

J-B Productions
9908 Santa Monica Boulevard
Beverly Hills, California 90212
Tel: 213-277-3881

Gary L. Jackson
1918 Broderick Street
San Francisco, California 94115
Tel: 415-563-5100

S. Jacoby Productions
8721 Sunset Boulevard
Los Angeles, California 90069
Tel: 213-652-5623

Henry Jaffe Enterprises, Inc.
5800 Sunset Boulevard
Los Angeles, California 90028
Tel: 213-469-3581

Jagro West
3905 Ventura Canyon
Sherman Oaks, California 91403
Tel: 213-986-7868

Jalem Productions, Inc.
141 El Camino Drive
Beverly Hills, California 90212
Tel: 213-278-7750

Jalmia Enterprises, Inc.
2715 Jalmia Drive
Los Angeles, California 90046
Tel: 213-874-3349

Jam Handy Organization
1680 North Vine Street
Los Angeles, California 90028
Tel: 213-463-2321

Jemmin, Inc.
1900 Avenue of the Stars
Los Angeles, California 90067
Tel: 213-553-7674

Johnson/Cowan, Inc.
6059 Carlton Way
Los Angeles, California 90028
Tel: 213-463-7181

Johnson-Nyquist Productions,
   Inc.
18414 Eddy Street
Northridge, California 91324
Tel: 213-349-2161

Don Jolly Productions
9348 Santa Monica Boulevard,
   Suite 101
Beverly Hills, California 90210
Tel: 213-273-3412

Frank Jones Associates
1150 West Olive Street
Burbank, California 91506
Tel: 213-843-2031

Kaleidoscope Films, Ltd.
6345 Fountain Avenue
Los Angeles, California 90028
Tel: 213-465-1151

Kaye Entertainment Enterprises
1680 North Vine Street, Suite 519
Los Angeles, California 90028
Tel: 213-462-6001

Stacy Keach Productions
5216 Laurel Canyon Boulevard
North Hollywood, California
   91607
Tel: 213-877-0472

Don Kelley Organization
1474 North Kings Road
Los Angeles, California 90069
Tel: 213-656-4787

Kerr-Gray Enterprises
22612 Sylvan Street
Woodland Hills, California 91364
Tel: 213-884-8810

Kess-Walk Productions, Inc.
1715 North Fairfax
Los Angeles, California 90046
Tel: 213-876-9721

King International Corporation
124 Lasky Drive
Beverly Hills, California 90212
Tel: 213-247-0333

Howard W. Koch Productions
5451 Marathon Street
Los Angeles, California 90038
Tel: 213-463-0100

Ken Kragen & Friends
451 North Canon Drive
Beverly Hills, California 90210
Tel: 213-273-5011

Stanley Kramer Productions
4000 Warner Boulevard
Burbank, California 91522
Tel: 213-843-6000

Steve Krantz Productions
6725 Sunset Boulevard
Los Angeles, California 90028
Tel: 213-461-4101

Kriton Productions
7906 Santa Monica Boulevard
Los Angeles, California 90046
Tel: 213-656-5964

Kurtz & Friends Films
6532 Sunset Boulevard
Los Angeles, California 90028
Tel: 213-461-8188

Kurtz Organization
8330 Elusive Drive
Los Angeles, California 90046
Tel: 213-656-0702

LMH Productions, Inc.
9134 Sunset Boulevard
Los Angeles, California 90069
Tel: 213-274-3400

N. Lee Lacy & Associates, Ltd.
8446 Melrose Place
Los Angeles, California 90069
Tel: 213-651-3610

Ely Landau Productions
10201 West Pico Boulevard
Los Angeles, California 90064
Tel: 213-277-2211

Landers/Roberts Productions
8899 Beverly Boulevard
Los Angeles, California 90048
Tel: 213-273-5050

Alan Landsburg Productions, Inc.
9200 Sunset Boulevard
Los Angeles, California 90069
Tel: 213-273-7400

Walter Lantz Productions
861 North Seward Street
Los Angeles, California 90038
Tel: 213-469-2907

Bob Larsen Productions
4842 Rigalo Road
Woodland Hills, California 91364
Tel: 213-346-1045

Lawrence-Grollnek Productions
4142 Benedict Canyon Boulevard
Sherman Oaks, California 91403
Tel: 213-985-1087

Alan Lee Productions
1040 North Las Palmas Avenue
Los Angeles, California 90038
Tel: 213-469-9011

Gerry Leider Productions
4000 Warner Boulevard
Burbank, California 91505
Tel: 213-843-6000

Sheldon Leonard Productions
8544 Sunset Boulevard
Los Angeles, California 90069
Tel: 213-652-7075

Lepard Productions
666 North Robertson Boulevar(
Los Angeles, California 90069
Tel: 213-657-4772

Gene Lester Productions
12642 Ventura Boulevard
Studio City, California 91604
Tel: 213-769-6160

Mark L. Lester Pictures
1737 Nichols Canyon Road
Los Angeles, California 90046
Tel: 213-876-8560

Alan J. Levi Productions
3431 Royal Woods Drive
Sherman Oaks, California 9140:
Tel: 213-784-2132

Jerry Lewis Films, Inc.
1900 Avenue of the Stars
Los Angeles, California 90067
Tel: 213-552-2200

Leyton Productions
4000 Warner Boulevard
Burbank, California 91522
Tel: 213-843-6000

Liboy Productions
4000 Warner Boulevard
Burbank, California 91522
Tel: 213-843-6000

Richard O. Linke Associates
4405 Riverside Drive
Burbank, California 91505
Tel: 213-843-6900

Lester Linsk Productions
10201 West Pico Boulevard
Los Angeles, California 90064
Tel: 213-277-2211

Lion's Gate Films, Inc.
1334 Westwood Boulevard
Los Angeles, California 90024
Tel: 213-475-4987

William Littlejohn Productions
23425 Malibu Colony Drive
Malibu, California 90265
Tel: 213-456-8620

Si Litvinoff
4000 Warner Boulevard
Burbank, California 91522
Tel: 213-843-6000

Jack Lloyd Productions
8440 Sunset Boulevard
Los Angeles, California 90069
Tel: 213-656-4607

Lori Productions, Inc.
6087 Sunset Boulevard
Los Angeles, California 90028
Tel: 213-466-7567

Lorimar Productions, Inc.
4000 Warner Boulevard
Burbank, California 91522
Tel: 213-843-6000

A. C. Lyles Productions, Inc.
2115 Linda Flora Drive
Los Angeles, California 90024
Tel: 213-476-7411

MCA-TV
100 Universal City Plaza
Universal City, California 91608
Tel: 213-985-4321

MLR Productions, Inc.
6251 Bellaire Avenue
North Hollywood, California
   91606
Tel: 213-762-1276

MacGillivray-Freeman Films
4173 Sunswept Drive
Studio City, California 91604
Tel: 213-980-3038

Madison Productions, Inc.
9028 Sunset Boulevard
Los Angeles, California 90069
Tel: 213-274-8671

Douglas Mador Productions
804 North Sierra Bonita Avenue
Los Angeles, California 90046
Tel: 213-651-1278

Lee Magid, Inc.
5750 Melrose Avenue
Los Angeles, California 90068
Tel: 213-463-2353

The Malpaso Company
Universal Studios
100 Universal City Plaza
Universal City, California 91608
Tel: 213-985-4321

Ted Mann Productions, Inc.
9255 Sunset Boulevard
Los Angeles, California 90069
Tel: 213-274-8831

Martin Manulis Productions
Box 818
Beverly Hills, California 90210
Tel: 213-476-2709

Marathon Productions
5478 Marathon Street
Los Angeles, California 90038
Tel: 213-462-9312

Mark VII Productions
100 Universal City Plaza
Universal City, California 91608
Tel: 213-985-4321

Marquee Enterprises
9200 Sunset Boulevard
Los Angeles, California 90069
Tel: 213-273-2473

Marten Company
8969 Sunset Boulevard
Los Angeles, California 90069
Tel: 213-274-9309

Jesse H. Martin Productions, Inc.
2913 Bentley Avenue
Los Angeles, California 90064
Tel: 213-270-4628

Matrix Image
6622 Variel Avenue
Canoga Park, California 91303
Tel: 213-883-6622

The Mayer Company
560 North Larchmont Boulevard
Los Angeles, California 90004
Tel: 213-462-6074

Rod McKuen Enterprises
8440 Santa Monica Boulevard
Los Angeles, California 90069
Tel: 213-656-7311

Meadowlane Enterprises
15201 Burbank Boulevard
Van Nuys, California 91401
Tel: 213-988-3830

Media Development Company
3000 West Alameda Avenue,
   Suite 2805
Burbank, California 91523
Tel: 213-845-7000

Mediarts, Inc.
9229 Sunset Boulevard
Los Angeles, California 90069
Tel: 213-278-8810

Melandrea, Inc.
6335 Homewood Avenue
Los Angeles, California 90028
Tel: 213-461-2791

Martin Melcher Productions, Inc.
4024 Radford Avenue
North Hollywood, California
   91604
Tel: 213-763-8411

Bill Melendez Productions, Inc.
439 North Larchmont Boulevard
Los Angeles, California 90004
Tel: 213-463-4101

Mentor Productions
9533 Brighton Way
Beverly Hills, California 90210
Tel: 213-278-2210

Merrick International Films
870 North Vine Street
Los Angeles, California 90038
Tel: 213-462-8444

Metro-Goldwyn-Mayer, Inc.
10202 West Washington
  Boulevard
Culver City, California 90230
Tel: 213-870-3311

Metro-Kalvar, Inc.
8927 West Exposition Boulevard
Los Angeles, California 90034
Tel: 213-837-7179

Metromedia Producers
  Corporation
8544 Sunset Boulevard
Los Angeles, California 90069
Tel: 213-652-7075

Herman Miller Project
4000 Warner Boulevard
Burbank, California 91505
Tel: 213-843-6000

Larry Miller Productions
Box 8094
Universal City, California 91608
Tel: 213-985-4071

Mirage Film Productions
6335 Homewood Avenue
Los Angeles, California 90028
Tel: 213-465-8130

Leon Mirell Productions, Inc.
6551 Commodore Sloat Drive
Los Angeles, California 90048
Tel: 213-933-3780

The Mirisch Corporation of
  California
100 Universal City Plaza
Universal City, California 91608
Tel: 213-985-4321

Mitman Productions
1418 North Highland Avenue
Los Angeles, California 90028
Tel: 213-462-1251

Monarch Productions
13914 Fairlock Avenue
Paramount, California 90723
Tel: 213-638-1263

Paul Monash Productions
100 Universal City Plaza
Universal City, California 91608
Tel: 213-985-4321

Moonstone Productions
1061 North Spaulding Avenue
Los Angeles, California 90046
Tel: 213-654-0890

Morgan-Steckler Productions
13025 Valleyheart Drive
North Hollywood, California
  91603
Tel: 213-789-3830

Mosaic Films, Inc.
2100 West Magnolia Boulevard
Burbank, California 91506
Tel: 213-848-5571

Motion Pictures International
9255 Sunset Boulevard
Los Angeles, California 90069
Tel: 213-273-5844

Motown Productions Company
6464 West Sunset Boulevard
Los Angeles, California 90028
Tel: 213-461-3011

Moustache Productions
9017 Harratt Street
Los Angeles, California 90069
Tel: 213-464-5161

The Movie Company Enterprises,
Inc.
9465 Wilshire Boulevard
Beverly Hills, California 90212
Tel: 213-271-7254

Movie-Tech
6518 Santa Monica Boulevard
Los Angeles, California 90038
Tel: 213-467-8491

Murakami/Wolf Films, Inc.
1463 Tamarind Avenue
Los Angeles, California 90028
Tel: 213-462-6474

Francis G. Murphy Productions
3060 Belden Drive
Los Angeles, California 90068
Tel: 213-466-2131

Mutual General Film
Corporation
9399 Wilshire Boulevard
Beverly Hills, California 90210
Tel: 213-274-8646

NBA Films
3215 Cahuenga Boulevard West
Los Angeles, California 90068
Tel: 213-466-1901

Jim Nabors Productions
P.O. Box 229
Beverly Hills, California 90210
Tel: 213-270-4434

Nassour Pictures, Inc.
9348 Santa Monica Boulevard
Beverly Hills, California 90210
Tel: 213-278-3952

Raymond Nassour Productions
12627 Moorpark Street
Studio City, California 91604
Tel: 213-877-3534

National Communications
Foundation
1041 North Las Palmas Avenue
Los Angeles, California 90038
Tel: 213-465-4111

National General Corporation
1 Carthay Plaza
Los Angeles, California 90054
Tel: 213-937-4100

National Screen Service
7026 Santa Monica Boulevard
Los Angeles, California 90038
Tel: 213-466-5111

Natoma Productions
1896 Rising Glen Road
Los Angeles, California 90069
Tel: 213-654-4400

Nawal Productions
3000 West Alameda Boulevard
Burbank, California 91505
Tel: 213-848-4916

Nemours Productions, Inc.
3518 West Cahuenga Boulevard
Los Angeles, California 90068
Tel: 213-851-3660

New World Pictures, Inc.
8831 Sunset Boulevard
Los Angeles, California 90069
Tel: 213-657-2201

Newman/Foreman Company
4000 Warner Boulevard
Burbank, California 91522
Tel: 213-843-7280

Next Stage Productions
1031 North La Brea Avenue
Los Angeles, California 90038
Tel: 213-851-0304

Nicholson Films, Inc.
6335 Homewood Avenue
Los Angeles, California 90028
Tel: 213-462-0878

Fred Niles Communication
  Centers, Inc.
5545 Sunset Boulevard
Los Angeles, California 90028
Tel: 213-462-7311

Wendell Niles Productions
4555 Ledge Avenue
North Hollywood, California
  91602
Tel: 213-985-2252

Norway Productions
4000 Warner Boulevard
Burbank, California 91505
Tel: 213-843-6000

Ocee Ritch Productions
1136 North Las Palmas Avenue
Los Angeles, California 90038
Tel: 213-461-9231

The Organization
4000 Warner Boulevard
Burbank, California 91522
Tel: 213-843-6000

Oriol Productions
175 North Sycamore Avenue
Los Angeles, California 90036
Tel: 213-933-1812

Orsatti Productions
10331 Riverside Drive
North Hollywood, California
  91602
Tel: 213-980-6430

Glenn Otto Studios
7408 Beverly Boulevard
Los Angeles, California 90036
Tel: 213-933-5679

Buck Owens Productions
  Company, Inc.
1225 North Chester Avenue
Bakersfield, California 93308
Tel: 805-393-1011

Oxford Films
1136 North Las Palmas Avenue
Los Angeles, California 90038
Tel: 213-461-9231

Paisley Productions, Inc.
6063 Sunset Boulevard
Los Angeles, California 90028
Tel: 213-461-2871

Pando Corporation
720 North Seward Street
Los Angeles, California 90038
Tel: 213-464-8331

Pantomime Pictures, Inc.
12144 Riverside Drive
North Hollywood, California
   91607
Tel: 213-980-5555

Paragon Films
7325 Santa Monica Boulevard
Los Angeles, California 90046
Tel: 213-851-0488

Paramount Pictures Corporation
Executive Offices
202 North Canon Drive
Beverly Hills, California 90210
Tel: 213-463-0100

Paramount Pictures Corporation
5451 Marathon Street
Los Angeles, California 90038
Tel: 213-463-0100

Paramount Television
5451 Marathon Street
Los Angeles, California 90038
Tel: 213-463-0100

Parthenon Pictures
2625 Temple Street
Los Angeles, California 90026
Tel: 213-385-3911

Pasetta Productions
4000 Warner Boulevard
Burbank, California 91505
Tel: 213-843-6000

Pax Enterprises
4000 Warner Boulevard
Burbank, California 91522
Tel: 213-843-6000

Peak Productions
6430 Sunset Boulevard
Los Angeles, California 90028
Tel: 213-461-4781

Pegasus Film Productions
1520 North Van Ness
Los Angeles, California 90028
Tel: 213-466-3571

Pen Communications, Inc.
2376 Westwood Boulevard
Los Angeles, California 90064
Tel: 213-474-6573

Arthur Penn Productions
4000 Warner Boulevard
Burbank, California 91505
Tel: 213-843-6000

Don Perry Enterprises, Inc.
8961 Sunset Boulevard
Los Angeles, California 90069
Tel: 213-278-8961

Peters & Company
1330 North Vine Street
Los Angeles, California 90028
Tel: 213-466-9351

The Petersen Company
1330 North Vine Street
Los Angeles, California 90028
Tel: 213-466-9351

Phaeton Film Productions
Box 48850
Los Angeles, California 90048
Tel: 213-275-3368

Phelps-Martin Productions
3617 Coty Road
Sherman Oaks, California 91403
Tel: 213-552-2226

Stuart Phelps Productions
1901 Avenue of the Stars
Los Angeles, California 90067
Tel: 213-552-2226

Phoenix Films Corporation
8157 Sunset Boulevard
Los Angeles, California 90046
Tel: 213-654-1660

The Picture Company
729 North Seward Street
Los Angeles, California 90038
Tel: 213-467-2683

Pingree Productions
10201 West Pico Boulevard
Los Angeles, California 90064
Tel: 213-277-2211

Playboy Productions
8560 Sunset Boulevard
Los Angeles, California 90069
Tel: 213-659-4080

Playhouse Pictures
1401 North La Brea Avenue
Los Angeles, California 90028
Tel: 213-851-2112

Plowshare Productions
1010 North Kings Road
Los Angeles, California 90069
Tel: 213-654-4678

Martin Poll Productions
10202 West Washington
  Boulevard
Culver City, California 90230
Tel: 213-870-3311

Paul Pompian Productions
8816 Sunset Boulevard
Los Angeles, California 90069
Tel: 213-657-0527

Price Filmakers
3491 Cahuenga Boulevard West
Los Angeles, California 90028
Tel: 213-851-3777

Producers Associates
3215 Cahuenga Boulevard
Los Angeles, California 90068
Tel: 213-851-4123

Production Associates, Inc.
3000 West Alameda Avenue
Burbank, California 91523
Tel: 213-845-7000

The Production Company
8612 West Pico Boulevard
Los Angeles, California 90035
Tel: 213-659-3940

Production House West
6671 Sunset Boulevard
Los Angeles, California 90028
Tel: 213-462-2378

Productions West
1134 North Highland Avenue
Los Angeles, California 90038
Tel: 213-464-0169

Project Films
3518 Cahuenga Boulevard West
Los Angeles, California 90028
Tel: 213-851-4320

Public Arts Productions
100 Universal City Plaza
Universal City, California 91608
Tel: 213-985-4321

Punkin Productions, Inc.
7800 Beverly Boulevard
Los Angeles, California 90036
Tel: 213-651-2345

Q-Ed Productions
2921 West Alameda Boulevard
Burbank, California 91505
Tel: 213-849-2275

Q-M Productions
1041 North Formosa Avenue
Los Angeles, California 90046
Tel: 213-851-1234

Qualis Productions
10889 Wilshire Boulevard, Suite
  1144
Los Angeles, California 90024
Tel: 213-477-1575

Quartet Films, Inc.
5631 Hollywood Boulevard
Los Angeles, California 90028
Tel: 213-464-9225

R & R Productions
8440 Santa Monica Boulevard
Los Angeles, California 90069
Tel: 213-656-7311

RFB Enterprises, Inc.
780 North Gower Street
Los Angeles, California 90028
Tel: 213-463-0100

RFD Productions
4000 Warner Boulevard
Burbank, California 91522
Tel: 213-843-6900

RFG Associates, Inc.
1132 North Highland Avenue
Los Angeles, California 90038
Tel: 213-466-2648

RKO-General Productions, Inc.
5670 Wilshire Boulevard
Los Angeles, California 90036
Tel: 213-462-2133

Rm Films International, Inc.
1725 North Ivar Avenue, Suite
  101
Los Angeles, California 90028
Tel: 213-466-7791

RSO Films (Robert Stigwood
  Organization)
8560 Sunset Boulevard
Los Angeles, California 90069
Tel: 213-652-5030

Martin Rackin Productions
4024 Radford Avenue
North Hollywood, California
  91604
Tel: 213-763-8411

Radnitz/Mattel Productions, Inc.
4024 Radford Avenue
North Hollywood, California
91604
Tel: 213-763-8411

Radoff-Deda Films, Inc.
6665 Franklin Avenue
Los Angeles, California 90028
Tel: 213-851-0322

Rainbow Productions, Inc.
Ralph Nelson
1801 Avenue of the Stars
Los Angeles, California 90067
Tel: 213-277-0700

Rainbow Productions, Inc.
911 Gateway West
Los Angeles, California 90067
Tel: 213-277-0700

Ramsgate Films
704 Santa Monica Boulevard
Santa Monica, California 90401
Tel: 213-394-8819

Martin Ransohoff Productions,
Inc.
9401 Wilshire Boulevard
Beverly Hills, California 90212
Tel: 213-463-0100

Rastar Productions
4000 Warner Boulevard
Burbank, California 91522
Tel: 213-843-6000

Red Lion Films
315 South Beverly Drive
Beverly Hills, California 90212
Tel: 213-553-0581

Reynolds Productions, Inc.
P.O. Box 5115
Beverly Hills, California 90210
Tel: 213-656-8121

Ridgerose Company
800 North Seward Street
Los Angeles, California 90038
Tel: 213-466-4271

Rivera Productions
6610 Selma Avenue
Los Angeles, California 90028
Tel: 213-462-8585

Alan Roberts Productions, Inc.
9000 Sunset Boulevard
Los Angeles, California 90069
Tel: 213-274-6628

Jack Robinette Productions
495 South Roxbury Drive
Beverly Hills, California 90212
Tel: 213-277-3134

Rocket Pictures, Inc.
1150 West Olive Avenue
Burbank, California 91506
Tel: 213-849-6078

Frederick K. Rockett Company
5451 Laurel Canyon Boulevard
North Hollywood, California
91607
Tel: 213-985-1090

Rogallan Productions
9000 Sunset Boulevard
Los Angeles, California 90069
Tel: 213-274-8518

Rohin Productions
Universal City Studios
Box 8044
Universal City, California 91608
Tel: 213-980-7375

Rojon Productions
6290 Sunset Boulevard
Los Angeles, California 90028
Tel: 213-462-1127

Glenn Roland Films
8543 Clifton Way
Beverly Hills, California 90211
Tel: 213-271-0533

Sam Rolfe Project
4000 Warner Boulevard
Burbank, California 91522
Tel: 213-843-6000

Pat Rooney Productions
4024 Radford
North Hollywood, California
  91604
Tel: 213-763-8411

Rosamond Productions, Inc.
501 South Fairfax Avenue
Los Angeles, California 90036
Tel: 213-933-7508

Rose-Magwood Productions of
  California, Inc.
948 North Cahuenga Boulevard
Los Angeles, California 90027
Tel: 213-466-8561

Robert M. Rosenthal
11744 Darlington Avenue
Los Angeles, California 90046
Tel: 213-826-0022

Herb Ross Productions
4000 Warner Boulevard
Burbank, California 91522
Tel: 213-843-6000

Stanley Ralph Ross Productions
407 North Maple Drive, Suite 210
Beverly Hills, California 90210
Tel: 213-275-7826

Richard Roth Unit
4000 Warner Boulevard
Burbank, California 91522
Tel: 213-843-6000

Roundtable Films, Inc.
113 North San Vincente
Beverly Hills, California 90211
Tel: 213-657-1402

Albert S. Ruddy Productions, Inc.
5451 Marathon Street
Los Angeles, California 90038
Tel: 213-463-0100

S-L Film Productions
5126 Hartwick Street
Los Angeles, California 90041
Tel: 213-254-8528

Sandler Films, Inc.
1001 North Poinsettia Place
Los Angeles, California 90046
Tel: 213-876-2021

Larry Sands Production
3625 Cahuenga Boulevard West
Los Angeles, California 90068
Tel: 213-876-4800

Savannah Productions
13063 Ventura Boulevard
Studio City, California 91604
Tel: 213-981-7575

Aubrey Schenck Enterprises, Inc.
7046 Hollywood Boulevard
Los Angeles, California 90028
Tel: 213-461-3426

Joseph M. Schenck Enterprises,
Inc.
190 North Canon Drive
Beverly Hills, California 90213
Tel: 213-274-8407

David Schine & Company
626 South Hudson Avenue
Los Angeles, California 90005
Tel: 213-937-5000

George Schlatter Productions
8321 Beverly Boulevard
Los Angeles, California 90048
Tel: 213-655-1400

Gerald Schnitzer Productions
1040 North Las Palmas Avenue
Los Angeles, California 90038
Tel: 213-467-7134

Screen Gems
Colgems Square
Burbank, California 91505
Tel: 213-843-6000

Joe Seide Productions
18416 Vanowen Street
Reseda, California 91335
Tel: 213-345-3072

Stan Seiden
1605 North Ivar Avenue
Los Angeles, California 90028
Tel: 213-464-7121

Walter Seltzer Productions, Inc.
4172 Stansbury Avenue
Sherman Oaks, California 91403
Tel: 213-788-1286

Selznick/Glickman Productions
9200 Sunset Boulevard
Los Angeles, California 90069
Tel: 213-271-1221

Sequoia Pictures, Inc.
4000 Warner Boulevard
Burbank, California 91522
Tel: 213-843-6000

Eric Sherman
P.O. Box 845
Malibu, California 90265
Tel: 213-456-3250

The Sidaris Company
8732 Sunset Boulevard, Suite 240
Los Angeles, California 90069
Tel: 213-657-2251

George Sidney Productions
9201 Wilshire Boulevard
Beverly Hills, California 90210
Tel: 213-274-7618

Signal Productions, Inc.
6223 Selma Avenue
Los Angeles, California 90028
Tel: 213-463-4173

Silver Screen Productions
924 Westwood Boulevard
Los Angeles, California 90024
Tel: 213-478-0887

Al Simon Productions
1040 North Las Palmas Avenue
Los Angeles, California 90038
Tel: 213-469-9011

Simpson & Company
650 North Bronson Avenue
Los Angeles, California 90004
Tel: 213-464-4771

Sinatra Enterprises
1041 North Formosa Avenue
Los Angeles, California 90046
Tel: 213-851-1234

Skirball Production Company
1900 Avenue of the Stars
Los Angeles, California 90067
Tel: 213-277-1664

Edward Small Productions, Inc.
1041 North Formosa Avenue
Los Angeles, California 90046
Tel: 213-851-1234

Smothers, Inc.
260 South Beverly Drive
Beverly Hills, California 90212
Tel: 213-278-8000

Snazelle Films, Inc.
5533 Sunset Boulevard
Los Angeles, California 90028
Tel: 213-466-4309

Soft/Lite Productions
9777 Wilshire Boulevard
Beverly Hills, California 90212
Tel: 213-279-2386

Solar Productions, Inc.
9134 Sunset Boulevard
Los Angeles, California 90069
Tel: 213-278-8600

Richard J. Soltys Productions
1615 Burbank Boulevard
Burbank, California 91506
Tel: 213-843-0373

Sombrero Pictures, Inc.
2373 Canyon Drive
Los Angeles, California 90068
Tel: 213-465-3603

South Street Productions, Inc.
9100 Sunset Boulevard
Los Angeles, California 90069
Tel: 213-273-8666

Jack Spear Productions
3215 Cahuenga Boulevard
Los Angeles, California 90068
Tel: 213-851-4123

Aaron Spelling Productions, Inc.
132 South Rodeo Drive
Beverly Hills, California 90213
Tel: 213-278-6700

Milton Sperling Productions, Inc.
9255 Sunset Boulevard
Los Angeles, California 90069
Tel: 213-273-4080

The Spunbuggy Works
8506 Sunset Boulevard
Los Angeles, California 90069
Tel: 213-657-8070

Stadmor Film Company, Inc.
143 Richmond Street
El Segundo, California 90245
Tel: 213-545-0603

Stanton Films
7934 Santa Monica Boulevard
Los Angeles, California 90046
Tel: 213-656-8656

Steam Camera Company
1018 Seward Street
Los Angeles, California 90038
Tel: 213-466-9244

Stellar Productions, Inc.
1258 North Highland Avenue
Los Angeles, California 90028
Tel: 213-461-2901

Stereovision International, Inc.
5700 Cahuenga Boulevard
North Hollywood, California
   91601
Tel: 213-762-7200

Don Stern Productions
3623 Cahuenga Boulevard West
Los Angeles, California 90068
Tel: 213-851-3673

Andrew L. Stone, Inc.
10478 Wyton Drive
Los Angeles, California 90024
Tel: 213-279-2427

The Story Company
P.O. Box 8486
Universal City, California 91608
Tel: 213-876-5899

The Strachan Company
666 North Robertson Boulevard
Los Angeles, California 90069
Tel: 213-659-4307

Straightley Films Ltd.
P.O. Box 1951
Beverly Hills, California 90213
Tel: 213-466-7807

Herbert L. Strock Productions
6500-02 Barton Avenue
Los Angeles, California 90038
Tel: 213-461-1298

Dick Strout Company
2040 Avenue of the Stars
Los Angeles, California 90067
Tel: 213-556-3341

Studio Center
4024 Radford Avenue
Studio City, California 91604
Tel: 213-763-8411

Burt Sugarman Productions
9000 Sunset Boulevard
Los Angeles, California 90069
Tel: 213-273-0900

Sullivan Productions, Inc.
8899 Beverly Boulevard
Los Angeles, California 90048
Tel: 213-278-2686

Summerhill Productions
1777 North Vine Street
Los Angeles, California 90028
Tel: 213-462-2207

Summit Pictures International,
Ltd.
1040 North Las Palmas Avenue,
Building 2
Los Angeles, California 90038
Tel: 213-4666-6111

Sundi Industries, Inc.
6640 Sunset Boulevard
Los Angeles, California 90028
Tel: 213-466-5181

Supercolossal Pictures
Corporation
3383 Barham Boulevard
Los Angeles, California 90068
Tel: 213-876-6770

TPS Productions
4000 Warner Boulevard
Burbank, California 91522
Tel: 213-843-6000

Talent Associates
4024 Radford Avenue
Studio City, California 91604
Tel: 213-763-8411

Tandem Productions, Inc.
1901 Avenue of the Stars
Los Angeles, California 90067
Tel: 213-553-3600

Tantalus, Inc.
1040 North Las Palmas Avenue
Los Angeles, California 90038
Tel: 213-465-4111

Taurean Films, S.A.
1041 North Formosa Avenue
Los Angeles, California 90046
Tel: 213-851-1234

Teleworld, Inc.
9000 Sunset Boulevard
Los Angeles, California 90069
Tel: 213-843-7430

Telsklew Productions, Inc.
100 Wilshire Boulevard
Santa Monica, California 90401
Tel: 213-451-5727

Teram, Inc.
4000 Warner Boulevard
Burbank, California 91505
Tel: 213-843-6000

R. Michael Terr Productions
2473 Crestview Drive
Los Angeles, California 90046
Tel: 213-654-7506

Danny Thomas Productions
P.O. Box 900
Beverly Hills, California 90213
Tel: 213-277-2211

Fred G. Thorne Productions
2780 Outpost Drive
Los Angeles, California 90068
Tel: 213-874-4800

Jerry Thorpe Productions
4000 Warner Boulevard
Burbank, California 91505
Tel: 213-843-6000

Toback & Associates
6532 Sunset Boulevard
Los Angeles, California 90028
Tel: 213-464-2157

C. Tobalina Productions, Inc.
1044 South Hill Street
Los Angeles, California 90015
Tel: 213-749-2067

Tomorrow Entertainment, Inc.
9200 Sunset Boulevard
Los Angeles, California 90069
Tel: 213-273-7610

Topaz Film Corporation
9145 Sunset Boulevard
Los Angeles, California 90069
Tel: 213-273-8640

Topel & Associates, Ltd.
1037 North Cole Avenue
Los Angeles, California 90038
Tel: 213-461-3066

Burt Topper Productions
6366 Santa Monica Boulevard
Los Angeles, California 90038
Tel: 213-464-3127

Trans Cinema, Inc.
9507 Santa Monica Boulevard
Beverly Hills, California 90210
Tel: 213-274-4701

Transcontinental Intermedia
  Productions
650 North Bronson Avenue
Los Angeles, California 90004
Tel: 213-464-2279

Translor Productions, Inc.
9229 West Sunset Boulevard
Los Angeles, California 90069
Tel: 213-274-8483

Transvue Pictures Corporation
14724 Ventura Boulevard, Suite
  909
Sherman Oaks, California 91403
Tel: 213-990-5600

Transworld Communications
4000 Warner Boulevard
Burbank, California 91522
Tel: 213-843-6000

Trio Productions, Inc.
932 North La Brea Avenue
Los Angeles, California 90038
Tel: 213-874-9400

Triplex Productions
9000 Sunset Boulevard
Los Angeles, California 90069
Tel: 213-274-9483

Trumball-Gruskoff Films
Box 1384
Studio City, California 91604
Tel: 213-340-5440

Twentieth Century–Fox Film
  Corporation
10201 West Pico Boulevard
Los Angeles, California 90064
Tel: 213-277-2211

Twentieth Century–Fox TV
Box 900
Beverly Hills, California 90213
Tel: 213-277-2211

UPA Pictures, Inc.
4440 Lakeside Drive
Burbank, California 91505
Tel: 213-842-7171

Unicorn Productions
1330 North Vine Street
Los Angeles, California 90028
Tel: 213-466-9351

United Artists
1041 North Formosa Avenue
Los Angeles, California 90046
Tel: 213-851-1234

United Artists TV
1041 North Formosa Avenue
Los Angeles, California 90046
Tel: 213-851-1234

United States Productions
9200 Sunset Boulevard
Los Angeles, California 90069
Tel: 213-271-5145

Universal Pictures
100 Universal City Plaza
Universal City, California 91608
Tel: 213-985-4321

Universal Television
100 Universal City Plaza
Universal City, California 91608
Tel: 213-985-4321

Vala Films
1280 Sunset Plaza Drive
Los Angeles, California 90069
Tel: 213-657-5515

George Van Valkenburg
   Productions
6253 Hollywood Boulevard
Los Angeles, California 90028
Tel: 213-461-4643

Viacom Enterprises
9229 Sunset Boulevard
Los Angeles, California 90069
Tel: 213-278-1050

Vik-Winkle Productions, Inc.
11350 Ventura Boulevard
Studio City, California 91604
Tel: 213-980-8648

Wabash Films
8910 Beverlywood Street
Los Angeles, California 90034
Tel: 213-559-1566

Wagner/International Cinema
   Corporation
427 North Canon Drive
Beverly Hills, California 90210
Tel: 213-278-5020

Alan Waite Productions
3753 Cahuenga Boulevard West
North Hollywood, California
   91604
Tel: 213-985-3905

Wakeford-Orloff Company
6528 Sunset Boulevard
Los Angeles, California 90028
Tel: 213-461-3771

Hal Wallis Productions
100 Universal City Plaza
Universal City, California 91608
Tel: 213-985-4321

Jay Ward Productions
8218 Sunset Boulevard
Los Angeles, California 90069
Tel: 213-654-3050

Warner Brothers, Inc.
4000 Warner Boulevard
Burbank, California 91522
Tel: 213-843-6000

Jerry Warner & Associates
8615 Santa Monica Boulevard
Los Angeles, California 90069
Tel: 213-655-4884

Watermark, Inc.
10700 Ventura Boulevard
North Hollywood, California
    91604
Tel: 213-980-9490

Lennie Weinrib Productions
9255 Sunset Boulevard
Los Angeles, California 90069
Tel: 213-654-2354

Adrian Weiss Productions
186 North Canon Drive
Beverly Hills, California 90210
Tel: 213-274-9991

Robert M. Weitman Productions
Columbia Pictures
Colgems Square
Burbank, California 91505
Tel: 213-843-6000

West Ho Films, Inc.
3611 Cahuenga Boulevard West,
    Suite A
Los Angeles, California 90068
Tel: 213-851-4277

Wexler Film Productions
801 North Seward Street
Los Angeles, California 90038
Tel: 213-462-6671

Ruth White Films
Whitney Building
Los Angeles, California 90034
Tel: 213-836-4678

Willcockson, Ltd.
1901 Avenue of the Stars
Los Angeles, California 90067
Tel: 213-821-9981

Elmo Williams Productions
10201 West Pico Boulevard
Los Angeles, California 90064
Tel: 213-277-2211

Winterbourne Productions, Ltd.
Box 2268
Los Angeles, California 90028
Tel: 213-461-5408

Glenn Winters Productions
8236 Blackburn Avenue
Los Angeles, California 90048
Tel: 213-653-3352

Wolper Pictures, Ltd.
Wolper Productions, Inc.
8489 West Third Street
Los Angeles, California 90048
Tel: 213-651-5010

World Film Services, Inc.
9489 Dayton Way, Suite 209
Beverly Hills, California 90210
Tel: 213-273-0622

World Wide Pictures
2520 West Olive
Burbank, California 91505
Tel: 213-843-1300

Frank Worth Productions
1850 North Whitley
Los Angeles, California 90028
Tel: 213-465-4121

Wrather Corporation
270 North Canon Drive
Beverly Hills, California 90210
Tel: 213-278-8521

Carter Wright Enterprises
6533 Hollywood Boulevard
Los Angeles, California 90028
Tel: 213-469-0944

Xanadu Productions
9134 Sunset Boulevard
Los Angeles, California 90069
Tel: 213-276-4174

Xerxes Productions, Ltd.
11130 1/2 McCormick Street
North Hollywood, California
   91601
Tel: 213-769-3061

Yongestreet Productions
357 North Canon Drive
Beverly Hills, California 90210
Tel: 213-273-8290

Max Youngstein Enterprises, Inc.
3727 Longridge Avenue
Sherman Oaks, California 91403
Tel: 213-987-7037

Yukon Pictures, Inc.
826 North Cole Avenue
Los Angeles, California 90038
Tel: 213-462-0701

The Zanuck/Brown Company
100 Universal City Plaza
Universal City, California 91608
Tel: 213-985-4321

Ervin Zavada Productions
6290 Sunset Boulevard
Los Angeles, California 90028
Tel: 213-461-8589

Felix Zelenka Productions
818 North La Brea Avenue
Los Angeles, California 90038
Tel: 213-466-3263

Zeppelin Associates
1012 North Hammond Street
Los Angeles, California 90069
Tel: 213-273-3766

San Francisco area:

American Zoetrope, Inc.
American Zoetrope Film Facility
827 Folsom Street
San Francisco, California 94107
Tel: 415-989-0600

Ampersand Films, Inc.
1736 Stockton Street
San Francisco, California 94133
Tel: 415-433-4135

Aratow Films
5915 Hollis Street
Emeryville, California 94608
Tel: 415-655-5794

Stephen Bafrey Productions
2774 Jackson Street
San Francisco, California 94115
Tel: 415-921-3607

Aubrey Bartlett
484 Frederick Street
San Francisco, California 94117
Tel: 415-752-6882

Marvin Becker, Film-Maker
2111 California Street
San Francisco, California 94115
Tel: 415-567-2160

Jon Beckjord
2121 Taylor Street
San Francisco, California 94133
Tel: 415-673-2974

Berkeley Film House
2908 Channing Way
Berkeley, California 94704
Tel: 415-843-6900

Bonanza Films
222 Agriculture Building, The
   Embarcadero
San Francisco, California 94105
Tel: 415-956-5660

Bravura Films
2259 Old Middlefield Way
Mountain View, California 94043
Tel: 415-969-2130

Cine-Idea Motion Picture
   Productions
23 Sequoyah View Drive
Oakland, California 94605
Tel: 415-569-3439

Cinema Financial of America,
   Inc.
680 Beach Street
San Francisco, California 94109
Tel: 415-885-5700

The Cinema
114 New. Mo
San Francisco
Tel: 415-566-6

The Coppola C
916 Kearny Street
San Francisco, California 94133
Tel: 415-788-7500

Davidson Films
3701 Buchanan Street
San Francisco, California 94123
Tel: 415-567-2974

Dawson Productions
44 Montgomery Street
San Francisco, California 94104
Tel: 415-391-7620

Leo Diner Films, Inc.
332-350 Golden Gate Avenue
San Francisco, California 94102
Tel: 415-775-3664

The Director's Company
827 Folsom Street
San Francisco, California 94107
Tel: 415-989-0600

Electrovision Productions
1080 Chestnut Street
San Francisco, California 94109
Tel: 415-433-3337

Entertainment Group
Winterland Arena
Post & Steiner Streets
San Francisco, California 94115
Tel: 415-921-5616

Essanay Motion Picture
  Productions Corporation
1935 Sixteenth Avenue
San Francisco, California 94116
Tel: 415-564-2886

The Film Works
75 Lansing
San Francisco, California 94109
Tel: 415-433-1277

Filmachine, Inc.
665 Harrison Street
San Francisco, California 94107
Tel: 415-956-4330

James Flocker Enterprises, Inc.
3080 La Selva
San Mateo, California 94403
Tel: 415-349-8000

Philip R. Freeman & Associates
77 Jack London Square
Oakland, California 94607
Tel: 415-451-7971

Furman Films
3466 21st Street
San Francisco, California 94110
Tel: 415-282-1300

Gambit Enterprises
119 Cuesta Drive
South San Francisco, California
  94080
Tel: 415-589-9158

Bill Graham Presents
1548 Market Street
San Francisco, California 94102
Tel: 415-863-2013

Randy Grochoske
253 Columbus Avenue
San Francisco, California 94133
Tel: 415-956-1860

Imagination, Inc.
443 Jackson Street
San Francisco, California 94111
Tel: 415-433-5480

Gary L. Jackson
1918 Broderick Street
San Francisco, California 94115
Tel: 415-563-5100

Korty Films, Inc.
200 Miller Avenue
Mill Valley, California 94941
Tel: 415-383-6900

Kriedt & Myers, Inc.
15 Tubbs Street
San Francisco, California 94107
Tel: 415-648-9002

Fred Lyon Pictures
Box 836
Sausalito, California 94965
Tel: 415-332-2056

Media Generalists
69 Clementina Street
San Francisco, California 94105
Tel: 415-433-3337

Medion, Inc.
1239 Polk Street
San Francisco, California 94109
Tel: 415-776-3440

Mitchell Brothers Film Group
895 O'Farrell Street
San Francisco, California 94109
Tel: 415-441-1930

J. C. Morgan Film Production
World Trade Center
San Francisco, California 94111
Tel: 415-392-5271

Motion Picture Service Company
125 Hyde Street
San Francisco, California 94102
Tel: 415-673-9162

Don Palmer Studios
563 Second Street
San Francisco, California 94107
Tel: 415-392-4449

Pitera Films
305 Richardson Street
Sausalito, California 94965
Tel: 415-332-2147

Production House, Inc.
665 Harrison Street
San Francisco, California 94107
Tel: 415-495-3086

Rinzler-Aratow Productions
159 Alvarado Road
Berkeley, California 94705
Tel: 415-653-7521

John Robert Productions
186 San Francisco Street
San Francisco, California 94133
Tel: 415-392-8408

Walter Schenk Films
1736 Stockton Street
San Francisco, California 94133
Tel: 415-398-1385

Skinner Studio
345 Sutter Street
San Francisco, California 94108
Tel: 415-986-5040

Snazelle Films, Inc.
155 Fell Street
San Francisco, California 94102
Tel: 415-431-5490

Stop Frame, Inc.
1736 Stockton Street
San Francisco, California 94133
Tel: 415-434-4413

Stuart-Sauter Company
100 Utah Avenue
San Francisco, California 94080
Tel: 415-761-0333

Tres Gatos Productions, Inc.
431 Bryant Avenue
San Francisco, California 94107
Tel: 415-957-1234

Colorado:

Another Production Company,
Inc.
1420 Blake Street
Denver, Colorado 80202
Tel: 303-623-6616

Arcuturus Film Productions
P.O. Box 6586
Denver, Colorado 80206
Tel: 303-322-5397

Barbre Productions, Inc.
1089 Bannock Street
Denver, Colorado 80204
Tel: 303-266-3601

Charles A. Bennett & Associates
4150 Fox Street
Denver, Colorado 80216
Tel: 303-433-3334

Broyles, Allebaugh & Davis, Inc.
2 Executive Park
Englewood, Colorado 80110
Tel: 303-771-5230

CVD Studios
15460 East Batavia Drive
Aurora, Colorado 80011
Tel: 303-341-5600

Cinema Arts Productions
4501 Elm Court
Denver, Colorado 80211
Tel: 303-455-7792

Cinema Service
P.O. Box 398
Eldorado Springs, Colorado
  80025
Tel: 303-443-4913

Computer Image Corporation
2475 West Second Avenue
Denver, Colorado 80223
Tel: 303-934-5801

Charles Deaton Productions, Inc.
Genesee Mountain
Golden, Colorado 80401
Tel: 303-277-0085

Entertainment Four Studios
1630 Chambers Road
Aurora, Colorado 80010
Tel: 303-341-5600

Espirit
3514 North Tejon
Colorado Springs, Colorado
  80907
Tel: 303-471-3376

Frisch Films, Ltd.
1365 South Dover Way
Denver, Colorado 80226
Tel: 303-985-7423

JPI
1420 Larimer Square
Denver, Colorado 80202
Tel: 303-623-0167

Kenneth A. Meyer Film
  Productions
2181 South Grape Street
Denver, Colorado 80222
Tel: 303-758-2534

Pade-Meale Productions
1901 East 47th Avenue
Denver, Colorado 80216
Tel: 303-623-1948

Stan Phillips & Associates
2245 West 30th Avenue
Denver, Colorado 80211
Tel: 303-433-3873

The Production House, Inc.
4150 Fox Street
Denver, Colorado 80216
Tel: 303-433-3334

Rainbow Pictures
4935 East 23rd Avenue
Denver, Colorado 80207
Tel: 303-322-7166

Summit Films, Inc.
538 East Alameda Avenue
Denver, Colorado 80209
Tel: 303-744-1319

Trans-World Films
260 Petroleum Club Building
110 Sixteenth Street
Denver, Colorado 80202
Tel: 303-266-0215

Trilogy Films
900 Sherman Street
Denver, Colorado 80203
Tel: 303-623-3167

World Film Productions, Inc.
P.O. Box 22361
Denver, Colorado 80220
Tel: 303-831-1140

District of Columbia:

Astrafilms
530 Eighth Street, S.E.
Washington, D.C. 20003
Tel: 202-543-1011

Creative Arts Studio
2323 Fourth Street, N.E.
Washington, D.C. 20002
Tel: 202-832-2600

Film Center
915 Twelfth Street, N.W.
Washington, D.C. 20005
Tel: 202-393-1205

Guggenheim Productions, Inc.
3121 South Street, N.W.
Washington, D.C. 20007
Tel: 202-337-6900

Hermes Films
3218 39th Street, N.W.
Washington, D.C. 20016
Tel: 202-244-3942

Florida:

A & R Films, Inc.
14875 N.E. Twentieth Avenue
North Miami, Florida 33161
Tel: 305-944-2911

ADCO Productions
5050 Biscayne Boulevard
Miami, Florida 33101
Tel: 305-751-3118

Allied Film Productions, Inc.
14875 N.E. Twentieth Avenue
North Miami, Florida 33161
Tel: 305-949-8117

Allmand-Newby Productions,
   Inc.
1435 South Miami Avenue
Miami, Florida 33101
Tel: 305-371-6271

Apple Productions
19 S.W. Sixth Street
Miami, Florida 33101
Tel: 305-379-2380

Associated Filmakers
   International
252 N.W. 29th Street
Miami, Florida 33101
Tel: 305-576-2827

Cinar Productions, Inc.
4522 West Kennedy Boulevard
Tampa, Florida 33609
Tel: 813-872-6326

Cinetron Corporation
1995 N.E. 150th Street
North Miami, Florida 33161
Tel: 305-947-8557

Colodzian Productions, Inc.
1944 N.E. 151st Street
North Miami, Florida 33161
Tel: 305-945-6746

Continental Cinema Corporation
Studios: c/o Studio City
P.O. Box 966
North Miami, Florida 33161
Tel: 305-949-2211

Coronado Studios
260 N.E. 70th Street
Miami, Florida 33101
Tel: 305-751-1853

Herb Dietz Enterprises
65 N.W. Third Street
Miami, Florida 33101
Tel: 305-379-8793

Film Artists Corporation
14875 N.E. Twentieth Avenue
North Miami, Florida 33161
Tel: 305-947-9056

GMC Productions
1075 95th Street
Bay Harbor Island, Florida 33154
Tel: 305-864-5955

Giralda Productions, Inc.
254 Giralda Avenue
Coral Gables, Florida 33134
Tel: 305-443-6343

William Grefé
14875 N.E. Twentieth Avenue
North Miami, Florida 33161
Tel: 305-944-2911

David Haylock Productions
801 N.W. Eleventh Street
Miami, Florida 33101
Tel: 305-754-4141

K & W Pictures Corporation
13911 N.W. Twentieth Court
Opa Loca, Florida 33054
Tel: 305-688-4795

Key Productions
350 Ocean Drive
Key Biscayne, Florida 33149
Tel: 305-361-9567

Jordan Klein
3131 N.E. 188th Street
Miami, Florida 33101
Tel: 305-931-2300

MJ Productions
4555 Ponce De Leon Place
Coral Gables, Florida 33146
Tel: 305-666-8055

McLeod Films, Inc.
17 Palmetto Drive
Miami Springs, Florida 33166
Tel: 305-887-1762

Luke Moberly Productions, Inc.
4810 S.W. 54th Terrace
Fort Lauderdale, Florida 33319
Tel: 305-581-7508

Poinciana Productions, Inc.
1150 S.W. First Street
Miami, Florida 33101
Tel: 305-545-8108

Screen Arts Corporation
13911 N.W. Twentieth Court
Opa Loca, Florida 33054
Tel: 305-681-6674

Studio Center, Inc.
14875 N.E. Twentieth Avenue
North Miami, Florida 33161
Tel: 305-944-2911

Trans-International Films
104 Crandon Boulevard
Key Biscayne, Florida 33149
Tel: 305-361-3341

Warren Sound Studios
35 N.E. 62nd Street
Miami, Florida 33101
Tel: 305-754-9539

Bert Williams Productions, Inc.
1414 N.E. 183rd Street
North Miami Beach, Florida
  33160
Tel: 305-947-5252

Woroner Films, Inc.
1995 N.E. 150th Street
North Miami, Florida 33161
Tel: 305-945-5465

Georgia:

AND, Inc.
1428-B Mason Street, N.E.
Atlanta, Georgia 30324
Tel: 404-876-1033

Bomark International
69 Pioneer Trail
Marietta, Georgia 30062
Tel: 404-422-4470

Centrum International Film
  Corporation
3958 Peachtree Road, N.E., Suite
  303
Atlanta, Georgia 30319
Tel: 404-233-4484

Color-Graphic Films
3184 Rosewell Road, N.W.
Atlanta, Georgia 30305
Tel: 404-233-2174

Film Ventures International
2351 Adams Drive, N.W.
Atlanta, Georgia 30318
Tel: 404-352-3850

Interfilm Corporation
6666 Powers Ferry Road
Atlanta, Georgia 30316
Tel: 404-394-3225

Jayan House
769 Peachtree Street
Atlanta, Georgia 30308
Tel: 404-874-4471

The Movie Company
455 East Paces Ferry Road
Atlanta, Georgia 30305
Tel: 404-237-6132

Provence Productions
2060 Peachtree Industrial Court,
  Suite 302
Atlanta, Georgia 30341
Tel: 404-451-4624

Reider Film & Television
1019 Amsterdam Avenue, N.E.
Atlanta, Georgia 30306
Tel: 404-874-8436

Seifferman Production Services,
  Inc.
5423 Woodberry Circle
Marietta, Georgia 30060
Tel: 404-993-1259

Shelton Productions, Inc.
677 Antone Street, N.W.
Atlanta, Georgia 30318
Tel: 404-355-0091

Storer-Harris Productions, Inc.
2863 Mabry Lane, N.E.
Atlanta, Georgia 30319
Tel: 404-237-7642

Synapse Films
619 Bonaventure Place
Atlanta, Georgia 30306
Tel: 404-876-8698

Vee Jay Productions, Inc.
P.O. Box 49605
Atlanta, Georgia 30329
Tel: 404-241-8081

Viscount Productions, Inc.
650 Miami Circle, N.E.
Atlanta, Georgia 30324
Tel: 404-261-6240

Wooster Productions, Inc.
445 Bishop Street
Atlanta, Georgia 30304
Tel: 404-874-2252

Hawaii:

Allison-Donnellan Productions
832 Halekauwila Street
Honolulu, Hawaii 96813
Tel: 808-537-4115

American Pacific Entertainment,
  Inc.
Box 9181
Honolulu, Hawaii 96820
Tel: 808-847-4875

Cine-Pic Hawaii
1847 Pacific Heights Road
Honolulu, Hawaii 96813
Tel: 808-533-2677

David Cornwell Productions
1358 Kapiolani Boulevard
Honolulu, Hawaii 96815
Tel: 808-949-7000

Tip Davis Films
2962 East Manoa Road
Honolulu, Hawaii 96822
Tel: 808-988-7122

Gregg-Kendall and Associates,
  Inc.
Llikai Hotel, Suite 101
1777 Ala Moana Boulevard
Honolulu, Hawaii 96815
Tel: 808-946-9577

Hawaii Production Center
1534 Kapiolani Boulevard
Honolulu, Hawaii 96814
Tel: 808-941-3011

Tom Matsumoto Motion Pictures
1618 South King Street
Honolulu, Hawaii 96814
Tel: 808-949-6003

Pacific Productions
Box 2881
Honolulu, Hawaii 96802
Tel: 808-531-1560

Spectrum Motion Pictures
2962 East Manoa Road
Honolulu, Hawaii 96822
Tel: 808-988-7122

Illinois:

Academy Film Productions, Inc.
123 West Chestnut Street
Chicago, Illinois 60610
Tel: 312-642-5877

Gilbert Altschul Productions, Inc.
909 West Diversey Avenue
Chicago, Illinois 60614
Tel: 312-525-6561

Behrend's, Inc.
161 East Grand Avenue
Chicago, Illinois 60611
Tel: 312-527-3060

Michael Birch, Inc.
600 North McClurg Court
Chicago, Illinois 60611
Tel: 312-329-9350

William H. Birch & Associates,
   Inc.
161 East Grand Avenue
Chicago, Illinois 60611
Tel: 312-527-2135

Cinemedia, Inc.
1944 North Cleveland Avenue
Chicago, Illinois 60614
Tel: 312-944-6606

Cinepac, Inc.
46 East Oak Street
Chicago, Illinois 60611
Tel: 312-787-2650

Creative Communications
676 North La Salle Street
Chicago, Illinois 60610
Tel: 312-337-7513

Cusack Productions
645 North Michigan Avenue
Chicago, Illinois 60611
Tel: 312-943-2118

Dexter Productions, Inc.
2728 Woodbine
Evanston, Illinois 60201
Tel: 312-328-1050

Directors, Inc.
17 East Chestnut Street
Chicago, Illinois 60611
Tel: 312-787-0414

Downie Productions, Inc.
1920 North Lincoln Avenue
Chicago, Illinois 60614
Tel: 312-787-6822

Cal Dunn Studios, Inc.
141 West Ohio Street
Chicago, Illinois 60610
Tel: 312-644-7600

Filmack Studios
1327 South Wabash Avenue
Chicago, Illinois 60605
Tel: 312-427-3395

Filmfair, Inc.
22 West Hubbard Street
Chicago, Illinois 60610
Tel: 312-822-9200

Alan M. Fishburn Productions
333 North Michigan Avenue
Chicago, Illinois 60611
Tel: 312-332-0657

GTR Productions, Inc.
600 North McClurg Court
Chicago, Illinois 60611
Tel: 312-337-2605

Goldsholl Associates, Inc.
420 Frontage Road
Northfield, Illinois 60628
Tel: 312-446-8300

Insight, Inc.
100 East Ohio Street
Chicago, Illinois 60611
Tel: 312-467-4350

Krebs Productions, Inc.
One IBM Plaza
Chicago, Illinois 60611
Tel: 312-337-3303

Les Images
1130 West Armitage Avenue
Chicago, Illinois 60614
Tel: 312-871-4700

Jack Lieb Productions, Inc.
1230 West Washington Boulevard
Chicago, Illinois 60607
Tel: 312-666-1220

Lippert/Saviano, Inc.
141 West Ohio Street
Chicago, Illinois 60610
Tel: 312-266-0123

Lukas Film Productions, Inc.
20 East Huron Street
Chicago, Illinois 60611
Tel: 312-944-6613

Don Meier Productions, Inc.
520 North Michigan Avenue
Chicago, Illinois 60611
Tel: 312-222-1755

Burt Munk Productions, Inc.
56 East Walton Place
Chicago, Illinois 60611
Tel: 312-337-0334

Fred A. Niles Communications
   Centers, Inc.
1058 West Washington Boulevard
Chicago, Illinois 60607
Tel: 312-738-4181

The Ken Nordine Group
6106 North Kenmore Avenue
Chicago, Illinois 60660
Tel: 312-262-8500

Pinnn
40 East Erie Street
Chicago, Illinois 60611
Tel: 312-787-8432

Producers Group, Ltd.
One IBM Plaza
Chicago, Illinois 60611
Tel: 312-467-1830

The Second Stage
3133 North Halsted Street
Chicago, Illinois 60657
Tel: 312-472-0940

Shield Productions, Inc.
161 East Grand Avenue
Chicago, Illinois 60611
Tel: 312-642-6441

The Shooting Gallery, Inc.
450 East Ohio Street
Chicago, Illinois 60611
Tel: 312-664-2447

Sight and Sound, Inc.
233 East Erie Street
Chicago, Illinois 60611
Tel: 312-337-6640

Studio Seven, Inc.
615 North Wabash Avenue
Chicago, Illinois 60611
Tel: 312-337-6264

Don Tait Enterprises, Inc.
161 East Grand Avenue
Chicago, Illinois 60611
Tel: 312-642-3986

Take Ten, Inc.
211 East Chicago Avenue
Chicago, Illinois 60611
Tel: 312-944-0455

Henry Ushijima Films, Inc.
600 North McClurg Court
Chicago, Illinois 60611
Tel: 312-266-9191

Wallace & Brown, Inc.
535 North Michigan Avenue
Chicago, Illinois 60611
Tel: 312-828-0080

Louisiana:

Pan-American Films
822 North Rampart Street
New Orleans, Louisiana 70116
Tel: 504-522-5364

Maryland:

Academy Film Productions
2423 Maryland Avenue
Baltimore, Maryland 21218
Tel: 301-338-0550

John D. Aherns, Inc.
2160 Rockrose Avenue
Baltimore, Maryland 21211
Tel: 301-542-8313

Associated Producers, Inc.
9020 Copenhaver Drive
Potomac, Maryland 20854
Tel: 202-529-7100

BF&J Productions, Inc.
3635 Woodland Avenue
Baltimore, Maryland 21215
Tel: 301-664-8311

Massachusetts:

Ballantine Films, Inc.
115 Newbury Street
Boston, Massachusetts 02116
Tel: 617-267-2160

Beacon Features, Inc.
708 Washington Street
Dedham, Massachusetts 02026
Tel: 617-329-9504

Films Production Corporation
80 Boylston Street
Boston, Massachusetts 02116
Tel: 617-426-8522

LMH Productions, Inc.
101 Monmouth Street
Brookline, Massachusetts 02146
Tel: 617-738-5888

Mass Media Films
343 Beacon Street
Boston, Massachusetts 02116
Tel: 617-536-0717

New Film Company, Inc.
331 Newbury Street
Boston, Massachusetts 02115
Tel: 617-261-3046

Woodshed Films
101 Monmouth Street
Brookline, Massachusetts 02146
Tel: 617-738-5888

Michigan:

Neil Douglas Productions
3030 Iroquois
Detroit, Michigan 48214
Tel: 313-923-0303

Regan Film Productions
19730 Ralston
Detroit, Michigan 48203
Tel: 313-368-3000

Minnesota:

K-tel Motion Pictures
421 Wilson Street, N.E.
Minneapolis, Minnesota 55413
Tel: 612-331-3070

Nebraska:

Chapman/Spittler, Inc.
1908 California Street
Omaha, Nebraska 68102
Tel: 402-348-1600

Nevada:

C & M Productions
26 Country Club Lane
Las Vegas, Nevada 89109
Tel: 702-734-2072

Film Arts Productions
2760 South Highland Drive
Las Vegas, Nevada 89102
Tel: 702-735-1711

Global Productions
1624 Mojave Road
Las Vegas, Nevada 89104
Tel: 702-457-2211

Matt Gregory Productions
5379 Tamarus
Las Vegas, Nevada 89109
Tel: 702-736-1600

K-B Productions
P.O. Box 12611
Las Vegas, Nevada 89112
Tel: 702-451-5290

Rancho Film Enterprises
5300 Paradise Road
Las Vegas, Nevada 89109
Tel: 702-736-9074

Sundance Productions
250 East Desert Inn Road
Las Vegas, Nevada 89109
Tel: 702-735-7511

Superstar International
  Productions, Inc.
P.O. Box 15267
Las Vegas, Nevada 89114
Tel: 702-735-4438

L. J. Wood Film Productions
P.O. Box 11291
Las Vegas, Nevada 89111
Tel: 702-739-7705

ew Jersey:

Henry Charles Motion Picture
  Studios
Plainfield Avenue
Edison, New Jersey 08817
Tel: 201-545-5104

Dubie-Do Productions, Inc.
1 Laurie Drive
Englewood Cliffs, New Jersey
  07632
Tel: 201-568-4214

Jersey Film Group, Inc.
15 Ramsay Road
Montclair, New Jersey 07042
Tel: 201-783-4789

Princeton Film Center
221 Nassau Street
Princeton, New Jersey 08540
Tel: 609-924-3550

Dick Roberts Film Company
341 Nassau Street
Princeton, New Jersey 08540
Tel: 609-924-9707

Worldwide Films
395 Main Street
Metuchen, New Jersey 08840
Tel: 201-494-9500

New Mexico:

Arlette Studio Film Production
1523 Elfego Baca Drive, S.W.
Albuquerque, New Mexico 87105
Tel: 505-855-9615

Bandelier Films, Inc.
2001 Gold Avenue, S.E.
Albuquerque, New Mexico 87106
Tel: 505-242-2679

Biotechnica Synergetic Movies
Madrid Highway
Santa Fe, New Mexico 87501
Tel: 505-982-1431

Bouche Productions
Box 5188
Santa Fe, New Mexico 87501
Tel: 505-982-0320

Max Evans Productions
1602 San Pedro Drive, N.E.
Albuquerque, New Mexico 87110
Tel: 505-255-8771

Multimedia International, Inc.
418 1/2 Montezuma Avenue
Santa Fe, New Mexico 87501
Tel: 505-982-2504

Fred Patton Productions
418 1/2 Montezuma Avenue
Santa Fe, New Mexico 87501
Tel: 505-982-2504

Rainbow Productions
100 East San Francisco
Santa Fe, New Mexico 87501
Tel: 505-982-9422

SKS Productions
First Northern Plaza
Santa Fe, New Mexico 87501
Tel: 505-982-2133

John Wagner Productions, Inc.
928 Avenida Manana, N.E.
Albuquerque, New Mexico 87110
Tel: 505-266-0460

New York:

ABC Pictures Corporation
1330 Avenue of the Americas
New York, New York 10019
Tel: 212-581-7777

Allied Artists Productions, Inc.
15 Columbus Circle
New York, New York 10023
Tel: 212-541-9200

The American Film Theatre, Inc.
1350 Avenue of the Americas
New York, New York 10019
Tel: 212-489-8820

American International Picture
165 West 46th Street
New York, New York 10036
Tel: 212-489-8100

Artists Entertainment Complex
641 Lexington Avenue
New York, New York 10022
Tel: 212-421-3760

Artscope, Ltd.
310 West 53rd Street
New York, New York 10019
Tel: 212-265-7420

Audubon Films
850 Seventh Avenue
New York, New York 10019
Tel: 212-586-4913

Berkshire Pictures Corporation
745 Fifth Avenue
New York, New York 10022
Tel: 212-752-5050

Brut Productions, Inc.
1345 Avenue of the Americas
New York, New York 10019
Tel: 212-581-3500

Bryanston Pictures
630 Ninth Avenue
New York, New York 10026
Tel: 212-581-5240

Cambist Films, Inc.
850 Seventh Avenue
New York, New York 10019
Tel: 212-586-5810

The Cannon Group, Inc.
405 Park Avenue
New York, New York 10022
Tel: 212-759-5700
Film Division

Centaur Releasing Corporation
165 West 46th Street
New York, New York 10036
Tel: 212-581-4980

Chancellor Films, Inc.
200 West 57th Street
New York, New York 10019
Tel: 212-246-4940

Cin-Art Motion Picture
  Productions
152 West 42nd Street, Suite 536
New York, New York 10036
Tel: 212-565-3517

Cinema 5, Ltd.
595 Madison Avenue
New York, New York 10022
Tel: 212-421-5555

Cinema Arts Associates, Inc.
333 West 52nd Street
New York, New York 10019
Tel: 212-246-2860

Cinemation Industries, Inc.
1350 Avenue of the Americas
New York, New York 10019
Tel: 212-765-3430

Cinerama, Inc.
1290 Avenue of the Americas
New York, New York 10019
Tel: 212-581-5858

City Film Productions
64-12 65th Place
Middle Village (Queens County)
New York, New York 11379
Tel: 212-456-5050

Columbia Pictures Industries, Inc.
711 Fifth Avenue
New York, New York 10022
Tel: 212-751-4400

D'Antoni Productions
8 East 63rd Street
New York, New York 10021
Tel: 212-688-4205

Darer Corporation
218 West 72nd Street
New York, New. York 10023
Tel: 212-799-1600

Dino De Laurentiis Corporation
One Gulf & Western Plaza
New York, New York 10023
Tel: 212-489-9575

Dico Productions, Inc.
99 Park Avenue
New York, New York 10017
Tel: 212-697-5125

Dioscuri Productions, Inc.
250 West Fifteenth Street, Suite 5
New York, New York 10011
Tel: 212-243-4251

Directors Group Motion Pictures,
  Inc.
870 Seventh Avenue
New York, New York 10019
Tel: 212-489-9611

Toni Ficalori Film Productions
28 East 29th Street
New York, New York 10016
Tel: 212-679-7700

Filmways, Inc.
540 Madison Avenue
New York, New York 10022
Tel: 212-758-5100

Fima Noveck Productions, Inc.
45 West 45th Street
New York, New York 10036
Tel: 212-757-3138

First Artists Productions, Inc.
600 Madison Avenue
New York, New York 10022
Tel: 212-935-4000

Gillwood Productions, Inc.
711 Fifth Avenue
New York, New York 10022
Tel: 212-753-6067

Gordon Films, Inc.
10 Columbus Circle
New York, New York 10023
Tel: 212-757-9390

Group W Productions, Inc.
90 Park Avenue
New York, New York 10016
Tel: 212-983-5081

Grove Press, Inc.
Kent E. Carroll, Director
53 East Eleventh Street
New York, New York 10003
Tel: 212-677-2400

Grove Press Film Division
53 East Eleventh Street
New York, New York 10003
Tel: 212-677-2400

Hemisphere Pictures, Inc.
445 Park Avenue, Suite 1405
New York, New York 10022
Tel: 212-759-8707

Horizon Pictures, Inc.
711 Fifth Avenue
New York, New York 10022
Tel: 212-421-6810

Independent-International Picture
  Corporation
165 West 46th Street
New York, New York 10036
Tel: 212-869-9333

Henry Jaffe Enterprises, Inc.
200 West 57th Street
New York, New York 10019
Tel: 212-245-2400

Jamel Productions, Inc.
850 Seventh Avenue
New York, New York 10019
Tel: 212-581-1780

Janus Films, Inc.
745 Fifth Avenue
New York, New York 10022
Tel: 212-753-7100

Kaleidoscope Films, Ltd.
353 West 57th Street
New York, New York 10019
Tel: 212-265-2377

The Ely Landau Organization,
Inc.
1350 Avenue of the Americas
New York, New York 10019
Tel: 212-489-8820

Dan Leeds Productions
45 West 45th Street
New York, New York 10036
Tel: 212-757-2897

Joseph E. Levine Presents, Inc.
345 Park Avenue
New York, New York 10022
Tel: 212-826-0370

Lorimar Productions, Inc.
565 Fifth Avenue
New York, New York 10017
Tel: 212-687-4960

Magenta Films, Inc.
600 Madison Avenue
New York, New York 10022
Tel: 212-758-4774

Melinda Productions Unlimited
301 East 38th Street
New York, New York 10016
Tel: 212-686-6921

Metro-Goldwyn-Mayer, Inc.
1350 Avenue of the Americas
New York, New York 10019
Tel: 212-977-3423

Metromedia Producers
Corporation
485 Lexington Avenue
New York, New York 10017
Tel: 212-682-9100

Nelson Morris Productions, Inc.
11 East 48th Street
New York, New York 10017
Tel: 212-753-1484

Charles A. Moses Company
12 West 55th Street
New York, New York 10019
Tel: 212-757-1900

New Line Cinema
121 University Place
New York, New York 10003
Tel: 212-674-7460

Palomar Pictures International
345 Park Avenue
New York, New York 10022
Tel: 212-644-3800

Paragon Pictures
40 West 57th Street
New York, New York 10019
Tel: 212-541-6770

Paramount Pictures Corporation
1 Gulf & Western Plaza
New York, New York 10023
Tel: 212-333-7000

Otto Preminger Films
711 Fifth Avenue
New York, New York 10022
Tel: 212-838-6100

QED Productions Inc.
21 West 46th Street
New York, New York 10036
Tel: 212-582-4291

Ramic Productions
58 West 58th Street
New York, New York 10019
Tel: 212-759-2300

Rastar Productions, Inc.
21 East 61st Street
New York, New York 10021
Tel: 212-486-0980

Walter Reade Organization
241 East 34th Street
New York, New York 10016
Tel: 212-683-6300

Republic Pictures International
655 Madison Avenue
New York, New York 10021
Tel: 212-838-8813

Hal Roach Studios
645 Madison Avenue
New York, New York 10022
Tel: 212-245-4135

Sagittarius Productions
375 Park Avenue
New York, New York 10022
Tel: 212-758-4530

Scotia American Productions
600 Madison Avenue
New York, New York 10022
Tel: 212-758-4775

Sigma Productions, Inc.
711 Fifth Avenue
New York, New York 10022
Tel: 212-838-6100

Silverstein International
Corporation
200 West 57th Street
New York, New York 10019
Tel: 212-541-6620

Howard Smith
732 Broadway
New York, New York 10003

Steckler Associates, Ltd.
227 East 56th Street
New York, New York 10022
Tel: 212-758-4150

The Robert Stigwood
Organization, Inc.
135 Central Park West
New York, New York 10023
Tel: 212-595-5011

The Strachan Company
443 West 50th Street
New York, New York 10019
Tel: 212-247-4610

Sullivan Productions, Inc
919 Third Avenue, 45th Floor
New York, New York 10022
Tel: 212-758-9103

Talent Associates–Norton Simon,
Inc.
747 Third Avenue
New York, New York 10017
Tel: 212-753-1030

Times Film International
Corporation
144 West 57th Street
New York, New York 10019
Tel: 212-757-6980

Trio Productions, Inc.
114 East 55th Street
New York, New York 10022
Tel: 212-838-3333

Twentieth Century–Fox Film
  Corporation
1345 Avenue of the Americas
New York, New York 10019
Tel: 212-582-6200

Two Roads Productions, Inc.
729 Seventh Avenue
New York, New York 10019
Tel: 212-575-4946

Unisphere Motion Pictures
165 West 46th Street
New York, New York 10036
Tel: 212-244-2233

United Artists Corporation
729 Seventh Avenue
New York, New York 10019
Tel: 212-575-3000

Universal Pictures
445 Park Avenue
New York, New York 10022
Tel: 212-759-7500

W & W Films, Inc.
1650 Broadway
New York, New York 10019
Tel: 212-541-9441

Andy Warhol Enterprises
33 Union Square
New York, New York 10003
Tel: 212-924-4344

Warner Brothers, Inc.
75 Rockefeller Plaza
New York, New York 10020
Tel: 212-484-8000

Ted White Productions
303 West 42nd Street
New York, New York 10036
Tel: 212-581-8833

Worldvision Enterprises, Inc.
660 Madison Avenue
New York, New York 10021
Tel: 212-832-3838

Wylde Films, Inc.
352 Park Avenue, South
New York, New York 10010
Tel: 212-685-1000

The Zanuck/Brown Company
445 Park Avenue
New York, New York 10022
Tel: 212-759-7500

North Carolina:

International Amusement
  Corporation
4325 Glenwood Avenue
Raleigh, North Carolina 27612
Tel: 919-782-6930

Jefferson Productions
1 Julian Prince Place
Charlotte, North Carolina 28208
Tel: 704-374-3823

Ohio:

Cinegraphs, Inc.
4653 Glendale Avenue
Toledo, Ohio 43614
Tel: 419-382-6974

Oklahoma:

CSI Productions
233 Mayo Building
Tulsa, Oklahoma 74103
Tel: 918-583-9146

Douglas Productions
1300 McGee Drive, Suite 106A
Norman, Oklahoma 73069
Tel: 405-321-1200

Oregon:

Cyclops Cinema
1423 S.W. Columbia Street
Portland, Oregon 97201
Tel: 503-222-2521

Pacific International Enterprises,
    Inc.
1133 South Riverside
Medford, Oregon 97501
Tel: 503-779-0990

Pennsylvania:

Capital Corporate Resources, Inc.
1700 Market Street
Philadelphia, Pennsylvania 19103
Tel: 215-864-7777

Gateway Films
Valley Forge, Pennsylvania 19481
Tel: 215-768-2042

Puerto Rico:

Creative Film Producers, Inc.
GPO Box 4069
San Juan, Puerto Rico 00936
Tel: 809-766-0235

Texas:

Bob Bailey Studios, Inc.
931 Yale Street
Houston, Texas 77008
Tel: 713-864-2671

Dale Berry and Associates, Inc.
9001 E R L Thornton Freeway
Dallas, Texas 75228
Tel: 214-324-0409

Carlocke/Langden, Inc.
4122 Main Street
Dallas, Texas 75226
Tel: 214-826-9380

Century Studios, Inc.
4519 Maple Avenue
Dallas, Texas 75219
Tel: 214-522-3310

Colordom Screen Productions
605 McGowen
Houston, Texas 77006
Tel: 713-522-9716

Charles M. Conner Productions
4713 Braeburn Drive
Bellaire, Texas 77401
Tel: 713-668-9900

William M. Hayes Productions
303 South Alamo Street
San Antonio, Texas 78205
Tel: 512-227-4073

Jamieson Film Company
6911 Forest Park Road
Dallas, Texas 75235
Tel: 214-350-1283

Kinetic Link, Inc.
303 South Alamo Street
San Antonio, Texas. 78205
Tel: 512-227-6206

MFC Film Production, Inc.
5915 Star Lane
Houston, Texas 77027
Tel: 713-781-7703

The Magus Film Group
9915 Powhatan Drive
San Antonio, Texas 78230
Tel: 512-696-8162

Mission Films International
9915 Powhatan, Suite E3
San Antonio, Texas 78230
Tel: 512-696-8163

Mulberry Square Productions
11411 North Central Expressway
Dallas, Texas 75231
Tel: 214-369-2430

Pearlman-McNee Productions,
Inc.
1622 West Alabama
Houston, Texas 77006
Tel: 713-523-3601

Piccadilly Films International
Company, Ltd.
1802 N.E. Loop 410, Gold Carpet
Suite
San Antonio, Texas 78246
Tel: 512-824-3548

Rawson and White, Inc.
2701 Westheimer
Houston, Texas 77006
Tel: 713-522-0888

Jack Robinette Productions
6227 Shady Brook
Dallas, Texas 75231
Tel: 214-368-1609

Sack Amusement Enterprises
1710 Jackson Street
Dallas, Texas 75201
Tel: 214-742-9445

Jim Seymour Associates
4100 Wildwood, Box 4821
Austin, Texas 78765
Tel: 512-454-1626

Shuler Productions
5327 North Central Expressway
Dallas, Texas 75205
Tel: 214-522-3250

Southwest Sound Films
1709 South Lamar
Dallas, Texas 75215
Tel: 214-747-3961

Ralph Stachon and Associates,
   Inc.
1322 Inwood Road
Dallas, Texas 75247
Tel: 214-638-6231

Bill Stokes Associates
5646 Dyer Street
Dallas, Texas 75206
Tel: 214-363-0161

TAC Productions
3508 Greenville Avenue
Dallas, Texas 75206
Tel: 214-327-1375

Utah:

American Cinema, Inc.
555 East Fourth South
Salt Lake City, Utah 84102
Tel: 801-521-8161

American National Enterprises,
   Inc.
556 East South
Salt Lake City, Utah 84102
Tel: 801-521-9400

Stockdale & Company
200 East First South
Salt Lake City, Utah 84111
Tel: 801-521-3505

Virginia:

Commonwealth Films
1500 Brook Road
Richmond, Virginia 23220
Tel: 804-649-8611

Dunn Productions
205 Nineteenth Street
Virginia Beach, Virginia 23451
Tel: 804-425-9422

Filmakers, Ltd.
Virginia Beach Municipal Center
2625 Princess Anne Road
Virginia Beach, Virginia 23456
Tel: 804-427-6101

Washington:

W. Brooks Baum Cinema
   Productions
715 First Avenue West
Seattle, Washington 98119
Tel: 206-283-6456

Cameron Film Productions
222 Minor North
Seattle, Washington 98109
Tel: 206-623-4103

George Carlson & Associates
Arcade Building
Seattle, Washington 98101
Tel: 206-623-8045

Cinecrest, Inc.
2800 Smith Tower
Seattle, Washington 98104
Tel: 206-623-6584

Cinema Associates
421 Minor Avenue North
Seattle, Washington 98109
Tel: 206-622-7378

Gardner/Marlow/Maes Corporation
Seattle Tower, Penthouse
Seattle, Washington 98101
Tel: 206-624-9090

Roger Hagan Associates
1019 Belmont Place East
Seattle, Washington 98102
Tel: 206-324-5034

JRB Motion Graphics
3323 Ninth Avenue West
Seattle, Washington 98119
Tel: 206-284-0834

King Screen Productions
320 Aurora Avenue North
Seattle, Washington 98109
Tel: 206-682-3555

Know Productions, Inc.
1003 Lenora Street
Seattle, Washington 98121
Tel: 206-682-6931

Oscar Productions, Inc.
1122 26th Avenue South
Seattle, Washington 98144
Tel: 206-324-9440

Pal Productions, Inc.
1003 Lenora Street
Seattle, Washington 98121
Tel: 206-682-1339

Stordahl's Place
3831 34th Avenue West
Seattle, Washington 98199
Tel: 206-285-3022

The Strachan Company
300 Metropole Building
Second at Yesler
Seattle, Washington 98104
Tel: 206-622-2373

Production Services

Colorado:

Allcom
302 South Peoria Circle
Aurora, Colorado 80011
Tel: 303-322-9719

Broyles-Allebaugh & Davis, Inc.
7901 East Belleview Avenue
Denver, Colorado 80237
Tel: 303-771-5230

Cinema Services
P.O. Box 398
Eldorado Springs, Colorado
80025
Tel: 303-443-4913

Complete Production Services
180 La Fayette Street
Denver, Colorado 80218
Tel: 303-744-9036

Concept Continuum
1551 South Pearl
Denver, Colorado 80210
Tel: 303-744-6441

Georgia:

A F E R
1846 Briarwood Road, N.E.
Atlanta, Georgia 30329
Tel: 404-633-4101

Avrum Fine
161 Spring Street, N.E.
Atlanta, Georgia 30303
Tel: 404-523-4669

Production Services Atlanta
2060 Peachtree Industrial Court,
N.E.
Atlanta, Georgia 30341
Tel: 404-451-4624

Nancy Sewell
3307 Stonecrest Court
Atlanta, Georgia 30341
Tel: 404-938-9782

Smith & Friends
2735-C Tallulah Drive, N.E.
Atlanta, Georgia 30319
Tel: 404-266-8717

New York:

City Film Productions
64-12 65th Place
Middle Village, New York 11379
Tel: 212-456-5050

Oblio Motion Picture Production
Service
217 East 27th Street
New York, New York 10016
Tel: 212-868-3330

Production Units, Mobile

As location shooting has become more widespread, due both to the demand for authentic backgrounds and the spiraling costs of studio production, mobile production units have become more prevalent and considerably more sophisticated. The principal suppliers of mobile systems are listed below.

California:
   Los Angeles area:

Howard A. Anderson Company
Paramount Studios
5451 Marathon Street
Los Angeles, California 90038
Tel: 213-463-0100
Ext: 2001

Audio Services/Mobile Sound
   Studios
1137 North McCadden Place
Los Angeles, California 90038
Tel: 213-464-3138

Birns & Sawyer Grip Trucks
1026 North Highland Avenue
Los Angeles, California 90038
Tel: 213-466-8211

The Burbank Studios
4000 Warner Boulevard
Burbank, California 91522
Tel: 213-843-6000

Cine Group
8560 Sunset Boulevard
Los Angeles, California 90069
Tel: 213-652-4800

Cinema "35" Center, Inc.
850 Colorado Boulevard
Los Angeles, California 90041
Tel: 213-255-1296

Cinemobile
8600 Sunset Boulevard
Los Angeles, California 90069
Tel: 213-652-4800

Columbia Pictures Industries
Colgems Square
Burbank, California 91505
Tel: 213-843-6000

Compact Video Systems
2813 West Alameda
Burbank, California 91505

F&B/CECO of California, Inc.
7051 Santa Monica Boulevard
Los Angeles, California 90038
Tel: 213-466-9361

Samuel Goldwyn Studios
1041 North Formosa Avenue
Los Angeles, California 90046
Tel: 213-851-1234

George Hill Mobile Studio
4010 Colfax Avenue
Studio City, California 91604
Tel: 213-769-8149

Hill Production Service, Inc.
835 North Seward Street
Los Angeles, California 90038
Tel: 213-463-0311

Hollywood Mobile Studios
5234 Vineland
North Hollywood, California
   91601
Tel: 213-769-5600

Lloyd-Davies Enterprises
1021 North McCadden Place
Los Angeles, California 90038
Tel: 213-462-1206

Mobile Production Systems
1225 North Vine Street
Los Angeles, California 90038
Tel: 213-465-7141

Movivan
906 North Atlantic Boulevard
Alhambra, California 91801
Tel: 213-283-3958

PSI-Production Systems Inc.
1123 North Lillian Way
Los Angeles, California 90038
Tel: 213-469-2704

Glen R. Roland, Jr.
8543 Clifton Way
Beverly Hills, California 90211
Tel: 213-271-0533

SOS/Photo-Cine Optics
7051 Santa Monica Boulevard
Los Angeles, California 90038
Tel: 213-466-9361

Soundco
932 North La Brea Avenue
Los Angeles, California 90038
Tel: 213-851-1622

Trans-American Video, Inc.
1541 North Vine Street
Los Angeles, California 90028
Tel: 213-466-2141

UPS Studio Rentals
6561 Santa Monica Boulevard
Los Angeles, California 90038
Tel: 213-461-1442

The Vidtronics Co., Inc.
855 North Cahuenga Boulevard
Los Angeles, California 90038
Tel: 213-466-9741

San Diego:

The Odyssey Corporation
1333 Camino Del Rio, Suite 316
San Diego, California 92108
Tel: 714-291-6830

San Francisco:

FERCO
363 Brannan Street
San Francisco, California 94107
Tel: 415-957-1787

Filmachine, Inc.
665 Harrison Street
San Francisco, California 94107
Tel: 415-956-4330

Manifest Productions Service
308 Eleventh Street
San Francisco, California 94102
Tel: 415-626-5596

The Phelps & Kopp Company
991 Tennessee Street
San Francisco, California 94107
Tel: 415-285-1900

Florida:

Cinema City Studios, Inc.
6015 Highway 301 North
Tampa, Florida 33610
Tel: 813-621-4731

Moviemobile
19812 North Twelfth Place
North Miami Beach, Florida
   33162
Tel: 305-891-2703

Hawaii:

Hawaii Production Center
1534 Kapiolani Boulevard
Honolulu, Hawaii 96814
Tel: 808-941-3011

The House of Eric Productions
1760 Ala Moana Boulevard
Waikiki, Hawaii 96815
Tel: 808-533-3877

Spectrum Motion Pictures
2962 East Manoa Road
Honolulu, Hawaii 96822
Tel: 808-988-7122

New York:

FERCO
419 West 54th Street
New York, New York 10019
Tel: 212-581-5474

Feature Systems, Inc.
513 West 26th Street
New York, New York 10001
Tel: 212-736-0447

The Film Van
333 Park Avenue
Wantagh, New York 11793
Tel: 516-221-8753

Filmtrucks–New York
512 West 39th Street
New York, New York 10018
Tel: 212-524-8668

New York Cinema
250 West 85th Street
New York, New York 10024
Tel: 212-947-1271

Texas:

Automated Commercial Training
   Systems, Inc.
9817 Westpark
Houston, Texas 77042
Tel: 713-783-1380

Washington:

W. Brooks Baum Cinema
   Productions
715 First Avenue West
Seattle, Washington 98119
Tel: 206-283-6456

Projection Equipment

Included here are both systems for viewing the finished product and systems used in connection with filming it, such as rear-projection apparatus.

California:

Los Angeles area:

Background Engineers
729 North Seward Street
Los Angeles, California 90038
Tel: 213-465-4161

Cinema "35" Center, Inc.
850 Colorado Boulevard
Los Angeles, California 90041
Tel: 213-255-1296

J. Dolan Projection Units
15415 Vanowen
Van Nuys, California 91406
Tel: 213-988-0120

Allan Gordon Enterprises
5362 North Cahuenga Boulevard
North Hollywood, California
91601
Tel: 213-985-5500

Harry McCune Sound Service,
Inc.
1420 West Ninth Street
Los Angeles, California 90015
Tel: 213-385-8238

Movie Tech
6518 Santa Monica Boulevard
Los Angeles, California 90038
Tel: 213-467-8491

Panavision, Inc.
18618 Oxnard Street
Tarzana, California 91356
Tel: 213-881-1702

Photo & Sound Company
870 Monterey Pass Road
Monterey Park, California 91754
Tel: 213-264-6850

Glen R. Roland, Jr.
8543 Clifton Way
Beverly Hills, California
Tel: 213-271-0533

SFS Projection Engineering Corp.
16055 Ventura Boulevard, Suite
700
Encino, California 91316
Tel: 213-789-9015

SOS/Photo-Cine-Optics
7051 Santa Monica Boulevard
Los Angeles, California 90038
Tel: 213-466-9361

San Diego:

The Odyssey Corporation
1333 Camino Del Rio, Suite 316
San Diego, California 92108
Tel: 714-291-6830

San Francisco:

Media Generalists
69 Clementina Street
San Francisco, California 94105
Tel: 415-433-3337

Harry McCune Sound Service,
   Inc.
951 Howard Street
San Francisco, California 94103
Tel: 415-777-2700

Harry McCune Sound Studio
991 Howard Street
San Francisco, California 94103
Tel: 415-777-2700

Sound Genesis, Inc.
445 Bryant Street
San Francisco, California 94107
Tel: 415-391-8776

District of Columbia:

Wilmo Corporation
3322 M Street, N.W.
Washington, D.C. 20007
Tel: 202-337-6680

Hawaii:

Thayer Sound
116 South Hotel Street
Honolulu, Hawaii 96809
Tel: 808-536-6161

New York:

A. V. Promotion Aids, Inc.
466 Lexington Avenue
New York, New York 10017
Tel: 212-679-4080

A. V. E. Corporation
250 West 54th Street
New York, New York 10019
Tel: 212-757-0552

Abbe Films & Equipment
417 West 44th Street
New York, New York 10036
Tel: 212-757-2219

E. J. Barnes & Company
630 Ninth Avenue
New York, New York 10036
Tel: 212-757-6600

Dura-Sell Corporation
41 East 42nd Street
New York, New York 10017
Tel: 212-687-1881

Jerome Menell Company
30 East 42nd Street
New York, New York 10017
Tel: 212-682-3452

Motion Picture Enterprises, Inc.
Tarrytown, New York 10591
Tel: 212-245-0969

Norelco
100 East 42nd Street
New York, New York 10017
Tel: 212-697-3600

Projection Systems International
730 Third Avenue
New York, New York 10017
Tel: 212-682-0995

Reliance Audio-Visual Corp.
619 West 54th Street
New York, New York 10019
Tel: 212-586-0435

Alan E. Starr
405 West 44th Street
New York, New York 10036
Tel: 212-246-8543

Washington:

National Theatre Supply
2415 Second Avenue
Seattle, Washington 98121
Tel: 206-624-7710

Props

The suppliers of properties categorized below can supply anything from a vintage Dusenberg touring car to plastic flowers guaranteed not to wilt under the heat of arc lights.

AUTOMOBILES (ANTIQUE)

California:

Horseless Carriage Club of
   America
9031 East Florence Avenue
Downey, California 90240
Tel: 213-862-6210

Movie World
6920 Orangethorpe Avenue
Buena Park, California 90620
Tel: 714-523-1520
Tel: 213-921-1702

Old Time Cars
1660 South La Cienega Boulevard
Los Angeles, California 90035
Tel: 213-278-7140

Pacific Auto Rental
310 South Berendo
Los Angeles, California 90052
Tel: 213-382-1186

Picture Cars Company
5639 Sunset Boulevard
Los Angeles, California 90028
Tel: 213-469-6351

Colorado:

Forney Transportation Museum
1416 Platte
Denver, Colorado 80202
Tel: 303-733-7241

Rippey Veteran Car Museum
2030 South Cherokee
Denver, Colorado 80223
Tel: 303-733-7241

Louisiana:

Thomas B. Favrot
1448 Fourth Street
New Orleans, Louisiana 70130
Tel: 504-897-3007

Richard Schmidt
4418 Majestic Oak Drive
New Orleans, Louisiana 70126
Tel: 504-242-7574

New Jersey:

Pennington Enterprises
72 Edmund Street
Edison, New Jersey 08818
Tel: 201-985-9090

New York:

The Obsolete Fleet
45 Christopher Street
New York, New York 10014
Tel: 212-255-6068

AUTOMOBILES (MODERN)

California:

AMF
500 Paula Avenue
Glendale, California 91201
Tel: 213-245-1204

Abbott & Hast Limousine Service
1000 Venice Boulevard
Los Angeles, California 90015
Tel: 213-746-1271

Armored Transport
1130 South Flower Street
Los Angeles, California 90015
Tel: 213-747-5604

Autos Unusual
431 South Crescent Drive
Beverly Hills, California 90212
Tel: 213-553-0775

Barris Kustom Industries, Inc.
10811 Riverside Drive
North Hollywood, California
  91602
Tel: 213-877-2352

Bob Bondurant School of High
  Performance Driving, Inc.
125 Nova Albion Way
San Rafael, California 94903
Tel: 415-472-3969

Brand-X Dune Buggy Group
532 Carol Place
Arroyo Grande, California 93420
Tel: 805-489-3410

Commercial Studio Rentals
809 North Cahuenga Boulevard
Los Angeles, California 90038
Tel: 213-462-6371

George Dockstader Rentals
6700 Fair Avenue
North Hollywood, California
  91606
Tel: 213-763-7167

Foremost Euro-Car
5430 Van Nuys Boulevard
Van Nuys, California 91401
Tel: 213-786-1960

Movie World
6920 Orangethorpe Avenue
Buena Park, California 90620
Tel: 213-921-1702
Tel: 714-523-1520

Pacific Auto Rentals
310 South Berendo Street
Los Angeles, California 90005
Tel: 213-382-1186

Peter Sartori Leasing, Ltd.
325 West Colorado Boulevard
Pasadena, California 91101
Tel: 213-795-8835

Snyder Ambulance Service
14122 Oxnard Street
Van Nuys, California 91401
Tel: 213-781-5151

TWA Film & TV Promotions
308 North Rodeo Drive
Beverly Hills, California 90210
Tel: 213-276-1194

U Sav Rent Any Car
5401 Lankershim Boulevard
North Hollywood, California
   91601
Tel: 213-980-1200

BOATING EQUIPMENT

Arizona:

Craig Pease Enterprises
P.O. Box 1118
Scottsdale, Arizona 85252
Tel: 602-945-4807

California:

The Blake Organization
2025 Avenue of the Stars
Los Angeles, California 90067
Tel: 213-277-3161

California Sailing Academy
14025 Panay Way
Marina Del Rey, California
   90291
Tel: 213-821-3433

Ed Cunningham & Son Marine
   Props & Rentals
12740 Culver Boulevard
Los Angeles, California 90066
Tel: 213-391-6319

Del Rey Marine Corporation
734 Washington Street
Marina Del Rey, California
   90291
Tel: 213-823-6331

Marine Activities
8850 Sunset Boulevard
Los Angeles, California 90069
Tel: 213-655-5555

Ted Turner
8850 Sunset Boulevard
Los Angeles, California 90069
Tel: 213-655-5555

Hawaii:

Hawaiian Divers
Box 572
Kailua-Kona, Hawaii 96740
Tel: 808-329-3407

BREAKAWAYS

California:

Ellis Mercantile
169 North La Brea Avenue
Los Angeles, California 90036
Tel: 213-933-7334

Krofft Enterprises
11347 Vanowen Street
North Hollywood, California
   91605
Tel: 213-877-3361

Mole-Richardson Company
937 North Sycamore Avenue
Los Angeles, California 90038
Tel: 213-851-0111

Motion Picture Enterprises
367 West Spazier
Burbank, California 91503
Tel: 213-842-9013

Olesen Company
1535 Ivar Avenue
Los Angeles, California 90028
Tel: 213-465-5194

Don Post Studios
5537 Cleon Avenue
North Hollywood, California
  91603
Tel: 213-877-1608

Shafton Associates
5255 Clinton Street
Los Angeles, California 90004
Tel: 213-461-2884

Showcraft, Inc.
9215 Cranford Street
Pacoima, California 91331
Tel: 213-768-1093

Silvestri Studios
1733 West Cordova Street
Los Angeles, California 90052
Tel: 213-735-1481

Special Effects Unlimited
752 North Cahuenga Boulevard
Los Angeles, California 90038
Tel: 213-465-3366

Colorado:

Stage Engineering & Supply, Inc.
Box 2002
Colorado Springs, Colorado
  80901
Tel: 303-635-2935

FIREWORKS

California:

Atlas Fireworks Co., Inc.
13500 Excelsior Drive
Norwalk, California 90650
Tel: 714-521-6767

California Fireworks Display Co.
3196 North Locust
Rialto, California 92376
Tel: 714-874-1645

De la Mare Engineering, Inc.
1910 First Street
San Fernando, California 91340
Tel: 213-365-9208

Jet Dragon Fireworks, Inc.
939 Terminal Way
San Carlos, California 94070
Tel: 415-591-5731

Mr. Effects
17812 Silverstream Drive
Saugus, California 91350
Tel: 805-252-5533

Special Effects Unlimited
752 North Cahuenga Boulevard
Los Angeles, California 90038
Tel: 213-465-3366

FURNITURE

California:

Joseph Basch Galleries Co.
5755 Santa Monica Boulevard
Los Angeles, California 90038
Tel: 213-463-5116

Cinema Mercantile Co., Ltd.
5857 Santa Monica Boulevard
Los Angeles, California 90038
Tel: 213-467-1151

Cinema Props Company
6161 Santa Monica Boulevard
Los Angeles, California 90038
Tel: 213-464-3191

Commercial Studio Rentals
809 North Cahuenga Boulevard
Los Angeles, California 90038
Tel: 213-462-6371

Ellis Mercantile Company
169 North La Brea Avenue
Los Angeles, California 90036
Tel: 213-933-7334

First Street Furniture Store, Inc.
1123 North Bronson
Los Angeles, California 90038
Tel: 213-462-6306

House of Props
1117 North Gower Street
Los Angeles, California 90038
Tel: 213-463-3166

McLean-Wasser, Inc.
8671 Melrose
Los Angeles, California 90069
Tel: 213-659-2690

Modern Furniture Rentals
5418 Sierra Vista Avenue
Los Angeles, California 90038
Tel: 213-462-6545

Omega Studio Rentals
5757 Santa Monica Boulevard
Los Angeles, California 90038
Tel: 213-874-7470

School Days Equipment
   Company
973 North Main Street
Los Angeles, California 90012
Tel: 213-223-3474

Silvestri Studio
1733 West Cordova Street
Los Angeles, California 90007
Tel: 213-735-1481

Spellman Desk Company
6159 Santa Monica Boulevard
Los Angeles, California 90038
Tel: 213-467-0628

Studio Specialties
1623 Palo Alto Street
Los Angeles, California 90026
Tel: 213-483-4950

United Design Associates, Inc.
812 North La Cienega Boulevard
Los Angeles, California 90069
Tel: 213-657-4202

Woodruff Antiques
4533 Sunset Boulevard
Los Angeles, California 90028
Tel: 213-666-9489

Billy Woolf Motion Picture
Accessories
1112 North Beechwood Drive
Los Angeles, California 90052
Tel: 213-469-5335

GENERAL

Arizona:

Old Tucson Studio
201 South Kinney Road
Tucson, Arizona 85705
Tel: 602-792-3100

Special Events Coordinators
3422 West Welden Avenue
Phoenix, Arizona 85017
Tel: 602-272-1337

California:
Los Angeles area:

AMF
500 Paula Avenue
Glendale, California 91201
Tel: 213-245-1204

Abbey Rents
600 South Normandie Avenue
Los Angeles, California 90005
Tel: 213-385-9241

Abbott & Hast Company
1948 South Figueroa Street
Los Angeles, California 90007
Tel: 213-746-1271

Barris Kustom Industries, Inc.
10811 Riverside
North Hollywood, California
91602
Tel: 213-877-2352

Joseph Basch Galleries Co.
5755 Santa Monica Boulevard
Los Angeles, California 90038
Tel: 213-463-5116

Beverly Hills Fountain Center
8574 Santa Monica Boulevard
Los Angeles, California 90069
Tel: 213-652-5297

Bischoff's Taxidermists
2798 Sunset Boulevard
Los Angeles, California 90026
Tel: 213-384-1123

The Burbank Studios
4000 Warner Boulevard
Burbank, California 91522
Tel: 213-843-6000

California Fireworks Display Co
P.O. Box 488
3196 North Locust Avenue
Rialto, California 92376
Tel: 714-874-1644

Cinema Mercantile Company
  Ltd.
5857 Santa Monica
Los Angeles, California 90038
Tel: 213-467-1151

Cinema Props Company
6161 Santa Monica Boulevard
Los Angeles, California 90038
Tel: 213-464-3191

Commercial Studio Rentals
809 North Cahuenga Boulevard
Los Angeles, California 90038
Tel: 213-462-6371

Coordinators 2
8113 1/2 Melrose Avenue
Los Angeles, California 90048
Tel: 213-653-6110

Creative Research Center
1666 1/2 Electric Avenue
Venice, California 90291
Tel: 213-821-3971

Ed Cunningham & Son Marine
  Props & Rentals
12740 Culver Boulevard
Los Angeles, California 90066
Tel: 213-391-6319

Dice, Inc.
6322 De Longpre Avenue
Los Angeles, California 90028
Tel: 213-461-9435

Larry Dorn Associates
9145 Sunset Boulevard
Los Angeles, California 90069
Tel: 213-274-7233

Ellis Mercantile Company
169 North La Brea Avenue
Los Angeles, California 90036
Tel: 213-933-7334

Fantasy Fair, Inc.
6617 Santa Monica Boulevard
Los Angeles, California 90038
Tel: 213-467-6141

Featherock, Inc.
6331 Hollywood Boulevard
Los Angeles, California 90028
Tel: 213-463-1119

Hill-Daves Productions
15300 Ventura Boulevard
Sherman Oaks, California 91403
Tel: 213-788-3595

Hollywood Fancy Feathers
  Company
512 South Broadway
Los Angeles, California 90013
Tel: 213-625-8453

Hollywood Toys, Inc.
6562 Hollywood Boulevard
Los Angeles, California 90028
Tel: 213-465-3119

House of Props, Inc.
1117 Gower Street
Los Angeles, California 90038
Tel: 213-463-3166

Hume's Sporting Goods Co.
140 North Victory Boulevard
Burbank, California 91502
Tel: 213-849-1614

Ray M. Johnson Studio
5555 Sunset Boulevard
Los Angeles, California 90028
Tel: 213-465-4108

Korky's Kustom Studios
16901 Roscoe Boulevard
Van Nuys, California 91406
Tel: 213-893-3818

Los Angeles Stage Lighting
1451 Venice Boulevard
Los Angeles, California 90006
Tel: 213-384-1241

Lennie Marvin Music Company
22320 Needles Street
Chatsworth, California 91311
Tel: 213-341-5315

Ray Mercer & Company
4241 Normal Avenue
Los Angeles, California 90029
Tel: 213-663-9331

Movie World
6920 Orangethorpe Avenue
Buena Park, California 90620
Tel: 213-921-1702

Native American
   Research/Consultants
526 South Reese Place
Burbank, California 91506
Tel: 213-848-6531

Omega Studio Rentals
5757 Santa Monica Boulevard
Los Angeles, California 90038
Tel: 213-466-8201

Don Post Studios
811 Milford Street
Glendale, California 91203
Tel: 213-245-4134

Ray Plastics
11565 Federal Drive
El Monte, California 91731
Tel: 213-579-4250

Roschu
6514 Santa Monica Boulevard
Los Angeles, California 90038
Tel: 213-469-2749

Scale Model Company
401 West Florence Avenue
Inglewood, California 90301
Tel: 213-674-1534

Shafton Associates
5255 Clinton Street
Los Angeles, California 90004
Tel: 213-461-2884

Showcraft, Inc.
9215 Cranford Street
Pacoima, California 91331
Tel: 213-768-1093

Silvestri Studio
1733 West Cordova Street
Los Angeles, California 90007
Tel: 213-735-1481

Special Effects Unlimited
752 North Cahuenga Boulevard
Los Angeles, California 90038
Tel: 213-465-3366
Tel: 213-467-8000

Stembridge Gun Rentals
5451 Marathon Street
Los Angeles, California 90038
Tel: 213-463-0100

Studio Set Service, Inc.
Producer's Studio
650 North Bronson Avenue
Los Angeles, California 90028
Tel: 213-465-4411

Universal City Studios
100 Universal City Plaza
Universal City, California 91608
Tel: 213-985-4321

Western Costume Company
5335 Melrose Avenue
Los Angeles, California 90038
Tel: 213-469-1451

Wolf & Vine Mannequins
490 Bauchet Street
Los Angeles, California 90012
Tel: 213-626-3125

Billy Woolf
1112 North Beechwood Drive
Los Angeles, California 90038
Tel: 213-469-5335
Tel: 213-766-4862

Yerkes Continental Circus
17721 Roscoe Boulevard
Northridge, California 91324
Tel: 213-344-4231

San Francisco :

Dance Art Company
222 Powell Street
San Francisco, California 94102
Tel: 415-392-4912

Horseless Carriage Club of
America
164 South Park
San Francisco, California 94107
Tel: 415-397-3111

William R. Johnson Advertising
66 Lansing Street
San Francisco, California 94105
Tel: 415-982-8389

The Phelps & Kopp Company
991 Tennessee Street
San Francisco, California 94107
Tel: 415-285-1900

Colorado:

Stage Engineering & Supply, Inc.
P.O. Box 2002
Colorado Springs, Colorado
80901
Tel: 303-635-2935

Florida:

Presentations, Inc.
6321 N.W. 37th Avenue
Miami, Florida 33101
Tel: 305-691-6300

Scenery, Inc.
7215 West Twentieth Avenue
Hialeah, Florida 33010
Tel: 305-821-7070

Hawaii:

Hawaii Production Center
1534 Kapiolani Boulevard
Honolulu, Hawaii 96814
Tel: 808-941-3011

Illinois:

Becker Studios, Inc.
2824 West Taylor Street
Chicago, Illinois 60612
Tel: 312-722-4040

Furniture Leasing Service
819 North Clark Street
Chicago, Illinois 60610
Tel: 312-642-0600

Hartman Furniture & Carpet Co.
218 West Kinzie Street
Chicago, Illinois 60610
Tel: 312-664-2800

The Scenery Works
2821 Central
Evanston, Illinois 60201
Tel: 312-864-1166

Gene Segal Antiques
431 North Wells Street
Chicago, Illinois 60654
Tel: 312-527-4474

Nevada:

Bonnie Springs Old Nevada
830 East Sahara Avenue, Suite
  One
Las Vegas, Nevada 89105
Tel: 702-732-2115

New York:

Imitation Food Company
197 Waverly Place
Brooklyn, New York 11201
Tel: 212-875-1268

Leonard Kaye Company
893 Third Avenue
New York, New York 10017
Tel: 212-753-5984

Kenmore Furniture Company
156 East 33rd Street
New York, New York 10016
Tel: 212-683-1888

Modern Artificial Flowers
457 West 46th Street
New York, New York 10019
Tel: 212-265-0414

Texas:

Elbee Company
P.O. Box 7408
821 West Commerce
San Antonio, Texas 78207
Tel: 512-223-4561

Performing Arts Supply Company
5734 Green Ash
Houston, Texas 77036
Tel: 713-667-8101

GUN RENTALS

California:

Alfonso of Hollywood
4850 Lankershim Boulevard
North Hollywood, California
  91601
Tel: 213-769-0362

Brass Rail Gun Shop
1136 North La Brea Avenue
Los Angeles, California 90038
Tel: 213-462-7458

Stembridge Gun Rentals
5451 Marathon Street
Los Angeles, California 90038
Tel: 213-463-0100

HORSE-DRAWN VEHICLES

California:

Myers & Wills Stables
Lakeview Terrace
11035 Osborne Street
San Fernando, California 91342
Tel: 213-899-8633

Randall Ranch
23870 Pine Street
Newhall, California 91321
Tel: 213-365-2119

Dick Webb Motion Picture
   Livestock & Equipment
23868 Pine Street
Newhall, California 91321
Tel: 213-365-3921

Colorado:

Colorado Coach Company
4530 Hoyt Street
Wheat Ridge, Colorado 80033
Tel: 303-421-3646

Hitch Rack Stables
310 South 31st Street
Colorado Springs, Colorado
   80904
Tel: 303-635-2051

Table Mountain Buggy Rentals,
   Inc.
7651 West 41st Avenue
Wheat Ridge, Colorado 80033
Tel: 303-422-4418

MOCK-UPS

California:

Barris Kustom Industries, Inc.
10811 Riverside Drive
North Hollywood, California
   91602
Tel: 213-877-2352

Culver City Studios
9336 West Washington Boulevard
Culver City, California 90230
Tel: 213-871-0360

Movie Tech
6518 Santa Monica Boulevard
Los Angeles, California 90038
Tel: 213-467-8491

Showcraft, Inc.
9215 Cranford Street
Pacoima, California 91331
Tel: 213-768-1093

Silvestri Studio
1733 West Cordova Street
Los Angeles, California 90007
Tel: 213-735-1481

Stereovision International, Inc.
5700 Cahuenga Boulevard
North Hollywood, California
   91601
Tel: 213-762-7200

TWA Film & TV Promotions
308 North Rodeo Drive
Beverly Hills, California 90210
Tel: 213-276-1194

Arthur Wallach & Associates
972 North La Cienega Boulevard
Los Angeles, California 90069
Tel: 213-655-6223

MODELS & MINIATURES

California:

Howard Anderson & Co.
5451 Marathon Street
Los Angeles, California 90038
Tel: 213-463-0100

Bob Baker Productions
1345 West First Street
Los Angeles, California 90026
Tel: 213-624-3973

Bob Clampett Productions
729 Seward Street
Los Angeles, California 90038
Tel: 213-466-0264

Hill-Daves Productions
15300 Ventura Boulevard
Sherman Oaks, California 91403
Tel: 213-788-3595

Ray M. Johnson Studio
5555 Sunset Boulevard
Los Angeles, California 90028
Tel: 213-465-4108

Krofft Enterprises
11347 Vanowen Street
North Hollywood, California
91605
Tel: 213-877-3361

Ray Mercer & Company
4241 Normal Avenue
Los Angeles, California 90029
Tel: 213-663-9331

Movie Tech
6518 Santa Monica Boulevard
Los Angeles, California 90038
Tel: 213-467-8491

Don Post Studios
Box 710
North Hollywood, California
91603
Tel: 213-877-1608

Ray Plastics
11565 Federal Drive
El Monte, California 91731
Tel: 213-579-4250

Scale Model Company
401 West Florence Avenue
Inglewood, California 90003
Tel: 213-674-1534

Shafton Associates
5255 Clinton Street
Los Angeles, California 90004
Tel: 213-461-2884

Showcraft, Inc.
9215 Cranford Street
Pacoima, California 91331
Tel: 213-768-1093

Studio Set Service, Inc.
Producer's Studio
650 North Bronson Avenue
Los Angeles, California 90004
Tel: 213-465-4411

PLANTS & FLOWERS

California:

Aldik Artificial Flowers
7651 Sepulveda Boulevard
Van Nuys, California 91405
Tel: 213-988-5970

Walter Allen Plant Rentals
5500 Melrose Avenue
Los Angeles, California 90038
Tel: 213-469-3621

George Barnes, Flowers
13205 Ventura Boulevard
North Hollywood, California
   91604
Tel: 213-877-4207

John Beistel, Inc.
Beverly-Wilshire Hotel
9500 Wilshire Boulevard
Beverly Hills, California 90210
Tel: 213-272-5616

Corham Artificial Flowers
11800 Olympic Boulevard
West Los Angeles, California
   90064
Tel: 213-477-4114

Flower Fashions
168 South Beverly Drive
Beverly Hills, California 9021?
Tel: 213-275-0159

Hill-Daves Productions
15300 Ventura Boulevard
Sherman Oaks, California 9140?
Tel: 213-788-3595

Moskatel's
733 San Julian
Los Angeles, California 90014
Tel: 213-627-1631

A. E. Schmidt Company
8222 Tujunga Avenue
Sun Valley, California 91352
Tel: 213-875-1434

Public Relations & Publicity

Through the magic of public relations and publicity, a grade-B spaghetti Western can be converted into a highly artistic statement of one man's inability to instill meaningful societal values in his fellow man—leading either to a ritualistic confrontation or a shootout.

California:

Los Angeles area:

Bob Abrams & Associates
6430 Sunset Boulevard
Los Angeles, California 90028
Tel: 213-461-4393

Ackerman-Egan Associates
324 South Beverly Drive
Beverly Hills, California 90212
Tel: 213-553-0814

Allan/Ingersoll/Segal
9301 Wilshire Boulevard
Beverly Hills, California 90210
Tel: 213-278-3670

John Allan Associates
553 North Hoover
Los Angeles, California 90004
Tel: 213-661-5748

Jay Allen
201 North Robertson Boulevard
Beverly Hills, California 90211
Tel: 213-274-6793

Joe Alvin & Company
1052 West Sixth Street
Los Angeles, California 90017
Tel: 213-680-1413

Sidney Balkin & Associates
1460 North Donhill Drive
Beverly Hills, California 90212
Tel: 213-275-2208

Fred Banker & Associates
3467 Wrightwood Drive
Studio City, California 91604
Tel: 213-877-0691

Bar-Lor Associates
428 North Palm Drive
Beverly Hills, California 90210
Tel: 213-278-1998

Aleon Bennett & Associates
8272 Sunset Boulevard
Los Angeles, California 90046
Tel: 213-656-1616

Jay Bernstein Public Relations
9110 Sunset Boulevard, Suite 250
Los Angeles, California 90069
Tel: 213-274-7656

Russell Birdwell
9250 Wilshire Boulevard, Suite
412
Beverly Hills, California 90212
Tel: 213-273-8477

Hilda Black
6311 Yucca Street
Los Angeles, California 90028
Tel: 213-464-1745

Joe Bleeden
10626 Wilshire Boulevard
Los Angeles, California 90024
Tel: 213-273-3414

Henri Bollinger Public Relations
9229 Sunset Boulevard, Suite 601
Los Angeles, California 90069
Tel: 213-274-8483

Booke & Company, Inc.
8920 Wilshire Boulevard
Beverly Hills, California 90211
Tel: 213-655-8363

Braverman-Mirisch, Inc.
9255 Sunset Boulevard
Los Angeles, California 90069
Tel: 213-272-8608

Burson-Marsteller Associates
3600 Wilshire Boulevard
Los Angeles, California 90017
Tel: 213-386-8776

Carl Byoir & Associates, Inc.
900 Wilshire Boulevard
Los Angeles, California 90017
Tel: 213-627-6421

James Byron
P.O. Box 2389
Los Angeles, California 90028
Tel: 213-276-2063

The Cambridge Company
8961 Sunset Boulevard
Los Angeles, California 90069
Tel: 213-274-4202

The Cardova Company
612 South Flower
Los Angeles, California 90017
Tel: 213-623-8177

The Carroll's Agency, Inc.
2001 North Curson Avenue
Los Angeles, California 90069
Tel: 213-876-5220

Carter/Craig Ltd.
14241 Ventura Boulevard
Sherman Oaks, California 91403
Tel: 213-872-2075

Wally Cedar Associates
Box 265
Beverly Hills, California 90213
Tel: 213-657-5858

The Chadwick Company
1717 North Highland Avenue
Los Angeles, California 90028
Tel: 213-851-1500

Esme Chandlee & Associates
195 South Beverly Drive
Beverly Hills, California 90212
Tel: 213-276-2369

Ben Cohn Company
1040 North Las Palmas Avenue
Los Angeles, California 90038
Tel: 213-469-9011

Paul Cooper
1100 North Alta Loma Road
Los Angeles, California 90069
Tel: 213-657-4040

Warren Cowan
250 North Canon Drive
Beverly Hills, California 90210
Tel: 213-272-0121

Tony DiMarco Company
Box 2329
North Hollywood, California
  91672
Tel: 213-662-0113

Michael B. Druxman & Associates
6464 Sunset Boulevard
Los Angeles, California 90028
Tel: 213-465-8886

James Eddy Company
8899 Beverly Boulevard
Los Angeles, California 90069
Tel: 213-278-3785

Daniel Edelman, Inc.
1901 Avenue of the Stars
Los Angeles, California 90067
Tel: 213-555-1560

Jay Faggen
1717 North Highland Avenue
Los Angeles, California 90028
Tel: 213-469-5367

Francis Feighan
9044 Shoreham Drive
Los Angeles, California 90069
Tel: 213-278-0176

Dick Fishell & Associates
120 El Camino Drive
Beverly Hills, California 90212
Tel: 213-275-4557

Pat Fitzgerald Company
9000 Sunset Boulevard
Los Angeles, California 90069
Tel: 213-273-0020

Jim Flood & Associates
9110 Sunset Boulevard
Los Angeles, California 90069
Tel: 213-274-0281

Jack V. Fogarty & Associates
9601 Wilshire Boulevard
Beverly Hills, California 90210
Tel: 213-274-8069

Maury Foladare & Associates
9229 Sunset Boulevard, Suite 611
Los Angeles, California 90069
Tel: 213-274-8847

Franken Public Relations
1115 South La Cienega Boulevard
Los Angeles, California 90034
Tel: 213-462-2395

Freeman & Best Public Relations
8732 Sunset Boulevard
Los Angeles, California 90069
Tel: 213-659-4700

Charles E. Fulkerson Associates
966 South Vermont
Los Angeles, California 90006
Tel: 213-388-2387

Furman Associates
3133 Lake Hollywood Drive
Los Angeles, California 90028
Tel: 213-851-3400

Cliff Gans
9100 Sunset Boulevard
Los Angeles, California 90069
Tel: 213-276-1334

Gardiner & Associates
124 North Clark Drive
Beverly Hills, California 90211
Tel: 213-659-3069

Mickey Garrett Associates
3349 Cahuenga Boulevard
Los Angeles, California 90068
Tel: 213-851-5075

The Garrett Company
8730 Sunset Boulevard
Los Angeles, California 90069
Tel: 213-657-1801

Gordon Gelford & Associates
8907 Wilshire Boulevard
Beverly Hills, California 90211
Tel: 213-652-6340

Gershenson & Dingilian
  Associates
120 El Camino, Suite 206
Beverly Hills, California 90212
Tel: 213-278-2343

Tom Gerst Associates
8746 Sunset Boulevard
Los Angeles, California 90069
Tel: 213-659-3921

Gibson/Stromberg/Jaffe
8780 Sunset Boulevard
Los Angeles, California 90069
Tel: 213-659-3565

Gifford/Wallace, Inc.
9800 West Olympic Boulevard
Beverly Hills, California 90212
Tel: 213-277-6747

The Goodman Organization
6464 Sunset Boulevard, Suite 990
Los Angeles, California 90028
Tel: 213-464-7241

Ed Greenberg
16770 Encino Hills Drive
Encino, California 91316
Tel: 213-789-4622

Guttman & Pam
1041 North Formosa Avenue
Los Angeles, California 90046
Tel: 213-851-2615

Hanson & Schwam Agency
9255 Sunset Boulevard
Los Angeles, California 90069
Tel: 213-278-1255

Harshe-Rotman & Druck, Inc.
3345 Wilshire Boulevard
Los Angeles, California 90010
Tel: 213-385-5271

Joe R. Hartsfield & Associates
4024 Radford Avenue
Studio City, California 91604
Tel: 213-763-8411

Doris Hellman
427 West Fifth Street
Los Angeles, California 90013
Tel: 213-628-2065

Harold Hilderbrand & Associates
6752 Selma Avenue
Los Angeles, California 90069
Tel: 213-467-1633

Hill & Knowlton, Inc.
5900 Wilshire Boulevard
Los Angeles, California 90036
Tel: 213-932-6271

Joe Hoening & Associates
195 South Beverly Drive
Beverly Hills, California 90212
Tel: 213-276-3121

Hoffman & Paladino & Landia
9000 Sunset Boulevard
Los Angeles, California 90069
Tel: 213-278-0024

Infoplan International, Inc.
3325 Wilshire Boulevard
Los Angeles, California 90210
Tel: 213-385-9021

Rick Ingersoll
1901 Avenue of the Stars
Los Angeles, California 90067
Tel: 213-277-3200

Sam Jacoby, Inc.
8721 Sunset Boulevard
Los Angeles, California 90069
Tel: 213-652-5623

Bob Jarzen & Associates
9220 Sunset Boulevard
Los Angeles, California 90069
Tel: 213-276-9994

Dan Jenkins Public Relations
4024 Radford Avenue
Studio City, California 91604
Tel: 213-763-8411

Ty Jurras
521 North La Cienega Boulevard
Los Angeles, California 90048
Tel: 213-655-6322

Milton Kahn & Associates
9454 Wilshire Boulevard, Suite
414
Beverly Hills, California 90212
Tel: 213-274-8641

Bernard F. Kamins Company
9720 Wilshire Boulevard
Beverly Hills, California 90210
Tel: 213-271-8141

Helen Kauffman
9017 Rangely Avenue
Los Angeles, California 90048
Tel: 213-275-3569

Kennett Public Relations
Associates
6640 Sunset Boulevard
Los Angeles, California 90028
Tel: 213-463-7191

Fred Kline
809 Cahuenga Boulevard
Los Angeles, California 90038
Tel: 213-462-6371

Kramer & Reiss Public Relations
9100 Sunset Boulevard
Los Angeles, California 90069
Tel: 213-273-3242

Lawrence Laurie & Associates
8899 Beverly Boulevard
Los Angeles, California 90048
Tel: 213-274-0851

Lee & Associates
8170 Beverly Boulevard
Los Angeles, California 90048
Tel: 213-651-2090

Herm Lewis & Associates
316 North Rossmore
Los Angeles, California 90004
Tel: 213-464-8189

The Lewis Company
8560 Sunset Boulevard
Los Angeles, California 90069
Tel: 213-655-9242

Frank Liberman & Associates
9255 Sunset Boulevard, Suite 510
Los Angeles, California 90069
Tel: 213-278-1993

Lipton Enterprises
1250 North Kings Road
Los Angeles, California 90069
Tel: 213-656-6842

Alex Litrov
9171 Wilshire Boulevard, Suite
540
Beverly Hills, California 90210
Tel: 213-274-7855

Rae Lynn
3670 Buena Park Drive
Studio City, California 91604
Tel: 213-761-6994

Jim Mahoney & Associates
120 El Camino Drive, Suite 104
Beverly Hills, California 90211
Tel: 213-274-8867

Paul Marsh & Associates
9255 West Sunset Boulevard
Los Angeles, California 90069
Tel: 213-278-7281

McFadden, Strauss & Irwin
1017 North La Cienega
Boulevard
Los Angeles, California 90069
Tel: 213-657-4330

William Meiklejohn
9250 Wilshire Boulevard, Suite
412
Beverly Hills, California 90048
Tel: 213-273-2556

The Mike Merrick Company
9000 Sunset Boulevard, Suite 717
Los Angeles, California 90069
Tel: 213-278-1211

Dan Merrin
General Service Studio
1040 North Las Palmas Avenue
Los Angeles, California 90038
Tel: 213-469-9141

Lee Merrin & Bruce Merrin
1040 North Las Palmas Avenue
Los Angeles, California 90038
Tel: 213-462-6791

Susan Meyer
308 South Rexford Drive
Beverly Hills, California 90212
Tel: 213-278-4357

Norman J. Millen
9100 Sunset Boulevard
Los Angeles, California 90069
Tel: 213-272-8461

Mirisch & Landia
9401 Wilshire Boulevard
Beverly Hills, California 90212
Tel: 213-274-5325

Morgan Company
2472 Beechwood Drive
Los Angeles, California 90068
Tel: 213-466-9757

Charles A. Moses Company
9256 Santa Monica Boulevard
Beverly Hills, California 90210
Tel: 213-550-0303

Stanley Musgrove
11010 Arleta
Mission Hills, California 91340
Tel: 213-465-2027

Ormond & Nicholson
6399 Wilshire Boulevard
Los Angeles, California 90048
Tel: 213-653-1755

Jerry Pam & Dick Guttman
  Associates
404 North Roxbury Drive, Suite
  422
Beverly Hills, California 90210
Tel: 213-278-6775

David F. Parry & Associates
5900 Wilshire Boulevard
Los Angeles, California 90036
Tel: 213-938-7138

Peggy Phillips
15155 Albright Street
Pacific Palisades, California
  90272
Tel: 213-454-1281

Pickwick Public Relations, Inc.
9744 Wilshire Boulevard, Suite
  209
Beverly Hills, California 90212
Tel: 213-273-7344

Charles A. Pomerantz Ltd.
15300 Ventura Boulevard
Sherman Oaks, California 91403
Tel: 213-872-0080

Joe Price & Associates
9000 Sunset Boulevard
Los Angeles, California 90069
Tel: 213-271-2116

Promo Productions
10643 Somma Way
Los Angeles, California 90024
Tel: 213-472-1067

Public Communications West
6252 Telegraph Road
Los Angeles, California 90040
Tel: 213-723-6401

Toni Redfield & Associates
6290 Sunset Boulevard
Los Angeles, California 90028
Tel: 213-465-5174

Melvin Rifkind & Associates
6505 Wilshire Boulevard
Los Angeles, California 90048
Tel: 213-651-5160

Roberts & Associates
9171 Wilshire Boulevard, Suite
310
Beverly Hills, California 90211
Tel: 213-273-0381

Rogers, Cowan & Taplinger, Inc.
250 North Canon Drive
Beverly Hills, California 90210
Tel: 213-275-4581

Henry Rogers
250 North Canon Drive
Beverly Hills, California 90210
Tel: 213-272-0121

Rothman-Kleiner Public
Relations
170 South Beverly Drive, Suite
135
Beverly Hills, California 90212
Tel: 213-278-7797

Ruder & Finn of Los Angeles, Inc.
9300 Wilshire Boulevard
Beverly Hills, California 90212
Tel: 213-274-8303

Stanley Sackin
1717 North Highland Avenue
Los Angeles, California 90028
Tel: 213-467-7425

Scannell Associates
1093 Broxton
West Los Angeles, California
90025
Tel: 213-879-9260

Scharf, Mann & Company
9056 Santa Monica Boulevard
Los Angeles, California 90069
Tel: 213-274-6222

Maurie E. Segal
12125 Riverside Drive, Suite 206
North Hollywood, California
91607
Tel: 213-980-2371

Edward Shaw & Associates
1901 Avenue of the Stars
Los Angeles, California 90067
Tel: 213-553-0307

Gene Shefrin & Associates, Inc.
812 South Robertson Boulevard
Los Angeles, California 90035
Tel: 213-657-2270

The Sherman Company
1940 North Las Palmas Avenue
Los Angeles, California 90038
Tel: 213-469-9011

Joseph Siegman, Inc.
9200 Sunset Boulevard, Suite 831
Los Angeles, California 90069 ·
Tel: 213-276-1014

Peter Simone & Associates
1717 North Highland Avenue
Los Angeles, California 90028
Tel: 213-461-4559

Jewel Smith
435 North Roxbury Drive
Beverly Hills, California 90210
Tel: 213-271-6613

Lou Smith Organization
9107 Wilshire Boulevard
Beverly Hills, California 90210
Tel: 213-272-4175

Solters/Sabinson/Raskin
9255 Sunset Boulevard
Los Angeles, California 90069
Tel: 213-275-5303

John Springer Associates, Inc.
1901 Avenue of the Stars
Los Angeles, California 90067
Tel: 213-277-3744

David Steinberg
8961 Sunset Boulevard
Los Angeles, California 90069
Tel: 213-278-3838

Alfred E. F. Stern
9021 Melrose Avenue
Los Angeles, California 90069
Tel: 213-272-6207

Dick Strout
1717 North Highland Avenue,
   Suite 618
Los Angeles, California 90028
Tel: 213-467-4106

Fred Stuart Associates
9126 Sunset Boulevard
Los Angeles, California 90069
Tel: 213-274-0674

Bob Suhosky Associates
9121 Sunset Boulevard, Suite 150
Los Angeles, California 90069
Tel: 213-274-9443

Swaney, Gershman & Gibson
8780 Sunset Boulevard
Los Angeles, California 90069
Tel: 213-659-3565

Ron Tepper & Associates
8961 Sunset Boulevard
Los Angeles, California 90069
Tel: 213-274-8569

Thomas & Associates
1549 North Vine
Los Angeles, California 90028
Tel: 213-464-2951

Thomas & Ford, Public Relations
8380 Melrose Avenue, Suite 306
Los Angeles, California 90069
Tel: 213-651-2350

Vandeburg-Linkletter Associates
1800 Avenue of the Stars
Los Angeles, California 90067
Tel: 213-879-4040

Vonne Associates Public
   Relations
1801 Avenue of the Stars
Los Angeles, California 90067
Tel: 213-553-1560

Waggoner Public Relations
7188 Sunset Boulevard
Los Angeles, California 90046
Tel: 213-876-1611

Sam Wall
1717 North Highland Avenue
Los Angeles, California 90028
Tel: 213-464-2760

Bill Watters & Associates
1271 St. Ives Place
Los Angeles, California 90069
Tel: 213-272-0148

Norman Winter & Associates
8255 Sunset Boulevard
Los Angeles, California 90046
Tel: 213-654-1473

Carlson Wolcott & Company
520 South Lafayette Park Place
Los Angeles, California 90057
Tel: 213-381-7201

Irwin Zucker
6565 West Sunset Boulevard
Los Angeles, California 90028
Tel: 213-461-3471

San Francisco area:

Wodell & Associates
Hobart Building Tower
Market & Montgomery Streets
San Francisco, California 94104
Tel: 415-391-1350

Illinois:

Harshe-Rotman & Druck
400 East Randolph Street
Chicago, Illinois 60601
Tel: 312-527-3730

Louisiana:

DiMaggio Associates
411 Frenchmen Street
New Orleans, Louisiana 70116
Tel: 504-945-2025

New Jersey:

Sol Abrams Associates, Inc.
1605 Lecmoine Avenue
Fort Lee, New Jersey 07024
Tel: 201-461-5300

New York:

David O. Alber Associates, Inc.
509 Madison Avenue
New York, New York 10022
Tel: 212-838-8300

R. C. Auletta & Co., Inc.
59 East 54th Street
New York, New York 10022
Tel: 212-355-0400

Barnes Associates
1271 Avenue of the Americas
New York, New York 10020
Tel: 212-245-1133

Buddy Basch
25 West 45th Street
New York, New York 10036
Tel: 212-586-7570

Myer P. Beck
729 Seventh Avenue
New York, New York 10019
Tel: 212-245-5552

Bernie Bennett
136 East 56th Street
New York, New York 10022
Tel: 212-751-0600

Paul W. Benson
340 West 57th Street
New York, New York 10019
Tel: 212-757-4635

The Lewis Bernard Company
37 West 57th Street
New York, New York 10019
Tel: 212-421-2650

Jay Bernstein
157 West 57th Street
New York, New York 10019
Tel: 212-489-6745

Billings Associates
250 West 57th Street
New York, New York 10019
Tel: 212-581-4493

Ivan Black
900 West 190th Street
New York, New York 10040
Tel: 212-568-2724

Roy Blumenthal International
  Assoc., Inc.
1 East 57th Street
New York, New York 10022
Tel: 212-838-2930

Mal Braveman
301 East 49th Street
New York, New York 10017
Tel: 212-758-3658

Herbert Breslin
119 West 57th Street
New York, New York 10019
Tel: 212-581-1750

Anita Helen Brooks Associates
155 East 55th Street
New York, New York 10022
Tel: 212-755-4498

Dick Brooks Organization
15 East 48th Street
New York, New York 10017
Tel: 212-751-7770

Gertrude Brooks
35 West 53rd Street
New York, New York 10019
Tel: 212-246-2235

Burke & Corbin Associates, Inc.
295 Madison Avenue
New York, New York 10016
Tel: 212-687-7777

Carl Byoir & Associates, Inc.
800 Second Avenue
New York, New York 10017
Tel: 212-986-6100

Calisch Associates, Inc.
730 Fifth Avenue
New York, New York 10019
Tel: 212-489-8420

Arthur H. Canton, Inc.
1501 Broadway
New York, New York 10036
Tel: 212-947-2445

Barbara Christensen
65 East 55th Street
New York, New York 10022
Tel: 212-593-3370

Nelson Clark, Ltd.
1014 Madison Avenue
New York, New York 10021
Tel: 212-628-1200

Communications Advisors, Inc.
551 Fifth Avenue
New York, New York 10017
Tel: 212-986-4235

Rima Corben
One Lincoln Plaza
New York, New York 10023
Tel: 212-799-9494

Bob Corcoran Associates
15 Minetta Street
New York, New York 10012
Tel: 212-477-2852

Jean Dalrymple Associates
130 West 56th Street
New York, New York 10019
Tel: 212-586-2828

Al Davis Publicity
444 Madison Avenue
New York, New York 10022
Tel: 212-753-4288

Connie De Nave's International
  Media Association
200 West 52nd Street
New York, New York 10019
Tel: 212-586-1330

Thomas J. Deegan, Co., Inc.
Time & Life Building
New York, New York 10020
Tel: 212-757-7070

Ted Deglin & Associates
40 East 80th Street
New York, New York 10021
Tel: 212-988-2797

Marvin Drager, Inc.
420 Madison Avenue
New York, New York 10017
Tel: 212-688-1078

Charlie Earle
250 West 57th Street
New York, New York 10019
Tel: 212-586-6994

Alan Eichler
1545 Broadway
New York, New York 10036
Tel: 212-765-5640

Max Eisen & Co.
234 West 44th Street
New York, New York 10036
Tel: 212-524-0872

Carl Erbe
29 West 56th Street
New York, New York 10019
Tel: 212-581-2710

Richard R. Falk Associates
220 West 42nd Street
New York, New York 10036
Tel: 212-244-5797

Lynn Farnol Group
50 Rockefeller Plaza
New York, New York 10020
Tel: 212-586-5777

Alan Foshko
305 West 52nd Street
New York, New York 10019
Tel: 212-582-2417

Richard Gersh Associates, Inc.
200 West 57th Street
New York, New York 10019
Tel: 212-757-1101

Gibson Stromberg Jaffe
15 West 72nd Street
New York, New York 10023
Tel: 212-799-8500

Gifford/Wallace, Inc.
136 East 96th Street
New York, New York 10028
Tel: 212-427-7600

Frank Goodman
251 West 57th Street
New York, New York 10019
Tel: 212-246-4180

Marian Graham
135 East 50th Street
New York, New York 10022
Tel: 212-753-7110

Peter Gravina
115 East 92nd Street
New York, New York 10028
Tel: 212-369-7086

Milton Gray
165 West 66th Street
New York, New York 10023
Tel: 212-799-6091

Grey & Davis
777 Third Avenue
New York, New York 10017
Tel: 212-752-2200

Gurtman & Murtha
162 West 56th Street
New York, New York 10019
Tel: 212-245-4771

Harsche-Rotman & Druck, Inc.
300 East 44th Street
New York, New York 10017
Tel: 212-661-3400

Kurt Hoffmann
2 West 45th Street
New York, New York 10036
Tel: 212-490-0744

Virginia Holden
4 East 88th Street
New York, New York 10028
Tel: 212-369-1311

Constance Hope Associates
225 West 57th Street
New York, New York 10019
Tel: 212-757-0515

Ted Howard Associates
16 West 55th Street
New York, New York 10019
Tel: 212-586-0946

Betty Lee Hunt
234 West 44th Street
New York, New York 10036
Tel: 212-354-0880

Bernie Ilson
65 West 55th Street
New York, New York 10019
Tel: 212-245-7950

Eddie Jaffe
140 West 55th Street
New York, New York 10019
Tel: 212-245-7355

Jurdem-Thomas Associates
37 West 57th Street
New York, New York 10019
Tel: 212-421-1461

Ade Kahn
250 East 52nd Street
New York, New York 10022
Tel: 212-421-8040

Marvin Kohn
234 West 44th Street
New York, New York 10036
Tel: 212-279-8458

Seymour Krawitz & Company
850 Seventh Avenue
New York, New York 10019
Tel: 212-247-1120

Saul Krieg Associates
488 Madison Avenue
New York, New York 10022
Tel: 212-688-6732

Laurence V. Laurie Associates,
   Inc.
551 Fifth Avenue
New York, New York 10017
Tel: 212-986-7278

Levinson & Associates
10 West 66th Street
New York, New York 10023
Tel: 212-595-3336

Peter Levinson
595 Madison Avenue
New York, New York 10022
Tel: 212-935-1036

Victoria Lucas Associates
1414 Avenue of the Americas
New York, New York 10019
Tel: 212-421-2586

Jim Mahoney & Associates
510 Madison Avenue
New York, New York 10022
Tel: 212-751-2060

Marshall & Bloom Associates, Inc.
7 West 51st Street
New York, New York 10019
Tel: 212-586-7833

Tex McCrary
161 East 61st Street
New York, New York 10021
Tel: 212-838-6220

McFadden, Strauss, Eddy & Irwin
509 Madison Avenue, Suite 1614
New York, New York 10022
Tel: 212-421-7610

Harry K. McWilliams Associates,
   Inc.
19 East 93rd Street
New York, New York 10028
Tel: 212-831-0211

The Mediary
200 West 57th Street
New York, New York 10019
Tel: 212-541-7590

Merlin Group, Ltd.
1560 Broadway
New York, New York 10019
Tel: 212-575-9680

Jan Morgan
250 West 57th Street
New York, New York 10019
Tel: 212-581-7068

Charles A. Moses Company
12 West 55th Street
New York, New York 10019
Tel: 212-757-1900

Howard Newman
250 West 57th Street
New York, New York 10019
Tel: 212-765-2566

Betsy Nolan
515 Madison Avenue
New York, New York 10022
Tel: 212-751-2150

Gustavus Ober Associates
500 East 77th Street
New York, New York 10021
Tel: 212-535-4060

Serge Obolensky Associates, Inc.
1010 Third Avenue
New York, New York 10021
Tel: 212-421-8266

Richard O'Brien
303 West 42nd Street
New York, New York 10036
Tel: 212-246-1970

Larry Penzell
575 Madison Avenue
New York, New York 10022
Tel: 212-759-3890

Bob Perilla Associates, Inc.
250 West 57th Street
New York, New York 10019
Tel: 212-581-5775

Pickwick
370 Lexington Avenue
New York, New York 10017
Tel: 212-889-6443

Arthur Pine
1780 Broadway
New York, New York 10019
Tel: 212-265-7330

Lee Posner
305 West 52nd Street
New York, New York 10019
Tel: 212-247-0715

Sy Presten
29 West 56th Street
New York, New York 10019
Tel: 212-246-9120

Public Relations Corp. of
  America
157 West 57th Street
New York, New York 10019
Tel: 212-757-1444

Harold Rand
919 Third Avenue
New York, New York 10022
Tel: 212-752-7411

Reggie Riccardi
400 East 56th Street
New York, New York 10022
Tel: 212-758-5677

Saul Richfield
200 West 57th Street
New York, New York 10019
Tel: 212-257-5907

Saul Richman
157 West 57th Street
New York, New York 10019
Tel: 212-757-1444

Richard H. Roffman Associates
675 West End Avenue
New York, New York 10025
Tel: 212-749-3647

Rogers, Cowan & Taplinger, Inc.
598 Madison Avenue
New York, New York 10022
Tel: 212-759-6272

Philip I. Ross Co., Inc.
20 Beekman Place
New York, New York 10022
Tel: 212-689-9770

Ruder & Finn, Inc.
110 East 59th Street
New York, New York 10022
Tel: 212-759-1800

David Rush Associates
408 West 57th Street
New York, New York 10019
Tel: 212-581-1036

Joe Russell Associates
218 West 47th Street
New York, New York 10036
Tel: 212-245-4848

Susan L. Schulman
115 West 86th Street
New York, New York 10024
Tel: 212-787-2309

Nancy Seltzer & Associates
140 East 56th Street
New York, New York 10022
Tel: 212-593-3352

Geraldine Shephard Associates
1199 Park Avenue
New York, New York 10028
Tel: 212-876-1040

Gerald Siegal
1650 Broadway
New York, New York 10019
Tel: 212-541-5460

Eve Siegel Associates
35 West 53rd Street
New York, New York 10019
Tel: 212-688-4598

Elinor Silverman
145 West 55th Street
New York, New York 10019
Tel: 212-246-0292

Solters/Sabinson/Roskin, Inc.
62 West 45th Street
New York, New York 10036
Tel: 212-867-8500

Benjamin Sonnenberg
20 Gramercy Park
New York, New York 10003
Tel: 212-986-5400

John Springer Associates, Inc.
667 Madison Avenue
New York, New York 10021
Tel: 212-421-6720

Gary Stevens Associates
42 East 52nd Street
New York, New York 10022
Tel: 212-753-1755

C. J. Strauss & Co.
221 West 57th Street
New York, New York 10019
Tel: 212-582-4102

Herb Streisfield
75 West 68th Street
New York, New York 10023
Tel: 212-873-0521

Marianne Strong Associates
1150 Fifth Avenue
New York, New York 10028
Tel: 212-249-1000

Stutman Associates, Inc.
1790 Broadway
New York, New York 10019
Tel: 212-247-2662

Robert S. Taplinger Associates,
    Inc.
415 Madison Avenue
New York, New York 10017
Tel: 212-752-7722

Jack Tirman Associates, Inc.
111 West 57th Street
New York, New York 10019
Tel: 212-247-7580

Mario Trombone Associates
40 East 49th Street
New York, New York 10017
Tel: 212-752-8660

Lewis Ufland
667 Madison Avenue
New York, New York 10021
Tel: 212-838-5944

Edgar Vincent Associates
156 East 52nd Street
New York, New York 10022
Tel: 212-752-3020

Tom Waller Associates
303 West 42nd Street
New York, New York 10036
Tel: 212-757-1588

Wartoke Concern
1545 Broadway
New York, New York 10036
Tel: 212-245-5587

Morton D. Wax & Associates
200 West 51st Street
New York, New York 10019
Tel: 212-247-2159

Gene Weber
866 United Nations Plaza
New York, New York 10017
Tel: 212-755-1614

Howard Weissman
135 East 50th Street
New York, New York 10022
Tel: 212-688-7262

Weston Associates, Inc.
50 Central Park West
New York, New York 10023
Tel: 212-874-2060

Nan Whitney
35 West 81st Street
New York, New York 10024
Tel: 212-877-6053

Alix B. Williamson
1860 Broadway
New York, New York 10023
Tel: 212-265-1758

Elizabeth Winston
119 West 57th Street
New York, New York 10019
Tel: 212-586-0987

Joe Wolhander, Inc.
211 East 51st Street
New York, New York 10022
Tel: 212-759-2050

Donegan Woods Co., Inc.
400 Madison Avenue
New York, New York 10017
Tel: 212-421-2929

Irving Zussman
60 East 42nd Street
New York, New York 10017
Tel: 212-697-1620

Pennsylvania:

Hal Weissman
1 Bala Avenue
Bala Cynwyd, Pennsylvania
   19004
Tel: 215-839-4017
Tel: 215-667-0582

Publications

The principal publications of the film industry and related segments of the entertainment business are included here.

California:

ACTION
Directors Guild of America
7950 Sunset Boulevard
Los Angeles, California 90046
Tel: 213-656-1220

Academy Players Directory
9011 Melrose Avenue
Los Angeles, California 90069
Tel: 213-278-8990

Advertising Age
6404 Wilshire Boulevard
Los Angeles, California 90048
Henry Bernstein, West Coast
Editor
Tel: 213-651-3710

The American Cinematographer
Published by American Society
of Cinematographers, Inc.
1782 North Orange Drive
Los Angeles, California 90028
Tel: 213-876-5080

American Cinemeditor
422 South Western Avenue
Los Angeles, California 90020
Tel: 213-386-1946

Amusement Business
9000 Sunset Boulevard
Los Angeles, California 90069
Tel: 213-273-7040

Back Stage
6325 Santa Monica Boulevard
Los Angeles, California 90038
Harry Lehman, Editor, West
Coast
Tel: 213-465-3376

Billboard Publications
9000 Sunset Boulevard, Suite
1200
Los Angeles, California 90069
Tel: 213-273-7040

Box Office
6425 Hollywood Boulevard
Los Angeles, California 90028
Tel: 213-465-1186

Branham-Maloney, Inc.,
Directory
4311 Wilshire Boulevard
Los Angeles, California 90010
Tel: 213-937-1930

Broadcasting Magazine
1680 North Vine Street
Los Angeles, California 90028
Tel: 213-463-3148

Broadcasting Magazine Yearbook
1689 North Vine Street
Los Angeles, California 90028
Tel: 213-463-3148

Brooks Standard Rate Book
1487 Glendon Avenue
Los Angeles, California 90024
Stanley Brooks, Editor
Tel: 213-651-4220

Business Screen
1901 West Eighth Street
Los Angeles, California 90057
Tel: 213-483-8530

Cash Box Magazine
6565 Sunset Boulevard
Los Angeles, California 90028
Tel: 213-469-2966

Celebrity Bulletin
8746 Sunset Boulevard
Los Angeles, California 90069
Tel: 213-652-1700

Cine/Grafic Publications
P.O. Box 430
Los Angeles, California 90028
Tel: 213-462-8670

Cinema Magazine
9667 Wilshire Boulevard
Beverly Hills, California 90212
Tel: 213-276-1578

Contact Book
8746 Sunset Boulevard
Los Angeles, California 90069
Tel: 213-652-1700

Daily Variety
1400 North Cahuenga Boulevard
Los Angeles, California 90028
Tel: 213-469-1141

Directors Guild of America
   Directory of Members
7590 Sunset Boulevard
Los Angeles, California 90046
Tel: 213-656-1220

Downbeat
6311 Yucca Street
Los Angeles, California 90028
Tel: 213-465-0119

Educational Broadcasting Journal
825 South Barrington Avenue
Los Angeles, California 90049
Ms. Bobby Atchison, West Coast
   Editor
Tel: 213-826-8388

Fame
1909 Manning Avenue
Los Angeles, California 90025
Dale Munroe, West Coast Editor
Tel: 213-474-4642

Film Quarterly
University of California Press
Berkeley, California 94720
Tel: 415-642-6333

Gambit
4400 Sunset Drive
Los Angeles, California 90027
Tel: 213-666-6500

Hollywood Film Production
   Manual
1036 North Avon Street
Burbank, California 91505
Tel: 213-848-1975

The Hollywood Reporter
6715 Sunset Boulevard
Los Angeles, California 90028
Tel: 213-464-7411

Hollywood Studio Magazine
Valley Hilton Hotel
15433 Ventura Boulevard
Sherman Oaks, California 91403
Tel: 213-789-9858

Hollywood Talent News
6223 Selma Avenue
Los Angeles, California 90028
Tel: 213-465-1011

International Motion Picture
  Almanac
1909 Manning Avenue
Los Angeles, California 90025
Tel: 213-474-4642

International Photographer
7715 Sunset Boulevard
Los Angeles, California 90046
Tel: 213-876-0160

Kemp's Film & Television
  Yearbook
2001 The Alameda
P.O. Box 6227
San Jose, California 95150
Tel: 408-296-1060

M.A.C. Western Advertising
6565 Sunset Boulevard
Los Angeles, California 90028
Tel: 213-465-2173

Modern Theatres
6425 Hollywood Boulevard
Los Angeles, California 90028
Tel: 213-465-1186

Movie Scope Magazine
6561 Santa Monica Boulevard
Los Angeles, California 90038
Tel: 213-461-1321

Pacific Coast Studio Directory
6331 Hollywood Boulevard
Los Angeles, California 90028
Tel: 213-467-2920

Record World Magazine
6290 Sunset Boulevard
Los Angeles, California 90028
Tel: 213-465-6126

Screen Actor
7750 Sunset Boulevard
Los Angeles, California 90046
Tel: 213-876-3030

Standard Rate & Data Service,
  Inc.
2975 Wilshire Boulevard
Los Angeles, California 90010
Tel: 213-383-4103

Studio Blu-Book
7046 Hollywood Boulevard
Los Angeles, California 90028
Tel: 213-464-0973

Talent News
6223 Selma Avenue
Los Angeles, California 90028
Tel: 213-465-6184

Theatrical Variety Publications
6855 Ben Avenue
North Hollywood, California
  91605
Tel: 213-764-2038

Variety
1400 North Cahuenga Boulevard
Los Angeles, California 90028
Tel: 213-469-1141

Videocassette Industry Guide
13273 Ventura Boulevard
Studio City, California 91604
Stephen Edward Poe,
   Editor-Publisher
Tel: 213-981-7100

West Coast Theatrical Directory
2001 The Alameda
P.O. Box 6227
San Jose, California 95150
Tel: 408-296-1060

Writers Guild Newsletter
P.O. Box 1644
Beverly Hills, California 90213
Tel: 213-276-4974

Illinois:

Cinefantastique
P.O. Box 270
Oak Park, Illinois 60303
Frederick S. Clarke,
   Editor/Publisher

Variety
400 North Michigan Avenue
Chicago, Illinois 60611
Tel: 312-337-4984

New York:

Ad Daily
400 East 54th Street
New York, New York 10022·
Tel: 212-421-3713

Advertising Age
708 Third Avenue
New York, New York 10017
Tel: 212-986-5050

Back Stage
165 West 46th Street
New York, New York 10036
Tel: 212-581-1080

Back Stage Film and Television
   Festival World Wide Directory
165 West 46th Street
New York, New York 10036
Tel: 212-581-1080

Back Stage Television, Film,
   Tape and Syndication
   Directory
165 West 46th Street
New York, New York 10036
Tel: 212-581-1080

Billboard
1 Astor Plaza
New York, New York 10036
Tel: 212-764-7300

Boxoffice
1270 Sixth Avenue, Room 2403
New York, New York 10020
Tel: 212-265-6370

Broadcasting
7 West 51st Street
New York, New York 10019
Tel: 212-757-3260

Business Screen
757 Third Avenue
New York, New York 10017
Tel: 212-754-4385

Cash Box
119 West 57th Street
New York, New York 10019
Tel: 212-586-2640

Catholic Film Newsletter
1011 First Avenue, Suite 1300
New York, New York 10022
Tel: 212-644-1880

Celebrity Bulletin
171 West 57th Street
New York, New York 10019
Tel: 212-757-7979

Contact Book
171 West 57th Street
New York, New York 10019
Tel: 212-757-7979

Downbeat
72 Green Avenue
Brooklyn, New York 11238
Tel: 212-857-0080

Editor & Publisher
850 Third Avenue
New York, New York 10022
Tel: 212-752-7050

Equity News
165 West 46th Street
New York, New York 10036
Tel: 212-757-7660

Fame
1270 Sixth Avenue
New York, New York 10020
Tel: 212-247-3100

Film Bulletin
1 East 42nd Street
New York, New York 10017
Tel: 212-661-8563

Film Comment
1865 Broadway
New York, New York 10036
Tel: 212-765-5100

Film News
250 West 57th Street
New York, New York 10019
Tel: 212-581-3596

Films in Review (Published by
    National Board of Review)
210 East 68th Street
New York, New York 10021
Tel: 212-988-4916

Greater Amusements and
    International Projectionist
1600 Broadway, Suite 514-D
New York, New York 10019
Tel: 212-246-4282

Hollywood Reporter
229 West 42nd Street
New York, New York 10036
Tel: 212-947-2470

IATSE Official Bulletin
1270 Avenue of the Americas
New York, New York 10020
Tel: 212-245-4369

The Independent Film Journal
1251 Avenue of the Americas,
    Suite 1179
New York, New York 10020
Tel: 212-246-6460

International Motion Picture
    Almanac
1270 Sixth Avenue
New York, New York 10020
Tel: 212-247-3100

Journal of the Society of Motion
  Picture and Television
  Engineers
Editorial Office; SMPTE
  Headquarters
862 Scarsdale Avenue
Scarsdale, New York 10583
Tel: 914-472-6606

Literary Market Place
1180 Avenue of the Americas
New York, New York 10036
Tel: 212-571-8800

Madison Avenue Handbook
17 East 48th Street
New York, New York 10017
Tel: 212-688-7940

Media News Keys
150 Fifth Avenue
New York, New York 10011
Tel: 212-924-0320

Motion Picture Product Digest
1270 Sixth Avenue
New York, New York 10020
Tel: 212-247-3100

Motion Picture, TV and Theatre
  Directory
Tarrytown, New York 10591
Motion Picture Enterprises
  Publications, Inc.
Warehouse: 432 West 45th Street
New York, NY, 10036
Tel: 212-245-0969

New Film Ventures
NFV Publishing Company
600 Madison Avenue
New York, New York 10022
Tel: 212-688-4480

Photography Market Place
Bowker Company, R. R.
1180 Avenue of the Americas
New York, New York 10036
Tel: 212-571-8800

Players' Guide
165 West 46th Street
New York, New York 10036
Tel: 212-245-8037

Public Relations Quarterly
305 East 45th Street
New York, New York 10017
Tel: 212-686-4100

Publishers Weekly
1180 Avenue of the Americas
New York, New York 10036
Tel: 212-764-5100

Ross Reports
Television Index, Inc.
150 Fifth Avenue
New York, New York 10011
Tel: 212-924-0320

Screen World
190 Riverside Drive
New York, New York 10024
Tel: 212-877-2154

Show Business
136 West 44th Street
New York, New York 10036
Tel: 212-586-6900

Television-Radio Age
666 Fifth Avenue
New York, New York 10019
Tel: 212-757-8400

Theatre World
190 Riverside Drive
New York, New York 10024
Tel: 212-877-2154

Theatrical Calendar
171 West 57th Street
New York, New York 10019
Tel: 212-757-7979

Variety
154 West 46th Street
New York, New York 10036
Tel: 212-582-2700

Writers' Newsletter
Madison Square Station
P.O. Box 251
New York, New York 10010
Tel: 212-254-8140

Washington:

"Movietone News"
Seattle Film Society
5236 Eighteenth Avenue, N.E.
Seattle, Washington 98105

Recording Studios

The studios included here are able to cope with the special requirements motion picture sound recording.

Arizona:

Arcoa International
2727 North Central Avenue
Phoenix, Arizona 85004
Tel: 602-263-6641

Copper State Recording
Company
815 Broadway
Tucson, Arizona 85719
Tel: 602-623-0318

Craig Pease Enterprises
P.O. Box 1118
Scottsdale, Arizona 85252
Tel: 602-945-4807

Spencer-Alquist Audio
6252 East Twentieth Street
Tucson, Arizona 85711
Tel: 602-886-2353

Swartwout Film Productions
6736 East Avalon Drive
Scottsdale, Arizona 85252
Tel: 602-945-8496

California:
Los Angeles area:

A & B Studios
9454 Wilshire Boulevard
Beverly Hills, California 90212
Tel: 213-278-2600

A D Recording Studio
1012 Oak Street
Burbank, California 91506
Tel: 213-848-9004

ADS Audio Visual Productions,
Inc.
1610 Argyle Avenue
Los Angeles, California 90038
Tel: 213-465-3672

Able Turntable
717 North Highland Avenue
Los Angeles, California 90038
Tel: 213-933-5701

Ace Playback
7834 Laurel Canyon Bouleva
North Hollywood, California
91605
Tel: 213-464-8311

Akkad International Production
Inc.
8730 Sunset Boulevard
Los Angeles, California 90069
Tel: 213-657-7670

American Recording Studio
11386 Ventura Boulevard
Studio City, California 91604
Tel: 213-769-5539

Ametron/American Electronics
  Supply, Inc.
1200 North Vine Street
Los Angeles, California 90038
Tel: 213-466-4321

Amigo Studios
11114 Cumpston Avenue
North Hollywood, California
  91601
Tel: 213-763-4396

Annex Studios
1032 North Sycamore Avenue
Los Angeles, California 90038
Tel: 213-464-7441

Artisan Sound Recorders
6430 Sunset Boulevard
Los Angeles, California 90028
Tel: 213-461-2751

Ascot Recording Studio
5904 Sunset Boulevard
Los Angeles, California 90028
Tel: 213-466-8355

Audio Arts Group
5611 Melrose Avenue
Los Angeles, California 90038
Tel: 213-469-5103

Audio Effects Company
1600 North Western Avenue
Los Angeles, California 90027
Tel: 213-469-3692

Audio Services/Mobile Sound
  Studios
3239 Cahuenga Boulevard West
Los Angeles, California 90028
Tel: 213-467-0152

Audio Tran
923 North Cole Avenue
Los Angeles, California 90038
Tel: 213-464-8307

B & B Productions
1313 North Vine Street
Los Angeles, California 90028
Tel: 213-461-3388

Bell Sound Studio
916 North Citrus Avenue
Los Angeles, California 90038
Tel: 213-461-3036

Mel Blanc Studios, Audiomedia
9454 Wilshire Boulevard, Room
  305
Beverly Hills, California 90212
Tel: 213-278-2600

The Burbank Studios
4000 Warner Boulevard
Burbank, California 91522
Tel: 213-843-6000

Buzzy's Recording Services
8719 Santa Monica Boulevard
Los Angeles, California 90069
Tel: 213-659-5444

Capitol Custom Services
1750 North Vine Street
Los Angeles, California 90028
Tel: 213-462-6252

Chappell Music Company
6255 Sunset Boulevard
Los Angeles, California 90028
Tel: 213-469-5141

Cherokee Ranch Recording
Studios
7235 Hollywood Boulevard, Suite
221
Los Angeles, California 90046
Tel: 213-998-8008

Cine Group
8560 Sunset Boulevard
Los Angeles, California 90069
Tel: 213-652-4800

Cinema "35" Center, Inc.
850 Colorado Boulevard
Los Angeles, California 90041
Tel: 213-255-1296

Cinesound
915 North Highland Avenue
Los Angeles, California 90038
Tel: 213-464-1155

Citadel Productions
6603 Independence
Canoga Park, California 91303
Tel: 213-348-4424

Clover Recorders
6232 Santa Monica Boulevard
Los Angeles, California 90038
Tel: 213-463-2371

Columbia Recording Studio, Inc.
6121 West Sunset Boulevard
Los Angeles, California 90028
Tel: 213-466-2481

Consolidated Film Industries
959 North Seward Street
Los Angeles, California 90038
Tel: 213-462-3161

Conway Recorders
655 North Saint Andrews Place
Los Angeles, California 90004
Tel: 213-463-2175

Crystal Recording Studios
1014 North Vine Street
Los Angeles, California 90028
Tel: 213-466-6453

Custom Fidelity, Inc.
7925 Santa Monica Boulevard
Los Angeles, California 90046
Tel: 213-654-4522

Custom Recorders
5530 Cahuenga Boulevard
North Hollywood, California
91601
Tel: 213-877-2557

Custom Recording Studio
5810 South Normandie
Los Angeles, California 90044
Tel: 213-753-5121

D C T Recorders
6414 Sunset Boulevard
Los Angeles, California 90028
Tel: 213-461-2841

Decca-Universal Recording
Studios
100 Universal City Plaza
Universal City, California 91608
Tel: 213-985-4321

Devonshire Prods
10729 Magnolia Boulevard
North Hollywood, California
91601
Tel: 213-985-1945

Edit-Rite
1213 North Highland Avenue
Los Angeles, California 90038
Tel: 213-465-6117

Richard Einfeld, Inc.
1512 North Las Palmas Avenue
Los Angeles, California 90028
Tel: 213-461-3731

El Dorado Recording Studio
1717 North Vine Street
Los Angeles, California 90028
Tel: 213-467-6151

Embassy Sound Productions
847 South Grand Avenue
Los Angeles, California 90017
Tel: 213-623-3266

Fat Chance Studios, Inc.
18434 Oxnard Street
Tarzana, California 91356
Tel: 213-342-2300

Film Technology Company, Inc.
6900 Santa Monica Boulevard
Los Angeles, California 90038
Tel: 213-465-4908

Gemini Recording
3374 Bennett Drive
Los Angeles, California 90068
Tel: 213-851-4844

General Music Corporation
6410 Willoughby Avenue
Los Angeles, California 90038
Tel: 213-462-0715

Glen Glenn Sound Corporation
6624 Romaine Street
Los Angeles, California 90038
Tel: 213-462-7221

Gold Star Productions
6252 Santa Monica Boulevard
Los Angeles, California 90038
Tel: 213-467-5132

Samuel Goldwyn Studios
1041 North Formosa Avenue
Los Angeles, California 90046
Tel: 213-851-1234

Gramophone Records Company
Box 921
Beverly Hills, California 90213
Tel: 213-276-2726

Harmony Recorders
6263 Leland Way
Los Angeles, California 90028
Tel: 213-463-2347

Wally Heider Recording
1604 North Cahuenga Boulevard
Los Angeles, California 90028
Tel: 213-466-5474

Hope Street Studio
805 1/2 Brent Avenue
South Pasadena, California 91030
Tel: 213-441-3044

I D Sound Studios, Inc.
1556 North La Brea Avenue
Los Angeles, California 90028
Tel: 213-462-6477

Independent Producers Service
7370 Melrose Avenue
Los Angeles, California 90046
Tel: 213-655-3599

Independent Recording Service
4028 Colfax Avenue
Studio City, California 91604
Tel: 213-877-2797

Jalmia Enterprises, Inc.
2715 Jalmia Drive
Los Angeles, California 90046
Tel: 213-874-3349

Kendun Recorders
619 South Glenwood Place
Burbank, California 91506
Tel: 213-849-6336

Bruce Kirby Sound Engineering
1016 North Highland Avenue
Los Angeles, California 90038
Tel: 213-462-6000

Larrabee Sound Recording
8811 Santa Monica Boulevard
Los Angeles, California 90069
Tel: 213-986-3994

C. P. MacGregor Recording
  Studios
729 South Western Avenue
Los Angeles, California 90005
Tel: 213-384-4191

Magnesonic Recording, Inc.
1680 North Vine Street
Los Angeles, California 90028
Tel: 213-469-1062

Major Independent Film Studios
1207 North Western Avenue
Los Angeles, California 90029
Tel: 213-461-2721

Manny's Filmmaker's Services
1135 North Cole Street
Los Angeles, California 90038
Tel: 213-464-4537

Mark Recording Studios
5505 Melrose
Los Angeles, California 90028
Tel: 213-467-7103

Matrix Image
6622 Variel Avenue
Canoga Park, California 91303
Tel: 213-883-6622

Metro-Goldwyn-Mayer, Inc.
10202 West Washington
  Boulevard
Culver City, California 90230
Tel: 213-836-3000

Movie Tech, Inc.
6518 Santa Monica Boulevard
Los Angeles, California 90038
Tel: 213-467-8491

Nagra Magnetic Recorders, Inc.
1147 North Vine Street
Los Angeles, California 90038
Tel: 213-469-6391

Newjack Sound Recorders
1717 North Highland Avenue
Los Angeles, California 90028
Tel: 213-466-6141

Parasound, Inc.
2825 Hyans Street
Los Angeles, California 90026
Tel: 213-462-3311

Producers Sound Service, Inc.
1223 North Highland Avenue
Los Angeles, California 90038
Tel: 213-462-6535

The Production Company, Inc.
8612 West Pico Boulevard
Los Angeles, California 90035
Tel: 213-659-3940

Quad-Teck Recording Studios,
    Ltd.
4007 West Sixth Street
Los Angeles, California 90020
Tel: 213-383-2155

Quality Sound, Inc.
5625 Melrose Avenue
Los Angeles, California 90038
Tel: 213-467-7154

RCA Records
6363 Sunset Boulevard
Los Angeles, California 90028
Tel: 213-461-9171

Ralke Company, Inc.
641 North Highland Avenue
Los Angeles, California 90036
Tel: 213-933-7111

Record Plant
8456–60 West Third Street
Los Angeles, California 90048
Tel: 213-653-0240

Rex Recording Studios
3041 East Gage Avenue
Huntington Park, California
    90255
Tel: 213-581-2774

Ryder Sound Services, Inc.
1161 North Vine Street
Los Angeles, California 90038
Tel: 213-469-3511

S & S Sound Company
6518 Santa Monica Boulevard
Los Angeles, California 90038
Tel: 213-467-8491

Sage & Sand Recording Studio
1511 Gordon Street
Los Angeles, California 90028
Tel: 213-469-1527

Al Schmitt
6671 Sunset Boulevard
Los Angeles, California 90028
Tel: 213-466-8556

Scottsound, Inc.
6110 Santa Monica Boulevard
Los Angeles, California 90038
Tel: 213-462-6981

The Silvery Moon Studios
326 1/2 North La Cienega
    Boulevard
Los Angeles, California 90048
Tel: 213-652-9255

Skyline Productions, Inc.
5609 Sunset Boulevard
Los Angeles, California 90028
Tel: 213-461-9271

Sound City, Inc.
15456 Cabrito Road
Van Nuys, California 91406
Tel: 213-787-3722

Sound Factory, Inc.
6357 Selma Avenue
Los Angeles, California 90028
Tel: 213-461-3096

Sound Services, Inc.
623 North La Cienega Boulevard
Los Angeles, California 90069
Tel: 213-653-3550

Sunset Editorial Enterprises
Colgems Square
Burbank, California 91505
Tel: 213-843-6000

Sunset Sound Recorders
6650 Sunset Boulevard
Los Angeles, California 90028
Tel: 213-469-1186

Sunwest Recording Studios, Inc.
5539 Sunset Boulevard
Los Angeles, California 90028
Tel: 213-466-9611

TV Recorders
6054 Sunset Boulevard
Los Angeles, California 90028
Tel: 213-469-8201

Tangerine Recording Studio
2107 West Washington Boulevard
Los Angeles, California 90018
Tel: 213-737-8000

Telaudio Centre
634 South Victory Boulevard
Burbank, California 91502
Tel: 213-876-3575

Theatratec
1237 Tenth Street
Santa Monica, California 90403
Tel: 213-395-6097

Todd-AO Corporation
1021 North Seward Street
Los Angeles, California 90038
Tel: 213-463-1136

United Artists Recording Studio
8715 West Third Street
Los Angeles, California 90048
Tel: 213-272-4483

United Recording Corporation
6050 Sunset Boulevard
Los Angeles, California 90028
Tel: 213-469-3983

Universal City Studios
100 Universal City Plaza
Universal City, California 91608
Tel: 213-985-4321

Valentine Recording Studios
5330 Laurel Canyon Boulevard
North Hollywood, California
    91607
Tel: 213-769-1515

Video Tape Mobile
Box 921
Beverly Hills, California 90213
Tel: 213-276-2726

Video View, Inc.
1617 North El Centro Avenue
Los Angeles, California 90028
Tel: 213-463-4179

The Village Recorder
1616 Butler Avenue
West Los Angeles, California
  90025
Tel: 213-478-8227

Watermark, Inc.
10700 Ventura Boulevard
North Hollywood, California
  91604
Tel: 213-980-9490

Western Recorders
6000 Sunset Boulevard
Los Angeles, California 90028
Tel: 213-463-6811

Whitney Recording Studio, Inc.
1516 West Glenoaks Boulevard
Glendale, California 91201
Tel: 213-245-6801

Glenn S. Winters Productions
8236 Blackburn Avenue
Los Angeles, California 90048
Tel: 213-653-3352

San Francisco area:

ALEMBIC, Inc.
60 Brady Street
San Francisco, California 94103
Tel: 415-864-3800

American Zoetrope, Inc.
American Zoetrope Film Facility
827 Folsom Street
San Francisco, California 94107
Tel: 415-989-0600

Marvin Becker Film-Maker
2111 California Street
San Francisco, California 94115
Tel: 415-567-2160

Roy Chen Recording Studios
130 Waverly Place
San Francisco, California 94108
Tel: 415-989-4004

Coast Recorders, Inc.
829 Folsom Street
San Francisco, California 94107
Tel: 415-397-7676

Leo Diner Films, Inc.
332–350 Golden Gate
San Francisco, California 94102
Tel: 415-775-3664

Edit Center
155 Fell Street
San Francisco, California 94102
Tel: 415-864-4644

Films for Information
190 California Avenue
Palo Alto, California 94306
Tel: 415-328-6516

James Flocker Enterprises, Inc.
3080 La Selva
San Mateo, California 94403
Tel: 415-349-8000

Funky Features Recording
142 Central
San Francisco, California 94117
Tel: 415-621-2646

Furman Films
3466 21st Street
San Francisco, California 94110
Tel: 415-282-1300

Gambit Enterprises
119 Cuesta Drive
South San Francisco, California
94080
Tel: 415-589-9158

Adolph Gasser, Inc.
5733 Geary Boulevard
San Francisco, California 92421
Tel: 415-751-0145

Wally Heider Recording
245 Hyde Street
San Francisco, California 94102
Tel: 415-771-5780

The Lacquer Channel, Inc.
2829 Bridgeway
Sausalito, California 94965
Tel: 415-332-6080

Mantra Corporation
2207 South El Camino Real
San Mateo, California 94403
Tel: 415-574-1500

Harry McCune Sound Service,
Inc.
951 Howard Street
San Francisco, California 94103
Tel: 415-777-2700

Motion Picture Service Company
125 Hyde Street
San Francisco, California 94102
Tel: 415-673-9162

Newcomb Recording Studio
4834 Bissell Avenue
Richmond, California 94805
Tel: 415-233-7487

Don Palmer Studios
563 Second Street
San Francisco, California 94107
Tel: 415-392-4449

W. A. Palmer Films, Inc.
611 Howard Street
San Francisco, California 94105
Tel: 415-986-5961

Pre-Dawn Enterprises, Inc.
501 Litho Street
Sausalito, California 94965
Tel: 415-332-5160

Pro-Tonics Company
2199 South El Camino Real
San Mateo, California 94403
Tel: 415-574-8511

Record Plant
2200 Bridgeway
Sausalito, California 94969
Tel: 415-332-6100

Sierra Sound Labs
1741 Alcatraz Avenue
Berkeley, California 94703
Tel: 415-655-7636

Skinner Studio
345 Sutter Street
San Francisco, California 94108
Tel: 415-986-5040

Snazelle Films, Inc.
155 Fell Street
San Francisco, California 94102
Tel: 415-431-5490

Sound Genesis, Inc.
445 Bryant Street
San Francisco, California 94107
Tel: 415-391-8776

The Sound Service
55 Stevenson Street
San Francisco, California 94105
Tel: 415-433-3674

Studio 16, Inc.
2135 Powell Street
San Francisco, California 94133
Tel: 415-982-2097

Colorado:

E. K. Edwards & Son Inc.
P.O. Box 22361
Denver, Colorado 80222
Tel: 303-757-5130

Jackson Sound Productions Ltd.
1401 South Lipan
Denver, Colorado 80223
Tel: 303-722-7019

Western Cine Service, Inc.
312 South Pearl Street
Denver, Colorado 80209
Tel: 303-744-1017

District of Columbia:

Byron Motion Pictures, Inc.
65 K Street, N.E.
Washington, D.C. 20002
Tel: 202-783-2700

Capital Film Laboratories, Inc.
470 East Street, S.W.
Washington, D.C. 20003
Tel: 202-347-1717

Koster Film Facilities, Inc.
1017 New Jersey Avenue, S.E.
Washington, D.C. 20003
Tel: 202-544-4410

Washington Film Laboratories,
   Inc.
1042 Wisconsin Avenue, N.W.
Washington, D.C. 20007
Tel: 202-333-1162

Florida:

American Sound Arts
983 S.W. First Street
Miami, Florida 33101
Tel: 305-377-2081

Cinema Sound, Inc.
1755 N.E. 149th Street
North Miami, Florida 33161
Tel: 305-949-8611

Criteria Recording, Inc.
1755 N.E. 149th Street
North Miami, Florida 33161
Tel: 305-947-5611

Film Sound, Inc.
1755 N.E. 149th Street
Miami, Florida 33101
Tel: 305-949-8611

Reela Film Lab., Inc.
65 N.W. Third Street
Miami, Florida 33161
Tel: 305-377-2611

Warren Sound Systems, Inc.
35 N.E. 62nd Street
Miami, Florida 33101
Tel: 305-754-9539

Georgia:

Acoustic Recording Co.
1279 Spring Street, N.W.
Atlanta, Georgia 30309
Tel: 404-872-2083

Doppler Studios, Inc.
417 Peachtree Street, N.E.
Atlanta, Georgia 30308
Tel: 404-873-6941

Kin-Tel Productions
1200 Spring Street, N.E.
Atlanta, Georgia 30309
Tel: 404-874-3668

Mastersound Recording Studios
1227 Spring Street
Atlanta, Georgia 30309
Tel: 404-873-6425

Sound Pit
125 Simpson Street
Atlanta, Georgia 30313
Tel: 404-522-8460

Trolly Tracks
3759 Main Street
Atlanta, Georgia 30337
Tel: 404-768-0057

Viscount Productions, Inc.
650 Miami Circle
Atlanta, Georgia 30324
Tel: 404-261-6241

Hawaii:

Commercial Recording, Inc.
333 Cooke Street
Honolulu, Hawaii 96813
Tel: 808-536-5439

The House of Eric Productions
1760 Ala Moana Boulevard
Waikiki, Hawaii 96815
Tel: 808-533-3877

Sounds of Hawaii
1084 Young Street
Honolulu, Hawaii 96814
Tel: 808-537-1442

Illinois:

Audio Arts
429 East St. Charles
Carol Stream, Illinois 60611
Tel: 312-668-6682

Audio Finishers, Inc.
46 East Walton Street
Chicago, Illinois 60611
Tel: 312-642-6465

Audio Mixers Recording
  Company
740 North Rush Street
Chicago, Illinois 60611
Tel: 312-943-4274

Barwig Recording Company
5254 West Agatite Avenue
Chicago, Illinois 60630
Tel: 312-283-2820

Boulevard Recording Studios,
  Inc.
609 North La Salle Street
Chicago, Illinois 60610
Tel: 312-944-2752

George W. Colburn Laboratory
164 North Wacker Drive
Chicago, Illinois 60606
Tel: 312-332-6286

Columbia Record Productions,
  CBS
630 North McClurg Court
Chicago, Illinois 60611
Tel: 312-944-6000

Consolidated Film Industries
222 East Chestnut Street
Chicago, Illinois 60611
Tel: 312-641-0028

Custom Audio, Inc.
110 South River Road
Des Plaines, Illinois 60016
Tel: 312-298-6680

db Studios, Inc.
676 North La Salle Street
Chicago, Illinois 60610
Tel: 312-944-3600

Downie Productions, Inc.
1920 North Lincoln Avenue
Chicago, Illinois 60614
Tel: 312-787-6822

Editel, Inc.
1920 North Lincoln Avenue
Chicago, Illinois 60614
Tel: 312-649-9707

Genesis Recording, Inc.
645 North St. Clair Street
Chicago, Illinois 60611
Tel: 312-649-5711

Glen-Warren Productions Ltd.
528 North Michigan Avenue
Chicago, Illinois 60611
Tel: 312-321-0494

International Recording Co.
1649 West Evergreen Avenue
Chicago, Illinois 60622
Tel: 312-227-2000

Robert L. Link, Inc.
600 North McClurg Court
Chicago, Illinois 60611
Tel: 312-664-8875

MBS Recording Studios
228 South Wabash Avenue
Chicago, Illinois 60604
Tel: 312-939-0866

Mills Recording Company
32 North State Street
Chicago, Illinois 60602
Tel: 312-332-4117

Paragon Recording Studios
9 East Huron Street
Chicago, Illinois 60611
Tel: 312-664-2412

Pinnn
40 East Erie Street
Chicago, Illinois 60611
Tel: 312-787-8432

George M. Ricci & Associates
625 North Michigan Avenue
Chicago, Illinois 60611
Tel: 312-787-5221

Sonic Film Recording, Inc.
1230 West Washington Boulevard
Chicago, Illinois 60607
Tel: 312-666-1220

Sound Haus, Ltd.
1026 Busse Highway
Park Ridge, Illinois 60068
Tel: 312-696-0610

Sound House, Inc.
22 West 381 Hillcrest Terrace
Medinah, Illinois 60157
Tel: 312-529-1001

Sound Market Recording Co.
664 North Michigan Avenue
Chicago, Illinois 60611
Tel: 312-664-4335

Sound Studios, Inc.
230 North Michigan Avenue
Chicago, Illinois 60611
Tel: 312-236-4814

Streeterville Studios, Inc.
161 East Grand Avenue
Chicago, Illinois 60611
Tel: 312-644-1666

Studio One, Inc.
430 North Michigan Avenue
Chicago, Illinois 60611
Tel: 312-337-5111

Tyler Recording & Film Services
5 West Hubbard Street
Chicago, Illinois 60610
Tel: 312-467-1456

Uniprocessors, Inc.
5 East Huron Street
Chicago, Illinois 60611
Tel: 312-266-0909

Universal Recording Corporation
46 East Walton Street
Chicago, Illinois 60611
Tel: 312-642-6465

WGN Continental Productions
Co.
2501 Bradley Place
Chicago, Illinois 60618
Tel: 312-528-2311

Webb Recording Company
812 North Dearborn Street
Chicago, Illinois 60610
Tel: 312-664-0705

Zenith Cinema Service, Inc.
3252 West Foster Avenue
Chicago, Illinois 60625
Tel: 312-478-2103

Kansas:

High Fidelity Recording
1059 Porter
Wichita, Kansas 67203
Tel: 316-262-6456

Montana:

Valtron Recording Studio
305 Allen Street
Helena, Montana 59601
Tel: 406-442-0734

Nebraska:

UPC Recording
2322 South 64th Avenue
Omaha, Nebraska 68106
Tel: 402-558-5770

Nevada:

Vic Beri Management–Vegas
   Music International, Inc.
3143 Industrial Road
Las Vegas, Nevada 89102
Tel: 702-732-1994

New York:

6 West Recording, Inc.
6 West 57th Street
New York, New York 10019
Tel: 212-246-7959

A-1 Sound Studios, Inc.
242 West 76th Street
New York, New York 10023
Tel: 212-362-2603

A & R Recording, Inc.
322 West 48th Street
New York, New York 10036
Tel: 212-582-1070

Ani-Live Film Service
45 West 45th Street
New York, New York 10036
Tel: 212-247-1800

Artscope, Ltd.
310 West 53rd Street
New York, New York 10019
Tel: 212-265-7420

Audio Transfers, Inc.
254 West 54th Street
New York, New York 10019
Tel: 212-265-6225

Aura Recording, Inc.
136 West 52nd Street
New York, New York 10019
Tel: 212-582-8105

Bell Sound Studios
237 West 54th Street
New York, New York 10019
Tel: 212-582-4812

Broadway Recording Studios
1697 Broadway
New York, New York 10019
Tel: 212-247-1690

Capitol Records, Inc.
1370 Avenue of the Americas
New York, New York 10019
Tel: 212-757-7470

Cine-Mix Corporation
1156 Avenue of the Americas
New York, New York 10036
Tel: 212-869-0100

Cinema Recording Corporation
21 West 46th Street
New York, New York 10036
Tel: 212-582-3744

Cinema/Sound, Ltd.
156 West 45th Street
New York, New York 10036
Tel: 212-687-5484

Columbia Records
49 East 52nd Street
New York, New York 10022
Tel: 212-765-4321

Cue Recordings, Inc.
1156 Avenue of the Americas
New York, New York 10036
Tel: 212-757-3641

Dimensional Sound, Inc.
245 West 55th Street
New York, New York 10019
Tel: 212-247-6010

East Coast Productions, Inc.
16 West 46th Street
New York, New York 10036
Tel: 212-765-4556

Don Elliot Studios
80 West 40th Street
New York, New York 10018
Tel: 212-524-9677

Eteilla Enterprises, Inc.
289 Church Street
New York, New York 10013
Tel: 212-431-8560

Fine Recording, Inc.
118 West 57th Street
New York, New York 10019
Tel: 212-245-6969

Generation Sound Studios
1650 Broadway
New York, New York 10019
Tel: 212-765-7400

Gotham Recording Corporation
2 West 46th Street
New York, New York 10036
Tel: 212-586-5577

Groove Sound
240 West 55th Street
New York, New York 10019
Tel: 212-581-4680

Hit Factory, Inc.
353 West 48th Street
New York, New York 10036
Tel: 212-581-9590

Image Sound Studio, Inc.
1619 Broadway
New York, New York 10019
Tel: 212-581-6717

Magno Recording Studios, Inc.
212 West 48th Street
New York, New York 10036
Tel: 212-757-8855

Manhattan Sound Studios
17 East 45th Street
New York, New York 10017
Tel: 212-757-9800

Mayfair Recording Studio, Inc.
701 Seventh Avenue
New York, New York 10036
Tel: 212-581-2178

Mediasound Studios
311 West 57th Street
New York, New York 10019
Tel: 212-765-4700

Charles Michelson, Inc.
45 West 45th Street
New York, New York 10036
Tel: 212-757-0695

Music Sound Track Service
1600 Broadway
New York, New York 10019
Tel: 212-246-4687

National Recording Studios
730 Fifth Avenue
New York, New York 10019
Tel: 212-757-6440

Olmstead Sound Studios, Inc.
80 West 40th Street
New York, New York 10018
Tel: 212-868-3342

RCA Records
110 West 44th Street
New York, New York 10036
Tel: 212-598-5900

RKO Sound Studios
1440 Broadway
New York, New York 10018
Tel: 212-764-6600

Record Plant
321 West 44th Street
New York, New York 10036
Tel: 212-581-6505

Reeves Cinetel, Inc.
304 East 44th Street
New York, New York 10017
Tel: 212-679-3550

Ross-Gaffney, Inc.
21 West 46th Street
New York, New York 10036
Tel: 212-582-3744

Sound Ideas Studio
Studio A: 151 West 46th Street
New York, New York 10036
Tel: 212-247-0815

Sound Ideas Studio
Studio B: 1595 Broadway
New York, New York 10019
Tel: 212-582-8776

Sound One, Inc.
35 West 45th Street
New York, New York 10036
Tel: 212-765-4757

The Sound Shop
321 West 44th Street
New York, New York 10036
Tel: 212-757-5837

Titra Sound Corporation
1600 Broadway
New York, New York 10019
Tel: 212-757-6681

Twelve East Recording, Inc.
12 East 44th Street
New York, New York 10017
Tel: 212-986-4747

United Recording Laboratories,
   Inc.
681 Fifth Avenue
New York, New York 10022
Tel: 212-751-4660

Thomas J. Valentino
151 West 46th Street
New York, New York 10036
Tel: 212-246-4675

Oregon:

M. P. Forde Labs
2153 N.E. Sandy Boulevard
Portland, Oregon 97232
Tel: 503-234-0553

Texas:

Automated Commercial Training
   System
9817 Westpark
Houston, Texas 77042
Tel: 713-783-1380

Century Studios, Inc.
4519 Maple Avenue
Dallas, Texas 75219
Tel: 214-522-3310

Houston Film Co-op, Inc.
P.O. Box 58932
Houston, Texas 77058
Tel: 713-482-7960

PSI Film Laboratory, Inc.
3011 Diamond Park Drive
Dallas, Texas 75347
Tel: 214-631-5670

Sound Techniques
1320 Inwood Road
Dallas, Texas 75247
Tel: 214-638-3256

Ralph Stachon & Associates, Inc.
1322 Inwood Road
Dallas, Texas 75247
Tel: 214-638-6231

Bill Stokes Associates
5646 Dyer Street
Dallas, Texas 75206
Tel: 214-363-0161

Utah:

Stockdale & Co., Inc.
200 East First Street
Salt Lake City, Utah 84111
Tel: 801-521-3505

Washington:

Aero Marc, Inc.
5518 Empire Way South
Seattle, Washington 98118
Tel: 206-725-1400

M. P. Forde Labs
306 Fairview Avenue North
Seattle, Washington 98109
Tel: 206-682-2510

JRB Motion Graphics
3323 Ninth Avenue West
Seattle, Washington 98119
Tel: 206-284-0834

Multi-Media Productions, Inc.
1200 Stuart Street
Seattle, Washington 98101
Tel: 206-624-8390

Sound Preservers Company
1915 North Quince Street
Olympia, Washington 98506
Tel: 206-352-9097

Research

Researchers and research facilities listed here can provide producers and designers with answers to questions involving costume and decor design to authenticate virtually any period, as well as provide custom research to answer any questions that may be new or novel.

Arizona:

Craig Pease Enterprises
P.O. Box 1118
Scottsdale, Arizona 85252
Tel: 602-945-4807

California:

American Film Institute Library
501 Doheny Road
Beverly Hills, California 90210
Tel: 213-278-8777

Celebrity Service, Inc.
8746 Sunset Boulevard
Los Angeles, California 90069
Tel: 213-652-1700

De Forest Research
780 North Gower Street
Los Angeles, California 90038
Tel: 213-469-2271

Film Technology Company, Inc.
6900 Santa Monica Boulevard
Los Angeles, California 90038
Tel: 213-465-4908

Metro-Goldwyn-Mayer Research
  Department
10202 West Washington
  Boulevard
Culver City, California 90230
Tel: 213-836-3000

Motion Picture & TV Research
  Center
8480 Beverly Boulevard
Los Angeles, California 90048
Tel: 213-653-2200

Native American
  Research/Consultants
526 South Reese Place
Burbank, California 91506
Tel: 213-848-6531

The Odyssey Corporation
1333 Camino Del Rio South
San Diego, California 92108
Tel: 714-291-6830

The Research Center of Los
  Angeles, Inc.
171 Del Amo Fashion Square
Torrance, California 90503
Tel: 213-542-1551

Colorado:

Albert M. Miller
1321 Gaylord Street
Denver, Colorado 80206
Tel: 303-355-5283

New York:

Celebrity Service, Inc.
171 West 57th Street
New York, New York 10019
Tel: 212-757-7979

Museum of Modern Art Film
   Library
11 West 53rd Street
New York, New York 10019
Tel: 212-245-8900

Douglas Blair Turnbaugh
460 East 79th Street
New York, New York 10021
Tel: 212-988-3509

Texas:

Piccadilly Films International Co.
1802 N.E. Loop 410, Gold Carpet
   Suite
San Antonio, Texas 78246
Tel: 512-824-3548

Scenic Backgrounds

That may or may not be Mount Fuji there in the background, but it certainly
looks real. Making the background look real is the job of the professional
listed below.

California:

Background Engineers
729 Seward Street
Los Angeles, California 90046
Tel: 213-465-4161

Coast Backing Company
924 North Formosa Avenue
Los Angeles, California 90046
Tel: 213-761-5167

Continental Camera Systems
16800 Roscoe Boulevard
Van Nuys, California 91408
Tel: 213-989-5222

Curran Productions & Lighting
Co.
1215 Bates Avenue
Los Angeles, California 90029
Tel: 213-662-8129

Dazian's Inc.
165 South Robertson Boulevard
Beverly Hills, California 90211
Tel: 213-272-1187

Frankel Associates, Inc.
321 South Robertson Boulevard
Los Angeles, California 90048
Tel: 213-878-1421

R. L. Grosh & Sons Scenic Studio
4114 Sunset Boulevard
Los Angeles, California 90029
Tel: 213-662-1134

Hansard Process
6647 Matilija Avenue
Van Nuys, California 91405
Tel: 213-780-2156

International Silks & Woolens
8347 Beverly Boulevard
Los Angeles, California 90048
Tel: 213-653-6453

J. C. Backing Corporation
10201 West Pico Boulevard
Los Angeles, California 90064
Tel: 213-277-0522

Jandelle
1034 South Los Angeles Street
Los Angeles, California 90015
Tel: 213-749-8243

Krofft Enterprises, Inc.
11347 Vanowen Street
North Hollywood, California
91605
Tel: 213-877-3361

Ray Mercer & Company
4241 Normal Avenue
Los Angeles, California 90029
Tel: 213-663-9331

Metro-Goldwyn-Mayer Studios
10202 West Washington
  Boulevard
Culver City, California 90230
Tel: 213-836-3000

Olesen Company
1535 Ivar Avenue
Los Angeles, California 90028
Tel: 213-465-5194

Pacific Studios
8315 Melrose Avenue
Los Angeles, California 90069
Tel: 213-653-3093

Paramount Pictures Studios
5451 Marathon Street
Los Angeles, California 90038
Tel: 213-463-0100

Scenic Backgrounds, Inc.
1041 North Formosa Avenue
Los Angeles, California 90046
Tel: 213-469-6161

Studio Specialties
1623 Palo Alto Street
Los Angeles, California 90023
Tel: 213-483-4950

Illinois:

Dazian's, Inc.
400 North Wells Street
Chicago, Illinois 60610
Tel: 312-467-1991

The Scenery Works
2821 Central
Evanston, Illinois 60201
Tel: 312-864-1166

Massachusetts:

Dazian's, Inc.
420 Boylston Street
Boston, Massachusetts 02116
Tel: 617-266-5040

New York:

Dazian's, Inc.
40 East 29th Street
New York, New York 10016
Tel: 212-686-5300

Texas:

Dazian's, Inc.
2015 Commerce Street
Dallas, Texas 75201
Tel: 213-748-3450

Southern Importers
4825 San Jacinto Street
Houston, Texas 77004
Tel: 713-524-8236

Screening Rooms

The screening rooms listed here all have 35mm interlock equipment and are available for rental. In New York the screening rooms of only some of the major production companies may be used on a fee basis. Consult the listing below.

Arizona:

Southwestern Studio
Box 105
Carefree, Arizona 85331
Tel: 602-946-3404

California:
Los Angeles area:

Academy Award Theatre
9038 Melrose Avenue
Los Angeles, California 90069
Tel: 213-278-8990

Charles Aidikoff Screening Room
9255 Sunset Boulevard
Los Angeles, California 90069
Tel: 213-274-0866

Beverly Hilton Hotel
9876 Wilshire Boulevard
Beverly Hills, California 90210
Tel: 213-274-7777

Centre Films, Inc.
1103 North El Centro Avenue
Los Angeles, California 90038
Tel: 213-466-5123

Cine Group
8560 Sunset Boulevard
Los Angeles, California 90069
Tel: 213-652-4800

Consolidated Film Industries
959 North Seward Street
Los Angeles, California 90038
Tel: 213-462-6171

Creative Film Arts
7090 Waring Avenue
Los Angeles, California 90038
Tel: 213-933-8495

Crest National Film Laboratories
1141 North Seward Street
Los Angeles, California 90038
Tel: 213-462-6696

De Luxe General
1546 North Argyle Avenue
Los Angeles, California 90028
Tel: 213-462-6171

Directors Guild of America
7950 Sunset Boulevard
Los Angeles, California 90046
Tel: 213-656-1220

F&B/CECO of California
1041 North Highland Avenue
Los Angeles, California 90038
Tel: 213-469-3601

Samuel Goldwyn Studios
1041 North Formosa Avenue
Los Angeles, California 90046
Tel: 213-851-1234

Gerald Gordon Enterprises
1451 North Las Palmas Avenue
Los Angeles, California 90028
Tel: 213-463-1845

Granada Theater
9000 Sunset Boulevard
Los Angeles, California 90069
Tel: 213-273-2266

Hollywood Screening Room
1800 North Highland Avenue,
  Suite 511
Los Angeles, California 90028
Tel: 213-462-9253

Stacy Keach Productions
5216 Laurel Canyon Boulevard
North Hollywood, California
  91607
Tel: 213-877-0472

Lion's Gate Films
1334 Westwood Boulevard
Los Angeles, California 90024
Tel: 213-475-4987

Major Independent Film
  Producers, Inc.
1207 North Western Avenue
Los Angeles, California 90029
Tel: 213-461-2721

Matrix Image
6622 Variel Avenue
Canoga Park, California 91303
Tel: 213-883-6622

Movie Tech, Inc.
6518 Santa Monica Boulevard
Los Angeles, California 90038
Tel: 213-467-8491

Donald H. Nosseck Theatre
9229 Sunset Boulevard, Suite 209
Los Angeles, California 90069
Tel: 213-274-4888

Preview House
7655 Sunset Boulevard
Los Angeles, California 90046
Tel: 213-876-6600

Joe Shore's Screening Room
9229 Sunset Boulevard, Suite 209
Los Angeles, California 90069
Tel: 213-274-4888

Sunset Strip Screening Room
9229 Sunset Boulevard, Suite 209
Los Angeles, California 90069
Tel: 213-274-4888

Theatrecraft Playhouse
7445 1/4 Sunset Boulevard
Los Angeles, California 90046
Tel: 213-876-3575

Trans-American Film
  Corporation
1680 North Vine Street
Los Angeles, California 90028
Tel: 213-466-7575

San Francisco area:

American Zoetrope, Inc.
American Zoetrope Film Facility
827 Folsom Street
San Francisco, California 94107
Tel: 415-989-0600

Marvin Becker Film-Maker
2111 California Street
San Francisco, California 94115
Tel: 415-567-2160

Berkeley Film House
2908 Channing Way
Berkeley, California 94704
Tel: 415-843-6900

Berkeley Film Institute
2908 Channing Way
Berkeley, California 94704

Bonanza Films
The Embarcadero
222 Agriculture Building
San Francisco, California 94105
Tel: 415-956-5660

Leo Diner Films
350 Golden Gate
San Francisco, California 94102
Tel: 415-775-3664

Edit-Center
155 Fell Street
San Francisco, California 94102
Tel: 415-864-4644

Furman Films
3466 21st Street
San Francisco, California 94110
Tel: 415-282-1300

JWA Screening Room
582 Market Street
San Francisco, California 94104
Tel: 415-391-1352

Motion Picture Service Company
125 Hyde Street
San Francisco, California 94102
Tel: 415-673-9162

Snazelle Films, Inc.
155 Fell Street
San Francisco, California 94102
Tel: 415-431-5490

The Sound Service
55 Stevenson Street
San Francisco, California 94105
Tel: 415-433-3674

Jack Wodell Associates
582 Market Street
San Francisco, California 94104
Tel: 415-391-1350

Colorado:

Barbre Products, Inc.
1089 Bannock
Denver, Colorado 80204
Tel: 303-266-3601

Century Screening Room
2100 Stout Street
Denver, Colorado 80205
Tel: 303-534-7611

Entertainment Four Studios
1630 Chambers Road
Aurora, Colorado 80010
Tel: 303-341-5600

The Flick Theatre
Larimer Square
Denver, Colorado 80202
Tel: 303-244-9155

Western Cine Service, Inc.
312 South Pearl Street
Denver, Colorado 80209
Tel: 303-744-1017

District of Columbia:

Byron Motion Pictures, Inc.
65 K Street, N.E.
Washington, D.C. 20002
Tel: 202-783-2700

Capital Film Laboratories, Inc.
470 E Street, S.W.
Washington, D.C. 20024
Tel: 202-347-1717

Koster Film Facilities, Inc.
1017 E Street, S.W.
Washington, D.C. 20024
Tel: 202-544-4410

Florida:

Cinema City Studios, Inc.
6015 Highway 301 North
Tampa, Florida 33610
Tel: 813-621-4731

Florida State Theatres Screening
  Room
Florida Theatre Building
128 East Forsyth Street
Jacksonville, Florida 32202
Tel: 904-356-1341

Post Production Services, Inc.
3808 San Nicholas Street
Tampa, Florida 33609
Tel: 813-253-0400

Georgia:

A F E R
1846 Briarwood Road
Atlanta, Georgia 30329
Tel: 404-633-4101

Atlanta Preview Theatre
161 Spring Street, N.W.
Atlanta, Georgia 30303
Tel: 404-523-0663

Cinevision
206 Fourteenth Street
Atlanta, Georgia 30304
Tel: 404-875-5616

Columbia Pictures
195 Luckie Street, N.W.
Atlanta, Georgia 30303
Tel: 404-523-1524

Craddock Films, Inc.
161 Spring Street, N.W.
Atlanta, Georgia 30303
Tel: 404-688-3492

Lanco Sound
3486 West Hospital Road
Atlanta, Georgia 30341
Tel: 404-457-1244

Master Sound Studios, Inc.
1227 Spring Street, N.W.
Atlanta, Georgia 30309
Tel: 404-873-6425

The Studio Center
445 Bishop Street, N.W.
Atlanta, Georgia 30318
Tel: 404-874-2252

Twentieth Century–Fox
    Exchange
197 Walton Street, N.W.
Atlanta, Georgia 30303
Tel: 404-523-3722

Hawaii:

Consolidated Amusement
    Company Ltd.
510 South Street
Honolulu, Hawaii 96812
Tel: 808-536-3571

Illinois:

ABC Great States, Inc.
175 North State Street
Chicago, Illinois 60601
Tel: 312-726-5300

H & E Balaban Theatres
190 North State Street
Chicago, Illinois 60601
Tel: 312-372-2262

Chicago International Film
    Festival
235 Eugenie
Chicago, Illinois 60614
Tel: 312-644-3400

Douglas Film Industries
10 West Kinzie Street
Chicago, Illinois 60610
Tel: 312-664-7455

Essaness Theatres Corporation
54 West Randolph Street
Chicago, Illinois 60601
Tel: 312-332-7465

Film Center, Incorporated
20 East Huron Street
Chicago, Illinois 60611
Tel: 312-337-2855

The Film-Makers, Inc.
2265 West St. Paul Street
Chicago, Illinois 60647
Tel: 312-342-3140

National General Pictures, Inc.
203 North Wabash Avenue
Chicago, Illinois 60601
Tel: 312-782-8310

Twentieth Century–Fox Film
    Corporation
550 West Jackson Boulevard,
    Room 420
Chicago, Illinois 60606
Tel: 312-372-1584

Universal Film Exchanges, Inc.
425 North Michigan Avenue
Chicago, Illinois 60601
Tel: 312-337-1100

Indiana:

Illinois Building Screening Room
Affiliated Theatre Service
Indianapolis, Indiana 46201
Tel: 317-253-1536

Kansas:

Commonwealth Amusement
Corporation
215 West Eighteenth Street
Kansas City, Kansas 66102
Tel: 913-471-2390

Dickinson Operating Company
5913 Woodson Road
Mission, Kansas 66222
Tel: 913-432-2334

Louisiana:

ABC Mid-South Theatres, Inc.
LaSalle Hotel, Fourth Floor
143 North Rampart Street
New Orleans, Louisiana 70112
Tel: 504-525-4181

Twentieth Century–Fox
200 South Liberty Street
New Orleans, Louisiana 70112
Tel: 504-525-9858

Maryland:

National Cine Laboratories
4319 Rhode Island Avenue
Brentwood, Maryland 20722
Tel: 202-779-6800

Massachusetts:

American Theatres Corporation
658 1/2 Washington Street
Boston, Massachusetts 02184
Tel: 617-426-4530

Cody Interlock Theatre
24 Dane Street
Somerville, Massachusetts 02143
Tel: 617-666-4540

E. M. Loew Theatres
164 Tremont Street
Boston, Massachusetts 02116
Tel: 617-482-9200

Metro-Goldwyn-Mayer, Inc.
46 Church Street
Boston, Massachusetts 02116
Tel: 617-426-0044

Sack Theatres
Music Hall Building
33 Hollis Street
Boston, Massachusetts 02116
Tel: 617-542-3334

Universal Pictures
60 Church Street
Boston, Massachusetts 02116

Michigan:

Fox Theatre Screening Room
2211 Woodward Avenue
Detroit, Michigan 48201
Tel: 313-961-9494

Point-of-Vue Screening Room
24300 Southfield Road
Southfield, Michigan 48075
Tel: 313-557-8111

Preview Projection Service
479 Ledyard Avenue
Detroit, Michigan 48201
Tel: 313-965-7729

Missouri:

Art Theatre Screening Company
3330 Olive Street
St. Louis, Missouri 63103
Tel: 314-535-8130

Nevada:

Nevada Audio Visual Services
3062 Sheridan Street
Las Vegas, Nevada 89102
Tel: 702-876-6272

New York:

Allied Artists Pictures
   Corporation
15 Columbus Circle
New York, New York 10023
Tel: 212-541-9200

Artscope, Ltd.
310 West 53rd Street
New York, New York 10019
Tel: 212-265-7420

Bonded Film Center Theatre, Inc.
630 Ninth Avenue
New York, New York 10036
Tel: 212-661-7600

Cine Metric Theatre, Inc.
2 West 45th Street
New York, New York 10036
Tel: 212-869-8670

Cinema 405, Inc.
405 Park Avenue
New York, New York 10022
Tel: 212-759-1930

Fifth Avenue Screening Room,
   Inc.
4 West 56th Street
New York, New York 10019
Tel: 212-541-5454

Magno Sound
212 West 48th Street
New York, New York 10036
Tel: 212-757-8855

Movielab Theatre Service, Inc.
619 West 54th Street
New York, New York 10019
Tel: 212-586-0360

Museum of Modern Art Film
   Library
11 West 53rd Street
New York, New York 10019
Tel: 212-245-8900

Park Avenue Screening
445 Park Avenue
New York, New York 10022
Tel: 212-688-3277

Precision Film Labs' Screening
   Theatre
630 Ninth Avenue
New York, New York 10036
Tel: 212-489-8800

Preview Theatre, Inc.
1600 Broadway
New York, New York 10019
Tel: 212-246-0865

Reeves Teletape
304 East 44th Street
New York, New York 10017
Tel: 212-679-3550

Rizzoli Screening Room
712 Fifth Avenue
New York, New York 10019
Tel: 212-245-0400

Ross-Gaffney, Inc.
21 West 46th Street
New York, New York 10036
Tel: 212-582-3744

Trans-American Film
Corporation
888 Seventh Avenue
New York, New York 10019
Tel: 212-582-7232

Westside Screenings, Inc.
311 West 43rd Street
New York, New York 10036
Tel: 212-489-1555

North Carolina:

Twentieth Century–Fox
Screening Room
308 South Church Street
Charlotte, North Carolina 28202
Tel: 704-332-7101

Ohio:

Twentieth Century–Fox Film
Corporation
617 Vine Street
Cincinnati, Ohio 45202
Tel: 513-241-6460

Twentieth Century–Fox Film
Corporation
2219 Payne Avenue
Cleveland, Ohio 44114
Tel: 216-861-2257

Pennsylvania:

Universal Screening Room
Universal Exchange Building
251 North Thirteenth Street
Philadelphia, Pennsylvania 19107
Tel: 215-564-3980

Texas:

Century Studios, Inc.
4519 Maple Avenue
Dallas, Texas 95219
Tel: 214-522-3310

Houston Film Co-Op, Inc.
P.O. Box 58932
Houston, Texas 77058
Tel: 713-482-7960

Washington:

JRB Motion Graphics
3323 Ninth Avenue West
Seattle, Washington 98119
Tel: 206-284-0834

Multi-Media Productions, Inc.
1200 Stuart Street
Seattle, Washington 98101
Tel: 206-624-8390

Pal Productions, Inc.
1003 Lenora Street
Seattle, Washington 98121
Tel: 206-682-1339

Wisconsin:

Centre Theatre Building
214 West Wisconsin Avenue
Milwaukee, Wisconsin 53203
Tel: 414-276-2220

Set Design

California:
 Los Angeles area:

Act Design & Execution
14106 Ventura Boulevard
Sherman Oaks, California 91403
Tel: 213-788-4219

Cinema Set Construction
6309 Eleanor Avenue
Los Angeles, California 90038
Tel: 213-464-9118

Coordinators 2
8113 1/2 Melrose Avenue
Los Angeles, California 90046
Tel: 213-653-6110

Curran Production & Lighting
 Company
1215 Bates Avenue
Los Angeles, California 90029
Tel: 213-662-8129

Spencer Davies
3115 West Olive Avenue
Burbank, California 91505
Tel: 213-845-9888

Design Arts/Normand Houle
6309 Eleanor Avenue
Los Angeles, California 90038
Tel: 213-464-9118

Graphicus, Inc.
11046 McCormick
North Hollywood, California
 91601
Tel: 213-769-5694

R. L. Grosh & Sons Scenic Studios
4114 Sunset Boulevard
Los Angeles, California 90029
Tel: 213-662-1134

Stacy Keach Productions
5216 Laurel Canyon Boulevard
North Hollywood, California
 91607
Tel: 213-877-0472

E. Jay Krause & Associates
3115 West Olive Avenue
Burbank, California 91505
Tel: 213-849-5502

Krofft Enterprises, Inc.
11347 Vanowen Street
North Hollywood, California
 91605
Tel: 213-877-3361

Seward Stages
6605 Eleanor Street
Los Angeles, California 90038
Tel: 213-466-8559

Studio Set Service, Inc.
Producer's Studio
650 North Bronson Avenue
Los Angeles, California 90004
Tel: 213-465-4411

Studio Specialties
1623 Palo Alto Street
Los Angeles, California 90026
Tel: 213-483-4950

San Francisco area:

The Phelps & Kopp Company
991 Tennessee Street
San Francisco, California 94107
Tel: 415-285-1900

Sound Effects

Most sound effects houses maintain libraries of stock sound effects such as crowd noises, slamming doors, gunshots and the like. Custom effects can be created upon request. For musical effects, see also "Music Libraries."

Arizona:

Craig Pease Enterprises
P.O. Box 1118
Scottsdale, Arizona 85252
Tel: 602-945-4807

California:
Los Angeles area:

Audio Effects Company
1600 North Western Avenue
Los Angeles, California 90027
Tel: 213-469-3692

B & B Productions
1313 North Vine Street
Los Angeles, California 90028
Tel: 213-461-3388

Buzzy's Recording Services
8719 Santa Monica Boulevard
Los Angeles, California 90069
Tel: 213-659-5444

Cinesound
915 North Highland Avenue
Los Angeles, California 90038
Tel: 213-464-1155

D.C.T. Recorders
6414 Sunset Boulevard
Los Angeles, California 90028
Tel: 213-461-2841

Edit International, Ltd.
6725 Sunset Boulevard
Los Angeles, California 90028
Tel: 213-463-1121

Edit-Rite, Inc.
1213 North Highland Avenue
Los Angeles, California 90028
Tel: 213-465-6117

Richard Einfeld, Inc.
1512 North Las Palmas Avenue
Los Angeles, California 90028
Tel: 213-461-3731

Embassy Sound Productions
847 South Grand Avenue
Los Angeles, California 90017
Tel: 213-623-3266

Filmagic
6362 Hollywood Boulevard
Los Angeles, California 90028
Tel: 213-464-5333

General Music Corporation
6410 Willoughby Avenue
Los Angeles, California 90038
Tel: 213-462-0715

Glen Glenn Sound Company
6624 Romaine Street
Los Angeles, California 90038
Tel: 213-462-7221

Independent Producers Service
7370 Melrose Avenue
Los Angeles, California 90046
Tel: 213-655-3599

Bruce Kirby Sound Engineering
1016 North Highland Avenue
Los Angeles, California 90038
Tel: 213-462-6000

Metro-Goldwyn-Mayer, Inc.
10202 West Washington
  Boulevard
Culver City, California 90230
Tel: 213-836-3000

Moustache Productions
9017 Harratt Street
Los Angeles, California 90069
Tel: 213-464-5161

Movie Tech, Inc.
6518 Santa Monica Boulevard
Los Angeles, California 90038
Tel: 213-467-8491

Mystic Sound Studio Library
Mystic Music Centre
6277 Selma Avenue
Los Angeles, California 90028
Tel: 213-464-9667

Newjack Sound Recorders
1717 North Highland Avenue
Los Angeles, California 90028
Tel: 213-466-6141

Olesen Company
1535 Ivar Avenue
Los Angeles, California 90028
Tel: 213-465-5197

The Petersen Company
1330 North Vine Street
Los Angeles, California 90028
Tel: 213-466-9351

The Production Co., Inc.
8612 West Pico Boulevard
Los Angeles, California 90035
Tel: 213-659-3940

Quality Sound, Inc.
5625 Melrose Avenue
Los Angeles, California 90038
Tel: 213-467-7154

Riviera Productions
6610 Selma Avenue
Los Angeles, California 90028
Tel: 213-462-8585

Sound City, Inc.
15456 Cabrito Road
Van Nuys, California 91406
Tel: 213-787-3722

Special Effects Unlimited
752 Cahuenga Boulevard
Los Angeles, California 90028
Tel: 213-465-3366

San Francisco area:

Parasound, Inc.
680 Beach Street
San Francisco, California 94109
Tel: 415-776-2808

Snazelle Films, Inc.
155 Fell Street
San Francisco, California 94102
Tel: 415-431-5490

Sound Genesis, Inc.
445 Bryant Street
San Francisco, California 94107
Tel: 415-391-8776

The Sound Service
55 Stevenson Street
San Francisco, California 94105
Tel: 415-433-3674

Colorado:

The Library
P.O. Box 18145
Denver, Colorado 80218
Tel: 303-778-9745

Western Cine Service, Inc.
312 South Pearl Street
Denver, Colorado 80209
Tel: 303-744-1017

Illinois:

Creative Sound Effects
9 East Huron Street
Chicago, Illinois 60611
Tel: 312-664-2412

New York:

Thomas J. Valentino, Inc.
151 West 46th Street
New York, New York 10036
Tel: 212-246-4675

Texas:

PSI Film Laboratory, Inc.
3011 Diamond Park Drive
Dallas, Texas 75347
Tel: 214-631-5670

Utah:

Stockdale & Company, Inc.
200 East First Street
Salt Lake City, Utah 84111
Tel: 801-521-3505

Washington:

JRB Motion Graphics
3323 Ninth Avenue West
Seattle, Washington 98119
Tel: 206-284-0834

Sound Equipment

Included in this category are suppliers who sell or rent the sound equipme necessary for motion picture production.

Arizona:

Spencer-Alquist Audio
6252 East Twentieth Street
Tucson, Arizona 85711
Tel: 602-886-2353

Studio Rentals Inc. of Arizona
2321 East University Drive
Phoenix, Arizona 85034
Tel: 602-252-5848

California:
Los Angeles area:

Acey-Decy Sound Company
3417 Cahuenga Boulevard West
Los Angeles, California 90068
Tel: 213-851-3550

Amertron/American Electronic
  Supply, Inc.
1200 North Vine Street
Los Angeles, California 90038
Tel: 213-466-4321

Audio Effects Company
1600 North Western Avenue
Los Angeles, California 90027
Tel: 213-469-3692

Audio Services/Mobile Sound
  Studios
3239 Cahuenga Boulevard West
Los Angeles, California 90028
Tel: 213-467-0152

Audio Tran
923 North Cole Avenue
Los Angeles, California 90038
Tel: 213-464-8307

Audio-Video Craft, Inc.
7710 Melrose Avenue
Los Angeles, California 90046
Tel: 213-655-3511

Birns & Sawyer, Inc.
1026 North Highland Avenue
Los Angeles, California 90038
Tel: 213-466-8211

Cine Group
8560 Sunset Boulevard
Los Angeles, California 90069
Tel: 213-652-4800

F. W. Corbett Productions
1823 Third Avenue
Los Angeles, California 90019
Tel: 213-733-5251

Custom Fidelity, Inc.
7925 Santa Monica Boulevard
Los Angeles, California 90046
Tel: 213-654-4522

F&B/CECO of California, Inc.
7051 Santa Monica Boulevard
Los Angeles, California 90038
Tel: 213-466-9361

John P. Filbert Company
1100 Flower Street
Glendale, California 91201
Tel: 213-247-6550

J. L. Fisher, Inc.
10918 Burbank Boulevard
North Hollywood, California
91601
Tel: 213-877-8848

Glen Glenn Sound Company
6624 Romaine Street
Los Angeles, California 90038
Tel: 213-462-7221

Alan Gordon Enterprises, Inc.
5362 North Cahuenga Boulevard
North Hollywood, California
91601
Tel: 213-985-5500

Hollywood Sound Systems
1526 North Ivar Street
Los Angeles, California 90028
Tel: 213-466-2416

Kendun Recorders
619 South Glenwood Place
Burbank, California 91506
Tel: 213-849-6336

Bruce Kirby Sound Engineering
1016 North Highland Avenue
Los Angeles, California 90038
Tel: 213-462-6000

Magnasync/Movieola, Inc.
1001 North Highland Avenue
Los Angeles, California 90028
Tel: 213-466-5233

Harry McCune Sound Service,
Inc.
1420 West Ninth Street
Los Angeles, California 90015
Tel: 213-385-8238

Mobile Production Systems
1225 North Vine Street
Los Angeles, California 90038
Tel: 213-465-7141

Movie Tech, Inc.
6518 Santa Monica Boulevard
Los Angeles, California 90038
Tel: 213-467-8491

Parasound, Inc.
2825 Hyans Street
Los Angeles, California 90026
Tel: 213-462-3311

Jack Pill & Associates
6370 Santa Monica Boulevard
Los Angeles, California 90038
Tel: 213-466-5391

Ryder Magnetic Sales
Corporation
1147 North Vine Street
Los Angeles, California 90038
Tel: 213-469-6391

Ryder Sound Services, Inc.
1161 North Vine Street
Los Angeles, California 90038
Tel: 213-469-3511

S & S Sound Company
6518 Santa Monica Boulevard
Los Angeles, California 90038
Tel: 213-467-8491

SOS/Photo-Cine-Optics, Inc.
7051 Santa Monica Boulevard
Los Angeles, California 90038
Tel: 213-466-9361

The Sound Center
319 North Beverly Drive
Beverly Hills, California 90210
Tel: 213-274-6951

Sound City, Inc.
15456 Cabrito Road
Van Nuys, California 91406
Tel: 213-787-3722

Westrex Corporation
390 North Alpine Drive
Beverly Hills, California 90213
Tel: 213-274-9303

San Francisco area:

Alembic, Inc.
60 Brady Street
San Francisco, California 94103
Tel: 415-864-3800

American Zoetrope Film Facility
827 Folsom Street
San Francisco, California 94107
Tel: 415-989-0600

Marvin Becker Film-Maker
2111 California Street
San Francisco, California 94115
Tel: 415-567-2160

Coast Recorders
829 Folsom Street
San Francisco, California 94107
Tel: 415-397-7676

Leo Diner Films, Inc.
332–350 Golden Gate
San Francisco, California 94102
Tel: 415-775-3664

Ferco
363 Brannan Street
San Francisco, California 94107
Tel: 415-957-1787

Furman Films
3466-21st Street
San Francisco, California 94110
Tel: 415-282-1300

Gambit Enterprises
119 Cuesta Drive
South San Francisco, California
    94080
Tel: 415-589-9158

Adolph Gasser, Inc.
5733 Geary Boulevard
San Francisco, California 94121
Tel: 415-751-0145

Harry McCune Sound Service,
    Inc.
991 Howard Street
San Francisco, California 94103
Tel: 415-777-2700

Motion Picture Service Company
125 Hyde Street
San Francisco, California 94102
Tel: 415-673-9162

Don Palmer Studios
563 Second Street
San Francisco, California 94107
Tel: 415-392-4449

W. A. Palmer Films, Inc.
611 Howard Street
San Francisco, California 94105
Tel: 415-986-5961

The Phelps & Kopp Company
991 Tennessee Street
San Francisco, California 94107
Tel: 415-285-1900

Skinner Studio
345 Sutter Street
San Francisco, California 94108
Tel: 415-986-5040

Snazelle Films, Inc.
155 Fell Street
San Francisco, California 94102
Tel: 415-431-5490

Sound Genesis
445 Bryant Street
San Francisco, California 94107
Tel: 415-391-8776

Studio 16, Inc.
2135 Powell Street
San Francisco, California 94133
Tel: 415-982-2097

Colorado:

Cinema Services
P.O. Box 398
Eldorado Springs, Colorado
    80025
Tel: 303-443-4913

Western Cine Service
312 South Pearl Street
Denver, Colorado 80209
Tel: 303-744-1017

Hawaii:

Hawkins Audio Engineers, Inc.
1160 North King Street
Honolulu, Hawaii 96817
Tel: 808-841-5031

The House of Eric Productions
1760 Ala Moana Boulevard
Waikiki, Hawaii 96815
Tel: 808-533-3877

Thayer Sound
116 South Hotel Street
Honolulu, Hawaii 96809
Tel: 808-536-6161

Nevada:

K-B Cine Supply
P.O. Box 12611
Las Vegas, Nevada 89112
Tel: 702-451-5290

Nevada Audio-Visual Services
3062 Sheridan Street
Las Vegas, Nevada 89102
Tel: 702-876-6272

Rugar Electronics
4515 Industrial Road
Las Vegas, Nevada 89103
Tel: 702-736-4331

Video Sound Engineering
2130 South Highland Avenue
Las Vegas, Nevada 89102
Tel: 702-385-4691

New Jersey:

Multi-Track Magnetics, Inc.
1 Ruckman Road
Closter, New Jersey 07624
Tel: 201-768-5037

New York:

The Camera Mart, Inc.
456 West 55th Street
New York, New York 10019
Tel: 212-757-6977

Ferco
419 West 54th Street
New York, New York 10019
Tel: 212-581-5474

Olmsted Sound Studios, Inc.
80 West 40th Street
New York, New York 10018
Tel: 212-868-3342

Texas:

Automated Commercial Training
  Systems
9817 Westpark
Houston, Texas 77042
Tel: 713-783-1380

Dale Berry & Associates, Inc.
9001 ERL Thornton Freeway
Dallas, Texas 75228
Tel: 214-324-0409

PSI Film Laboratory
3011 Diamond Park Drive
Dallas, Texas 75347
Tel: 214-631-5670

Utah:

Stockdale & Company, Inc.
200 East First Street
Salt Lake City, Utah 84111
Tel: 801-521-3505

Washington:

Aero Marc, Inc.
5518 Empire Way South
Seattle, Washington 98118
Tel: 206-725-1400

Gibson Sound Company
501 North 36th Street
Seattle, Washington 98105
Tel: 206-633-1180

National Theatre Supply
2415 Second Avenue
Seattle, Washington 98121
Tel: 206-624-7710

Stordahl's Place Productions
3831 34th Avenue West
Seattle, Washington 98199
Tel: 206-285-3022

Special Effects

If the script calls for the invasion of Manhattan by an army of outsized cockroaches, you're going to need a special effects person. Listed below are some of the leading professionals. See the listings under "Props" if the job calls for mock-ups, models, or miniatures.

California:

Howard A. Anderson Company
5451 Marathon Street
Los Angeles, California 90038
Tel: 213-463-0100
Ext: 2001

Anicam
6331 Homewood Avenue
Los Angeles, California 90028
Tel: 213-465-4114

Bob Beck & Associates
1538 Cassil Place
Los Angeles, California 90028
Tel: 213-462-7093

Braverman Productions, Inc.
8961 Sunset Boulevard
Los Angeles, California 90069
Tel: 213-278-5444

Wally Bulloch Animation
    Camera Service, Inc.
1113 North Formosa Avenue
Los Angeles, California 90046
Tel: 213-851-0400

Butler-Glounder
1438 North Gower Street
Los Angeles, California 90028
Tel: 213-462-3111

Lee Chaney & Associates
6362 Hollywood Boulevard
Los Angeles, California 90028
Tel: 213-464-5333

Cinefx/ACME Laboratories, Inc.
1161 North Highland Avenue
Los Angeles, California 90038
Tel: 213-464-7474

Cinema Research Corporation
6860 Lexington Avenue
Los Angeles, California 90038
Tel: 213-461-3235

Cinema Service, Inc.
1459 Seward Street
Los Angeles, California 90028
Tel: 213-463-3178

Consolidated Film Industries
959 North Seward Street
Los Angeles, California 90038
Tel: 213-462-3161

Robert Costa Productions
1615 Colorado Boulevard
Los Angeles, California 90041
Tel: 213-255-1841

Creative Film Arts
7070 Waring Avenue
Los Angeles, California 90038
Tel: 213-933-8495

Elliot Periscope Lens
932 North La Brea Avenue
Los Angeles, California 90038
Tel: 213-874-9400

Film Effects of Hollywood, Inc.
1140 North Citrus Avenue
Los Angeles, California 90038
Tel: 213-469-5808

Filmagic
6362 Hollywood Boulevard
Los Angeles, California 90028
Tel: 213-464-5333

Golden West Videotape
8500 Sunset Boulevard
Los Angeles, California 90012
Tel: 213-469-3181

Imagic, Inc.
845 North Highland Avenue
Los Angeles, California 90038
Tel: 213-461-3744

Ray Mercer & Company
4241 Normal Avenue
Los Angeles, California 90029
Tel: 213-633-9331

Metro-Goldwyn-Mayer Studios
10202 West Washington
   Boulevard
Culver City, California 90230
Tel: 213-836-3000

National Screen Service
   Corporation
7026 Santa Monica Boulevard
Los Angeles, California 90038
Tel: 213-466-5111

Opticals West
7026 Santa Monica Boulevard
Los Angeles, California 90038
Tel: 213-466-5111

Pacific Title and Art Studio
6350 Santa Monica Boulevard
Los Angeles, California 90038
Tel: 213-464-0121

Photo-Effex
3701 Oak Street
Burbank, California 91505
Tel: 213-849-6959

Special Effects Unlimited
752 North Cahuenga Boulevard
Los Angeles, California 90038
Tel: 213-465-3366

Trans-American Video, Inc.
1541 North Vine Street
Los Angeles, California 90028
Tel: 213-466-2141

Universal City Studios Title &
   Optical Department
4050 Lankershim Boulevard
Universal City, California 91608
Tel: 213-985-4321

Westheimer Company
736 North Seward Street
Los Angeles, California 90038
Tel: 213-466-8271

Colorado:

Special Effects, Inc.
P.O. Box 246
Morrison, Colorado 80465
Tel: 303-697-8493

Stage Engineering & Supply, Inc.
P.O. Box 2002
Colorado Springs, Colorado
    80901
Tel: 303-635-2935

Florida:

International Animated Cartoons
14875 N.E. Twentieth Avenue
North Miami, Florida 33161
Tel: 305-947-2983

Mako Engineering
3131 N.E. 188th Street
Miami, Florida 33101
Tel: 305-931-2300

Persistence of Vision
1492 West Flagler Street
Miami, Florida 33101
Tel: 305-541-2554

Warren Sound Studios
35 N.E. 62nd Street
Miami, Florida 33101
Tel: 305-754-9539

New York:

Animation Productions of
    America
230 West Tenth Street
New York, New York 10014
Tel: 212-929-9436

Special Services

Included here are service organizations peculiar to the motion picture industry, such as box office monitoring and fan mail services.

AIRLINE MOVIES

New York:

Inflight Services, Inc.
485 Madison Avenue
New York, New York 10022
Don Zimmet, Vice-President,
Sales
Tel: 212-751-1800

Inflight Services provides motion picture and audio entertainment for the airline industry. Over 30 worldwide airlines are served, and over 500 aircraft are equipped with the Inflight projection system. Subsidiaries include a film processing laboratory in Hollywood and a joint venture theater chain operation.

CELEBRITY INFORMATION

California:

Celebrity News International
1717 North Highland Avenue
Los Angeles, California 90028
Tel: 213-466-4207

New York:

Celebrity Service, Inc.
171 West 57th Street
New York, New York 10019
Tel: 212-757-7979

Celebrity Service is the international clearing house for information on celebrities and public figures. Celebrity Service offers subscribers up-to-date information by telephone inquiry on the location and movement of celebrities. Nonsubscribers may obtain the service on a special report basis. *Theatrical Calendar, Contact Book,* and *Celebrity Bulletin* are published by Celebrity Service in connection with their information service on public figures. The organization is also able to provide specialized public relations services, arrange endorsements and special events, and provide specially screened lists of names.

Celebrity Service maintains offices in New York, Hollywood, London, Paris, and Rome.

FAN MAIL SERVICES

California:

Studio Fan Mail Service
1122 South Robertson Boulevard
Los Angeles, California 90035
Tel: 213-275-6122

United Fan Mail Service
8966 Sunset Boulevard
Los Angeles, California 90069
Tel: 213-274-8226

VIP Fan Mail Service
9157 Sunset Boulevard
Los Angeles, California 90069
Tel: 213-278-2561

Texas:

Picadilly Films International Co.,
Ltd.
1802 N.E. Loop 410, Gold Carpet
Suite
San Antonio, Texas 78246
Tel: 512-824-3548

HOTEL-MOTEL MOVIES

California:

First Cine-Tel Communications
Corporation
9000 West Sunset Boulevard
Los Angeles, California 90069
Tel: 213-273-2188

New York:

Computer Cinema
A Division of Computer
Television, Inc.
15 Columbus Circle
New York, New York 10023
Tel: 212-489-6622

Through an advanced communications system, Computer Cinema
presents movies in hotel and motel
rooms. Related services include com-
puterized room status, message, and
security functions.

MARKETING INFORMATION

Georgia:

Marketing Information Service
1730 N.E. Expressway Access
Road, N.E.
Atlanta, Georgia 30329
Gary Harper
In New York: Bill Smith,
National account executive for
motion pictures
Tel: 404-325-3221
Tel: 212-832-7127

Marketing Information Service is
a custom research house providing the
following services: audience reaction
in theaters; nonpatron interviews;
advertising awareness surveys; super-
vision of four-wall distributions, including hosting and monitoring services, daily reports to the distributor
and deposit of cash receipts; open
checking; monitoring of television
advertising spots.

New York:

Certified Reports, Inc. (CRI)
101 West 57th Street
New York, New York 10019
Mr. Harold Roth
Tel: 212-541-4545

Provides theater monitoring and
box office checking services, as well as
specialized motion picture industry
research.

MOTION PICTURE FINANCING

New York:

International Film Management
1225 Park Avenue
New York, New York 10028
Tel: 212-876-1626

SUBSCRIPTION FILMS

New York:

American Film Theatre
1350 Avenue of the Americas
New York, New York 10019
Tel: 212-489-8820

American Film Theatre presents
filmed versions of plays on a sub-
scription basis in designated theaters
throughout the country on a limited
run basis.

TELEVISION MONITORING

California:

Audio-Video Craft, Inc.
7710 Melrose Avenue
Los Angeles, California 90046
Tel: 213-655-3511

Crest Monitoring & Reports
Corporation
6922 Hollywood Boulevard
Los Angeles, California 90028
Tel: 213-463-6967

International Color TV
Monitoring
6100 Beeman Avenue
North Hollywood, California
91606
Tel: 213-766-3130

Overseas TV Reports
223 South Beverly Drive
Beverly Hills, California 90212
Tel: 213-278-3810

THEATER CHECKING & BOX OFFICE MONITORING

Georgia:

Marketing Information Service
1730 N.E. Expressway Access
Road, N.E.
Atlanta, Georgia 30329
Tel: 404-325-3221
Tel: 212-832-7127

New York:

Certified Reports, Inc. (CRI)
101 West 57th Street
New York, New York 10019
Tel: 212-541-4545

Dale System, Inc.
200 Garden City Plaza
Garden City, New York 11530
Tel: 516-741-2070

Hanover Security Systems, Inc.
17 Battery Place
New York, New York 10004
Tel: 212-425-8555

Stock Shots

You don't want to send a camera crew to Nairobi just to get the necessary shot of a 747 taking off from Nairobi airport. You shop the suppliers of stock shots and footage and find a supplier with such a sequence at Dar-es-Salaam. You sign up for the Dar-es-Salaam footage, gambling that the audience won't detect the difference.

Arizona:

Craig Pease Enterprises
P.O. Box 1118
Scottsdale, Arizona 85252
Tel: 602-945-4807

California:
Los Angeles area:

American Airlines
3449 Cahuenga Boulevard, West
Los Angeles, California 90068
Tel: 213-465-3911

American Stock Photos
202 West First Street
Los Angeles, California 90053
Tel: 213-624-2444

Associated Press Photos
202 West First Street
Los Angeles, California 90053
Tel: 213-624-2444

Lem Bailey
7934 Santa Monica Boulevard
Los Angeles, California 90038
Tel: 213-654-9550

Creative Photographic Library
2038 Milan Avenue
South Pasadena, California 91030
Tel: 213-682-3131

Elmer Dyer
711 North La Jolla
Los Angeles, California 90046
Tel: 213-939-8308

William R. Eastabrook
  Photography
3281 Oakshire Drive
Los Angeles, California 90068
Tel: 213-851-3281

Evco Film Library
838 North Seward Street
Los Angeles, California 90038
Tel: 213-464-9252

Fotos International
4230 Ben Avenue
Studio City, California 91604
Tel: 213-762-2181

Gornick Film Productions/
  Environmental
  Marine Enterprises
4200 Camino Real
Los Angeles, California 90065
Tel: 213-223-8914

Sherman Grinberg Film
  Libraries, Inc.
1040 North McCadden Place
Los Angeles, California 90038
Tel: 213-464-7491

Ron Grover
145 Maple Street
Burbank, California 91505
Tel: 213-842-6643

Lenstour Photo Service
5301 Laurel Canyon
North Hollywood, California
  91607
Tel: 213-877-0181

L. McFadden Studios
1210 1/2 North La Brea Avenue
Los Angeles, California 90038
Tel: 213-272-1544

Mercury Archives
1574 Crossroads of the World
Los Angeles, California 90067
Tel: 213-466-1441

NBC Library
3000 West Alameda
Burbank, California 91503
Tel: 213-845-7000
Ext: 640

Producers Library
7325 Santa Monica Boulevard
Los Angeles, California 90038
Tel: 213-466-4374

Allan Sandler
1001 North Poinsettia Place
Los Angeles, California 90046
Tel: 213-876-2021

Ray Stuart
2007 North Hobart Boulevard
Los Angeles, California 90027
Tel: 213-464-4614

UPI-Compix
1265 South Cochran
Los Angeles, California 90019
Tel: 213-933-5741

United Air Lines
625 Wilshire Boulevard
Los Angeles, California 90017
Tel: 213-482-2000

Wolfe Worldwide Films
1657 Sawtelle Boulevard
Los Angeles, California 90025
Tel: 213-879-1360

San Francisco area:

Above San Francisco Company
444 Market Street
San Francisco, California 94111
Tel: 415-981-1135

Gerald L. French Photography
908 Fox Plaza
San Francisco, California 94102
Tel: 415-621-6555

Curt W. Kaldor Photography
603 Grandview Drive
South San Francisco, California
  94080
Tel: 415-583-8704

Gabriel Moulin Studios
444 Montgomery Street
San Francisco, California 94104
Tel: 415-362-6680

Florida:

Bruco Enterprises
1370 Washington Avenue
Miami Beach, Florida 33139
Tel: 305-534-6122

Hawaii:

Cal-Hawaii Photographics
1240 Kaumualii, Box 9451
Honolulu, Hawaii 96820
Tel: 808-841-4335

Camera Hawaii, Inc.
206 Koula Street
Honolulu, Hawaii 96813
Tel: 808-536-2302

Eastman Kodak Company
1065 Kapiolani
Honolulu, Hawaii 96814
Tel: 808-531-6565

Pacific Productions
P.O. Box 2881
Honolulu, Hawaii 96802
Tel: 808-923-9429

Nevada:

Las Vegas News Bureau
Convention Center
3150 Paradise Road
Las Vegas, Nevada 89109
Tel: 702-735-3611

New York:

Fotosonic, Inc.
15 West 46th Street
New York, New York 10036

Sherman Grinberg Film
Libraries, Inc.
630 Ninth Avenue
New York, New York 10036
Tel: 212-765-5170

UPI-Compix
220 East 42nd Street
New York, New York 10017
Tel: 212-682-0400

Winik Films Corporation
1619 Broadway
New York, New York 10019
Tel: 212-541-7150

Texas:

Automated Commercial Training
Systems
9817 Westpark
Houston, Texas 77042
Tel: 713-783-1380

Storage

See also "Film Storage" and "Film Vaults."

California:

Bekins Film Center
1025 North Highland Avenue
Los Angeles, California 90038
Tel: 213-466-9271

Bonded Services
8290 Santa Monica Boulevard
Los Angeles, California 90046
Tel: 213-654-7575

Cobar Enterprises
814 North Cole Street
Los Angeles, California 90038
Tel: 213-469-8366

Consolidated Film Industries
959 Seward Street
Los Angeles, California 90038
Tel: 213-462-3161

Evco Refrigerated Film Vaults
838 North Seward Street
Los Angeles, California 90038
Tel: 213-464-9252

Hollywood Film Company
956 Seward Street
Los Angeles, California 90028
Tel: 213-462-3284

Producers Film Center
948 North Sycamore Avenue
Los Angeles, California 90038
Tel: 213-851-1122

Seward Film Vaults
1010 North Seward Street
Los Angeles, California 90028
Tel: 213-464-0141

TV/Recorders
6054 Sunset Boulevard
Los Angeles, California 90028
Tel: 213-469-8201

United Theatrical Amusement
1658 Cordova Street
Los Angeles, California 90007
Tel: 213-734-0510

Illinois:

Consolidated Film Industries
333 North Michigan Avenue
Chicago, Illinois 60601
Tel: 312-641-0028

New York:

Consolidated Film Industries
15 Columbus Circle
New York, New York 10023
Tel: 212-581-1090

Rapid Film Technique, Inc.
37-02 27th Street
Long Island City, New York
11101
Tel: 212-786-4600

Studios

Included here is a listing of sound stages suitable for indoor motion picture production throughout the United States. Some of the Hollywood listings have outdoor sets and back lots as well.

Arizona:

Apacheland Movie Ranch
Route 1, Box 1700
Apache Junction, Arizona 85220
Tel: 602-969-8093

Old Tucson Movie Locations and
  Studio
201 South Kinney Road
Old Tucson, Arizona 85705
Tel: 602-792-3100

Rawhide, Arizona
P.O. Box 548
Scottsdale, Arizona 85252
Tel: 602-992-6111

Southwestern Studio
P.O. Box 1014
Carefree, Arizona 85331
Tel: 602-946-3403

California:
Los Angeles area:

ABC Television Center
4151 Prospect Avenue
Los Angeles, California 90027
Tel: 213-663-3311

Aldrich Studios
201 North Occidental Boulevard
Los Angeles, California 90026
Tel: 213-386-5630

Howard A. Anderson Company
5451 Marathon Street
Los Angeles, California 90038
Tel: 213-463-0100

Beckett Stages
1224 North Vine Street
Los Angeles, California 90038
Tel: 213-465-7141

R. L. Bevington Stage Rental
650 North Bronson Avenue
Los Angeles, California 90004
Tel: 213-466-7778

The Burbank Studios
4000 Warner Boulevard
Burbank, California 91522

CBS Studio Center
4024 North Radford Avenue
North Hollywood, California
  91604
Tel: 213-763-8411

CBS Studios
6309 Eleanor Avenue
Los Angeles, California 90038
Tel: 213-464-9118

CBS Television City
7800 Beverly Boulevard
Los Angeles, California 90036
Tel: 213-651-2345

Carthay Studio
5907 West Pico Boulevard
Los Angeles, California 90035
Tel: 213-938-2101

Columbia Pictures Industries
Colgems Square
Burbank, California 91505
Tel: 213-843-6000

Culver City Studios
9336 West Washington Boulevard
Culver City, California 90230
Tel: 213-871-0360

Walt Disney Productions
500 South Buena Vista Street
Burbank, California 91503
Tel: 213-845-3141

F&B/CECO of California, Inc.
7051 Santa Monica Boulevard
Los Angeles, California 90038
Tel: 213-466-9361

F-M Motion Picture Services
733 North Highland Avenue
Los Angeles, California 90038
Tel: 213-937-1622

Jerry Fairbanks Productions
826 North Cole
Los Angeles, California 90038
Tel: 213-462-1101

Falcon Studios
5526 Hollywood Boulevard
Los Angeles, California 90028
Tel: 213-462-9356

Family Films
5823 Santa Monica Boulevard
Los Angeles, California 90038
Tel: 213-462-2243

General Service Studios
1040 North Las Palmas Avenue
Los Angeles, California 90038
Tel: 213-469-9011

Samuel Goldwyn Studios
1041 North Formosa Avenue
Los Angeles, California 90046
Tel: 213-851-1234

International Studios
846 Cahuenga Boulevard
Los Angeles, California 90038
Tel: 213-466-3534

Ray M. Johnson Studio
5555 Sunset Boulevard
Los Angeles, California 90028
Tel: 213-465-4108

Major Independent Film Studios,
  Inc.
1207 North Western Avenue
Los Angeles, California 90029
Tel: 213-461-2721

Burt Martin Studio
3805 West Magnolia Boulevard
Burbank, California 91505
Tel: 213-848-8229

Ray Mercer & Company
4241 Normal Avenue
Los Angeles, California 90029
Tel: 213-663-9331

Metro-Goldwyn-Mayer, Inc.
10202 West Washington
  Boulevard
Culver City, California 90230
Tel: 213-836-3000
Ext: 404

Mole-Richardson Company
937 North Sycamore Avenue
Los Angeles, California 90038
Tel: 213-654-3060

NBC Television
3000 West Alameda Avenue
Burbank, California 91503
Tel: 213-845-7000

Paramount Pictures Corporation
5451 Marathon Street
Los Angeles, California 90038
Tel: 213-463-0100

Pegasus Film Productions, Inc.
1520 North Van Ness
Los Angeles, California 90028
Tel: 213-466-3571

Producers Studio, Inc.
650 North Bronson Avenue
Los Angeles, California 90004
Tel: 213-466-3111

Rampart Studios
2625 Temple Street
Los Angeles, California 90026
Tel: 213-385-3911

SOS/Photo-Cine-Optics, Inc.
7051 Santa Monica Boulevard
Los Angeles, California 90038
Tel: 213-466-9361

Seward Stages
6605 Eleanor Street
Los Angeles, California 90038
Tel: 213-466-8559

Studio One
6650 Santa Monica Boulevard
Los Angeles, California 90038
Tel: 213-466-4393

TV & Film Production Center
3805 West Magnolia Boulevard
Burbank, California 90621
Tel: 213-845-3709

Twentieth Century–Fox Film
  Corporation
10201 West Pico Boulevard
Los Angeles, California 90035
Tel: 213-277-2211

U.P.A. Pictures, Inc.
4440 Lakeside Drive
Burbank, California 90621
Tel: 213-842-7171

Universal City Studios
Universal City Plaza
Universal City, California 91608
Tel: 213-985-4321

Warner Brothers, Inc.
4000 Warner Boulevard
Burbank, California 91522
Tel: 213-843-6000

San Francisco area:

Blancheri-Zaga Studios
465 Geary Street
San Francisco, California 94102
Tel: 415-474-1275

Cinerent West, Inc.
155 Fell Street
San Francisco, California 94102
Tel: 415-864-4644

Fugazi Hall
678 Green Street
San Francisco, California 94133
Tel: 415-362-7884

Motion Picture Service Company
125 Hyde Street
San Francisco, California 94102
Tel: 415-673-9162

W. A. Palmer Films
611 Howard Street
San Francisco, California 94105
Tel: 415-986-5961

The Phelps & Kopp Company
991 Tennessee Street
San Francisco, California 94107
Tel: 415-285-1900

Snazelle Films, Inc.
155 Fell Street
San Francisco, California 94102
Tel: 415-431-5490

Studio 16, Inc.
2135 Powell Street
San Francisco, California 94133
Tel: 415-982-2097

Colorado:

CVD Studios
15460 East Batavia Drive
Aurora, Colorado 80011
Tel: 303-341-5600

Entertainment Four Studios
1630 Chambers Road
Aurora, Colorado 80010
Tel: 303-341-5600

Florida:

Cinema City Studios, Inc.
6015 Highway 301 North
Tampa, Florida 33610
Tel: 813-621-4731

Coronado Studios
266 N.E. 70th Street
Miami, Florida 33101
Tel: 305-751-1853

Film World Studio
Sheridan Street
Dania, Florida 33004
Tel: 305-581-7508

Luke Moberly Studios
4810 S.W. 54th Terrace
Fort Lauderdale, Florida
Tel: 305-581-7508

Reela Films Studio
65 N.W. Third Street
Miami, Florida 33101
Tel: 305-374-2611

Studio Center, Inc.
14875 N.E. Twentieth Avenue
North Miami, Florida 33161
Tel: 305-944-2911

Hawaii:

CBS Hawaii 5-O
Diamond Head Road
Honolulu, Hawaii 96816
Tel: 808-732-5577

David Cornwell Productions, Inc.
1358 Kapiolani Boulevard
Honolulu, Hawaii 96814
Tel: 808-949-7000

Hawaii Production Center
1534 Kapiolani Boulevard
Honolulu, Hawaii 96814
Tel: 808-941-3011

Spectrum Motion Pictures
2962 East Manoa Road
Honolulu, Hawaii 96822
Tel: 808-988-7122

Illinois:

Gilbert Altschul Productions, Inc.
909 West Diversey Avenue
Chicago, Illinois 60614
Tel: 312-525-6561

Asch & Associates Film &
  Videotape Production, Inc.
875 West Buckingham Place
Chicago, Illinois 60657
Tel: 312-477-1920

Betzer Productions, Inc.
450 East Ohio Street
Chicago, Illinois 60611
Tel: 312-664-3257

Michael Birch, Inc.
600 North McClurg Court, Suite
  1711-A
Chicago, Illinois 60611
Tel: 312-329-9350

William H. Birch & Associates,
  Inc.
161 East Grand Avenue
Chicago, Illinois 60611
Tel: 312-527-2135

Christopher Productions
161 East Erie Street
Chicago, Illinois 60611
Tel: 312-642-2280

Directors, Inc.
17 East Chestnut Street
Chicago, Illinois 60611
Tel: 312-787-0414

Cal Dunn Studios, Inc.
141 West Ohio Street
Chicago, Illinois 60610
Tel: 312-644-7600

The Harwald Company, Inc.
1245 Chicago Avenue
Evanston, Illinois 60611
Tel: 312-491-1000

Lawrence-Phillip Studios
343 South Dearborn Street
Chicago, Illinois 60604
Tel: 312-922-1945

Jack Lieb Productions, Inc.
1230 West Washington Boulevard
Chicago, Illinois 60607
Tel: 312-666-1220

Lippert/Saviano Inc.
141 West Ohio Street
Chicago, Illinois 60611
Tel: 312-266-0123

Fred A. Niles Communications
Centers, Inc.
1058 West Washington Boulevard
Chicago, Illinois 60607
Tel: 312-738-4181

Scientific Film Company
211 East Chicago Avenue
Chicago, Illinois 60611
Tel: 312-943-0320

Sonic Film Recording, Inc.
1230 West Washington Boulevard
Chicago, Illinois 60607
Tel: 312-243-2600

Topel & Associates
3133 North Halsted Street
Chicago, Illinois 60657
Tel: 312-929-1000

Master Motion Picture Company
50 Piedmont Street
Boston, Massachusetts 02116
Tel: 617-426-3592

New England Film Service, Inc.
300 Second Avenue
Waltham, Massachusetts 02154
Tel: 617-890-2700

Professional Films, Inc.
136 Arlington Street
Boston, Massachusetts 02116
Tel: 617-423-0007

Telavix Studios
216 Tremont Street
Boston, Massachusetts 02108
Tel: 617-542-9161

Michigan:

Massachusetts:

Atoz Rental Center
1000 Main Street
Malden, Massachusetts 02148
Tel: 617-321-0980

Dekko Film Productions, Inc.
126 Dartmouth Street
Boston, Massachusetts 02109
Tel: 617-536-6160

Fitzgerald Motion Picture
Service, Inc.
176 Newbury Street
Boston, Massachusetts 02109
Tel: 617-266-2512

Bartlett Film Services
70 West McNichols
Detroit, Michigan 48203
Tel: 313-868-0778

Cinema 8
11820 Harper
Detroit, Michigan 48213
Tel: 313-371-7879

Jam Handy Productions
2821 East Grand Boulevard
Detroit, Michigan 48203
Tel: 313-875-2450

Pathway
505 Abbey Street
Muskegon, Michigan 49442
Tel: 616-766-5480

Regan Film Productions
19730 Ralston
Detroit, Michigan 48203
Tel: 313-883-4334

New Jersey:

Allscope, Inc.
33 Witherspoon Street
Princeton, New Jersey 08540

New York:

3-G Stage Corporation
236 West 61st Street
New York, New York 10023
Tel: 212-247-3130

339 Focus Stage
339 East 48th Street
New York, New York 10017
Tel: 212-371-3703

95th Street Studio, Inc.
206 East 95th Street
New York, New York 10028
Tel: 212-831-1946

ABZ Studios
266 East 78th Street
New York, New York 10021
Tel: 212-628-1310

Biograph Studios, Inc.
807 East 175th Street
New York, New York 10460
Tel: 212-299-5500

Boken, Inc.
349 West 48th Street
New York, New York 10036
Tel: 212-581-5507

Cameo Stages, Inc.
21-29 45th Road
Long Island City, New York
   11101
Tel: 212-937-6486

The Camera Mart, Inc.
456 West 55th Street
New York, New York 10019
Tel: 212-757-6977

Cine Centrum, Inc.
1414 Avenue of the Americas
New York, New York 10019
Tel: 212-593-3464

Cine Studio
241 West 54th Street
New York, New York 10019
Tel: 212-581-1916

City Film Center, Inc.
Middle Village
64-12 65th Place
Queens, New York 11379
Tel: 212-456-5050

F&B/Ceco Studio
460 West 54th Street
New York, New York 10019
Tel: 212-581-5590

Filmways, Inc.
246 East 127th Street
New York, New York 10035
Tel: 212-427-6796

Daniel Jones, Inc.
314 Grand Street
New York, New York 10002
Tel: 212-766-1400

Lance Productions, Inc.
353 West 57th Street
New York, New York 10019
Tel: 212-757-6167

Mother's Studio
435 West Nineteenth Street
New York, New York 10011
Tel: 212-243-8064

Michael Myerberg Studios
Roosevelt Field
Garden City,
Long Island, New York 11530
Tel: 212-886-0308

Nelson Studios, Inc.
1079 Nelson Avenue
New York, New York 10052
Tel: 212-588-5310

Anthony Nolles Studio
45 West 45th Street
New York, New York 10036
Tel: 212-581-5507

Phoenix Studios, Inc.
537 West 59th Street
New York, New York 10019
Tel: 212-581-7721

Production Center
221 West 26th Street
New York, New York 10001
Tel: 212-675-2211

Ready Made Stages, Inc.
314 Grand Street
New York, New York 10002
Tel: 212-766-1400

Reeves Production Services
304 East 44th Street
New York, New York 10017
Tel: 212-679-3550

Ross-Gaffney, Inc.
21 West 46th Street
New York, New York 10036
Tel: 212-582-3744

Stage 20 West
20 West End Avenue
New York, New York 10023
Tel: 212-586-3753

Stage 54 West
429 West 54th Street
New York, New York 10019
Tel: 212-757-2030

Stage 90
423 East 90th Street
New York, New York 10028
Tel: 212-582-1441

Ohio:

Cine-Craft Productions, Inc.
2515 Franklin Avenue
Cleveland, Ohio 44113
Tel: 216-781-2300

Escar Motion Picture Service, Inc.
7315 Carnegie Avenue
Cleveland, Ohio 44103
Tel: 216-361-2707

Herb Faris Studios, Inc.
1706 Euclid Avenue
Cleveland, Ohio 44115
Tel: 216-781-4323

Oklahoma:

Douglas Productions
1300 McGee Drive, Suite 106A
Norman, Oklahoma 73069
Tel: 405-321-1200

Texas:

Automated Commercial Training
    Systems, Inc.
9817 Westpark
Houston, Texas 77042
Tel: 713-783-1380

Dale Berry & Associates, Inc.
9001 ERL Thornton Freeway
Dallas, Texas 75228
Tel: 214-324-0409

Bill Stokes Associates
5646 Dyer Street
Dallas, Texas 75206
Tel: 213-363-0161

Virgin Islands:

Station WTJX
P.O. Box 5077
St. Thomas, Virgin Islands 00801
Tel: 809-774-6255

Washington:

Multi-Media Productions, Inc.
1200 Stuart Street
Seattle, Washington 98101
Tel: 206-624-8390

Stunts

At the last minute Robert Redford decides he doesn't want to plunge off the 150-foot cliff into the circle of burning napalm, so you need a quick substitute. Some of your best bets are listed below. The stunt industry trade associations are included as well.

California:

Art Scholl Aviation
4130 Mennes
Riverside, California 92509
Tel: 714-686-0510

Black Stuntmen's Association
8949 West 24th Street
Los Angeles, California 90034
Tel: 213-837-2985

Briles Wing & Helicopter
3011 Airport Avenue
Santa Monica, California 90405
Tel: 213-390-3554

OBS Air Shows, Inc.
P.O. Box 1253
Santa Ana, California 92701
Tel: 714-547-2888

Stunt Women of America
202 Vance Street
Pacific Palisades, California
    90272
Tel: 213-454-8228

Stuntmen's Association
15300 Ventura Boulevard
Sherman Oaks, California 91403
Tel: 213-462-2301

Stuntmen's Association of Motion
    Pictures, Inc.
4810 Whitsett Avenue
North Hollywood, California
    91607
Tel: 213-766-4334

Stunts Unlimited
3518 Cahuenga Boulevard West
Los Angeles, California 90068
Tel: 213-874-0050

Sunny Woods Stunts
1410 Morningside Drive
Burbank, California 91506
Tel: 213-846-1766

Yerkes Productions
17721 Roscoe Boulevard
Northridge, California 91324
Tel: 213-344-4231

Colorado:

Joe Allan Cabrera
5755 West 37th Avenue
Wheat Ridge, Colorado 80212
Tel: 303-423-0087

Eddie Eldon
Route 1, Box 102
Avondale, Colorado 81022
Tel: 303-947-3470

Titles

The use of cleverly designed titles or title sequences is one way to increase a film's initial visual impact. Listed below are some of the principal title houses supplying motion pictures and television films. See also "Animation" for title sequences relying heavily on animation techniques.

Arizona:

Don Heraldson Animated Film, Inc.
8213 East Fairmont
Scottsdale, Arizona 85251
Tel: 602-947-0696

California:
Los Angeles area:

Akkad International Productions
8730 Sunset Boulevard
Los Angeles, California 90069
Tel: 213-657-7670

Howard A. Anderson Company
5451 Marathon Street
Los Angeles, California 90038
Tel: 213-463-0100

Saul Bass Associates
7039 Sunset Boulevard
Los Angeles, California 90028
Tel: 213-466-9701

Bob Beck & Associates
1538 Casill Place
Los Angeles, California 90028
Tel: 213-462-7093

Braverman Productions, Inc.
8961 Sunset Boulevard
Los Angeles, California 90069
Tel: 213-278-5444

Cinema Research Corporation
6860 Lexington Avenue
Los Angeles, California 90038
Tel: 213-461-3235

Consolidated Film Industries
959 North Seward Street
Los Angeles, California 90038
Tel: 213-462-3161

Robert Costa Productions
1615 Colorado Boulevard
Los Angeles, California 90041
Tel: 213-255-1841

Craftsman Company
1050 North Cahuenga Boulevard
Los Angeles, California 90038
Tel: 213-469-5594

Creative Film Arts
7070 Waring Avenue
Los Angeles, California 90038
Tel: 213-933-8495

Dimensional Design
11046 McCormick Street
North Hollywood, California
 91601
Tel: 213-769-5694

Sandy Dvore, Inc.
9100 Wilshire, Suite 212
Beverly Hills, California 90212
Tel: 213-278-4343

Richard Einfeld Productions
1512 North Las Palmas Avenue
Los Angeles, California 90038
Tel: 213-461-3731

Ray Engle & Associates
626 South Kenmore Street
Los Angeles, California 90005
Tel: 213-381-5001

Film Effects of Hollywood, Inc.
1140 North Citrus Avenue
Los Angeles, California 90038
Tel: 213-469-5808

Wayne Fitzgerald Film Design,
 Inc.
8430 Santa Monica Boulevard
Los Angeles, California 90069
Tel: 213-654-8261

Earl Hays Press
1121 North Las Palmas Avenue
Los Angeles, California 90038
Tel: 213-466-2495

Frank Jones Associates
1150 West Olive Avenue
Burbank, California 91506
Tel: 213-843-2031

Kaleidoscope Films, Ltd.
6345 Fountain Avenue
Los Angeles, California 90028
Tel: 213-465-1151

Manny's Filmaker's Services
1135 North Cole Street
Los Angeles, California 90038
Tel: 213-464-4537

Matrix Image
6622 Variel Avenue
Canoga Park, California 91303
Tel: 213-883-6622

Ray Mercer & Company
4241 Normal Avenue
Los Angeles, California 90029
Tel: 213-663-9331

National Screen Service
 Corporation
7026 Santa Monica Boulevard
Los Angeles, California 90038
Tel: 213-466-5111

Nicholson Films, Inc.
6335 Homewood Avenue
Los Angeles, California 90028
Tel: 213-462-0878

Phill Norman, Ltd.
1203 North Wetherly Drive
Los Angeles, California 90069
Tel: 213-659-5925

Opticals West
7026 Santa Monica Boulevard
Los Angeles, California 90038
Tel: 213-466-5111

Pacific Title & Art Studio
6350 Santa Monica Boulevard
Los Angeles, California 90038
Tel: 213-464-0121

Photo-Effex
3701 Oak Street
Burbank, California 91505
Tel: 213-849-6959

J. D. Sawchak & Associates
11046 McCormick Street
North Hollywood, California
   91601
Tel: 213-980-1533

Willard Tidwell Motion Picture
   Titles
808 North Highland Avenue
Los Angeles, California 90038
Tel: 213-465-8555

Title House, Inc.
800 North Cole Avenue
Los Angeles, California 90038
Tel: 213-469-8171

Titles
P.O. Box 1151
Los Angeles, California 90028
Tel: 213-784-2210

Universal City Studios Title &
   Optical Dept.
4050 Lankershim Boulevard
Universal City, California 91608
Tel: 213-985-4321

Van Der Veer Photo Effects
3518 West Cahuenga Boulevard
Los Angeles, California 90068
Tel: 213-851-4333

Westheimer Company
736 North Seward Street
Los Angeles, California 90038
Tel: 213-466-8271

Cornett Wood Television Art
1959 Cahuenga Boulevard
Los Angeles, California 90028
Tel: 213-467-3717

Felix Zelenka Productions
818 North La Brea Avenue
Los Angeles, California 90038
Tel: 213-466-3263

San Francisco area:

W. A. Palmer Films, Inc.
611 Howard Street
San Francisco, California 94105
Tel: 415-986-5961

Skinner Studio
345 Sutter Street
San Francisco, California 94108
Tel: 415-986-5040

Stop Frame, Inc.
1736 Stockton Street
San Francisco, California 94133
Tel: 415-434-4413

District of Columbia:

Creative Arts
2323 Fourth Street, N.E.
Washington, D.C. 20002
Tel: 202-832-2600

Hawaii:

Cine-Pic Hawaii
1847 Pacific Heights Road
Honolulu, Hawaii 96813
Tel: 808-533-2677

Spectrum Motion Pictures
2962 East Manoa Road
Honolulu, Hawaii 96822
Tel: 808-988-7122

Illinois:

Consolidated Film Industries
333 North Michigan Avenue
Chicago, Illinois 60601
Tel: 312-641-0028

New York:

A. A. Title Service
228 East 45th Street
New York, New York 10017
Tel: 212-986-9468

Consolidated Film Industries
15 Columbus Circle
New York, New York 10023
Tel: 212-581-1090

HP Colortype
13 East 47th Street
New York, New York 10036
Tel: 212-752-9575

Hot Press Company
2 West 46th Street
New York, New York 10036
Tel: 212-245-6350

I. F. Studios, Inc.
328 East 44th Street
New York, New York 10017
Tel: 212-683-4747

Kaleidoscope Films, Ltd.
353 West 57th Street
New York, New York 10019
Tel: 212-265-2377

Knight Title Service
145 West 45th Street
New York, New York 10036
Tel: 212-265-2080

A. Paganelli
21 West 46th Street
New York, New York 10036
Tel: 212-582-2899

Toro Titles
319 East 44th Street
New York, New York 10017
Tel: 212-679-5589

Texas:

A-V Corporation
2518 North Boulevard
Houston, Texas 77006
Tel: 713-523-6701

Houston Film Co-op, Inc.
P.O. Box 58932
Houston, Texas 77058
Tel: 713-482-3683

K & H Productions
3601 Oak Grove
Dallas, Texas 75204
Tel: 214-526-5268

Washington:

Gardner/Marlow/Maes Corporation
Seattle Tower, Penthouse
Seattle, Washington 98101
Tel: 206-624-9090

JRB Motion Graphics
3323 Ninth Avenue West
Seattle, Washington 98119
Tel: 206-284-0834

Translations

Listed below are sources of translations for scripts, either for shooting or dubbing in another language.

California:

All-World Language Institute
208 South Beverly Drive
Beverly Hills, California 90212
Tel: 213-278-5950

A. J. Amateau
1336 North Harper
Los Angeles, California 90038
Tel: 213-654-0638

Benemann Translation Center
760 Market Street, Suite 1048
San Francisco, California 94102
Tel: 415-982-7658

Berlitz Translation Service
3345 Wilshire Boulevard
Los Angeles, California 90010
Tel: 213-380-1144

Foreign Language Service Co.
7046 Hollywood Boulevard
Los Angeles, California 90028
Tel: 213-467-5128

International Translation Bureau
426 South Spring Street
Los Angeles, California 90013
Tel: 213-629-1990

Amador H. Solis & Associates
304 South Broadway, Suite 224
Los Angeles, California 90013
Tel: 213-661-5633

Translations Unlimited
1150 West Olive Avenue
Burbank, California 91506
Tel: 213-843-2031

Underwater Photography & Equipment

Underwater photographers and equipment suppliers are concentrated in tropical areas where water visibility and temperature favor underwater camera action. The underwater photography trade association is listed here as well as the individuals and organizations operating in the field.

California:

California Sailing Academy
14025 Panay Way
Marina Del Rey, California
  90291
Tel: 213-821-3433

Commercial Diving Center
272 South Fries
Wilmington, California 90744
Tel: 213-834-2501

Alan Gordon Enterprises, Inc.
5362 North Cahuenga Boulevard
North Hollywood, California
  91601
Tel: 213-985-5500

Gornick Film Productions/
  Environmental
  Marine Enterprises
4200 Camino Real
Los Angeles, California 90065
Tel: 213-223-8914

Independent Artists Productions
P.O. Box 5165
Sherman Oaks, California 91403
Tel: 213-463-4811

Stacy Keach Productions
5216 Laurel Canyon Boulevard
North Hollywood, California
  91607
Tel: 213-877-0472

Marine Enterprises
4200 Camino Real
Los Angeles, California 90065
Tel: 213-223-8914

Oceanic Films, Inc.
c/o International Products
  Service
3518 Cahuenga Boulevard West
Los Angeles, California 90068
Tel: 213-851-3595

Photo-Sonics, Inc.
820 South Mariposa Street
Burbank, California 91506
Tel: 213-849-6251

Photomarine International
7126 Reseda Boulevard
Reseda, California
Tel: 213-881-4545

SOS/Photo-Cine-Optics, Inc.
7051 Santa Monica Boulevard
Los Angeles, California 90038
Tel: 213-466-9361

Sawyer Rental & Sales
6820 Santa Monica Boulevard
Los Angeles, California 90038
Tel: 213-466-6114

Don Stern Productions
3623 Cahuenga Boulevard West
Los Angeles, California 90068
Tel: 213-851-3673

M. Stewart & Company
205 South Beverly Drive
Beverly Hills, California 90212
Tel: 213-272-0103

Underwater Motion Picture
    Association
1500 South Second Street
Alhambra, California 91801
Tel: 213-282-4117

Zihla Enterprises
9967 Milburn Drive
Sun Valley, California 91352
Tel: 213-767-5663

Florida:

Jordan Klein
3131 N.E. 188th Street
Miami, Florida 33101
Tel: 305-944-1476

Schulke Underwater Films
8305 S.W. 72nd Avenue
Miami, Florida 33143
Tel: 305-667-5671

Hawaii:

Cal-Hawaii Photographics
P.O. Box 9451, 1240 Kaumalli
Honolulu, Hawaii 96820
Tel: 808-841-4335

David Cornwell Productions, Inc.
1358 Kapiolani Boulevard
Honolulu, Hawaii 96814
Tel: 808-949-7000

Hawaiian Divers (Division of
    Undersea Safaris, Inc.)
P.O. Box 572
Kailua-Kona, Hawaii 96740
Tel: 808-329-3407

McWayne Marine Supply Ltd.
1125 Ala Moana
Honolulu, Hawaii 96814
Tel: 808-521-3411

Pacific Instrumentation
5388 Papai Street
Honolulu, Hawaii 96821
Tel: 808-373-1287

Pacific Marine Frontiers, Inc.
850 Kam Highway
Honolulu, Hawaii 96782
Tel: 808-455-1480

Skindiving-Hawaii
1651 Ala Moana
Honolulu, Hawaii 96815
Tel: 808-941-0548

South Seas Aquatics
1125 Ala Moana
Honolulu, Hawaii 96814
Tel: 808-538-7724

Spectrum Motion Pictures
2962 East Manoa Road
Honolulu, Hawaii 96822
Tel: 808-988-7122

Massachusetts:

The Film Group, Inc.
2400 Massachusetts Avenue
Cambridge, Massachusetts 02140
Tel: 617-354-5695

Texas:

Dale Berry & Associates, Inc.
9001 ERL Thornton Freeway
Dallas, Texas 75228
Tel: 214-324-0409

Houston Film Co-op, Inc.
P.O. Box 58932
Houston, Texas 77058
Tel: 713-482-7960

The Ocean Corporation
2120 Peckham Street
Houston, Texas 77019
Tel: 713-526-8957

Wardrobe

Wardrobe houses are normally able to clothe a whole regiment or chorus, as required. Some costume houses, however, deal in small numbers or the creation of custom designs. See also "Costumes."

Arizona:

Old Tucson Studio
201 South Kinney Road
Tucson, Arizona 85705
Tel: 602-792-3100

California:
Los Angeles area:

A-Cinema Costumers of
  Hollywood
1773 Cahuenga Boulevard
Los Angeles, California 90028
Tel: 213-466-2959

Frank Acuna
8212 Sunset Boulevard
Los Angeles, California 90046
Tel: 213-656-1413

Berman's Costume Company
1040 North Las Palmas Avenue
Los Angeles, California 90038
Tel: 213-466-6454

The Burbank Studios
4000 Warner Boulevard
Burbank, California 91522
Tel: 213-843-6000
Costume Carousel

Fantasy Fair, Inc.
6617 Santa Monica Boulevard
Los Angeles, California 90038
Tel: 213-467-6141
Higby O'Daniel Design

The Costume Place
7211 Santa Monica Boulevard
Los Angeles, California 90046
Tel: 213-876-7979

Hollywood Tuxedo
1552 North Highland Avenue
Los Angeles, California 90028
Tel: 213-465-6101

I. C. Costume Company
6121 Santa Monica Boulevard
Los Angeles, California 90038
Tel: 213-496-2056

Ice Capades, Inc.
6121 Santa Monica Boulevard
Los Angeles, California 90038
Tel: 213-469-2767

Inner City Cultural Center
1308 South New Hampshire
  Avenue
Los Angeles, California 90006
Tel: 213-387-1161

International Costume Company
8336 Melrose Avenue
Los Angeles, California 90069
Tel: 213-653-2446

Invincible Sales Corporation
2303 West Ninth Street
Los Angeles, California 90006
Tel: 213-383-1685

Krofft Enterprises
11347 Vanowen Street
North Hollywood, California
  91605
Tel: 213-877-3361

A. Levy Uniform Company
235 South La Brea Avenue
Los Angeles, California 90036
Tel: 213-938-5204

Myers' Costume
5538 Hollywood
Los Angeles, California 90028
Tel: 213-465-6589

Native American Research/
  Consultants
526 South Reese Place
Burbank, California 91506
Tel: 213-848-6531

Norcostco, Inc.
15976 East Francisquito Avenue
La Puente, California 91744
Tel: 213-968-6459

Proshaska Animal Creations
1438-A 25th Street
Santa Monica, California 90404
Tel: 213-462-2301

A. Scotti Manufacturing Co.
746 South Los Angeles Street
Los Angeles, California 90014
Tel: 213-622-3972

Shipstads & Johnson Ice Follies
1001 North La Brea Avenue
Los Angeles, California 90038
Tel: 213-874-8800

Showcraft, Inc.
9215 Cranford Street
Pacoima, California 91331
Tel: 213-768-1093

Silwani & Company
6519 Hollywood Boulevard
Los Angeles, California 90028
Tel: 213-469-6819

Les Steinhardt
110 East Ninth Street
Los Angeles, California 90015
Tel: 213-627-2437

Tuxedo Center
7360 Sunset Boulevard
Los Angeles, California 90046
Tel: 213-874-4200

Universal City Studios
100 Universal City Plaza
Universal City, California 91608
Tel: 213-985-4321

Western Costume Company
5335 Melrose Avenue
Los Angeles, California 90038
Tel: 213-469-1451

San Francisco area:

Dance Art Company
222 Powell Street
San Francisco, California 94102
Tel: 415-392-4912

Encore Theatrical Supply
5929 MacArthur Boulevard
Oakland, California 94605
Tel: 415-568-1881

Eunice's Costume Design
1325 Ocean Avenue
San Francisco, California 94112
Tel: 415-586-2553

Masquerade Costumes
1049 Irving Street
San Francisco, California 94122
Tel: 415-661-2443

Stagecraft Studios
1854 Alcatraz Avenue
Berkeley, California 94703
Tel: 415-653-4424

Colorado:

American Costume Company
830 Eighteenth Street
Denver, Colorado 80202
Tel: 303-244-6066

Colorado Costume Company
2100 Broadway
Denver, Colorado 80205
Tel: 303-825-6874

Nevada:

Avey Design, Inc.
1040 Matley Lane, Building 5
Reno, Nevada 89502
Tel: 702-323-3540

Williams Costume Rental
226 North Third Street
Las Vegas, Nevada 89101
Tel: 702-384-1384

New York:

Brooks–Van Horn Costume
    Company
117 West Seventeenth Street
New York, New York 10036
Tel: 212-989-8000

Eaves Costume Company, Inc.
151 West 46th Street
New York, New York 10036
Tel: 212-757-3730

Texas:

Performing Arts Supply Company
5734 Green Ash
Houston, Texas 77036
Tel: 713-667-8101

If you would like to order additional copies of the 1976–1977 edition of MOTION PICTURE MARKET PLACE, send a check or money order for $12.95/copy to:

Direct Mail Department
Little, Brown and Company
34 Beacon Street
Boston, Massachusetts 02106

Please add 75¢ per copy for postage and handling, and sales taxes where applicable.